The Talmud's Theological Language-Game

SUNY series in Jewish Philosophy

Kenneth Seeskin, editor

The Talmud's Theological Language-Game

A Philosophical Discourse Analysis

◖ Eugene B. Borowitz ◗

State University of New York Press

Published by
State University of New York Press, Albany

© 2006 State University of New York

All rights reserved

Printed in the United States of America

No part of this book may be used or reproduced in any manner whatsoever without written permission. No part of this book may be stored in a retrieval system or transmitted in any form or by any means including electronic, electrostatic, magnetic tape, mechanical, photocopying, recording, or otherwise without the prior permission in writing of the publisher.

For information, address State University of New York Press,
194 Washington Avenue, Suite 305, Albany, NY 12210-2384

Production by Judith Block
Marketing by Michael Campochiaro

Library of Congress Cataloging-in-Publication Data

Borowitz, Eugene B.
  The Talmud's theological language-game : a philosophical discourse analysis / Eugene B. Borowitz.
    p. cm. — (SUNY series in Jewish philosophy)
  Includes bibiographical references and index.
    ISBN 0-7914-6701-5 (hardcover : alk. paper) — ISBN-13: 978-0-7914-6702-2 (pbk. : alk. paper)
  1. Aggada—Philosophy. 2. Aggada—History and criticism—Theory, etc. 3. Samuel ben Naḥman, 3rd/4th cent.—Knowledge—Aggada. 4. Discourse analysis. I. Title. II. Series.

BM516.5.B67 2006
296.1'27606—dc22   2005012109

ISBN-13: 978-0-7914-6701-5 (hardcover : alk. paper)

10 9 8 7 6 5 4 3 2 1

The classic (1965) text updated:

❦ *"To my beloved Estelle (1925–2004), who (for fifty-seven years) [has] taught me the meaning of existence in covenant."* ❧

Contents

Preface	ix

Part One. Entering the Maze of Rabbinic Diction

	Introduction to a Religious Puzzle	1
1.	What Is the *Aggadah* Problem?	7

Part Two. Scrutinizing Talmudic *Aggadah* at Three Levels

2.	The Surface Characteristics	31
3.	The Substantive Concerns	49
4.	The "Logic"	67
5.	Does Extending the Sample Alter the Findings?	83

Part Three. The Limits and Nature of *Aggadah*

6.	Is Aggadic Discourse Self-Limiting?	115
7.	Positively, What Is *Aggadah*?	145
8.	Reconstruing the *Aggadah* Problem	179

Afterwords

Can We Theologize as the Rabbis Did?	191
On Concluding	193

Notes	195
Bibliography of Works Cited COMPILED BY TINA WEISS	281
Index of Text Citations	293
Index of Subjects and Proper Names	307

❦ Preface ❧

For a half century or more now, thinking about thinking—philosophy examining its own roots—has substantially concentrated on how language shapes what we can and cannot meaningfully say. Ludwig Wittgenstein pioneered that linguistic turn and gave it the lasting gift of his notion of a "language-game." By devising an imagined set of conditions of what one may or may not do, one can create a small world of pleasure or frustration for all who are ready to abide by the rules of the game. Writ large, something like that seems to be what makes it possible for people in many diverse areas of life to communicate with one another and to express a depth of meaning and command that often perplexes those who have no feel for the particular language-game involved.

For well over three decades now it has seemed to me that we products of Western culture and its academies will better understand the classic Jewish religious mind and its enduring manifestation, rabbinic literature, if we could appreciate the rabbinic language-game. Alas for the scholar with only one lifetime in which to work on such a grand scale. The rabbinic tradition itself knows that there are two major verbal universes intertwined in its linguistic universe: *halakhah*, its world of mandated action, and *aggadah*, all the rest of its concerns, most particularly for my theological concerns, the explicit statement of authoritative opinions (sic) on matters of Jewish religious belief. Against the odds—so it has seemed to me—I have long sought to understand the linguistic game rules of aggadic utterance. I am therefore especially grateful to the people and institutions whose help, personal and material, has enabled me to bring this task to this point of closure.

Institutionally, this work could not have come into being without the perennial assistance of student-aid and research funds that the Hebrew Union College-Jewish Institute of Religion made available for this project. A generation or more of students have spent their summers—and, some, a few winters—searching libraries, finding and photocopying studies and texts of potential interest, writing up their reactions to these materials, and, more recently, utilizing the databases that have eased the task of retrieval. None of this would have been possible without the faith and personal support of old deans and dear friends, Paul M. Steinberg, of blessed memory, and Norman Cohen, and their recent successor, Aaron Panken. At a very early stage of this project, the then cultural arm of the Jewish Material Claims Conference made a helpful grant that kept the work going forward. Dr. Philip Miller, director of the Klau Library at the New York School of the HUC-JIR, has been untiring in his efforts to provide me with the wide range of materials cited in this work and many others that did not merit inclusion. Through his knowledgeable and genial efforts, the exceptional holdings of our Cincinnati School Library have also smoothly come to me. Tina Weiss of the New York Library staff brought her fine skills to the arduous task of creating the bibliography. I learned very much and should probably have cited more of the insightful comments Rick Sarason of our Cincinnati School faculty made to the first version of this manuscript. An author is fortunate indeed to have so able and willing a colleague devote his time and learning to a friend's work. Nan and Andrew Langowitz gave me considerable insight into how computer networks work, thus enabling me to develop my idea that the nonlinear structure of aggadic utterance might now best be understood in terms of the dynamics of network logic. And Andrew, with exemplary patience and knowledge, helped me resolve a host of computing problems. Ken Seeskin, eminent philosopher and *mentsh*, was kind enough to see the merits of this work and commend it to the SUNY Press. I am indebted to the staff of the SUNY Press for the high professionalism and personal courtesy with which, as the Hebrew idiom puts it, they "brought this book into the light." My particular thanks go to Judith Block for the kind and imaginative efficiency she brought to this project, to Wyatt Benner for the strength of intellect and unflagging dedication he brought to the challenges of integrating the style of this work, to Elise Brauckmann whose graphic talent turned a book cover into an evocative commentary on my text, and to Nancy Zibman for the excellent indexes, which greatly add to the usefulness of the book. My thanks and gratitude to the Ultimate One who made possible this work and so much else are expressed in the final paragraphs of this volume.

Part One

Entering the Maze of Rabbinic Diction

❦ Introduction to a Religious Puzzle ❧

Many world religions know the distinction between scripture—a centrally significant sacred text—and tradition, the less sacred accompaniment to scripture that has subsidiary authority in theory but, as the official interpreter of scripture, practical preeminence. In Judaism's case, scripture comes to be called the Written Torah (or the Written Law) and, with that development, it gained a companion revelation on Sinai called the Oral Torah (or Oral Law). But Judaism seems unique among religions in formally understanding Tradition, the Oral Torah, as bipartite. That is, it has two identifiable, closely related modes of discourse that differ in authority, areas of concern, and the "logics" by which they set forth their propositions and seek to have them accepted. The more authoritative, because normative, diction is termed the *halakhah*, what came to be seen as the personal and communal duties of Jews to God under the Covenant, or simply, "the law." The less authoritative part of God's revelation of Oral Torah is the *aggadah*, or simply, all else in rabbinic literature. Explicit reflection on Jewish belief—the Jewish equivalent of "theology" in Christianity—takes place in the *aggadah*. This principle is so deeply embedded in rabbinic diction but so fully evidenced in rabbinic texts that it has the quasi-authoritative status of not requiring statement or demonstration; it is taken for granted. This book arises from this Jewish understanding that its classic statements concerning its beliefs are in the *aggadah*—but before saying more about this, let me briefly set these abstract statements about Judaism in historical perspective.

Judaism's foundation is God's revelation as given in various forms in the Hebrew Bible, but the religious life that grew from it over the centuries was shaped not only by its explicit language but by the interpretation of its texts. By the time of the Roman domination of the Land of Israel, as the Common Era was beginning, its ongoing way of life and thinking was more and more shaped by the dynamic reading and interpretation of the Bible (and the traditions associated with them) by "the Rabbis," the sages mentioned in the Mishnah and the Talmud. The Mishnah, the increasingly authoritative, orderly studybook of halakhic dicta and its significant minority of aggadic statements, is the rabbis' earliest documentary record, edited about 200 CE. The Babylonian Talmud ("the" Talmud, also called "the Bavli"), which became Judaism's classic document of Tradition, is a sprawling account of the mostly later rabbis' analyses of the Mishnah's meaning and that of various notions associated with them. It seems to have reached its present form about 600 CE. All later movements to reexplain Judaism, whether driven by sociocultural, rationalistic, mystic, modernizing, or feminist concerns, have had to come to terms with Talmudic Judaism if they sought welcome in the community discussion that vitalizes the continuity of Judaism.

Contemporary Jewish thinkers have a number of special problems in this regard, not the least of them being the thoroughgoing sexism of rabbinic teaching, partially mitigated though it is by occasional efforts to improve the second-class status of women. Since this book is concerned with faithfully understanding rabbinic discourse in its own terms (as these can interface with our own), I believe I need to be true to their disturbing attitude toward women, an attitude and practice I am happy a substantial sector of contemporary Jewry keeps trying to put more effectively behind it. Another difficulty arises from our considerable doubts today about how we can utilize history, that mainstay of modern interpretations of classic Jewish documents, in relation to rabbinic literature, very much of which seems more ideological and imaginative than factual. In this work, I follow a well-trodden path in modern Jewish studies by bracketing the issues of historicity and speak only of what the literature indicates. However, as I am normally concerned with contemporary rather than historical Jewish thought, the problem that mostly drives this investigation is that of Jewish authenticity. It arises from the special genius that enables modern Jewish thinkers to bring fresh insight to their readings of Judaism, namely, the expertise Western academic accomplishment has in understanding culture generally. Applying any one or several of the hermeneutics that it offers carries with it the potential threat that reading Judaism with modern lenses will transform Judaism unacceptably. The problem also has a significant religious aspect. Western culture is permeated by Christianity and, in the United States, by Protestant Christianity. Particularly in the realm of religious thought, the categories—like "revelation," "faith," "salvation," and such, and the ways of organizing them, like "religion," "theology," "dogma," and such—remain permeated by the Christian model. And this problem lingers despite the laudable academic efforts to broaden the horizon of Western thinking to include Eastern "religions" and other ways of shaping the seriously spiritual life. For some decades now, Jewish academics have become conscious of this difficulty and, more recently, the increased Jewish self-respect of thinkers has given this matter of authenticity a significant place on the agenda of contemporary Jewish thought.

One major recent response to this issue has been the emergence of the textual reasoning movement, largely spurred on by Peter Ochs. Still young, it has indicated how, by working with classic Jewish or modern texts in conscious emulation of the rabbis, albeit with a Western academic sophistication, one might make a newly cogent statement of Judaism.[1] A different approach is taken in this book, one whose first document goes back to a term paper I wrote in 1957 for a graduate course in religion at Columbia University. That work gave me special insight into the linguistic philosophy of Ludwig Wittgenstein[2] and it got me to thinking about a fresh hermeneutic for understanding and explicating classic Jewish belief. Specifically, his later writings stress the manner in which different "forms of life" created their own "language-games" and thought patterns. This set me to wondering about the rabbis' language-game and the consequences of theological issues being assigned to the *aggadah*. It also enabled me to fend off the aggressive empirical dogmatism of analytic philosophy, which long dominated American philosophy, and kept me receptive to the later flood of writing closely linking thought and the language patterns in which it was expressed. And by helping me look at the rabbis with fresh eyes, it led me to dissociate my religious thought from the common Jewish intellectual practice of the day, which was to look to the medieval Jewish philosophers as the models of a proper interface with contemporary culture. But if even these great thinkers had to explain the relationship of their "modern" philosophy to rabbinic teaching, I concluded that our contemporary concern for Jewish authenticity would be more fully satisfied by seeking to understand how the rabbis thought about their beliefs and to what extent we might then emulate them.[3]

Working with these Wittgensteinian lenses, it quickly became evident that, except in the rarest cases, rabbinic verbalization about belief took place only in their aggadic—that is, their nonlegal—discourse. To be sure, it was often implicit in their halakhic, their legal, statements, but inferring from a law's dictates the values and beliefs underlying it is a highly uncertain practice, one whose results seem inevitably debatable. The aggadic setting of rabbinic ideas has its own special challenge, for the "rules of the [*aggadah*] language-game" seem utterly elusive and have long defied efforts to dig them out and give them comprehensive statement. Yet it is just in this linguistic mode that the rabbis thought it best to express Jewish faith, thereby creating an intellectuality deserving of study and perhaps emulation.

This book is motivated by a theological concern—my desire to give a reasonably authentic contemporary statement of the nature of Judaism—but its content is, in fact, primarily the analysis of literature carried on with a focus on how it seeks to achieve cogency, a mode of study that may be called philosophical. Thus, it employs a complex interdisciplinary perspective indeed, but one whose several intersecting methodologies must peacefully coexist if this study is to be true to the data under examination and the motivation that initiated and drives it. In that spirit I have regularly tweaked the standard translations of the Bible and the rabbinic texts cited in this book to accommodate the spirit the rabbis brought to them and have employed a simplified transliteration system for the terms and texts cited in the original languages. In sum, what follows is the culmination of a decades-long effort in that spirit to understand the *aggadah* as a language-game.

I cannot emphasize too strongly that, as used here, *the term* aggadah *and its derivatives (pl.* aggadot, haggadah/haggadot, aggadeta*) are not to be taken as the equivalent of* midrash, *biblical interpretation of various kinds.* While *aggadah* and *midrash* are terms whose meanings substantially overlap, there is such a thing as halakhic *midrash*, and a large amount of *aggadah*, unlike the *midrash*, is not related to the Bible or to imaginative narrative. In this investigation, the term *aggadah* follows the common definition modern students of Judaism give it, namely, *aggadah* is all that part of rabbinic discourse which is not *halakhah*. To emphasize that these terms are not being used as loose, imaginative interpretations but with considerable terminological specificity, I employ two linguistic devices. First, I always italicize the terms *aggadah* and *midrash*. Second, in particularly sensitive contexts, I remind the reader that I am rigorously committed to *aggadah*'s embracing meaning as Non-Halakhic Discourse by occasionally utilizing the intentionally disruptive acronym NHD.

The argument I have made for employing a vaguely Wittgensteinian linguistic analysis to comprehend NHD should not be understood as suggesting that I think *aggadah* should always be studied in this manner. There is, I hope, too much reference to the important work of other students using other methods of investigating this material to support such an exclusive notion. Rather, I hope that, in their efforts to understand the rabbis, other scholars will find a place for the philosophical insight that rabbinic thought created a postscriptural, two-branched language-game that allowed them to extend and amplify what God had revealed to their forebears. This device nurtured the extraordinary freedom of religious thought and imagination that has long characterized Judaism. Much that is admirable in later Jewish intellectual life is explained by the rabbis' extraordinary linguistic accomplishment.

Chapter 1

ꤷ What Is the *Aggadah* Problem? ꤸ

The term *aggadah* is so widely used in the Talmud and early related literature that one would think it easy to ascertain its meaning. But the Talmudic masters do not provide us with formal definitions of their procedural terms. As it were, they seem too busy with their Torah work to step away from it and initiate outsiders into the nature of their analytic tools. Their terminological pragmatics was emulated by those who transmitted their teachings and the redactors who reduced these oral records to the written texts we still study. Since the rabbinic study tradition has never died out, this practice is, to a considerable extent, satisfactory. But particularly for those interested in how the rabbis thought about their belief—their "philosophizing" in a quite loose sense of the word—this absence of definition is disturbing and barely relieved by the common expedient of defining *aggadah* in terms of what it is not, namely, that it is Jewish law's nonlegal accompaniment.

A philological approach to a positive understanding does not help us much. Though the Hebrew root of the term, *n-g-d*, is well attested in the Bible and carries the primary meaning of "tell," the noun form with its collective sense appears only in rabbinic literature. Wilhelm Bacher's pioneering efforts to trace a path from the biblical "telling" to the polysemy of the rabbinic usage has not convinced most later scholars and their several alternative proposals have themselves not resolved the issue.[1]

Turning to the Talmud, we quickly encounter a reason for some of this terminological indeterminacy when we look at the use of the Hebrew version of this term, *haggadah*. It has three distinct and essentially unrelated uses. It may refer either to: testimony acceptable in the Jewish legal process;[2] or, the ritual retelling of the Exodus story at the home dinner-service, the seder, which begins the Passover festival;[3] or, overwhelmingly, to a surprising diversity of matters whose lack of an integrating character has led to the catchall definition, "any nonlegal passage." As a result, it has become customary to signal that one is not talking about the Haggadah of the seder (or a Jewish court procedure) but a critical kind of rabbinic discourse, by using the term's Aramaic form, *aggadah*.

We can most easily gain some positive insight into the nature of this discourse by studying what the sages directly said about the *aggadah* and then look at what one of its noted practitioners did in his nonlegal Talmudic statements. Specifically, we shall first focus on the rabbis' attitudes toward it compared to their views of the *halakhah*; then, we shall look at its appearance or absence in different lists of components of the Oral Torah; and, lastly, examine its content in the nonlegal teachings of an acknowledged master-aggadist, R. Samuel b. Naḥman.

The Unexpected Rabbinic Ambivalence to *Aggadah*: The Positive Side

In the Talmud and other early rabbinic literature there is widespread appreciation of the *aggadah* as a major constituent of the Oral Torah. R. Joshua b. Levi said that at Mt. Sinai God revealed "Bible and *mishnah* [?[4] sometimes: the general study of the Oral Torah; mostly: R. Judah the Nasi's orderly compilation of these traditions, the Mishnah]; *talmud* [? not yet set texts but a general term for the analytic study of biblical and rabbinic teachings]; *halakhot* [laws] and *aggadot* [? whose meaning is the subject of this study]. Even what an experienced disciple would in the future teach before his *rav* [master] was already told Moses at Sinai."[5] The reader should bear in mind that in this book the citations adduced for a given point are almost always a selection of the material available. Most of the aggadic passages cited in it could be used to substantiate many other observations about aggadic discourse, but to exhibit as much diverse rabbinic opinion as practical, most texts have been cited sparingly. Thus, the evidence for the various opinions put forward here is not limited to just what is cited in their support but is substantially cumulative; much of the citation in the entire work grounds much of what is asserted throughout. On this type of "logic," see the material on network organization in chapter 7. More generally, "The *Dorshe Haggadot* [the *Aggadah* Expounders, an otherwise unknown group] say: 'If you wish to recognize The-one-who-spoke-and-the-world-came-into-being, study *haggadah*, for by this you will recognize The-one-who-spoke-and-the-world-came-into-being and cling to His ways.' "[6]

As a consequence, study of the *aggadah* is an important duty for a disciple of the sages. Dt. 32:47 is understood to caution against distinguishing between easy and difficult Bible passages to study, even if we wish to concentrate on the difficult ones. So, too, we may not say we've learned enough *halakhot* "for the verse says not 'a commandment' or 'the commandment' but '*all* this commandment.' Hence you must study *midrash* [interpretation], *halakhah*, and *haggadah*," a view that Dt. 8:3 is cited as substantiating.[7] (This is the first of many passages indicating that Talmudic usage often links the term *aggadah* with biblical interpretation that is distinguished from *midrash*.) Elsewhere, R. Dimi chides Abaye for disputing an exegesis of his by asking, "Why aren't you familiar with the *aggadah*?"[8] In this vein, too, an anonymous view asserts that one cannot really know the mettle of a disciple of the sages until one has heard him teach *midrash*, *halakhot*, and *haggadot*.[9] Some rabbis are considered masters of *aggadah* (see below), and so R. Yoḥanan advises that when we hear R. Eliezer b. R. Yose Hagelili discoursing in *aggadah* we should "make our ears like a hopper" to take in his words.[10] Yet the study of *aggadah* should not be considered an easy thing (see below). Thus, when R. Simlai came to R. Yoḥanan to study *aggadah*, the master demurred teaching him on the basis of a family tradition not to teach Babylonians or southerners "for they are thick-witted and Torah lightweights"—but he agreed to teach him a halakhic matter which was, in fact, quite complex.[11] Instruction in *aggadah* as well as *halakhah* seems the usual practice, as we learn from the tale of R. Ami and R. Assi each asking their master to teach them the other discipline.[12]

Not only is there an imperative to study *aggadah*, but many of the laws concerning the study of *halakhah* apply equally to aggadic study. Thus, when such study has included ten men (the quorum for a fuller liturgy), at its conclusion the group recites the *kaddish derabbanan*, the standard full doxology with a special insertion for the rabbis and their disciples.[13] Or, as deep mourning precludes study of the *halakhah*, it equally proscribes study of the *aggadah*,[14] and since the observance of the Ninth of Av fast is based on the laws of mourning, aggadic study is also outlawed then.[15]

The great attraction of the *aggadah* is its wide and immediate appeal (an attribute that, as we shall see, also makes it troublesome). It is frequently compared to water, which, in an arid climate, "draws the heart of a man,"[16] but occasionally also to wine.[17] The result is that it can be pleasingly taken in by everybody.[18] R. Joshua, informed of the content of the Sabbath *aggadah* lecture that he had missed, called it a "precious pearl" and chided his students for being reticent to tell him about it.[19] R. Ḥananiah needed the support of R. Ḥiyya b. Ba to walk in Sephoris, but when R. Ḥiyya told him that everyone was running to hear R. Yoḥanan expound Torah, he blessed God for letting him see the fruits of his labor, since he had taught him "all the *aggadah* but that for Proverbs and Ecclesiastes."[20] (R. Ḥananiah apparently considered *aggadah* a special kind of biblical discipline.) R. Joshua b. Levi, praising the person who regularly does charity, says his reward will be sons who are "wise, wealthy and learned in *aggadah*."[21]

The *Aggadah* Disparaged

Though the *aggadah* is an integral part of God's Sinaitic revelation of the Oral Torah, it troubles many of the Talmudic masters, and this gives us an early indication of what will grow into the later problem more reflective generations had with this discourse. Thus, the rabbis' great appreciation of the *aggadah* is often offset by efforts to denigrate it and give it a status decidedly subsidiary to the *halakhah*, the dialectic study/teaching of mandatory Jewish religious duty. Thus, the glorious restoration of the Jewish people to God's favor is described in Hos. 14:8 as a state in which "they shall make the grain grow, they shall flower like the vine." The grain, the basic necessity, is *talmud* (the study/teaching dialectic mostly centered on halakhic matters), and the flowers, which provide beauty but not nutrition, are *aggadah*.[22] Here, as often, the deprecation of the *aggadah* is tempered by an appreciation of it as another aspect of Oral Torah. The same comparative strategy appears in a rabbinic comment on riches. The one who is rich in possessions and pomp, that is a master of *aggadot*; the one who is rich in money and oil, that is a master of *pilpul* (advanced study dialectic); and one who is rich in goods and storerooms, that is a master of *shemuot* (legal traditions); but all of them have need of the master of grain, *gemara* (the study/teaching dialectic based on the Mishnah).[23]

This hierarchy of value is correlated with a sense of the appropriately greater mental demands laid upon students of the *halakhah*, as we see in a tale about R. Jeremiah and his master, R. Zeira. When R. Jeremiah invited the sage to begin the instruction, R. Zeira begged off on the grounds that he was not feeling well. Whereupon R. Jeremiah suggested that he might perhaps still teach some *aggadah*, which he then did.[24] A group version of this sense of values occurs in tales about scholars who come to communities and cannot respond to the questions publicly put to them. When, for example, Levi b. Sisi failed to answer the first question—on a halakhic matter—put to him by the people of Simonia, they thought that, though Judah the Nasi had recommended him, he might only be a master of *aggadah,* so they then asked him a question in that realm to which, as it turned out, he also could not respond.[25] Something of this disparaging attitude lies behind the tale of R. Ḥiyya the Elder's surprising snub of R. Yishmael b. R. Yose in the bathhouse. When asked about this affront, R. Ḥiyya said he hadn't seen him since he was busy going over the *aggadah* of the whole book of Psalms.[26] That this eminent sage considered it appropriate amid the nakedness of the bathhouse to study aggadic traditions is an indication of the lesser seriousness he attached to them.

We get a rare general description of *aggadah* in R. Ḥinenah b. Papa's exposition of the first commandment of the Decalogue. He understands it as asserting God's unity despite the many aspects in which we meet God, in this instance the four "faces" shown in His revelation. Where the Bible shows us a threatening "face," the Mishnah an ordinary one, and the *talmud* a welcoming, explanatory one, the *aggadah* shows us a "playful face."[27] Some rabbis apparently felt that much aggadic teaching and exegesis is simply frivolous (a theme examined in later chapters) and a foray into "entertainment" unworthy of rabbinic leadership. This attitude lies behind the accounts of sages who come to speak in a community, with the one speaking on halakhic matters later disconsolate that most people rushed off to hear his colleague's aggadic discourse. When this happened to R. Ḥiyya b. Abba, he was consoled by his aggadic colleague, R. Abbahu, by being reminded that when one merchant sells precious stones and the other small wares, the masses naturally go to what they can afford, the cheap goods.[28] R. Yitzḥak blamed the same unhappy state on the economic suffering resulting from Roman rule, insisting that when times were good people had been eager to hear a Mishnah or *talmud* lesson but now only yearned to hear a biblical or aggadic teaching.[29]

To what extent the *aggadah*'s "playfulness" of content and process engendered its secondary status cannot be determined. Yet it is clear that frivolousness may easily cross the murky border into unacceptability even in a religiosity that allows extraordinary openness to the spiritual imagination. Remarkably enough, the rabbinic tradition preserves a reminder of such indecency. The rabbis interpreted Num. 15:30, "But the person who acts defiantly . . . shall be cut off" [from the Israelite people], to apply to "Menasseh b. Ḥizkiyah who sat and expounded [the technical phrase for formal teaching] *aggadot shel dofi* [tainted or reproachful *aggadot*]. Did Moses have nothing better to write than 'And the sister of Lotan was Timnah; and Timnah was the concubine of Elifaz'? [Gen. 36:12; or] 'And in the days of the wheat Reuben went and found mandrakes in the field'?" [Gen. 30:14]. A Heavenly Voice then uttered several condemnatory verses condemning such behavior.[30] Astonishingly, this cautionary tale is then followed by an *aggadah* in which Menasseh's question is reopened and an acceptably serious response to it is given. Aggadic freedom thus threatens to validate near-heretical exposition.

The rabbinic denigration of *aggadah* also has a substantive foundation. R. Levi interpreted the four gifts of God in Eccl. 6:2 to refer to Bible, *halakhot*, *tosafot* (non-Mishnaic Tannaitic traditions), and great Mishnah collections. But R. Levi said that when the verse refers to one whom God does not give the power to enjoy them, this referred to a master of *aggadah*. Such a teacher, for all his learning, "can neither prohibit nor permit, declare ritually impure nor ritually pure," which functions are God's supreme gifts of religious significance to the master of *talmud*.[31] Rabbinic Judaism cares preeminently about what one must do—a religious perspective with considerable biblical precedent. The authority for determining this is granted only to those who are masters of the halakhic process and, despite the aggadic competence required to be a sage of the Oral Torah, having that learning alone denies one the most significant Jewish authority.

R. Zeira[32] is the most outspoken critic of aggadic method, as we see from an extended passage in yMaas. 3.10. Sitting studying with R. Abba b. Kahana and R. Levi, he upbraided the aggadists, calling their books "magic books." When R. Abba b. Kahana challenged R. Zeira to give him a verse to interpret, R. Zeira produced the unclear Ps. 76:10: "For the wrath of men shall praise You; You will restrain the remainder of the fury." R. Abba b. Kahana interpreted the first phrase as referring to this world and the second phrase as refering to the world to come. This led R. Zeira to demonstrate that one might just as intelligently interpret it the other way around. R. Levi then sought to resolve the conflict by amalgamating the two interpretations into one. This led R. Zeira to say, "This one turns it and this one twists it, but we don't learn anything from it at all! Jeremiah, my son, sharpen up your study of the pruning shear [the halakhic matter they had previously been analyzing], for it is better than all of this [*aggadah*]."

Yonah Frenkel (= Fraenkel) seeks to mitigate the denunciatory effect of this passage and others that disparage the *aggadah*,[33] but not only does the weight of the negative passages count against him, but so, too, does the practice of serious-minded scholars of rabbinics to belittle the *aggadah* from the rabbis' time to our own. Raphael Patai gave this epitome of their attitude: "[I]n the Yeshivot ... which to this day are centers of traditional studies as they have been pursued for many centuries, all non-halakhic material is treated with much condescension as mere 'agad'te,' non-serious exercise of fancy, which can well be skipped or glossed over."[34] David Stern notes how late this attitude persisted even among university academics. The Hebrew University in Jerusalem, whose Institute of Jewish Studies began when the school was established, took half a century to find a specialist in *midrash* worthy of a professorship (of Hebrew literature, to be sure). Stern calls this "perhaps the ultimate sign that midrash had 'arrived' as a fully recognized subject within the Jewish literary curriculum."[35]

A somewhat circuitous deprecation of *aggadah* may also be seen in the appearance of books of *aggadot* (discussed later in this chapter) despite a strong polemic attitude against using written works for formal study-recitation.[36] Perhaps it was the lesser status of the *aggadah* that made it possible for works devoted to it to begin what some surely saw as the slippery descent to the oxymoron of a written Oral Torah.

This small collection of evidence about the curious realm of religious discourse called the *aggadah* prompts a deeper study of its nature and operation. Since usage seems the soundest way to achieve that, two relatively specific ways the term is often used suggest themselves as the areas with which to begin. The first usage, of which we have already had examples, is in lists of elements of the Oral Torah in which *aggadah* regularly but not inevitably has a place. These should, at least, provide an indication of what sectors of the Oral Torah the rabbis understood to be different from *aggadah* and of the extent to which they employed the "all that is not *halakhah*" definition. The second usage of the term, which derives from the first, is the designation of certain sages as "masters of *aggadah*." Studying what masters of *aggadah* do and what others ask of them should enable us to have an initial sense of what questions should guide our in-depth study of the nature of the *aggadah*.

Aggadah in Lists of Components of Oral Torah: Lists of Two or Three

In the course of many discussions, halakhic and aggadic alike, the rabbis specify various bodies of traditional teaching as parts of Oral Torah. These comments follow no regular form and cannot be said to supply a homogenous database that might yield a tightly drawn picture of what the rabbis included in Oral Torah and how the parts related to one another. Nonetheless, their statements in this vein are sufficiently frequent that they may give us a significant indication of their attitude to the *aggadah*.

The data quickly discloses that the term *aggadah* mostly occurs in lists with two or three other terms (besides the Bible—the Written Torah), though there are a number of statements that list more items. Nowhere in these enumerations do we find one that states the present general understanding that Oral Torah consists of *halakhah* and nonhalakhic material, the latter termed *aggadah*.[37] The closest we come to such a full scale bi-furcation of rabbinic literature is contrasts between public lecturers on halakhic and then on aggadic themes; occasional legal rulings, such as Judah the Nasi's that one who had a nocturnal emission might then teach *halakhah* but not *aggadah*; and the juxtaposition of various study options, such as the anonymous dictum that one asking a formal question about *halakhah* or *aggadah* must do so from a standing position.[38] We have here not only a repetition of the rabbinic ambivalence toward *aggadah* for its crowd appeal but also its equivalence with *halakhah* in the one case, offset by its distinction in another.

Two speculative reactions—the one substantive, the other linguistic—seem pertinent. These several rulings all concern public activities. It is not clear what their propounders would say about their relevance in the private realm, such as the solitary disciple's review of the day's learning. Moreover, two of these three texts do not speak of *halakhah* and *aggadah* but rather of *halakhot* and *aggadot*, a usage that, in fact, is predominant in such lists. The distinction between the singular and plural forms suggests the possibility that they refer to different understandings of the terms. The use of the singular lends itself to an integrated vision of the material—a class or a category—while the plural may reflect a less reflective, practical focus on statements which share a certain vague "family resemblance." But we clearly need much more data before drawing any conclusions here.

The lists with three components (besides Bible) mostly come in two forms, but there are a few anomalous lists as well. The two frequent forms seem almost formulaic, and perhaps the choice of opening term determines what then follows. Thus, the lists of three that begin with *mishnah* mostly continue with *talmud* and *aggadah*, while the ones that begin with *midrash* mostly continue with *halakhot veaggadot* (note the prior discussion of the plural forms).[39] One might conjecture that if *talmud* is understood as study of the Mishnah, then the lists appear to follow a logical order. That, however, makes it odd to then add *aggadah* to the list, since the Mishnah as it has come down to us includes considerable aggadic material. Furthermore, the absence of the term *halakhah* in this list is troubling, though it might simply be assumed to be part of *talmud* as rabbinic study. The other formula raises its own issues. Since it begins with *midrash*, it seems odd that *aggadot* are later mentioned separately, the two terms being so close, as indicated by the fact that the verb *d-r-sh*, which gives the one domain its name, is frequently used to describe someone teaching *aggadah*.[40] That leads to the suggestion that, in this list, *midrash* is a comprehensive term for rabbinic study, allowing us to substantiate the common rule that *halakhot* and non*halakhot*—that is, *aggadot*—are the constituent parts of Oral Torah. Since we do have works of so-called halakhic *midrash*— namely, *Mekhilta*, *Sifra*, and *Sifre*—as well as numerous books of aggadic *midrash*, the proposal has a certain appeal. Before analyzing it further, the anomalous lists of three should be noted. In *San.* 33b we hear that when R. Meir gave a public lecture, he devoted a third of it to halakhic traditions, a third to *aggadah*, and a third to parables. In *Mek. Vayasa* 1 (H/R 157) God's revelation is understood as *aggadot, gezerot* [harsh decrees], and *halakhot*. In *AdRN* 14 the two formulas are mixed to produce *mishnah, halakhot veaggadot*.

Louis Finkelstein published the most significant defense of the notion that the *midrash* formula was the earliest curriculum of rabbinic Jewish study, and thus, I infer, a comprehensive introduction to Oral Torah.[41] There are many reasons to question this view. The *mishnah* formula occurs as frequently and, in a number of such instances, Finkelstein can only suggest that the text really should read *"midrash."* Moreover, there are even more four-term than three-term formulas in early rabbinic literature and a few that grow to five or six terms. If we can most reliably try to understand the term *aggadah* by exploring its usage, the bulk of the evidence is against its being understood by the rabbis as one of the two parts that alone make up the Oral Torah.

Aggadah in Lists of Components of Oral Torah: Lists of Four or More

Where the lists including only two or three constituents of Oral Torah largely take two forms, the variety in form increases when we examine the large number of lists containing four components (aside from Bible). The obvious candidate for a longer list formula would seem to be one that includes both *mishnah* and *midrash*, but almost twice as many more lists follow *mishnah* with *talmud*, an initial sequence popular also in lists with more than four members. And whether the lists of four items begin with either *mishnah, midrash* or *mishnah, talmud*, these pairs then regularly conclude with *halakhot veaggadot* (with some variation).[42] None of the previous material prepares us for four additional *mishnah, talmud* passages (all found in aggadic works) in which *tosefet*, "supplement" (the Tosefta?) replaces *halakhah*.[43] Thus, in these lists, we do not find the *halakhot veaggadot* formula at all, adding a further bit of evidence against its serving as an axiom of rabbinic discourse in this period. Two further variants of the list of four occur, one that follows *mishnah* with *gemara* rather than *midrash* or *talmud*,[44] and the other with the unique reading *midrash vehalakhot, veaggadot vetoseftot*.[45]

All the major terms—*mishnah, talmud, midrash, halakhot ve-aggadot*—are united in a list of five found in a halakhic passage applying the study rules with regard to mourners to the general observance of the Ninth of Av fast.[46] What may be called a list of six occurs in a charming colloquy between God and the Torah, personified as a woman. She dresses in mourning because people turn verses from the Song of Songs into drinking-place songs. When God inquires what people should be occupying themselves with at banquets, she responds, "If they are masters of *mishnah* let them occupy themselves with *mishnah, halakhot ve-haggadot* and if they are masters of *talmud* let them occupy themselves with the laws of [whichever of the three] festivals [on which they are feasting]."[47] The curriculum R. Akiba mastered in the tale recounted of his becoming a student at age forty provides us with another list of six study topics: *targum* [the Aramaic interpretive translation of the Bible], *midrash, halakhot ve-aggadot, siḥin* [languages of various creatures], and *meshalim* [parables]. "He learned them all."[48] A list of eight occurs in an interpretation of Dt. 32:13 and includes *mishnah, talmud*, inferences from minor to major, analogies, laws, answers to legal inquiries, *halakhot*, and *haggadot*.[49]

However, the undoubted champion of all lists of study material is detailed in praise of R. Yoḥanan.

> They said about R. Yoḥanan b. Zakkai that he did not neglect [studying] Bible, *mishnah, gemara, halakhot, aggadot*, the details of the Torah [text], the details of rabbinic traditions, inferences from minor to major, analogical reasoning, eras, numerical equivalents, launderers' fables, fox

fables, the language of spirits, the language of palm trees, and the language of the ministering angels, a great matter—the Work of the Chariot—and a small matter—the arguments of Abaye and Rava.[50]

We must also take into account that, as even an informal survey indicates, there are a small but not negligible number of lists in this vein that do not include *aggadah* at all. Many of these lists seek to provide a concise indication of what a sage ought to know. Their simplest form is perhaps R. Pinḥas's tradition of R. Joshua's observation that before Vespasian destroyed them, Jerusalem had four hundred Houses of Assembly, each with a general school and a *talmud* school, the former teaching Bible and the latter *mishnah*.[51] R. Joshua describes the study of God's Torah-revelation as divided into the Written Torah, the Bible as a whole, and the Oral Torah, whose major elements are *mishnah* and *talmud*.[52]

What We Learn from *Aggadah* in Rabbinic Lists

From the appearance and absence of the term *aggadah* in a variety of rabbinic lists, we see that it is a significant part of Oral Torah, one far more significant than *tosefet*, for example, and one adduced more frequently than *gemara*, though that term may be included in the frequently appearing *talmud*. *Aggadah* mostly appears as a collective singular, as befits its being another of the subgenres of the Oral Torah. However, references to this discourse regularly use the plural form, *aggadot*, with a conjunction linking it to *halakhot* (*halakhot ve-aggadot*, though the conjunction may merely indicate the conclusion of the list as a whole). In contemporary discussions about rabbinic Judaism the singular and plural forms are generally taken as equivalents, but a nuance should also be considered: that while the singular points to an integrated sense of the domain, the plural may signify only an atomistic understanding. These rabbis may only be referring to bodies of traditions rather than a developed realm of discourse (a way of speaking that has not yet developed into a "game"). And despite the possible conjunction of *halakhah* and *aggadah* noted above, the one realm where the two types of discourse are regularly linked and contrasted is public presentations. The audience may be either the community at large or the disciples, but the lecturer is described as speaking in one or the other of the modes or perhaps dividing his time between them in a certain way. Thus far, only in such circumstances does our evidence indicate that, as the common rule has it, rabbinic discourse operates in either a halakhic or a nonhalakhic, aggadic, mode.

These observations provide a context for understanding some additional data concerning the *aggadah*. We are not surprised when we hear from R. Tanḥuma that he knows how to resolve the clash between the Torah's specification of the dimensions of the Tabernacle and the Holy of Holies because of a *masoret aggadah*, an aggadic tradition.[53] Some further examples of data explicitly identified as aggadic traditions are that Nebuchadnezzar was murdered by his mother's husband,[54] that Jacob's children were the destined conquerors of Esau's descendants,[55] and that Seraḥ [daughter of Asher] was made a mill slave in Egypt.[56] Such traditions seem utterly consonant with the orality of the Oral Torah. Then, too, we hear of specialists in this branch of the teaching. Some rabbis—some young enough not to have completed their disciplehood—serve their teacher as his *mesader aggadeta*, literally, "orderer" (more likely, "reciter" or "reviewer" of *aggadah*), another clearly oral activity.[57] Others, as we heard above, are called *baalei aggadah*, masters of this material.[58] But a variety of terms is used for such scholars, like *baki baaggadah*, steeped in *aggadah*, as we hear of R. Yishmael[59] and of R. Joshua b. Levi;[60] and *rabanan deaggadeta*, sages who are specialists in *aggadah*.[61] Elsewhere we are warned not to confuse R. Isaac b. Aḥa, who is a halakhist, *deshemaata*, and R. Isaac b. Pinḥas, who is an aggadist, *deaggadah*.[62] Occasionally we read of certain teachers who have no aggadic title but are nonetheless reported to have studied *aggadah* intently, such as R. Papa and R. Huna.[63] The most outstanding of these untitled aggadic masters is R. Elazar Hamodai, who four times is honored as the resolver of disputes about biblical meanings, with the senior sage involved reciting the formula, "[The matter remaining unsettled] We still need [the teaching of] the Modai."[64] The prevalence of such experts may perhaps be gauged from R. Joshua b. Levi's account of his effort—despite himself being a recognized aggadic expert—to get a satisfactory explanation of the difficult verse, Gen. 46:1. "I went back and forth among all the *baalei aggadah* in the south and couldn't get a satisfactory answer until I came to Judah b. Pedayah."[65]

That the *aggadah* is so fully a part of the traditions of Oral Torah makes it all the more surprising that the Talmud has numerous references to its being written down, something we do not hear of any other components of the Oral Torah noted above. This practice evoked considerable controversy, and only occasionally are books of *aggadah* spoken of positively, as when R. Ḥisda directed his student R. Taḥlia b. Abina to write [the meaning of] two uncommon Hebrew words into his *aggadah* book.[66] Perhaps we may say the same of R. Yaakov b. Aḥa's nonjudgmental citation of a teaching he had seen in an *aggadah* book. However, that dictum turns out to be a halakhic statement pertinent to the rabbinic discussion of the especially lenient procedural laws that apply to prosecutions of non-Jews as against those that apply to Jews.[67] Many statements about aggadic books are ambivalent toward them, some strikingly so. Thus, R. Joshua b. Levi's anathema of those who write such books, speak from them, or listen to such presentations is followed by his account of the one occasion when he looked into one and discovered an admittedly fine insight into Abraham's longevity. But the account then notes, "Even so, I was fearful that night."[68] The same play of two attitudes occurs in the report that R. Yoḥanan and Resh Lakish deeply studied an aggadic book on Shabbat. This immediately engenders the (rhetorical?) objection, "But this material was not given so as to be written," and the response—ultimately the classic justification for writing down other bodies of the Oral Torah—"When necessity demands it [we invoke Ps. 119:26] 'It is time to work for *Adonai*, [therefore] they [may] break with your Torah.' "[69] The ambivalence may also be seen in the practice of respected figures. Both R. Yoḥanan and R. Naḥman are reported to have given their *aggadah* books the respect due them by asking their disciples to hold them when they went into the privy. Yet they did not then take off their phylacteries. They explained, saying that since the rabbis had mandated the phylacteries they would protect the sages in this dangerous locale, but the rabbis had not sanctioned aggadic books, so carrying them into the privy would add to their [spiritual] risk.[70] And in three places we hear that Rava authorized seizing *aggadah* books and other property inherited by orphans and returning them to a believable claimant to their ownership, because they were articles people customarily lent or hired out.[71]

This line of inquiry has expanded our understanding of *aggadah* as one among other constituents of the Oral Torah, but it has only given us some hints about its special area of concern and, more importantly for our purposes, even less information about its particular way of shaping the content it presents. For an initial foray into these matters we take a look at the dicta ascribed to a recognized *baal aggadah*, R. Samuel b. Naḥman (sometimes, "Naḥmani").

The Aggadic Practice of R. Samuel b. Naḥman

Four stories with a common rhetorical form testify to R. Samuel b. Naḥman's aggadic eminence.[72] They begin with the flattering formula: "Because I have heard that you are a *baal aggadah*," and then ask "what is the meaning of . . . ," a biblical verse troubling them. R. Simon b. Yehotzedek has a feasability problem and wants to know the source of the light God created for the universe (Gen. 1:3). The other three inquirers are troubled by certain biblical assertions: R. Judah the Nasi II, that God rides the clouds (Ps. 68:5); R. Ami, that God's righteousness extends to the [heavenly] heights (Ps. 71:19); and R. Ḥelbo, that God has now made the clouds a barrier to prayer (Lam. 3:43). R. Samuel b. Naḥman then unhesitatingly gives an explanatory response and generally, but not always, climaxes his statement with a supporting biblical verse.

These accounts provide unique insight into the nature and process of aggadic discourse, for they are the only ones that identify the discourse they are involved in as *aggadah*. R. Simon b. Naḥman is approached explicitly because he is known to be an expert in that realm and is asked a question pertinent to his expertise. There is good reason for considering the rest of the texts adduced in this volume (including many others of R. Samuel b. Naḥman) as *aggadah*, but those texts do not so label themselves; we judge them to be aggadic. The specificity of these four tales about R. Samuel b. Naḥman may tempt us to generalize from them and insist that they constitute a template for all aggadic discourse, but we must soberly consider them only a limited, if excellent, example of *aggadah*. However, limited as this data is, it provides us with valuable guidance for moving on to study our many other texts in considerable depth.

Thus, the questions posed to the aggadic master all concern meaning rather than action. Something in what the Bible says clashes with the way in which these rabbis normally understand things to occur. R. Simon b. Yehotzedek cannot understand how light can be created merely by God's words, and R. Judah the Nasi II, R. Ami and R. Ḥelbo are taken aback by biblical wording that violates their understanding of accepted Jewish teaching. To that R. Samuel b. Naḥman responds in cultural or biblical terms that his hearer will find meaningful and then generally elaborates on his response by the citation of a supporting biblical verse.[73] Mostly he does not seek to demonstrate that something in the troubling text itself prompts his response, though he demonstrates this possibility to R. Judah the Nasi II by reading what seems clearly meant as God's name (here with a preposition) as a word meaning "government," and thus a textual prop for his argument by analogy.[74] Furthermore, he draws on a considerable body of nonbiblical knowledge for many of his answers. Thus, the response to R. Ami assumes he agrees that the (heavenly) heights—an impersonal designation—are occupied by heavenly creatures; the instruction to R. Ḥelbo is based on the analogy of prayer to a *mikveh*, "ritual bath," and of repentance to the sea; and that given to R. Judah the Nasi II, appropriately enough, refers to the nature of government.[75]

From this limited sample we may say that *aggadah* is principally concerned with biblical interpretation, though in ways that apparently distinguish it from *mikra*, Bible (the Written Torah), and *midrash*, biblical exegesis that embraces halakhic as well as aggadic topics. The relationship of *midrash* and *aggadah* in this period is not clear, though the former seems closely bound to its textual base, while the latter seems here less focused on exegesis—even imaginatively creative exegesis—than on traditions of the text's meaning whose origins are not specified. Aggadists presume that the text is meant to be intelligible to the informed but not specialist reader and that there is an ideal integrity to biblical meaning that the rabbis seek to elucidate and propound to their students and the public. In that effort, they find analogies to ordinary life a useful tool in elucidating this integrated meaning. Yet—and here we move from the data of the four accounts to the contexts in which we now find them—no matter how convincing their teachings seem to us, they are not presented as mandatory, as the way we are required to understand a given text. In fact, aggadic views are often presented to us, as here, as one of a number of informed opinions about this theme.[76] (It should come as little surprise, then, that, as we shall see later, the multiplication of additional insights into a text is considered religiously meritorious.)

None of our four paradigmatic stories of R. Samuel b. Naḥman occurs in the Babylonian Talmud, the classic work that grounds all later Judaism and thus is the major focus of our study. To see what R. Samuel b. Naḥman's aggadic practice was as the Bavli records it, we must accept the limited certainty that comes with identifying the data by the commonly accepted definition of *aggadah*: that which is not *halakhah*. By that standard, the aggadic passages attributed to him in the Talmud seem to follow four major patterns: the largest number, by far, explain a verse but with no textual exegesis; some do build on an exegesis of a biblical text; others merely conclude with a verifying text; and the remaining passages make their point without any reference to a biblical text. Let us look at some examples of each category.

Most of the time, R. Samuel b. Naḥman will indicate what a verse teaches but then provides little indication of how he got from the text itself to what he tells us about it. Thus, when Boaz invites Ruth not only to eat her meal near him at the threshing floor but also suggests that she feel free to dip it into the vinegar condiment, we are told that this foretells that one of her descendants will be the nefarious King Menasseh.[77] The metaphors used by the proverb about finding joy in the wife of one's youth indicate that there is something delightfully erotic about Torah study.[78] When the Hallelujah Psalm moves from praising God's mighty acts to glorifying the person who does righteousness at all times, that high ideal becomes an encomium for one who raises orphans and then enables them to marry.[79] The prophet's ecstatic vision of the precious stones that will decorate the walls of postexilic Jewish settlements is obscure enough in some of its terms that R. Samuel b. Naḥman pictures the archangels Michael and Gabriel in heaven debating the meaning of the word *kadkhod*.[80]

He can, however, also move to his message by direct exegesis. Sometimes this involves meticulous attention to the details of the text. If the place name Ramat-Zophim concludes with a plural there must be two such places;[81] if we read that one "goes up" to Timnah as well as one "goes down" to get there, that must be because there are two such places;[82] and if a verb in the singular introduces the Judean exiles to Babylonia—namely, Daniel, Ḥananiah, Mishael, and Azariah—it must be because only Daniel was a descendant of the tribal progenitor Judah.[83] At other times, the exegesis seems more a product of the imagination. At its simplest, this involves direct word-association, as when the exegete notes that the same verb is used to describe a victory of Moses as well as one of Joshua, indicating that the sun stood still for both of them.[84] Mostly, however, the associations are more creative than textually motivated: as when the reward of "precious," *toafot*, silver promised in Job 22:25 means it will fly directly to you, since the verb "to fly," *uf*, is implied by the adjective;[85] or when the vowels of *befarekh*, "rigor[?]," used to describe the workload of Egyptian slavery in Ex. 1:13, are changed and the letter *heh* is added to make *beferikah*, which may, perhaps, be freely read as "by the book";[86] and where King Asa's bier was piled with *besamim uzenim*, diverse [?] spices, R. Samuel b. Naḥman, noting the similarity of *uzenim* to the verbal root *z-n-h*, meaning "to whore," disparages this rabbinic villain by saying that even in death he wallowed in aphrodisiacs.[87] His imagination can also reach quite far: the condemnation of foolish behavior in Prov. 30:32 is inverted to praise one who suffers in order to learn and condemns the withdrawn student;[88] the shift of noun from *naarah*, lass, to *almah*, young woman, in Ex. 2:8 points by means of the root of that term (ʿ- l-m) to Jochebed having hid her familial interest in rescuing the baby Moses from the Nile;[89] and the vision in Ez. 47:12 of streams emerging from a restored Temple producing trees whose leaves heal illness becomes in the aggadist's view leaves that make scholars' faces beautiful.[90]

On occasion R. Samuel b. Naḥman will state his message first and only adduce a substantiating biblical text as the climax and conclusion of his teaching. Thus, his response to a community beset by famine and pestilence asking which of these to petition God to take away counsels praying instead for abundance, since it is given for the living, a notion he sees in Ps. 145:16;[91] in Ex. 2:3 the basket with the baby Moses is laid in the *suf* along the Nile's banks, which brings to mind the reeds of Is. 19:5;[92] agreeing with sages who deprecate starting a task but not finishing it, R. Samuel b. Naḥman adds to the punishments of incompletion that the miscreant will bury his wife and children, as happened to Judah, according to Gen. 38:12 and 46:12;[93] he touchingly says, "All things can be replaced except the wife of one's youth" and cites Is. 54:6 to "prove" it;[94] and after two other statements are given about the length of time the sun stayed still for Joshua, he is cited as agreeing that it did the same for Moses and then quoting Dt. 2:25.[95] This final Talmudic text is of particular interest, because R. Samuel b. Naḥman introduces his text by saying, "*Migufeih* [from the body of the text] you learn this," but the verse only talks about peoples fearing Moses so that "they shall tremble and quake because of you." He assumes that everyone will hear in these words the echo of what was later said to Joshua, thus allowing the identification of what happened to the one to be true of the other. It is an extraordinary example of what "close reading" can become when practiced by an aggadist.

Were this all the aggadic material in the Talmud attributable to R. Samuel b. Naḥman, we would be justified in presuming that aggadic discourse was a special variety of biblical study, one less focused on the text than *mikra* or on its exegesis than is nonlegal *midrash* (with which, clearly, it overlaps). But we also find a small but significant number of his nonhalakhic teachings that have no relation to a specific biblical text. Two of these bear on biblical personalities. In the first case, a disciple asks why, when Jacob removed the birthright from Reuben, he bestowed it on Joseph. He is answered by an analogy from the case of a grateful orphan who, on becoming rich, showered his benefactor with kindness (as Joseph did to Jacob and his extended family in Egypt).[96] The second case is simpler, R. Samuel b. Naḥman simply saying that the angel who wrestled with Jacob at the ford of the Jabbok had the appearance of a heathen.[97] The three other instances are completely independent of the Bible: the *maamad*, the community representatives at the Temple for a certain period, had to fast on Sunday because that was the third day after the creation of man;[98] one who has the merit of having studied *mikra* and *mishnah* but has never given a disciple's personal service to a master is simply a boor;[99] and the returnees from exile could find the site of the innermost structure in the utterly destroyed Temple area by the smell that the old incense still gave off, and so, too, they could find the site of the altar by the odor of the limbs that had been sacrificed there.[100]

This data, preliminary though it be, prompts a critical question with regard to the nature of *aggadah*: how did what appears at this stage to be an area focusing on biblical meanings and associations come to be understood as one embracing every nonlegal statement, regardless of a relation to the Bible? Moreover, most of R. Samuel b. Naḥman's dicta occur as one of several differing opinions, and some of these are objected to by other sages on the basis of contrary data or opinion. Considering, too, the hints we have had about how strongly imaginative aggadic exegesis can be, one cannot help but wonder with R. Zeira what the point is of such freely flowing aggadic discourse.

Extending our coverage of R. Samuel b. Naḥman's teaching to include the Jerusalem Talmud (the Yerushalmi) and early *midrash* collections like *Genesis Rabbah*, *Leviticus Rabbah*, and *Lamentations Rabbah* does not resolve these issues. If anything, such broader study of his aggadic discourse gives us further reason for puzzling over them. The Yerushalmi has forty-six different aggadic passages attributed to R. Samuel b. Naḥman (plus ten others that substantially duplicate some of these), about the same amount of aggadic material we find in the Bavli. These readily conform to the four patterns of his aggadic utterance in the Babylonian Talmud. Again the bulk of his *aggadah* is in the form of general, nonexegetic comments on biblical verses, but the Yerushalmi has hardly any aggadic statements by him grounding his interpretation of a verse on its close reading.[101] The rest of his comments are about evenly divided between those climaxing the teaching by citing a supporting biblical verse and dicta made without reference to a verse, about the same distribution of these forms that we found in the Bavli.[102]

Turning our attention now to citations of R. Samuel b. Naḥman in *Genesis Rabbah, Leviticus Rabbah,* and *Lamentations Rabbah* does not materially alter the view of *aggadah* we have thus far gained. True, the proportion of his nonhalakhic comments that do not cite a biblical verse is drastically lessened in these works—seven out of a total of one hundred twenty-eight—but that is not surprising in works devoted to teaching about the Bible. In each of these *midrash* works the use of a text to clinch a previously stated position is the predominant form of the passage, but, in contrast to the Yerushalmi, *Gen. R.* and *Lev. R.* report him often closely reading the text he is expounding, as seems appropriate for a *midrash* book.[103] We encounter some relatively lengthy aggadic passages in these books, though it is difficult to determine how much of them after the introductory exposition is his teaching or the work of energetic redactors. In the uncommon series of introductory presentations that precede the comments on the book of Lamentations, there is one of considerable length that demonstrates considerable artistic merit and is attributed to R. Samuel b. Naḥman (but would be quite uncommon for a single sage).[104] Rhetorical and redactional considerations seem to lie behind other such lengthy statements. *Genesis Rabbah* and *Leviticus Rabbah* record slightly different versions of the master's rule that the verb form *vayehi*, "and it came to pass," connotes trouble, while the same verb in the form *vehayah*, "and it happened," connotes joy. This assertion unleashes a cascade of objections that allow the aggadist to teach the proper interpretation of many other Bible texts. This structure is rhetorically grounded, since aggadic discourse is broadly hospitable to diverse opinion, as demonstrated by R. Yoḥanan's contrary view that introduces this passage.[105] However, other such rhetorical devices may similarly be deployed. Commenting on why Gen. 38:2 says "These are the generations of Jacob" and then immediately names Joseph and not Reuben, Jacob's firstborn, the aggadist responds with a torrent of parallel happenings in the lives of Jacob and Joseph (but without mentioning the biblical verses to substantiate this, apparently because he expects his hearers will be able to do this for themselves).[106] Or, in another such lengthy, rhetorically shaped passage, we have the unhesitating comparison of God's mourning over the destruction of the Temple, Lam. 3:28, to the mourning of an earthly king. Anthropomorphic teaching shows its special power as R. Samuel b. Naḥman introduces his theme by having

God inquire of the Ministering Angels, "What does a human king do [in such a situation]?" and, on receiving their response, poignantly saying, "That is what I will do."[107]

Some exceptional, briefer texts demand citation here. One charmingly relates the childhood circumstances (and gives us some insight into how the rabbis lived) in which R. Samuel b. Naḥman heard about R. Meir's Torah scroll. This text did not have the usual statement that the creation was very (*meod*) good, but that death (*mavet*) was good. The tale says he heard about this when R. Simeon b. Elazar discussed it one day as the youngster was seated on his grandfather's shoulder during the walk from their town to Kefar Ḥana.[108] Perhaps the most astonishing of all the imaginative exegeses of R. Samuel b. Naḥman is that of Gen. 35:8, which says that the oak under which Deborah, Rebecca's nurse, was buried was therefore called *Alon Bakhut*, customarily understood as "the oak of weeping." R. Samuel b. Naḥman blithely says of this name, "It is Greek, in which *alon* means 'another,'" and he goes on to say, without direct textual basis, that his mother had also died.[109] If aggadic discourse allows one to interpret the Bible as written in languages other than Hebrew (and Aramaic), one wonders what limits, if any, there are for its grant of freedom and what sense of this discourse its hearers must have brought to such potentially uninhibited instruction—and this becomes an important aspect of the "*aggadah* problem" already at this early stage in rabbinic discourse.

We might gain some insight into these matters if we could resolve the baffling dictum of R. Samuel b. Naḥman extending the view of his teacher, R. Jonathan, that God permitted three people to ask things of Him, Solomon, Ahaz, and King Messiah. To this R. Samuel b. Naḥman is reported to have said, "We can adduce two more from the *haggadah*." He then cites two verses indicating that Abraham and Jacob thanked God for what God would be giving them—from which the master aggadist infers that the assurance that prompted the thanks must have come from God's previously inviting them to ask.[110] But what does R. Samuel b. Naḥman teach us about the "*haggadah*" here? Surely R. Jonathan's remarks are also "*haggadah*," being a nonlegal statement based on explicit biblical instructions. Is the disciple saying that his additions, despite their being a considerably inferential interpretation of texts, are also *haggadah*? If that is all he is saying, then why only two additions, since such imaginative reading would allow for many further candidates for this honor? Or is R. Samuel b. Naḥman saying that he is applying a special form of discourse that yields his lesson? Intriguing as the usage is here, I do not see that we can find anything in this text that enables us to resolve the enigma of the character of "*haggadah*."

If we are to get some deeper insight into the nature and process of *aggadah* we must change the scope of our investigation, moving from a direct study of the term "*aggadah*" to a study of a substantial sample of the Rabbis' nonhalakhic discourse. This shift to a description and analysis of NHD itself again comes with the lessened certainty that all the data is *aggadah*, since these statements are not explicitly designated as in that category. However, working inductively with the material that the common scholarly definition (NHD) says is *aggadah* should allow us to say what can be said with a textual basis about its character and the manner in which its kind of thinking is shaped. Our inquiry, therefore, will now proceed in two major steps. First, we shall select a substantial sample of NHD in the Babylonian Talmud, the classic Jewish rabbinic text, and see what its details indicate about the nature and process of aggadic discourse. Second, after extending our database to include further material from the Talmud as well as data from the Yerushalmi and the early *midrash* books, we shall seek to determine what limits aggadic discourse and then consider what might explain the uncommon character of the *aggadah*. The book closes with a brief personal reflection on how these findings might bear on the work of Jewish theology today.

Part Two

Scrutinizing Talmudic *Aggadah* at Three Levels

Chapter 2

⋖ The Surface Characteristics ⋗

Establishing a representative sample of Talmudic *aggadah* for investigation is a contentious enterprise. By following a mathematical procedure I tried to randomize the selection process somewhat, thus reducing its inevitable subjectivity to manageable proportions. I therefore first selected a medium-sized Talmudic tractate to examine in its entirety, considering several likely to be dealing with law actually in practice and not primarily theoretical. I chose *Shevuot* (hereafter *Shev.*), "Oaths," of the order *Nezikin*, "Damages." I then supplemented this tractate with a chapter each from tractates of the five other orders of the Talmud, both tractate and chapter having roughly an increasing ordinal position. Thus, the universe for selecting the sample consisted of chap. 1 of *Berakhot* (*Ber.*), "Blessings," chap. 2 of *Eruvin*, (*Er.*), "Sabbath and Holy Day Bounds," chap. 3 of *Nedarim*, (*Ned.*), "Vows," chap. 4 of *Hullin*, (*Hul.*), "Unconsecrated Animals," and chap. 5 of *Niddah*, (*Nid.*), "The Menstruant."[1]

The Problem of Determining What Is *Halakhah*

The first difficulty confronting this investigation arose from the accepted definition of *aggadah* as all the material in rabbinic discourse that is not *halakhah*. However, the Talmud text does not explicitly distinguish *aggadah* from *halakhah*, either by placement, specific terms, or other device. Hence to discover the aggadic data meant first finding the halakhic discourse and bracketing it. But just how does one identify *halakhah* in this period, the time of the conclusion of the Talmud?[2] When one knows the Torah's commands and the Mishnah's mandates, one can feel somewhat more confident of one's judgments in this matter, but the literary style of Talmudic discussion so tightly interweaves the legal topics and their ancillary themes that distinguishing between them seems largely an act of the investigator's imagination.[3]

Exhortative passages constitute a typically ambiguous borderline category. They may speak of a required act and thus appear to be *halakhah*. But rather than specify just what one must do, they may only indicate the great desirability of acting this way.[4] In such cases I judged that the rabbis teaching in this fashion were not speaking with full juridic authority and enjoining a discipline, *halakhah*, but giving important but not mandated guidance, *aggadah*.[5]

The dynamics of legal development also complicate this method of identifying Talmudic *aggadah*. What once was a valued but voluntary act often later was legally enjoined and thus became a law. However, the codes, which clarify such matters, are centuries later than the period we are talking about. Surely, one should not judge texts from the first six centuries of the Common Era by what the great law codes of much later times declare the *halakhah* to be.

Let me illustrate something of these difficulties by turning to two tales of R. Samuel b. Nahman (a recognized master aggadist, as we saw) that, upon deliberation, I classified as more halakhic than should be included in a study of *aggadah*. In the one instance the rabbis were debating whether a ban pronounced on one of their number for sexual transgression should be lifted because of his great expertise in certain areas of the Oral Law. R. Samuel b. Nahman is quoted as objecting that if the rabbis had not lifted a ban against one of their colleagues who had been anathematized for a lesser infraction, then they certainly should not do so in this case.[6] I hesitated in this case, because the account of the case reflects a fine sense of narrative and moves toward a climax that occurs on the death of the miscreant. These are not the customary attributes of halakhic diction but of a certain kind of aggadic rhetoric. Yet what is reported about R. Samuel b. Nahman indicates a legal stance of his. Thus, with some misgivings, I eliminated it from the aggadic data used above to study R. Samuel b. Nahman as an aggadist. He is also a significant figure in another passage dealing with a sexual issue, this time of a man who became so obsessed with a certain woman that it threatened his life.[7] The physicians indicated that he would die if the rabbis insisted that he not only could not have intercourse with her or see her naked but even talk to her, sight unseen, from the other side of a cloth. On this issue, too, R. Samuel b. Nahman ruled stringently, despite the danger. In this account the rhetorical aspects of the exposition are even clearer. The case seems more likely to be a heuristic device, more theoretical *halakhah* than practical, but, for our purposes, it is more halakhic than aggadic discourse. I also thought it unlikely that the definition of the terms ought to be applied so rigidly that this material should be judged to be aggadic up to the words where a legal ruling is made. The rabbis seem to me quite satisfied operating with imprecise rules for their "language-game" and comfortable in their community practice of something like what moderns might term "fuzzy logic." So I also barred this passage from the study of R. Samuel b. Naḥman's *aggadah*.

These caveats about the sampling and other that will emerge should be kept in mind as the study moves forward. In this first section of this book, it does so by analyzing the Talmudic sample on three levels in vertical sequence, as it were, moving from its surface manifestations to its underlying "logic." This chapter describes the broad, external characteristics of the aggadic sample. The next chapter delves into its thematic content and the customary manners of expressing it. The last of these chapters then seeks to expose the operations that structure nonhalakhic discourse in the Talmud.

Where Do Aggadic Passages Occur in the Talmud?

Overwhelmingly, Talmudic *aggadah* is embedded in a halakhic context. Occasionally, an aggadic passage (or several together) seems quite independent of its surrounding text and, rarely, *aggadah* goes on at length to become a lengthy series of *aggadot*. In three of the tractates in the sample, including all of tractate *Shevuot*, there was little *aggadah* indeed, roughly between 1 and 3 percent of the whole. In chapters 2 of *Eruvin* and 3 of *Nedarim*, about 25 percent of the text was aggadic. Chapter 1 of *Berakhot* is well known for its high aggadic content, perhaps as much as 65 percent of its bulk. The variation in these findings approximates what students of the Talmud have previously reported.

No single theory consistently explains this eccentric distribution. In *Shevuot*, though the smallest chapters have the least *aggadah*, the largest chapters do not have the most. The Mishnah topics on which the Talmudic discussions center generally have little relationship to the amount of subsequent aggadic material. In *Ber.* chap. 1, the Mishnah's legalistic discussion of the correct time for saying the Shema prayers leads into a far-ranging discussion of prayer and liturgical etiquette, generalities that invite aggadic comment. In *Er.* chap. 2, however, the bulk of the aggadic texts are engendered by a discussion about which enclosures of a public well halakhically qualify them to be considered the legal equivalent of private property and, hence, areas in which one might carry burdens on the Sabbath. For some reason, a small anthology of aggadic comment occurs here, much of it a series of comments on the word "two," which was critical to two efforts to clarify the legal niceties involved.[8] More logically, Ḥul. chap. 4, which details what animals may or may not be eaten, has little *aggadah*, and the aggadic Mishnah text of *Ned.* 3:11 generates the substantial cluster of *aggadah* on folios 31b–32b. However, though the theme of vows leads to the considerable *aggadah* of *Ned.* chap. 3, tractate *Shevuot*, all of which treats of oaths, has little nonhalakhic content.

The simplest explanation for the eccentric occurrence of *aggadah* in the Talmud seems to be that it roughly recapitulates the Mishnah in this regard. The older text is centrally halakhic and only sporadically aggadic, and so is the Talmud, though the Talmud's far looser form of organization permitted the aggadic material to accrete to the halakhic texts rather randomly. (For a comparison of the Babylonian and Jerusalem Talmuds in this regard, see chapter 5.)

This mention of randomness should not be taken as ruling out the possibility of seeing a certain logic to a given *aggadah* occurring where it does. Very often, some form of association—sometimes quite imaginative from our point of view—lies behind such an occurrence. Verbal connections predominate. Thus, a reference to the uncircumcised elicits an opprobrious comment on that state; the alleged identity of "false" and "vain" oaths produces a reminder of God's ability to simultaneously command the two versions of the Decalogue's Sabbath law, "Remember" (Ex. 20:8) and "Observe" (Dt. 5:12); a ruling on odd animal births elicits an observation about normal animal births; a law based on repetitive erections prompts information about the eye's capacity to tear.[9]

Mostly, as we have seen, nonhalakhic discourse is biblically oriented and thus substantially intertextual. But a given *aggadah* may also extend a halakhic dictum, as when a law is followed by a preachment about the consequences of observing or violating it.[10] Or it may make its hortatory point by means of an example taken from the Bible or from life;[11] it may reverse the sequence and explore how a halakhic ruling suggests interpreting certain biblical texts afresh.[12] Aggadic material may itself spur further aggadic comment. A statement on the evils of losing one's temper is followed by an anecdote telling of Ulla's remorse for once encouraging a murderer he fell in with.[13] Whether the precipitating prior passage is legal or not, the *aggadah* connected to it is often rhetorically introduced by the query, *minayin* or *minalan*, "What biblical verse underlies this teaching?"[14]

The link to the previous passage may, however, be quite loose indeed. A teacher may suddenly make a personal judgment about a colleague or introduce new data, like giving the authorship of a book previously referred to.[15] Or we may get a generalization relevant to a previous discussion.[16] Since much legal reasoning is done by analogy, the parallel case may itself lead a teacher to new ground.[17] Or the *aggadah* may introduce a different analogous area to the original halakhic topic, as in the move to a discussion of anger as part of the discussion of people's propensity to make vows.[18]

The connection with the prior passage may also be relatively formal. One teaching by a sage may elicit others of his dicta regardless of their subject matter but sometimes all on the given theme.[19] The citation of a verse may produce one or more fresh comments upon it[20] or a certain topic may, for reasons not clear, engender an aggadic minianthology about it.[21]

Some Initial Impressions of the Talmud's *Aggadah*

The sample of the Talmud studied here demonstrates why we cannot equate *aggadah*, nonhalakhic discourse, and *midrash*, the exegesis of biblical texts. The tractates with the least amount of *aggadah* also had the fewest passages containing exegesis: in *Ḥul.* chap. 4, only one aggadic text utilized a biblical verse; in *Nid.* chap. 5, only two did. In tractate *Shevuot* about twice as many passages eschewed exegesis as utilized it. Where *aggadah* abounds, the proportion of *midrash* increases: in *Ber.* chap. 1 and *Ned.* chap. 3, about twice as many *aggadot* adduced verses as did not, while in *Er.* chap. 2, the margin was even greater, being about three to one.[22] The two terms may overlap but should not be substituted, one for the other.

We also find considerable variation in the extent to which passages are presented in the name of an authority or are anonymous. In the *Ḥullin* and *Niddah* chapters, the *aggadah* occurs mainly in asides in halakhic debates, and perhaps this explains why it is transmitted as the words of certain named sages (since great care with such ascription is demanded in halakhic discourse). In *Shevuot* and the chapters of *Eruvin*, *Berakhot*, and *Nedarim*, respectively, the ratio of named to unnamed statements rose from less than three to one, to three to one, to nearly four to one.[23]

A metaphor drawn from the field of chemistry may prove helpful in gaining an overall sense of the *aggadah*. Scientists considering the chemical elements have long noticed that ones with a similar subatomic configuration share certain significant behavioral traits, though they are otherwise quite distinct. They thus speak of a "family of elements," and a similar line of reasoning leads humanists to speak of various idea or style patterns as demonstrating "family resemblances," though not because they are a clearly definable group. At this stage of our study, it may be helpful to borrow this notion to describe *aggadah* in the Talmud. Nonhalakhic passages exhibit certain family resemblances, even though just what unites them otherwise cannot easily be stated.

Extending our chemical metaphor gives us an important insight, albeit by differentiation, into large aggadic units. That is, the atoms of common aggadic expression occasionally link up with one another to form larger, quasi-molecular structures of some length. But whereas the chemical elements that undergo molecular combination are dramatically transformed by this process, the discrete units of Talmudic *aggadah* remain largely themselves even when gathered into integrated chains. They may be said more to agglomerate than to integrate. And, to shift to another metaphor, even when we can gain an overall picture of a lengthy set of aggadic passages we come across in a Talmudic tractate, the effect is generally more of a blurry mosaic than of a realistic painting. (By contrast, the *midrash* books, as we shall later see, often weave their materials into artistically integrated wholes.)

Because Talmudic *aggadah* often occurs as complex aggregations of discrete units, some of which may themselves be complex, how can we know just which segments of the whole should be considered individual aggadic utterances? For example, prooftexts are occasionally heaped up at the conclusion of a passage, but which of these exegeses also might stand alone cannot be settled.[24] Often, too, rhetorical questions introduce new turns in the argument. Did the original speaker employ these aggadic devices, or were they added by a later teacher or the text's redactor?[25] As the passages lengthen or become convoluted, the questions multiply. Various portions of the exposition might as likely be integral to the original *aggadah* as later appended to it.[26] Moreover, the discrete units may themselves contain divergent items of information, complicating what one can say about the parts and the whole. Thus, an aggadic compilation may, almost as an aside, contain an identification of a name or a term given in a few words,[27] or an exegesis given in a sentence or two, or more if it studies a series of several clauses.[28] If anecdotes are included, we may then be dealing with short paragraphs or long ones reaching the equivalent of twelve or fourteen English sentences.[29]

Much of this aggadic complexity may stem from its being one branch of Talmudic reasoning as a whole, whose central method of developing ideas is the open dialectic of challenge and response. Thus, a straightforward passage may indicate one rabbi's statement, another's challenge, and then the response of the first.[30] Or, with greater sinuousness, it may tease out some important though subtle religious distinctions, as, for example, those which distinguish the righteous from the wicked.[31]

The infinite possibilities of exegetic ingenuity ramify the possibilities of *aggadic* complexity. Two masters may be cited as having different interpretations of a verse, and these exegeses then follow.[32] Two or more verses may be juxtaposed as complementary or contradictory and, whatever the case, this itself is made to yield a new lesson.[33] When subtle dialectic is linked with complex exegesis, the resulting passage may impress contemporary readers as quite convoluted.[34]

When Aggadic Texts Are Linked Together at Some Length

To our eyes, the extended aggadic passages of the Talmud move along quite eccentrically, a development difficult to convey in concise English description. Three such passages occurred in the sample.

The *aggadah* in *Ned.* 31b–32a was unique among these texts, because it could build on the substantial aggadic material provided by the *mishnah* that is the focus of this section of the tractate. Thus, the second of the six parallel mishnaic statements there that extol the virtue of circumcision refers to Moses's punishment for delaying it in his sons (Ex. 4:24). This elicits two efforts seeking to lift this opprobrium from Moses. Another statement then seeks to elaborate the biblical story, leading on to some ingenious speculation as to what Moses did and then a controversy concerning this which, in turn, evokes a resolution of the perceived difficulty. We are then presented with some different versions of the *mishnah* material plus some other statements with a similar form that also extol the significance of circumcision. The last of these, it is noted, contradicts a similar statement of a sage with regard to Torah, so the focus of the passage now shifts to Abraham, the great exemplar of the rite of circumcision. This brings on an antiastrology exegesis followed by two encomia of people who seek to be wholehearted with God and two statements about those who do and do not practice enchantment. Three explanations of the Egyptian servitude of Abraham's descendants then occur and are succeeded by four comments on Abraham's servants, Eliezer in particular. The last one having made its point by *gematria*, the numerical equivalent of words, three additional numerological points are made, all attributed to one master, R. Ammi b. Abba, with the middle one having no relation to Abraham. Another of his dicta is then given, this one dealing with the power of the Evil Urge. This leads on to an anonymous, roughly related text, whose exegesis contains a euphemistic reference to the penis. A complex, multiversed exegesis on the relation of Melchizedek to Abraham concludes this section of the Talmud, and the next *mishnah* follows. One who is at home with Talmudic literature will not find this meandering attention to shifting topics and different modes of presentation strange, even though the length of this aggadic passage is unusual.

The aggadic excursus in *Er*. 18a–19a is lengthier than that of *Ned*. 31b–32a and especially noteworthy, because it contains two aggadic *sugyot*, Talmudic literary units of dialectical analysis. Loosely, nine comments by R. Jeremiah b. Elazar provide the structure for much of these three folios. Subjected to rabbinic study, two textual terms yield the meaning "two," spurring the first of R. Jeremiah's comments, this one proving scripturally that Adam had two faces. Rav and Samuel are then cited, the one saying that the "rib" from which Eve was fashioned was a full face, the other insisting it was a tail. This begins the first *sugya*. Four times the "face" position is shown to have little difficulty accommodating another biblical text, while the "tail" interpretation has to work to provide an acceptable explanation of the challenge verse. (Only in the first instance is there an interpolated rejection of the assumption about the "face" view, but it is quickly reinstated by exegesis.) A fifth analysis reverses the role of the two positions and leads on to an additional interpretation of the challenge verse. The succeeding biblical phrase is used to prove that God acted as Adam's groomsman. The discussion now turns to Rav's "full [two] face" theory. Since one of the faces was Eve's, that engenders the halakhic problem of which face walked in front as provided in the law—which is then mentioned—that husbands should walk before their wives, a practice whose importance is then stressed. A dictum on the analogous sin of counting money directly into a woman's hand follows. Three statements then debate the religious stature of Manoah and other married biblical personages as a prelude to an exhortation about the evil of walking behind a woman. Seven statements by R. Jeremiah b. Elazar now follow consecutively, the first accompanied by an interpolated objection and its resolution, and the last leading into statements by other sages. R. Jeremiah's diverse themes are that Adam begot demons after the expulsion from Eden (no—he was a saint; nonetheless, the demons arose from his nocturnal emissions); that a person should offer only a little praise in someone's presence and all of it only in his absence; what Noah's dove's olive branch might teach us; that studying at night protects one's house; that since the destruction of the Temple "YH" is a sufficient mention of the tetragrammaton; that the curse of Babylon extended to her neighbors, but not that of Samaria; and that when the government takes a life the sufferer is rebellious, but when God does so there is acceptance. A corroborating exegesis extends this to the acceptance of Gehenna, the place of afterlife punishment, but another is cited contradicting this view, thus effectively introducing the second *sugya*, which centers on questions concerning Gehenna.

The contradiction about how sinners accept God's punishment, death and Gehenna, is resolved by referring the positive attitude to Jewish sinners but the negative one to gentiles. This is substantiated by showing its consistency with something else taught by one of the sages involved. An objection is raised based on Ps. 84:7, which implies universal salvation. That is rejected by teaching that Abraham saves everyone but not the most despicable sinners. On exegetic grounds, R. Kahana rejects the concept of the continuing rebellion of sinners in Gehenna. The dialectic discussion of reactions to punishment ends there, and the text continues with the teachings of individual rabbis on the topic of Gehenna: R. Jeremiah b. Elazar is cited for the ninth time, indicating where the three gates of Gehenna are located. A fourth location is proposed and then conflated with one in the previous statement. We then get biblical proof that Gehenna has seven names. An eighth and ninth name are then suggested and rejected by reinterpreting the reasons offered in their support. Resh Lakish specifies where Gehenna might be if it is in three countries. Two teachers then praise the fruit of certain locations in Babylon, bringing this uncommonly lengthy aggadic passage to an end.

Similar continuities and shifts of topic characterize the sample's third unusually long aggadic passage, *Ber.* 4b–8b. Over thirty clumps of aggadic discussion agglomerate here, some of them quite complex internally. While the connection between passages here is often thematic, strings of statements by a given teacher on various topics also frequently appear: R. Levi b. Ḥama cites R. Simeon b. Yoḥai twice; Abba Benjamin is represented four times; Rabin b. R. Adda transmits R. Isaac's words three times; R. Ḥelbo gives seven of R. Huna's dicta (though the second presents R. Huna without R. Ḥelbo); R. Yoḥanan cites R. Yose five times; R. Yoḥanan provides eight comments by R. Simeon b. Yoḥai; R. Ḥiyya b. Ammi presents Ulla's views three times; R. Huna b. Judah's words are then given twice without indicating who transmitted them. But these small collections of nonexegetic statements do not nearly exhaust the material found on these folios. If *aggadah* is that which is not *halakhah*, this material indicates why, in its entirety, it should not be equated with narrative, homiletics, textual comment, or any other such single Western literary genre.

Passages such as these three explain why Western readers often find the Talmud's rhetoric puzzling and even repugnant. Not only is the development of its longer passages foreign to our sensibilities but, as we shall see in detail later, the diction of its shorter pieces often appears cryptic, compressing its substance to the point of omitting needed information or steps in its logical development. We might perhaps reduce our perplexity with this discourse if we could specify the social situation in which this kind of discourse originated and was in use, but modern scholarship has not gone much beyond learned conjecture of what is likely to have been the case. One significant matter, however, is widely accepted: that the rabbinic tradition was essentially an oral activity, though that was early accompanied by a certain concern for written text. But just what that implies textually and the extent to which texts were written (and when) and the balance between the oral and the protowritten remain disputed matters. We will return to this topic in chapter 7.

Literary Forms That May Surface in Nonhalakhic Discourse

These comments about the uncommon aesthetic sensibility of Talmudic *aggadah* should not be taken as denying that the rabbis had any sense of what we know as literary form. Many nonhalakhic passages are aesthetically fashioned so as to enhance the appreciation of their message, often by the widespread pattern of presenting the substance so as to create a tension in order to relieve it climactically. A favorite rabbinic strategy is to set forth a startling assertion and then validate it by means of rabbinic logic, thus creating a sense of pleasant surprise. The tension is often increased by introducing various possible explanations, none of which is shown to be satisfactory, thereby enhancing the meaning and aesthetic delight with the final acceptable solution.[35] At some level, the framers of such statements recognized that giving their thought such rhetorical shaping would enhance its acceptability.

A number of Western literary forms turned up in the sample. The aggadic anecdote is probably the best known of these. In the equivalent of a few sentences we are told of something noteworthy that happened; more likely than not in our sample, it happened to a sage, the tale often being told to instruct others about ideal behavior or the idiosyncrasies of famous figures. Thus, we find two stories about R. Yoḥanan visiting the sick and another about his being visited when he was sick.[36] Often the tale is clearly shaped to teach a moral.[37] Most of the accounts are well within our experience, but some recount what we would call wonders, like R. Yoḥanan baring his arm to illumine a room or, like many another master, instantly healing the sick.[38] Some of the accounts are legends, like the story of the harp that hung above King David's bed and played itself each midnight.[39] All show the artistry of created tension and its resolution.[40] Parable, *mashal*, a concise invented tale, is particularly useful to the rabbis for bridging the gap between God and human beings and is often introduced by the formula, "A parable—to what may this be compared? To a king who . . ." In our sample it occurs mainly as a device for contrasting God's qualities with those of human beings in order to teach what the rabbis considered ideal human behavior.[41] But the sample has nothing remotely close to the self-conscious story form exhibited in the apocryphal books of Judith and Tobit and well known to the rabbis from the biblical accounts of Ruth and Esther.

Something similar may be said of the dialogue form, which occurs frequently. It rarely extends beyond a limited number of exchanges and nowhere approaches the expansive working out of ideas preeminently exemplified in the works of Plato. (So, too, the epistle form has no clear parallel in the Talmud.) Some aggadic dialogues are presented to us with such crispness that they seem like the report of someone present.[42] Others impress one as so nicely shaped that they appear to be the creations of those who passed on the traditions.[43] Those who transmitted these accounts probably felt somewhat freer to shape the aggadic traditions they had received or created, since they knew they were not working with legal material where verbal exactitude was stressed. Perhaps, too, they were influenced by the Greco-Roman practice of creating speeches for the heroes and villains they depicted.

A tangential observation may be in order here. Much of the *aggadah* is a self-conscious, second-level literature. That is, it is intertextual, taking off from previous verbalizations. Sometimes these sources are treated with great reverence, as in the case of words from the Bible, or simply with great respect, as when the statements are attributed to a sage, to a rabbinic "house," or to the rabbis corporately. A metaliterary consideration lies behind the piety the rabbis bring to their intertextuality: their creativity functions in relation to and in continuation of God's revelation. Within limits, they should be seen as dependent, rather than independent, creative spirits; typically, they did not adulate originality and innovation as modern writers do. Perhaps that helps explain why they did not often utilize such biblical forms as the extended tale, short or long poetry, or historical narrative.

The Rhetorical Touch in Aggadic Utterance

The rabbis often shape their lesson to make it more convincing. Even when they were deducing something from a biblical text, they might enhance their assertion by comparing or contrasting it with other biblical texts or personages.[44] They occasionally argue logically, asserting that if such and such is true in a lesser matter, how much more will it be true with a more significant one.[45] They regularly employ simile and metaphor to make their case. Thus R. Joseph and R. Simeon b. Avishalom tell us about travelers' crises and debtors' worries, and a woman consulting R. Akiba about her marital status compares her situation to a baby who cries the first time its finger is stuck into honey but not thereafter.[46] The rhetorical question occurs with great frequency (though many instances may equally be read as an exchange between scholars).[47] Personification, already present in the Bible, as in the account of Balaam's ass, occurs only rarely in this sample,[48] and reification also is infrequent.[49] Euphemism was widely used, particularly where sexual matters were concerned, though it was balanced by instances where the rabbis spoke with a directness that would still be considered improper in much Western academic diction.[50]

They also frequently used proverbs, particularly, perhaps, to help convey their thoughts to the community at large, often introducing such adages with the phrase, "As people say . . ."[51] And some of their comments seem more like folk wisdom than scholarly insight, like R. Ḥisda's homey observation that women's bodies are shaped like a storehouse, narrow above, wide below.[52] Their formulations often exhibit a certain verbal artfulness whose most common pattern is word association, like the lesson about human nature drawn by punning off the term *yotzri*, "my Creator," to get to *yitzri*, "my evil urge."[53] Or they may put their teachings into a series of parallel expressions, lending a certain rhythmic intensity to them.[54] In general, they prefer compact formulations of their messages, as if they hoped allusiveness would increase the impact of their words.[55] They play with numbers for a similar effect, though this sometimes seems to become more a scholars' competition than a way of influencing people.[56]

Hyperbole, however, is the distinctive aggadic trope, for it appears all through this material and therefore merits special treatment.

Some Varieties of Aggadic Hyperbole

The rabbis regularly speak of the most fundamental religious truths in terms that are variously playful, purposefully shocking, wildly imaginative and, to the case in point, extravagantly exaggerated. They and their community must have shared a rich context of acceptable communication, one we can only partially dig out. Taking many of their aggadic statements literally leads to a misunderstanding of rabbinic Judaism generally, as wide knowledge of rabbinic literature makes plain. We also cannot dismiss the statements as mere whimsy, for the rabbis considered them part of the Oral Torah God gave to Moses on Sinai. But unlike halakhic dicta, which the rabbis invested with normative force, it remains difficult to specify what kind of credence their community brought to these nonhalakhic materials.

Moreover, the sages do not value personal detachment. They believe in and live what they teach to the point of martyrdom, should it be necessary. They not only want to enunciate a lesson but get people to accept and live by it. Hence, they utilize many devices to emphasize the point they are making, the most common being their citation of the Bible. By connecting their teachings to God's own words, the Written Torah, they have invested them with powerful authority. But it is clear to them and their listeners that they are a step removed from prophecy and God's verbal instruction. To invest what they say with appropriate divine weight they often clothe their words with great emphasis. Sometimes this is done directly, as when R. Isaac not only lists one punishment for a certain infraction and adds "and more, he [the sinner]..." but also piles on "and (even) more, he..."[57] His colleagues find ingenious other ways to extend the punishments or rewards, as when R. Simeon b. Lakish "proves" R. Yose's three stripes are one hundred, or when R. Joseph "demonstrates" that Moses' progeny numbered six hundred thousand.[58] Exegesis may likewise be utilized to intensify a punishment to include what is usually contradictory, like simultaneous fire and water, or rabbinic logic may be employed to insist that some Jewish sinners will not share the common redemption from Gehenna.[59] Some rabbis seek to lend greater authority to their teaching by calling the action they are advocating a *mitzvah*, a "commandment," though most other masters considered them merely meritorious but optional.[60]

The rabbis realized exaggeration could be a problem, for they sometimes utilize a term signaling that they do not mean to be taken literally: *keʾilu*, "as if." R. Isaac says that when one recites the bedtime Shema prayers, it is as if he held a two-edged sword.[61] R. Abbahu teaches that if one felicitates a groom it is as if he had offered a Temple thanksgiving sacrifice; R. Naḥman b. Isaac remarks that it is as if he had restored one of the ruins of Jerusalem.[62] God, too, can be invoked in such imagery. One who studies Torah, does benevolent deeds and prays with a congregation is esteemed by God as if he had "redeemed Me and My children from among the nations of the world."[63]

The line dividing simple emphasis and hyperbole is most indistinct (as we have already seen). In hyperbole, the speakers' enthusiasm pushes their words beyond the bounds of plausibility, and though meant quite seriously, it probably signals their listeners—who are familiar with such diction—to take them with a considerable discount. That reality did not inhibit the rabbis from expressing themselves freely in hyperbolic terms; if anything, this permitted them to explore the fine line between what one can understand and what one can believe. It is tempting—and not a little "orientalist"—to ascribe this wide use of hyperbole to a general Near Eastern ethos, but the Bible writers generally do not resort to hyperbole as freely and with the near abandon of the Talmudic masters. While we do not know what made hyperbole so congenial to them, it is clear that the community in which the rabbis functioned apparently welcomed this manner of instructing and entertaining them at the same time.

The sanctity with which the rabbis regarded the Bible seems, if anything, to have encouraged them to treat its heroes and villains hyperbolically. Thus, when we hear of Abraham's 318 servants (Gen. 14:14), some rabbis can take that as a reference to the ever-faithful and resourceful Eliezer, for 318 is the numerical equivalent of the letters of his name.[64] While other kings glory in their pomp, King David busied himself with the messy evidence involved in making halakhic judgments about menstrual blood, the fetus, and the placenta, in order to permit Jewish wives to their husbands.[65] King Solomon, too, is also pictured as a functioning rabbi. R. Judah cited Samuel, who said that when Solomon ordained the laws of ʿeruv (the boundaries of permitted movement on Sabbath and festive days) and hand washing, a Heavenly Voice (*bat kol*) proclaimed Prov. 23:15, praising him.[66] And the 3,000 proverbs and 1,005 songs ascribed to him (1 K. 5:12) were, according to R. Hamnuna, really the number of proverbs he created for each word of the Torah, while the "songs" were actually the reasons he gave for each rabbinic dictum.[67] Hyperbole is also used to extend God's glory, as in R. Jeremiah b. Elazar's exaggeration of the piety with which people accept natural death by contrast to their reaction to execution by the government. R. Joshua b. Levi pushes this notion even further, giving us a vision of the wicked in Gehenna coming piously to accept the legitimacy of God's judgment on them.[68]

As passionate advocates of a way of living, the rabbis also regularly resort to hyperbole to esteem or disparage certain behaviors. What we consider the discourtesy of not returning greetings can be denounced by a teacher as making one worthy to be called a robber.[69] Seeking to establish the importance of worship in the synagogue, Abba Benjamin said that one's prayer is heard only in a synagogue.[70] He also said that when two enter a synagogue to pray and one finishes and then leaves before the other, his prayer is "torn up to his face"; more, he causes the *Shekhinah*, God's indwelling presence, to depart from the Jewish people.[71] A man who once said his prayers outdoors, with his back to a synagogue, was visited by Elijah, who not only rebuked him but drew a sword and slew him.[72] Three rabbis report a tradition of R. Eliezer b. Jacob that to eat first [on arising] and only then pray draws God's own contumely.[73]

The rabbis cannot find praise enough for the person who lives up to their standards. Of one who fears God and keeps the commandments (Eccl. 12:13), R. Abba b. Kahana said he is equal in value to the whole world; R. Simeon b. Azzai said the whole world was created for him; R. Elazar said the whole world was created for his sake only [which contradicts the similar evaluation of circumcision in *Ned.* 3:11].[74] Esteeming repentance, Rava b. Hinena said that one who commits a sin and is ashamed of it has all his sins forgiven.[75] Resh Lakish insisted that even Jewish sinners have as many merits as a pomegranate has seeds.[76]

Similarly, the sages lavishly praise the exemplars of their ideals, those who study the Torah and, thus, those who are its sages; they also uninhibitedly excoriate those who scorn them. R. Ḥisda cited Mari

b. Mar's lengthy exegesis to show that the entire universe is but $1/3200$ of the extent of the Torah.[77] He also transmitted Mar Ukba's boast that it was possible to heap up mounds of exposition on every pen stroke in the Torah.[78] R. Jeremiah b. Elazar said that a house in which Torah is studied at night will never be destroyed.[79] Rava said that to study is to taste meat.[80] He also said that only the person who could be cruel (frugal) to his family (so that he was free to study) would ever plumb the Torah's depths, while Rabbah merely required that he deprive himself of food to the point where his face blackened.[81] Rava contrasted the luxury and decadence of townspeople with the utter poverty and saintliness of scholars.[82] R. Papa cited R. Aha b. Ulla, who said that one who scoffs at the sages' words will be condemned to boiling in excrement;[83] an anonymous comment simply says that one who transgresses a rabbinic enactment deserves death.[84]

The term designating the unlettered, ʿam haaretz, hyperbolically the enemy of the scholar, is a vile rabbinic epithet, applied in our sample only to Manoah, the father of Samson, for walking behind his wife.[85] Piling hyperbole on hyperbole, R. Ashi then "proves" that he must not have gone even to a child's Scripture school or he would have known better from Gen. 24:61, which shows that Rebecca and her maidens knew they had to follow behind Eliezer.[86] Another form of verbal reprobation, denying someone the great felicity of life in the world to come, is wielded against one who crosses a river behind a (married) woman by R. Nahman b. Isaac, who had a tradition to that effect.[87] The converse of that condemnation is, of course, the highest possible reward, and the rabbis often promise it for what they are then advocating. R. Yohanan guarantees admittance to the future life to those who, without pause, join the 18/19 benedictions of the Tefilah (the "prayer" par excellence of Jewish services) to the Geʿulah prayers (the "redemption" litany that concludes the several prayers of proclaiming the Shema).[88] R. Elazar b. Avina is even more enthusiastic about reciting Psalm 145 thrice daily (perhaps intending thereby the three services this psalm introduces), assuring such a worshiper that he "may be certain that he is a son of the world to come."[89] But let someone transgress rabbinic standards, and indignation flames into hyperbole. If he counts money from or to a woman's hand so that he might look at her, "even if his merits are as great as those of Moses, our master, who received the Torah at Sinai, he will not be free from the punishments of Gehenna."[90]

Are There Distinctive Aggadic Literary Usages?

It will be helpful, even at this early stage in this study, to venture some tentative general observations suggested by the material in the sample. Other than its heavy recourse to hyperbole, there seems little that sets off the style of the Talmudic *aggadah* from that of the *halakhah*. One might perhaps make a case for the *aggadah* exhibiting a certain element of artistic creativity, as when dialogue is put into the mouth of biblical figures or various people in rabbinic times. Yet here, as in most of the other literary forms noted above, we can more easily speak of a difference of degree rather than of kind. Invention and fantasy are to be found in halakhic passages, not only in the exegeses that are used as their textual foundations but in the dialectic examination of conflicting opinions and in the creation and analysis of various hypothetical law-testing situations. We shall pursue this comparison further in chapter 6.

It should also be noted that perusing the Talmudic *aggadah* from the perspective of its external form has, incidentally, brought us little surprise as to its contents. Mostly, as we saw in the prior chapter, it is concerned with the Bible, the wording of its texts, the stories of its heroes and villains, the historical events it relates, and the practices it enjoins. But a significant amount of this material is not at all biblical, thus continuing the old perplexity about what one should say positively about the nature of *aggadah*. And the further indication that a religion has a sacred discourse, the Oral Torah, a major part of which glories in overexaggeration and casually transmits comments on quite trivial and mundane matters, makes us puzzle further about the limits of aggadic utterance. Let us see how these questions reshape themselves based on our further study of the sample.

Chapter 3

ୄ The Substantive Concerns ୨ୢ

In this chapter and the next, authorial decisions so significantly interpose themselves between the description of Talmudic *aggadah* offered and what the contemporary Western reader encounters in the Talmudic text that they deserve explicit notice. Generalizations—such as this one and its many successors—are most infrequent in aggadic diction not only in the sample but, in my experience, also in the Talmud generally; when they do occur, as we shall see later, they tend to be a form of rhetorical emphasis rather than a reliable observation about aggadic practice as a whole. We moderns seek to understand a specific datum by turning it into an instance of a class or category, but the rabbis are content to speak specifically and let the general religious perspective they share with their hearers validate the place of their statement in the overall scheme of things. Indeed, the data we are studying, the discrete aggadic texts, are almost always presented to us as the statement of this or that individual teacher and only quite rarely as what might be the rabbis' consensus view (which might be understood from the term *vehakhamim omrim*, "but the sages say," which, ironically, we often meet in a contrast of some group's opinion with that of one or more of their colleagues). Thus statements about "the rabbis" or the like, which occur here, are only my judgments that a specific statement is characteristic of a view held more broadly in the sample or elsewhere in the Talmud.

The same problem confronts us in seeking to gain a sense of the concerns manifested in aggadic passages. Merely to list these as they occurred in the sample (as was done in the prior chapter) would be truest to the text but leave us with a sense that aggadic discourse was only a motley collection of opinions rather than part of what it was to those who spoke or heard it; a functioning religious worldview.

Responding to our cognitive urge to categorize, I have brought the rabbis' aggadic interests together under seven broad themes prominent in the sample: God, the Torah, the Sages, Jewish Duty, Israel and the Nations, Humankind, and the World, the whole being summarized in some conjectures on the topics about which the rabbis are silent. This arrangement belies the usual atomism and fragmentariness of most nonhalakhic discourse. Except where the *midrash* books give us what seem to be compressed versions of synagogue or other public presentations, or where redactors have artfully shaped thematic aggadic anthologies, most nonhalakhic discourse, certainly in the Talmud, is found as brief statements rather than as developed, searching examinations of a topic. I must ask the reader to balance this loss of verisimilitude against the gain of comprehending the breadth of aggadic intellectuality.

The rabbis' equivalent of a general term for all this religious truth was "Torah," the term being used in its broadest compass. Westerners commonly translate the Hebrew word *torah* as the "Law," which is quite misleading. True, religious commandment is one of its chief ingredients, but even in the Bible, and certainly for the rabbis, "law," *halakhah*, is clearly not the entirety of Torah. We come closer to the self-understanding of the Talmudic masters if we remember that "Torah" is a noun-derivative from the Hebrew verb root *y-r-h*, one of whose conjugational forms (and the nouns derived from it) denotes the act of teaching or instruction. Early in one's study of Hebrew one meets it in the noun for "teacher," *moreh/ah*. Thus, a less-inadequate English word to provide an overarching generalization for this religious perspective is "the Teaching"—it being understood that ultimately the one, sovereign God of the universe is the Instructor, a truth that gives this teaching its unique quality. The rabbis are, in their quite human way, channels of the Divine Instruction. This axiom underlies their tradition of the Torah having both Written and Oral aspects, and the further understanding that the Oral Torah is constituted of two intermingled forms of discourse, *halakhah* and *aggadah*, an axiom that grounds our inquiry into the latter.

If we can tolerate some latitude in description, nonhalakhic discourse is a species of instruction, one that may be seen as extending the reach of the book of Proverbs, a treatise that taught about God but was more substantially concerned with human existence, mundane matters, and the trivia of everyday life. The rabbinic expansion of this biblical horizon of divine wisdom leads to the often astonishing range of tone and content in aggadic discourse and largely creates our common inability to characterize the *aggadah* by a simple English category.

One further reservation about my analysis of the Talmudic sample should be noted: I have separated the study of the content of this material (this chapter) from that of its forms of gaining cogency (the next chapter). Surely that is further to distort the reality of the texts themselves. But each of these topics is highly complex, so the risk of separating them may claim heuristic value. Moreover, this separation allows us to give separate attention to each of our two continuing problems—the nature of *aggadah* and the "logic" by which it regulates argument as permissible or not. Notice having been given, we continue.

The Teaching: God

The rabbis in our sample assert little about God that students of the Bible will not recognize (though they sometimes give these themes a surprising slant), but whereas the Bible writers affirm God's oneness by continually polemicizing against idolatry, the aggadists here tend to emphasize God's uniqueness. They steadfastly affirm as well that despite God's transcendence, God is also nearby and available. For God is king but simultaneously father,[1] one who prefers His mercy to His justice,[2] Who knows everything with certainty,[3] yet can be a model for human beings.[4] God's power is so great that He can create a two-faced, two-gendered Adam[5] or exempt Israel from the natural astrological forces that determine the fate of every other nation.[6] God is not unreasonable if given an opportunity to be responsive,[7] and should a petition not be granted, God must have a reason.[8] Nonetheless, there are barriers to reaching God.[9] One should also have proper respect for God, recognize certain limits to the questions one asks, and never ever curse God.[10] In this sample, three terms describe God's involvement with people. The one, *ruaḥ hakodesh*, "the holy spirit," is a biblical locution that becomes a term used in the Talmud to describe the heavenly influence that enables those endowed with it to foresee the future.[11] The two other terms are wholly rabbinic. One, *bat kol* (literally, "the daughter of a voice," connotes a gentle voice from heaven, in one passage here, reciting certain biblical verses to praise Solomon.[12] The other term is *Shekhinah*, "God's indwelling presence," a feminine noun developed from the verb the Torah employs to describe God's residing among the Israelites. Rabin b. R. Adda taught that the *Shekhinah* is with every ten men (the quorum needed for a full service) engaged in prayer, and also with every three men sitting as a court, and even with two studying together.[13]

As in the Bible, God is not impassible but can change His mind, for example, when a person deserving punishment does good.[14] One can calculate God's moods and know the best time for approaching Him.[15] For God can be deferential,[16] though He clearly has reason to be angry when Israel misbehaves.[17]

However, no aspect of God's reality draws as much aggadic attention as does God's justice. Surely, the destruction of the Temple and the national degradation and human suffering that followed from it could not be far from the rabbis' minds. Yet their comments in this sample deal far more with individual than with social theodicy. Various sages firmly assert that God is just,[18] that He keeps records on which he bases His judgment.[19] He may be relied on to reward the righteous[20] and the doers of good deeds.[21] Therefore, one should not become anxious about receiving one's proper rewards, such as sons,[22] or long life,[23] possibly even by means of a wonder.[24] One's good deeds also bring one the merit that offsets one's sins.[25] Abstractly, one acquires merit before God,[26] but the rabbis more generally speak of specific everyday benefits that come to the observant. Thus, various teachers promised that for doing various acts one will have one's sins forgiven,[27] a long life,[28] no mishaps all day,[29] protection all night,[30] one's enemies defeated,[31] and people saying good things about one after one's death.[32] The climax of all rewards and a major focus of rabbinic exhortation is life after death, entry into "the-World-to-Come."[33]

By contrast, it is good to avoid suffering[34] since God punishes sinners appropriately,[35] always having a just reason for His dispensation,[36] with certain sins identified with certain sufferings.[37] Even trivial matters can bring on chastisement,[38] and no one is so great as to be exempt from it.[39] If, then, evil should come upon one, it should be viewed as a punishment,[40] which may be extreme,[41] but generally God follows the rule of measure for measure,[42] such as humbling the one who humbled others.[43] The preachment may as easily take a negative stance, connecting condemnation with given acts.[44] God is depicted as inquiring about the lapse or becoming angry at it.[45] More commonly, the rabbis inveigh against doing certain acts simply on the basis of their own authority.[46] Or they may show a sin's gravity by saying one should do an obviously heinous deed rather than commit this despicable misdeed,[47] or they compare its depravity to that of an utterly horrid malefaction.[48] And they do not hesitate to shift their reprobation from the act to the person, warning him of the disgusting names he will be called for such a sin.[49] Sometimes the threat is of future punishment. Such teachings can take the form of cautionary tales,[50] or, more frequently, the dire results are specified: one may lose one's prior merit,[51] bring exile upon oneself and one's children,[52] invite one's death,[53] be punished in Gehinnom after one's death,[54] perhaps even be sentenced to be boiled in excrements there,[55] or have to remain in Gehinnom when others will be released.

This fervently held belief does not blind the rabbis to the reality that often the righteous are not being rewarded while the wicked are not being punished.[56] Jewish piety allows one to raise questions about God's justice[57] and various responses are offered to these. Thus, suffering might lead the wicked to turn to God (a pragmatic justification of their punishment).[58] The chastisement may result from the vicarious guilt that family solidarity produces.[59] Similarly, the Israelites' Egyptian slavery stemmed from Abraham's sin,[60] though we more commonly hear of Abraham's vicarious merit.[61] When all other answers fail, the rabbis suggest an idea unknown from the Bible: sufferings may come as God's "chastisements of love." God may send undeserved suffering upon the righteous so that their reward will be greater in the World-to-Come.[62] Otherwise inexplicable suffering should induce one to ask whether these are, perhaps, chastisements of love.[63]

Ultimately, faith in the World-to-Come with its promise of reward and punishment sustains the rabbis' theodicy. They expect that era to be ushered in by the painful wars of Gog and Magog (foretold by Ezek. 38:2).[64] Gehinnom and its retributive suffering await the many who will be sent there.[65] But by his merit Abraham will obtain the release of all the Jews still in Gehinnom (giving them entry to the bliss of the World-to-Come).[66]

The Teaching: The Torah

Though God is the solid foundation of rabbinic belief and practice, the rabbis are far more concerned with their views about Torah and their activity of Torah study and elaboration. Their biblically unknown form of religiosity and leadership is built on their unshakable faith that the one God of the universe gave the people of Israel God's unique Written Instruction, Torah, together with an accompanying Oral Instruction that added content and provided a process for the Torah's continued amplification. All this was given to Moses at Mt. Sinai by God. R. Simeon b. Lakish, as reported by R. Levi b. Ḥama, interpreted Ex. 24:12 to show that Moses received not only the Decalogue and Pentateuch there but also the Mishnah, the Prophets and Writings, and the Gemara (here apparently a general term for the rabbis' analytic study method).[67]

If one chooses to call the many such statements of belief "rabbinic theology," one should remember that the Written Torah, the Bible, says very much less about God than it does about the people of Israel and how they ought to live, individually and collectively (and to a much lesser extent, about humankind and its duties). Hence rabbinic "theology" is, as it were, less concerned with "theos" than with the rabbinic "logos" of the Written and, particularly, the Oral Torah, the beliefs that undergird and inform it, the life it enjoins as ideal and reality, and the scholarly community that transmits this to the people God has chosen to live by Torah. For where God had communicated directly with Moses and the prophets, in postbiblical times the sages (and all Jewry) only had the record of the prior revelation with its infinite layers of meaning and the divinely revealed traditions of how it should be understood and appropriately interpreted. The sages reverently acknowledge that the Written Torah has a theological priority that gives it unique authority, but they also enjoin the most serious possible penalties for not following their legal rulings (which are Oral Torah).[68] They also do not hesitate to call their traditions and activity of study, interpretation, and instruction (Oral) Torah and apply that term to their own creative teachings.[69] Aggadic hyperbole prompts one master to declare that since the destruction of the Temple, God's only earthly dwelling place is the limited world of *halakhah*.[70] As previously noted, such expressions of aggadic enthusiasm should not be taken as an indication of how the rabbis halakhically ranked a given law and even less, what the people did in daily practice.

The teachers in our sample see revelation as so extraordinary a benefit that R. Adda b. Ḥanina aggadically seeks to mitigate the evil of the biblical Israelites' sin by noting that it precipitated the prophetic books.[71] The term "Torah," when referring to the Written Torah, is not limited to the Pentateuch, the Torah proper, but may refer to any part of the rest of the Bible;[72] being God's revelation, facts cannot truly contradict it.[73] It was given only once and hence is entirely homogenous (thereby validating a major aspect of rabbinic exegesis, as we shall see).[74] The sages generally assume that their listeners know the context of the verses they employ,[75] that they may now aggadically supply new dialogue to God and Moses (or any other Bible figures),[76] explain Moses's motivation,[77] discuss King David's sleeping habits,[78] read the Song of Songs as an exchange between Israel and God,[79] identify the Kohelet of the book of Ecclesiastes as King Solomon,[80] or even indicate what the animals in a given story said.[81] In fact, they believe that every aspect of the Written Torah—its letters, for example, and not merely its words or phrases—can yield "heaps of exposition,"[82] so that the Written Torah might yield a near infinity of meaning. Yet some teachers are also extraordinarily down-to-earth, teaching that "the (Written) Torah speaks in ordinary human language," and others comment that its demands for religious expenditure are made "with compassion for the people of Israel's money."[83]

As Yitshak Heinemann pointed out in his pioneering literary study of the *aggadah*, making creative additions to the received accounts of biblical figures and incidents is one of the rabbis' major interpretive procedures.[84] What follows are examples from our sample: Adam was created with two faces, but though one sage believes Eve was created from one of them, another insists she was shaped from his tail (usually, rib).[85] Abraham's age when he first acknowledged God is variously figured as 3, 172, and 364.[86] He was God's most perfect servant, one who "armed" his servants with the protection gained by the merit of Torah study,[87] one who first called God "Lord," one whose merits were so great that Daniel's prayers centuries later were heard only on his account.[88] When his name was changed from Abram to Abraham ("father of nations," as per Gen. 17:5), he was given control over (those sources of sin) his eyes, his ears, and his genitals.[89] His and Sarah's changed names (Sarai to Sarah, "princess") signified their universal importance.[90] His piety was so much greater than that of Melchizedek that his descendants merited the Temple priesthood. Yet his failings caused his children later to become slaves in Egypt.[91] Though his grandson Jacob was told "Your name shall not be called 'Jacob' any more" (Gen. 35:10), the patriarch's original name was not obliterated, merely made secondary.[92] Jacob's wife Leah was the first person to praise God, and her son Reuben was not jealous that his brother Judah received his birthright.[93]

Lesser figures and events also evoke comment. No human being has ever been able to calculate the exact instant when God's anger flares as could Balaam, the gentile prophet, and this talent made his curses exceptionally effective.[94] Barak, the general who assisted the female judge Deborah, is said to have interdicted the inhabitants of Meroz for not joining his forces by sounding four hundred trumpet blasts when he proclaimed the ban on them.[95] Manoah, the father of Samson, was a boor, an *am haaretz*, for walking behind his wife, which any elementary school child would know was improper.[96] Saul repented of having killed the inhabitants of Nob, and God forgave him.[97]

David's psalms, the basis for innumerable rabbinic homilies, show him to be deeply grateful to God, as in his praises for five aspects of his existence: his growth in his mother's womb, his emergence into the world, his nurture at his mother's breast, his beholding the downfall of the wicked, and even in his anticipation of the day of death.[98] R. Simeon b. Abishalom read Psalm 3 to say that God's punishment of him would come at the hands of a rebellious son rather than at those of a merciless slave or bastard.[99] Solomon, R. Judah says, instituted the (Talmudic) rules requiring laypeople to wash their hands before certain rituals. He also taught how special areas might be created for the Sabbath and festivals in which carrying would be permitted.[100] Elijah during the contest with the prophets of Baal on Mt. Carmel entreated God not to let the people believe his miracles had been done by sorcery.[101] Since his death, when he was taken up to heaven, he has flown on his missions as angels do, though not as speedily as the greatest of them.[102] The chamber the Shunamite woman prepared for the convenience of his disciple, Elisha, is divergently described by Rav and Samuel on the basis of 2 K. 4:10.[103]

The rabbis, we are told, approved of three things King Hezekiah did but also disapproved of three others. Two judgments of each category roughly follow the Bible's account. One then turns a simple description into Hezekiah's improperly following rabbinic usage, while the remaining positive one is for his banning (literally, "hiding") the otherwise unknown *Book of Cures*.[104] Other teachers ponder why Ezra's leadership of the reentry of the people of Israel to the Land after their exile was not accompanied by a miracle, as was the original entry under Joshua, allowing them to say (pointedly to their listeners, no doubt) that the people's sins prevented this.[105]

The Teaching: The Sages

Particularly because of their devotion to and expertise in the Oral Torah, the rabbis consider themselves, their scholarly community, and the community's activity the chief glory of the people of Israel. R. Ḥiyya b. Ammi reported that Ulla said that, since the day the Temple was destroyed, God has had no place in the world other than "the four cubits of *halakhah*."[106] Abaye and R. Ammi and R. Assi are noted as acknowledging that since hearing this statement, they only prayed where they studied.¹⁰⁷ Obviously, with God so closely identified with them, the masters of *halakhah* had incomparable spiritual status. Perhaps the single figure most celebrated as a model of the sage is R. Akiba.¹⁰⁸ But all the sages unself-consciously claim vast knowledge, e.g., how gentile kings live¹⁰⁹ and how God observes Jewish law.¹¹⁰

Knowing Torah conveys spiritual power of a practical sort. The formal effect is stated in the boast of one sage that he and a colleague, having studied all the relevant law, are qualified to rule authoritatively in a given area.¹¹¹ But having studied yields more tangible benefits, for assiduity at the House of Study brings one great reward,¹¹² as does personal suffering to acquire Torah.¹¹³ It would arm one against the night and its special threats¹¹⁴ and protect one against bodily temptation.¹¹⁵ Some masters also have the power to do wonders, like instantly healing the sick.¹¹⁶ All of them, because of their special status, have a special responsibility to pray for others.¹¹⁷ However, despite their attainments they know there are limits to what they can do, as in their custom of not gathering at the home of a sick colleague for study lest they provoke Satan.¹¹⁸ It is no wonder, then, that those wives who enable their husbands to study are most praiseworthy.¹¹⁹ And laymen who do not know more Torah than a woman or a primary school student are a disgrace.¹²⁰ Those who could attend the House of Study but do not do so are deprecated, and the fate of the scholars who as they age begin forgetting their (orally acquired) learning is most poignant.¹²¹

Three important aspects of the study process are more assumed than asserted. First, the theoretical activity of deriving laws from Scripture is both valid and meritorious.¹²² Second, sages should undertake the responsibility of rendering decisions as to practice, an activity that ideally should be supervised by one's teacher.¹²³ Third, the Torah is enhanced when rabbis seek to correlate their teachings with one another and with everyday experience.¹²⁴ Other aspects of their activity are verbalized. Thus, some teachers suggest that certain sins are worse than others¹²⁵ or that a distinction exists between major and minor commandments.¹²⁶ Or we are told who taught a certain rabbi,¹²⁷ because this may explain why he derived a given law as he did.¹²⁸

Despite their adulation of study, rabbinic realism also asserts itself. A sage can question the worth of the rabbinic enterprise¹²⁹ or acknowledge that certain folk sayings parallel their teachings.¹³⁰ They seem to have little inhibition about recounting their human fallibility, as in the report of their getting drunk and rowdy at the wedding feast of

R. Joshua b. Levi's son.[131] They also do not seem reticent about making personal comments about one another. Some are complimentary: Ulla wishes that he could be like Rav and Samuel,[132] R. Adda b. Mattena praises Rava's acuity by saying, "His knife is sharp,"[133] and Rava himself is reported to have said of Rabbah that "he [mentally] draws water from a deep pit."[134] However, readers expecting academic civility among the rabbis will be shocked by the negativity of some of their remarks. R. Yoḥanan rejects an argument of R. Simeon b. Lakish by saying, "Any schoolchild knows that."[135] Rav derides R. Papa's apparent lack of worldly information by remarking, "You eat in the forest."[136] When Rabbah sat before R. Ḥisda and recited a certain law, the latter taunted him, "Who listens to you and R. Yoḥanan, your teacher?"[137] And R. Papi does not hesitate to suggest that a certain ruling has slight support, for those who make it are frail.[138]

Though all these statements closely identify Torah with rabbinic study, the Oral Torah equally drives toward wide-scale community observance of the law and the teaching, a practice of piety whose requirements devolve upon the learned and unlearned alike. Thus, the sages take for granted[139] and participate in a regimen of Jewish prayer unknown to the Bible and largely created by their community.[140] Their conduct sets a standard for general Jewish behavior.[141] This includes rebuking their colleagues[142] and accepting suffering patiently,[143] though more is often expected of them than of ordinary Jews.[144] They may disclose the details, even intimate ones, of their observance,[145] and they surely teach the necessary details of proper practice.[146] If they appear to have made a mistake in teaching or practice, there must have been some significant reason.[147] They are quite human, appreciating having their words listened to[148] and weeping at tragedy,[149] and, though occasionally foolish, they remain effective teachers.[150]

The manner of discipleship in this guild is intimated in the verb usually employed to describe it: *leshamesh*, "to serve," or "wait upon," the sage. The learning is intensely interpersonal and not mere attendance at the teacher's lectures. So disciples should reside in one's master's town, though rabbinic realism allows for the independent minded not to do so.[151] Those who cannot take on the rigors of full discipleship should nonetheless see to the needs of scholars, an act which can hyperbolically be called even greater than study.[152] So one who entertains the rabbis can be said to acquire merit as if he had offered up the daily sacrifice in the Temple.[153] By contrast, heretics are the sages' great vexation.[154]

The Teaching: The Range and Tone of Jewish Duty

The Torah specifies the acts and virtues that should fill a Jewish life. While the *halakhah* seeks to define just what constitutes one's obligation, the *aggadah* often attempts to supply the theological and historical foundation of Jewish duty; so to speak, a major function of aggadic theology is to explicate Judaism's metahalakhic foundations. The *aggadah* also often extends the *halakhah*'s required discipline by stating what is religiously desirable yet cannot be made mandatory. In these activities, individual aggadists speak only for themselves, though their counsel carries the weight of being Oral Torah and may become the consensus opinion. Considerable aggadic utterance exhorts the Jewish people to do their duty and avoid specific sins. Examples of each tendency follow; first there are some comments concerning various laws, then some general ethical appeals, and finally some instances of the rabbis' exhortation, positive and negative.

The opening chapter of the tractate *Berakhot*, "Blessings," is replete with advice on the proper way to pray. Going to the synagogue, one should run; leaving it, one should take small steps.[155] One should arrive there early and leave late.[156] Upon entering, one should not stay near the door but come in a fair distance.[157] R. Helbo asks for special care about the afternoon prayers, while R. Yohanan and R. Nahman b. Isaac said the same about the evening and morning prayers, respectively.[158] R. Helbo also reported that R. Huna urged people to have a fixed place in the synagogue for saying their prayers.[159] Among the various special occasions on which one surely ought to pray are finding a wife, when studying Torah, at a death, at a grave, and at a privy.[160] R. Yosi b. Hanina emphasized the importance of praying from a low place and further urged, in the name of R. Eliezer b. Jacob, that one say one's morning prayers before eating.[161] Guidance with regard to proper prayer is not limited to this tractate but is found frequently elsewhere in the Talmud. Thus, an aside in tractate *Hullin* calls on sufferers to make their plight known so that others will begin praying for them.[162] Praying is not a unique duty when it comes to such urging, for almost every other duty specified in the *halakhah* receives similar treatment in Talmudic *aggadah*.

Matters of character, though important to the sages, could not be made a matter of law. Instead the rabbis communicated their values through the *aggadah*. Since all else stems from it, the rabbis highly esteem the fear of God.[163] Thus, R. Yohanan reminded R. Elazar that it was one's relation to God, not the extent of one's suffering, that was significant;[164] and a similar comment is made anonymously about the sacrifices one brings to the Temple.[165] Yet the rabbis also commend the responsible human will. "Rabbi said, 'What is the correct course that one should choose for oneself? The one which he feels is honorable to himself and will bring him honor from others.' "[166] The righteous are characterized by promising little but doing much.[167] Simeon b. Tarfon observed that one tends to become like those with whom one associates.[168] R. Yoḥanan, who counseled against trying to placate someone who was angry,[169] did permit confronting the wicked with his wickedness, but R. Isaac warned against doing this when fortune was smiling on him.[170] Self-reproach is commended as a far better corrective than the lashes the Bible often prescribes.[171] Sometimes the advice is far more practical, as when Abaye is quoted as saying that a pious person need not hesitate accepting an offer of hospitality if he wishes to do so.[172]

The community is also exhorted by various sages to embody a virtue that that particular teacher holds dear, such as hospitality,[173] serving as a groomsman (even for someone of inferior social status),[174] giving and returning greetings to others,[175] visiting the sick,[176] praying even though one feels one is doomed,[177] and reciprocating favors to others.[178] So, too, certain acts are strongly reprobated, such as making vows,[179] losing one's temper,[180] recourse to magic,[181] walking behind a woman or even counting money into her hand so as to look at her,[182] taking too much on oneself,[183] and, naturally, any sort of immorality, heresy, or idolatry.[184]

The Teaching: The People of Israel; the Nations

The sample yielded very few direct comments on the national groups in rabbinic times, preferring to express its attitudes on such matters in the course of its other teachings. The astute reader will, in the course of this work, gain a good sense of the rabbinic attitudes toward Israel and toward the nations by the many allusions to them in the texts cited. What they did say does, however, provide a useful entry into their attitudes in this area.

The glory of Torah, which the rabbis believed so distinguished them from the rest of Israel, similarly gives the people of Israel its utter preeminence among the nations of the world. R. Yoḥanan sums up this faith in his statement that God granted Moses's request that God's Presence rest upon the Jewish people but not upon idolaters.[185] Israel's unique character as the people of Torah requires them to be spiritually responsible for one another.[186] As against the natural order of things, they are immune to the astrological forces that affect individuals and peoples.[187] Simeon b. Lakish boasts that even Israel's sinners are as stuffed with good deeds as a pomegranate is filled with seeds.[188]

By contrast, "the nations" do not live by Torah, not even by the seven laws given to the Children of Noah; hence, they commonly are identified as *reshaim*, "wicked," the antithesis of the righteousness found in Israel. Rome is often simply called "wicked Rome" or is referred to as "the arrogant kingdom," though the rabbis respect its worldly dominance.[189] While R. Akiba is reported to have admired certain practices of the Medes and R. Gamaliel esteemed some of those of the Persians, the text then notes that R. Joseph asserted that all "the nations" are destined for Gehinnom.[190]

The Teaching: Humankind

The rabbis inherited a general view of human nature from the Bible, which they then developed in their own fashion, notwithstanding their acceptance of the existing Near Eastern social patterns with their hierarchy of status and responsibility.[191] Thus, they expect fathers to provide for their families and wives to accept this appreciatively.[192] Moreover, true to the culture, they can esteem males highly[193] though believing them particularly susceptible to temptation,[194] a condition associated with having a penis.[195] However, feminists have justly observed that their views, whether received or creative, speak of humankind with a distinctively masculine model in mind. They relegate women to the status of an "other" whose special nature is understood in terms of the rabbinic standard, "man"; thus, in the comments about a couple walking in file, the issue is always the man's position, and the reason for it is given in terms of male proclivities. Explicit comments on women as a group were rare in our sample and were, in male eyes, positive: women's sexual organs are built the way a good storehouse is, spacious above and narrow beneath (a male view; no one asked a woman for her view);[196] women have more "understanding," *binah*, of things than men (*sic*) do;[197] and they are better able to recognize the character of their guests than are men (*sic*).[198]

As to humankind generally, they believe life is good, and attacks on it are unwarranted.[199] R. Shimi b. Ukba provided a religious foundation for this thinking by indicating five ways in which the human soul emulates God. Even as God is pure, abides in the innermost recesses, sees but is not seen, feeds the world and fills it, so the soul is pure, innermost, unseen, nurturing, and everywhere in the body.[200] They deem it wise to seek medical advice[201] and think the death of one's child one of the worst forms of suffering.[202] There is a decisive difference between the near-human status of an embryo, even if it should move after its mother's death, and the full human nature of a one-day-old child.[203] While the rabbis have great respect for one's biological inheritance, they place even greater emphasis upon how a child is reared, insisting, for example, that the name one bestows upon the child will influence his or her character.[204] One can sometimes read people's human situation from the look on their faces, certainly in the case of poverty.[205] Social status does not delimit what people may do, for just as a son, Absalom, could rebel against his father, so slaves may rebel against their owner.[206] The rabbis would not be surprised were a slave or a *mamzer*, "an illegitimately conceived Jew," to be cruel, but surely a normal Jewish son would not be cruel to his father.[207] Most people will reciprocate one's generosity,[208] and some few are saintly, to which their asceticism may testify,[209] though more commonly it is their humility.[210] Similarly, we should not accept suffering but seek to avoid it.[211] Thus, one should avoid living in cities where temptations abound.[212]

The ubiquity and persistence of sin troubles the rabbis as much as it did the authors of the Bible. Simple observation made plain to them that most people spurn life's most significant concerns for relatively trivial matters.[213] To some extent, they believed our bodies are responsible for our poor sense of values, for a man's hands and feet, his eyes and ears, his mouth and penis, regularly lead him to sin; the eyes and ears may be the major channels motivating sin, but sexuality is the passion most likely to traduce us.[214] Therapeutically, the sages take a dialectical approach to overcoming one's predilection to sin, for they see us torn between our urge to do evil and our urge to do good. They had no illusions about the great power of the urge to do evil and the weakness of the urge to do good, requiring people to struggle against the evil urge and, despite the tools given them for doing so, they may lose the battle.[215] Nonetheless, they believe that the urge to do good can prevail.[216] R. Simeon b. Lakish is reported to have suggested the following strategy: one should use his will power against the evil; that failing, one should immerse himself in study; if necessary then, he should recite the Shema; and as a last resort, let him remind himself of his day of death [and subsequent judgment by God].[217]

The Teaching: The World, Natural and Supernatural

The rabbis tell us a good deal about their understanding of the environment, mostly as such matters come up in connection with issues of law or interpretation. So God's anger rises each day when the cock's comb is white and it stands on one leg.[218] We are told that young pigeons have tender skin,[219] an ass's skin is loathsome,[220] and the skin of serpents is generally smooth[221] and striped.[222] Stories are told about unusual animals, like the serpent in King Shapur's day who devoured thirteen stables filled with straw.[223]

The sample's *aggadah* also includes information about plants, like the value of the wild onion as a therapy for heart trouble,[224] but more commonly about the way people live. They paint trees red so that people will pray for their recovery.[225] They use beet juice in the dish known as *elaiogaron* and that of all kinds of boiled vegetables in *oxygaron* (neither otherwise known).[226] Peoples' dreams have predictive power.[227] Kings usually do not arise until the third hour,[228] and holy men may be recognized either by no flies coming near their table or their not having nocturnal emissions.[229] Babylon's evil influence is seen in its neighbors being cursed merely because it was cursed, while only Samaria (the kingdom of Israel) was punished by God for its own sins.[230] Yet, a comment may be as casual as an incidental description of a certain neighborhood in Pum Nahara in Babylon[231] or what distinguishes a courtyard described as "Tyrian."[232]

The sages take it for granted that extraordinary events occur in nature,[233] that luck and fate are real,[234] that astrology is usually reliable and witchcraft works.[235] Their world also includes angels[236] and demons with whom people interact,[237] even begetting them (by nocturnal emission).[238] The demons do not have human form.[239] They are the cause of many ailments; they mingle in the crowd during the scholars' study month; and, though they are normally invisible and often horrible, one can see them by special acts.[240] Satan is very powerful, and one should avoid provoking him.[241] There is very little material in these folios about angels, though we do hear of the angel of death. We also learn that the angel Michael (the People of Israel's guardian) has greater status than Gabriel.[242] Elijah, though not an angel, can also come from heaven and punish an evildoer.[243]

The rabbis affirm the biblical faith that human and natural history will move toward its climax with the rebellion of Gog and Magog, producing suffering worse than anything Israel has heretofore experienced.[244] In the new era that begins the Days of the Messiah, we are assured that the remembrance of the Exodus will still be part of Israel's life.[245] The likely entry to the place of eschatological punishment, Gehinnom, is discussed at some length, as are its various names[246] eventually leading on to a debate over the fate of the Jews who are sent there.[247] So, too, the place of eschatological reward, Eden, is the subject of some speculation,[248] and while we never receive much detail about it, the expectation of great reward awaiting righteousness is a central tenet of rabbinic faith.[249]

About What Is the *Aggadah* Silent?

These aggadic statements involve so many different themes it seems unlikely that anything significant to people in rabbinic times has been omitted. Yet moderns know that what remains unspoken, perhaps carefully ignored, often has the greatest significance for one's values and life—and the same is true of cultures and their ethos. But how can we gain insight into the unspoken assumptions of a way of life without living contact with the person or society we seek to understand? What we impute to others often says more about us than about them. We can perhaps guard against flagrant eisegesis by attending to their patterns of avoidance, such as in euphemism, or look for elaborate strategies of denial or evasion. Nonetheless, we must be modest in such an effort, since what a symbol most significantly conveys can best be stated, if ever, by the one who utilizes it. In short, the Greek logicians were wise in suggesting that arguments from silence are notoriously weak. That being understood, some tentative observations may prove of value.

The rabbis have no difficulty speaking of sex when they wish to do so. They can discuss sexual organs[250] and intercourse,[251] sexual temptation,[252] and operations to reverse circumcision.[253] Yet they do not make this the subject matter of ordinary talk, preferring, as their use of euphemism indicates,[254] to treat sex with a certain privacy. They are rather more restrained about excrement, but not to the point of inhibition.[255]

None of this seems very significant, though it may yield the judgment that, considering what Westerners tend to expect of religious literature, rabbinic spirituality is uncommonly down-to-earth. In terms of their inner lives, they do not engage much in biography, confession, or mystical speculation other than an occasional tantalizing hint (none occurred in this sample). More surprisingly, in contrast to biblical literature, the rabbis speak only incidentally of Jewish history and politics, largely ignoring the social changes that had lasting consequences for later events. This historical unconcern has prompted speculation that their silence betokens a considered strategy that testifies tellingly to their living faith.

How much importance we should attach to this rabbinic silence is quite uncertain. Clearly, they are not avoiding the social realities and do not seem to be ruled by emotional strain in attending to a variety of troubling topics. They acknowledge with sadness that the Temple has been destroyed and that this has had a devastating human and spiritual effect; they suffer under Rome's tyrannical rule and realistically assess the Parthians as less powerful and somewhat more humane.[256] Both matters, it would seem, have little new to say to a people that has the Bible to tell it God's truth about history. Their sacred book has taught them that the Temple can be destroyed and was, after an ethnic exile, restored. Though the dislocations of Jewish life disturb them greatly, they do not generate radical cognitive dissonance. Rome and Parthia, Christianity and Zoroastrianism, are only the latest versions of Babylonians and idolaters. The rabbinic unconcern about politics and history may well be indicative of the faith they simply take for granted that God will punish His people but He will not abandon them and will, one day, gloriously restore them to their patrimony.

Chapter 4

❦ The "Logic" ❧

No Talmudic master left us a manual of the rules for cogent nonhalakhic discourse (NHD). To gain some insight into the patterns by which the sages sought to win thinking assent, we must proceed inductively, by extrapolation from the aggadic teaching that the rabbinic community transmitted to us. That daunting task is made more complex by the fact that this is religious thinking, and, with the Bible as the sages' foundation document, far more than Aristotelian logic is involved in seeking to communicate the truth of Torah. To begin with, aggadic "logic" substantially overlaps with aggadic rhetoric. To understand how the rabbis thought about their beliefs we must also pay some attention to the manner in which their appeal to the mind lived comfortably with an affective reach for persuasion. Thus, this chapter concentrates primarily on four illuminating modes of rabbinic appeal to the mind and then concludes with some comments on several major rhetorical strategies in their teaching. Specifically, we shall investigate what our sample of Talmudic nonhalakhic discourse discloses about seeking intellectual assent based on the Written Torah as guided by the Oral Torah; seeking it on the basis of Oral Torah alone; the acceptable challenges to these kinds of teaching; the acceptable responses to such challenges; and their accompanying key rhetorical devices: question and answer, hyperbole, retrojective synchronicity, and anthropomorphism. This thematization of the data is, of course, not that of our Talmudic texts but is a scheme imposed upon it to help make Talmudic intellection accessible to our own ways of thinking.[1]

Warrants for Assent Based on the Written Torah as Guided by the Oral Torah

Because the Bible is God's instruction to Israel and humankind, it contains infinite layers of meaning encased in ordinary human language. This may be said to have led the rabbis to identify two main modes of reading it, one conscious of its human intent, the other of its divine authorship. The first of these, reading for the *peshat*, seeks to convey what rabbinic culture understands the simple meaning of a biblical text to be.[2] Thus, interpretations conveying the *peshat* of the Bible will largely read it like an ordinary book, expecting it to be grammatical,[3] diachronic,[4] mathematically exact,[5] and verbally consistent.[6] A sage can then make his point by what his community considered a straightforward reading[7] of the text. So the most common warrant for a teaching is a scriptural verse; it quickly authenticates a lesson,[8] substantiates a commonly accepted notion,[9] or bolsters the interpretation of another text.[10]

The *peshat* may be somewhat more complex than a direct reading, as when a verse from one section of the Bible (say, the Prophets, or the Writings) is used to interpret a verse in another section (say, the Torah proper). Such an imported text may be a direct parallel to the original text,[11] or expand its meaning,[12] or make something unusual seem less exceptional,[13] or add a contrast that yields a richer understanding.[14] In such passages verses with what seems to us only a loose verbal or thematic connection to the verse being interpreted may be introduced,[15] and a blizzard of citations seems to add special weight to the point being made.[16] But rabbinic boundary lines in such matters being quite indistinct, perhaps we have already crossed the line into the second, more notorious mode of rabbinic exegesis. As this is the realm in which the creative genius of the *aggadah* is particularly manifest, we shall discuss it at somewhat greater length.

The rabbis, despite their reverence for the Written Torah, are not literalists. Because they believe the Oral Torah was revealed by God to Moses and faithfully transmitted to them in all its dynamism, they knew themselves to be empowered to interpret the Bible with what we deem to be extraordinary freedom. Their terms for this process derive from the verb root *d-r-sh*, whose meaning is "search," or "inquire"[17]—that is, into the infinite depths of God's written and oral teaching. The less-used term for this hermeneutic is *derash*, the process, or an instance of its use; its more widely used one is *midrash*, also an instance of this method or a collection of such interpretations. Both *peshat* and *derash*, it should be noted, are utilized in both *halakhah* and *aggadah*, though we are concerned here only with their use in nonhalakhic discourse.[18]

The spirit of aggadic *derash* is suffused with the conviction that a high religious merit is attached to amplifying the message of the Written Torah. The term often used to signal this multiplication of textual meanings is *davar aḥer*, literally, "another word or matter," but in interpretive contexts it is an idiom marking another interpretation of the verse being analyzed.[19] A somewhat similar spirit is conveyed by the phrase *im baᶜet, ema*, "if [by rejecting my prior textual proof] you require it, I will say ... ," and then adducing another text.[20]

Their specific creative procedures may, with some aggadic license, best be described by separating those that arise from the revelation's microfullness from those generated by its macrofullness. In the former category, the Torah being God's document for humans, no detail of it is superfluous; every aspect of it might convey many meanings.[21] Should a phrase, a word, or even a letter appear to be unnecessary, that may only be a cue to teach a lesson or avoid a false interpretation.[22] Odd spellings or calligraphy—itself part of the revelation—will communicate meaning to the astute exegete.[23] The common Hebrew reduplication of terms for emphasis may indicate two separate events.[24] A shift of terms in a passage implies an additional lesson[25] and personal names or place-names, when read for their literal meaning, may yield valuable lessons.[26] The changed spelling of a personal name allows for a special message beyond the Bible's.[27]

The plethora of meaning given the Bible by revelation extends to its words, phrases, and sentences as well as its details. What surprises the modern reader is that the *derash* may also substantially transform the meaning of the *peshat*. A literal phrase may be interpreted figuratively,[28] or the reverse,[29] and various other images, such as of humans and the Divine, may be substituted for one another.[30] Sages may split a word in two to expose a fresh meaning, or change the accepted vowels of a word,[31] or alter its consonants.[32] We might, to improve meaning or flow, propose dividing verses differently than does the traditional Hebrew Bible, but we are unlikely to do so to derive a new teaching[33] or one different from the text's simple meaning[34] or one that reverses it[35] by drawing a negative inference from a verse whose *peshat* is positive.[36] Some of these practices may be justified, because, as the rabbis indicate, biblical texts may themselves say daring things, e.g., about God, that we would not be permitted to say had they not been in the Bible.[37] Another means of expounding a verse's meaning is by adducing otherwise unknown data, like Adam's saintly fasting and abstention from sexual intercourse.[38] More commonly, they will utilize some form of wordplay,[39] or pun on a word to produce a fresh interpretation.[40] This comes to something of a climax when the Hebrew letters, which can serve as numerals, are read numerologically, a process called *gematria*. This can itself yield new meaning or can do so by the process of equating a word with an arithmetic equivalent, allowing the original text to be interpreted in terms of this new notion.[41] Sometimes a rabbi will simply read a text creatively by an exercise of his imagination.[42] However, it must be emphasized that despite all this freedom of interpretation the rabbis are devoted to the fundamental authority of the Bible as evidenced by their practice that when a colleague enunciates a nonscriptural lesson, a rabbi may reasonably demand to know its scriptural basis.[43]

Warrants for Assent Based on Oral Torah

The rabbis are the inheritors and masters of the traditions of the Oral Torah that God gave Moses and through him and his successors to the people of Israel. A major aspect of that revelation was not only the proper manner of interpreting the Written Torah but of teachings independent of it (though sometimes directly related to it) and how those teachings might continually be amplified. The result has been the record of *halakhah* and *aggadah* that not only interprets the Written Torah but, logically speaking, that sometimes operates directly in terms of the authority of the Oral Torah. It is to the nature of argumentation in this kind of nonhalakhic discourse that we now turn.

Sages often state a truth but give no textual basis for it, apparently simply relying on their authority as teachers of God's Oral Torah.[44] R. Yoḥanan identified David's son Kileab as Daniel[45] as well as R. Yose as the author of the book *Seder Olam*.[46] R. Zeira says that Arioch, an otherwise obscure Babylonian teacher, is really but another name for Samuel.[47] Resh Lakish suggested that if the eschatological Garden of Eden would be in the Land of Israel, its gate would be in Bet Shean, if in Arabia it would be in Bet Gerem, if in Iraq it would be in Dumaskanin.[48]

As above, one theme of such nontextual statements is the transmission of data. Another is what certain sages did or preferred. Thus, we are informed of Abba Benjamin's concern that his bed should be oriented north and south;[49] or Rava's injunction to litigants to appear before him with proper humility;[50] or R. Meir's willingness to learn from his wife, the learned Beruriah.[51] So, too, we unexpectedly come across a list of seven rabbis identifying the specially meritorious aspect of various religious activities.[52] Other passages inform us about unusual happenings like R. Sheshet's manner of bowing and rising in prayer[53] or R. Yoḥanan's crying about the prospective loss of his beauty in death.[54] In some passages, the experience of non-Jews is recounted for what it may teach, even in unusual cases.[55] Sometimes the statement is merely a conjecture about what a master was doing that might explain a report of his teaching.[56] Citing an authority,[57] or indicating that a given message is paralleled by that of another teacher or a rabbinic tradition, adds conviction.[58] Thus, as with biblical texts, the very multiplication of confirming opinions further establishes the lesson,[59] occasionally becoming a comparatively lengthy development of the theme.[60] The masters often do not speak from their own authority alone but as transmitters of received traditions of other teachers whom they name.[61] The tradition sometimes recounts what occurred to a rabbi.[62] Yet on occasion, a teaching may be ascribed to tradition in general, and the term *gemara* may be used to indicate this.[63]

The teachings become a species of argument when they appeal to something other than the teacher's authority. The simplest form this takes is an appeal to what everyone knows[64] or common sense.[65] Some matters are self-evident, a judgment conveyed by the term *mistabra*.[66] There are also appeals to everyday behavior,[67] or life,[68] common experience,[69] or well-known facts,[70] or accepted wisdom.[71] An unusual occurrence may be related,[72] or events of interest,[73] or a generally accepted religious rule utilized.[74]

The appeal may be more abstract. Comparisons are a regular means of making a point, and forms of the root *d-m-h*, to be like, are often used in them. The objects of such reasoning may be model figures[75] or accepted values,[76] with analogies providing another such line of thought.[77] Exposition by contrast is also steadily used.[78] Mathematics, serious and highly creative, seems to have a special appeal to the rabbis,[79] but they only occasionally make their aggadic case by logical inference.[80]

Challenges to a Position That Evoke a Response

Aggadic discourse seems so open it is surprising that objections to some rabbinic assertions arouse a response. An examination of what may cause problems in aggadic statement should give us some perspective into what may be aggadically troublesome. Such difficulties may be generated by the biblical text itself. An unclear word or phrase may produce a request for an explanation—perhaps introduced by such terms as *may* or *may mashma*—and one or several answers may be given. In the school of R. Yannai they interpreted the contentless particle *na* (which occasionally accompanies Hebrew verbs) as a nicety of entreaty, such as "I pray you."[81] So, too, in commenting on the acrostic Psalm 145, R. Yoḥanan turns the missing letter *nun* with its associations of calamity into an argument for Israel's inevitable rise from such depths.[82] The opposite may also be the case, as when the sages, idealizing a certain parsimony in the revelation, wonder why a text was needed to give an obvious lesson and ask *may dikhetiv*, "why is it written"?[83] Similarly, R. Yoḥanan dismisses R. Simeon b. Lakish's teaching from Job 5:7 as something so obvious even schoolchildren would know it from Ex. 15:26.[84] In response to a series of exegeses proving God's presence is with fewer and fewer people praying or studying, even one, a challenge is raised as to why, then, all the prior demonstrations were necessary.[85]

Anomalies in the biblical text are assumed to be God's prompts for comment, and the rabbis may say of such verses that they "require," *mibaʿeh leh*, a different Hebrew word, hence the given one must indicate another lesson.[86] The warning against making many books in Eccl. 12:12 cannot suggest the illegitimacy of writing books of Oral Torah like the Mishnah.[87] A master may say that one colleague's aggadic exegesis is surpassed by another colleague's reading of the text (without explaining the basis for that judgment).[88] Since texts can often be read literally or figuratively, a "corrective" exegesis is a legitimate basis for a challenge.[89]

When the Bible apparently contradicts itself, we reach something of a climax in the problems created by anomalous biblical texts. So Abraham was anxious when God asked him to "be a blessing" but was calmed when God then promised to protect him.[90] Jacob became fearful though God had earlier promised to care for him, because, nobly, he feared he might have sinned and thus forfeited that blessing.[91] Ben Zoma and the sages trade verses and interpretations in an argument about whether the Exodus will be remembered in the days of the Messiah.[92] The repetition in one verse of the Song of the Sea (Ex. 15:16) of God's people "crossing over" educes the possibility of two crossings.[93] Similarly, the conflicting texts of God's forgiveness and nonforgiveness of sinners become the occasion for a series of comments on theodicy.[94] A complicating but elegant extension of the juxtaposition of opposing texts occurs when the contending exegeses are then subjected to mutual challenge.[95]

Biblical verses that might seem to contradict accepted Jewish belief are a major stimulus to aggadic comment. Is it possible to say, as R. Ḥiyya b. Abin's interpretation of 1 Chr. 17:21 implies, that God sings Israel's praise?[96] Or that, as R. Joshua b. Levi points out, Dt. 7:10 seems to suggest that one could hate God to His face?[97] Surely, as R. Ḥisda pointedly asserts of S. S. 7:14, the Torah was not given on two occasions.[98] As against R. Yoḥanan's teaching based on Prov. 3:12, his colleagues say that neither Torah study nor prayer would be prevented by God's chastisements of love.[99] Despite Amos 5:2, the people of Israel will never fall and not be raised up.[100] R. Huna insists Habakkuk's allusion to the wicked "swallowing up the righteous" (1:13) is offset by two verses assuring the righteous of God's protection.[101] R. Ishmael rejects the implication of Gen. 14:18 that the gentile Melchizedek was intended to be the father of the priesthood.[102] R. Yose is appalled that R. Joshua b. Korḥa would read Ex. 4:24 as suggesting that Moses delayed his son's circumcision.[103] When God promised to be with Israel in every future servitude, Ex. 3:14, Moses complained about the implied future suffering.[104] Can we imagine that, as that verse also hints when it says "about midnight," that Moses did not know exactly when the Exodus would begin[105] or that he literally saw God's back, as Ex. 33:23 plainly indicates?[106]

Aggadic teachings set forth without a textual base can also be subjected to dialectical challenges (though these were scarce in our sample). In two respects the difficulties raised were like those directed at textual teachings: lack of clarity and apparent clash with accepted belief. Thus, what did Rava have in mind when he prohibited "sitting on the bed of an Aramean woman"?[107] or when R. Ammi said that the Egyptians gave treasures to the Jews "against their will," whose will was he thinking of?[108] if a sage teaches that Adam was created with two faces, male and female, which faced forward when he walked?[109] if the worst form of death is that of "the croup," what is that like?[110] Accepted belief was at stake in various debates, such as that between R. Eliezer and R. Joshua as to whether God's promises are always fulfilled;[111] or justifying God's justice system and the belief that individual transgression brings on corporate suffering;[112] or the reality of old men in Babylonia when long life is only promised those who dwell in the Land of Israel.[113] Faith also lies behind the rabbinic utilization of euphemisms (in both textual and nontextual teachings) to replace language that would curse or denigrate the people of Israel.[114] An extended aggadic passage in *Ber.* 5a–b displays most of their characteristic reactions: that study of the Torah is the best preventative of suffering; that even righteous people may be suffering from sins they had forgotten; that some suffering (here, leprosy) comes to help us expiate our sins.[115]

Some questions arise that seem particularly germane to teachings that do not begin from a textual base. The most obvious of these is a request for the scriptural support for the teaching, and it may be signaled by terms like *minayin*, *minalan* (two forms of "whence") or *may kera*, "what verse."[116] The uncommon notion that had the people of Israel not sinned after entering the Land of Israel they would not have received the prophetic books is justified this way.[117] There are also problems when a rabbinic dictum appears to contravene accepted practice: Can Jews be told to paint trees red, a heathenish custom?[118] Or, if there are only four cases in an arm phylactery, why does a teacher provide five verses for them?[119] But piety alone does not create cognitive dissonance here. Common sense or everyday experience also can do so, since God's words are not the basis of the teaching. Thus, R. Judah b. Simeon rejects a statement that a certain collection includes eighteen psalms when one can count nineteen there.[120] R. Zeira rejects R. Yose's assurance that a given pattern of prayer will protect one from injury, since that was not his experience.[121] This also appears to be behind a rejection of R. Yoḥanan's teaching that leprosy may be God's chastisement of love.[122] And natural phenomena, like the behavior of white cocks or the reality of giant serpents, can militate against some rabbinic opinions.[123]

Against the usual flow of the discourse, questions may arise when an aggadic view appears to contradict the views of another sage.[124] A teacher wonders how one can counsel living in the village of one's master when other teachers forbid it.[125] So, too, the possibility that a sage's opinion might conflict with another of his aggadic views motivates a defense of his consistency.[126] But a rabbi can also be sufficiently disturbed by his own behavior that he and others comment on it.[127]

Matters that do not reach the level of contradiction may also elicit an inquiry, but by far the most common form of the challenge is to leave it with the reader by leaving us with sages holding clashing aggadic views: R. Yoḥanan and R. Isaac's on contending with the wicked;[128] Resh Lakish's difference with R. Jeremiah and R. Joshua on whether sinners repent at the gate of Gehinnom;[129] R. Meir and R. Jeremiah on Adam as saint or sinner;[130] R. Meir and R. Yoḥanan on whether Moses was granted two or three requests (here signaled by the technical term for clashing rabbinic opinions: *peliga*, a division);[131] two anonymous views on whether Balaam could tell the split-second of God's anger when he couldn't even read the mind of his ass;[132] and Rabbi and R. Nathan on whether there are three or four watches during the night.[133]

How Do the Rabbis Respond to Intellectual Challenges?

Aggadic discourse in the Talmud is substantially dialectical, proceeding mostly by statement and response. Like all such modes of eliciting the truth, its "logic" permits a variety of responses to a colleague's dialectical probe, though these responses are nowhere made explicit. Three aspects of this process may be discerned in the material under analysis: the direct response, the reconciliation of the positions, and the coexistence of diverse views. We will consider them in turn.

A dialectical thrust occurs when a rabbi is asked, or rhetorically asks himself, what a given word or phrase means. The simplest response is to supply it. But often a challenge has such cogency that it produces a defensive modification of the original view. A simple way of doing this, particularly in exegetic *aggadah*, is to give a fresh meaning to a troublesome term. Thus, when God says he is *ehyeh*, "I will be," Moses pleads that the future reading of that term not replace its present sense, "I am."[134] Moses's imprecision in saying God will come "about" midnight is quickly explained away by reading the Hebrew prefix in its more customary comparative sense of "like," turning what seemed like God's imperfection into the more acceptable "like the midnight when God killed the Egyptian firstborn."[135] Daniel's shift to the third person when addressing God in prayer can be justified as a reverential reference to Abraham, the first to call God "Lord."[136] R. Eliezer charges that an exegesis of R. Joshua implies that God does not keep His promises, a point of such cogency that R. Joshua reworks his exegesis to preserve God's faithfulness.[137] In a similar bind, R. Yose juxtaposed the promise of Dt. 9:14 and the list of names in 1 Chr. 23:15–17 to prove God is so anxious to fulfill His promises that He fulfills even His conditional blessings, though the conditions were not satisfied.[138]

More broadly, what a rabbi says can be defended by turning the literal into the figurative or the opposite. When Rava puzzlingly said one should not sit on the bed of an Aramean woman, that can be understood to mean "Don't marry a proselyte" or even "Don't go to bed at night before saying the prescribed prayers."[139] R. Ḥisda urged one to enter two doors into a synagogue, which is read as the interior distance of two doors.[140] As in the Bible, names like Gehinnom easily translate into meanings.[141] The unseemly description of Manoah walking "after" his wife merely means he followed her counsel.[142] In a similar strategy, to be discussed below, clashing opinions can be defended as meant to apply only to different, specific situations.[143] An abstract term, like "indignation," can be read concretely, as the name of an angel.[144]

The defense becomes more elaborate when new data is introduced to justify the original statement. Thus, a bird called the *kerum* changes colors as a shamed sinner will;[145] David had a harp that awakened him each midnight by its playing;[146] David, fleeing from Absalom, could rejoice in psalmody, because his foe was his child rather than a merciless slave or bastard;[147] hopelessly guilty sinners will be redeemed from Gehinnom by Abraham's merit;[148] and God's "building" of Adam's rib into Eve is really the use of a sea-town verb, "to plait" hair, for He was getting her ready to meet her spouse.[149]

Despite the broad range of these strategies, a sage may, in extremis, admit his challenger is correct but calmly indicate that he counts nineteen psalms as eighteen in number,[150] or six verses as four,[151] in each case uniting two passages to get the desired number.

A second manner of responding to challenges is to reconcile the two positions involved. Perhaps the simplest way of accomplishing this is by bringing in a new verse. This seems reasonable when the issue is the meaning of a somewhat obscure Hebrew word, like *neshef*, customarily understood as "evening," and contending that it can mean "morning" as well.[152] But many nonexegetical issues are also resolved by bringing in an additional verse: phylacteries give Israel strength;[153] for a fellow scholar one must pray to the point of making oneself ill;[154] one who could study but neglects doing so is chastised by God;[155] and Jews rightfully reject the criticism of sectarian antagonists of their practice of doing exegesis by the synchronic juxtaposition of verses, *semukhin*.[156] Perhaps the equivalent of this maneuver is changing the vocalization of the original verse to yield the meaning one said was to be found there.[157] (We shall discuss this further in chapter 5.)

Perhaps the most common strategy for mediating between a thesis and its challenge is to suggest that the supposed alternatives are, in fact, speaking of different situations. In our sample, personal, chronological, and geographical differences are so treated. Can or cannot leprosy and childlessness be chastisements of God's love? Yes, if the disease is hidden, but not if it is obvious; yes, if one had children and lost them, but not if one never had them.[158] Does or does not God visit the iniquity of fathers on their children? Yes, if they follow in their footsteps, but not if they do not.[159] May or may one not contend with the wicked? Yes, over matters of religion, but not over private matters.[160] May one or may one not live in the same town as one's teacher? Yes, if one is submissive but not if one is not.[161] Will or will not sinners accept God's rule and repent when they reach Gehinnom? Yes, if they are Jewish sinners, but not if they are gentile.[162]

Similarly, clashing statements can be reconciled by suggesting that each refers to a different time. Were humans created as man and woman, or just as man? God first thought to create man and woman, but then decided to make man first.[163] Did God speak in five voices (exegetically deduced) at Sinai or with one? Before giving the Decalogue God utilized five voices, but at the theophany proper, only one.[164] Even if one is wicked in religious as against private matters and thus merits reproof, should one contend with him? Yes, if fortune is not smiling on him, but not when it is.[165] Though R. Elazar b. Azariah and R. Akiba agree that the Exodus took place during daytime (Nu. 33:3), but disagree whether the preceding evening was also redemptive, R. Abba reconciles them by saying they were redeemed in the evening (Dt. 16:1) but departed only in the daytime.[166] Sometimes the reconciliation is hesitant, as when Adam's righteousness is maintained by attributing his sin to a nocturnal emission (and hence was involuntary),[167] or when a suggested additional, fourth gate to Gehinnom is, "perhaps," the same as one of those already identified.[168] Moreover, only once in this sample was a difference reconciled by assigning it to the different positions of the teachers of the Land of Israel and those of Babylon—namely, as to whether leprosy can or cannot be a chastisement of God's love.[169]

The third manner of dealing with differing views is simply to let them stand, side by side. Only rarely in our sample do we find an aggadic passage that appears to favor one side in a nonhalakhic disagreement. Thus, R. Yoḥanan's unanswerable query about the biblical grounds for a Tana's considering the death of one's children a chastisement of God's love is tantamount to its rejection, but a certain elder's exegesis then resolves that issue.[170] Similarly, a statement in the name of Rav seems a decisive climax to the presentation of a difference of opinion between R. Ḥanina, R. Elazar, and an anonymous teacher.[171]

However, aggadic discourse regularly accommodates sharp, unresolved differences of opinion, a "logic" the Western mind does not associate with the authoritative extension of revelation. Examples of such "tolerance" abound. Though all agree that a sin of Abraham caused the Egyptian slavery, R. Elazar, Samuel, and R. Yoḥanan differ as to what it was. The first said it was pressing scholars into his service; the second, that he tested God too much; and the third, that he prevented people from proselytizing.[172] Though R. Joshua b. Korḥa is cited in the Mishnah to the effect that Moses was lax in circumcising his son, R. Yose denies that laxity was involved.[173] While some call Psalm 91 the psalm of plagues, *negaim*, others call it the psalm of evil occurrences, *pegaim*.[174] R. Ḥaggai agrees with R. Ila that God is long-suffering with the righteous, but he maintains God is similarly gracious to the wicked.[175] R. Elazar had stated that Torah was the reason heaven and earth endured, while an anonymous statement gives the commandment of circumcision that honor.[176] Rabbi and R. Simeon b. Elazar disagree as to whether boys or girls mature earlier.[177] While the rabbis say one should judge one's neighbors generously, R. Joseph limits the imperative to one who is religiously observant.[178] Chastisements of God's love never impede either study or prayer;[179] and, as we have seen, *neshef* can mean both evening and morning.[180]

Some Accompanying Rhetorical Devices

In the aggadic operations analyzed above, the "logical" efforts to win consent are enhanced by the employment of various rhetorical strategies (though this heuristic division between the cognitive and imaginative emphases belies the essential integrity of the discourse). Four rhetorical practices stand out, and though they are familiar from the prior discussions, they deserve some special notice. They are the question and answer, hyperbole, retrojective synchronicity, and anthropomorphism.

Making one's exposition more appealing by creating and then relieving a tension by raising a question and then answering it is the familiar "rhetorical question." We cannot be certain whether an anonymous question following a rabbinic statement was a rhetorical device of the sage doing the teaching or of the Stammaim (the anonymous post-Amoraic editors of the Talmud) or the inquiry of a perplexed disciple or thoughtful colleague. Whatever the case, this pattern is ubiquitous in Talmudic dialectic and in its aggadic strand.[181] Even a woman who comes to ask a halakhic question of R. Akiba, as the story informs us, adds a pertinent fact after hearing his decision.[182]

Many aggadic teachings are set forth with an enthusiasm that seems to modern eyes gross overstatement. R. Nathan said that making a vow is like building an idolatrous high place, and fulfilling it is like offering sacrifices there.[183] Rava b. Hinena cited Rav as saying said that one who sins and is ashamed of it has all his sins forgiven.[184] R. Ḥiyya b. Ammi reported that Ulla insisted that living from one's labor is a greater achievement than the fear of Heaven.[185] R. Jeremiah b. Elazar asserted that at their execution criminals must be physically prevented from cursing the government but the righteous approach death with praise of God's righteousness. R. Joshua b. Levi, not to be outdone in hyperbole, proclaims that even the wicked do this.[186]

The sages so identify with the Oral Torah and the life it engenders—Torah scholars being Israel's true glory,[187] its proper heroes,[188] its authentic royalty,[189]—that they retrojectively envisage the great figures of Bible times living as they do. Adam, who was created with male and female faces, would certainly have walked with the male one forward.[190] After being punished with expulsion from Eden, Adam lived in *nidui*, one form of the rabbinic ban.[191] Noah's dove engaged in *derash*, "rabbinic exegesis."[192] King David functioned as a rabbinic judge,[193] and Solomon not only had a teacher in rabbinica[194] but instituted the rabbinic laws of lay ritual washing and the permissible extension of the Sabbath boundary.[195] Isaiah convoked a rabbinic study session at King Hezekiah's door so that its merit would help cure his illness.[196]

The range of aggadic anthropomorhism seems, if anything, greater than that of the Bible. One sage sees God seated on His throne and hears Him speaking and then nodding in approval of the rabbi's statement.[197] God prays to Himself that he may be able to overcome His inner conflict between justice and mercy.[198] Indeed, like any good Jew, God has *tefilin*, "phylacteries," for prayer, one for the arm and another for His head.[199] He sits on His throne, roaring like a lion at His pain over the destruction of the Temple and Israel's exile.[200] God even may be said to need atonement[201] and redemption.[202] The latter passage uses a technical term, *ke'ilu*, "as if," which signals the use of a bold anthropomorphism (and perhaps the rabbinic ambivalence about doing so). They sometimes use another term, *kiveyakhol*, literally "as if one could," which more emphatically signifies "not really ... but think about it."[203] While daring aggadic anthropomorphisms regularly occur without either term being utilized, the two signifiers testify to a rabbinic consciousness that aggadic freedom allows them to dare the limits of permissible statement.

Aggadic Thinking, Some Preliminary Observations

Having now examined the sample of Talmudic *aggadah* on three levels, some comment is in order about what we have learned, particularly in relation to the two perplexing issues that arose from our initial look at nonhalakhic discourse: What, positively put, is the nature of this mode of communication? And what are the limits of acceptable statement in it?

In every aspect, aggadic discourse is extraordinarily diverse. As the Talmud presents them, the aggadists display extraordinary competence, discussing an astonishing range of topics and, unfazed, responding to challenging questions or counterarguments. In the *halakhah*, some questions are left for Elijah to decide when he comes heralding the Messiah (so a number of texts outside our sample, e.g., *Men.* 45a). There is no such modesty in the *aggadah* we have examined. In this realm the sages appear to exercise unflagging intellectual stamina. None ever says, "You can't ask that question" (though inquiries dealing with mysticism might evoke that ban; no such matter arose in the sample). They do not hearken to the anonymous aggadist who counseled, "Let your tongue acquire the habit of saying, 'I know not,' lest you be led into lying."[204]

This enveloping embrace of the world as they knew it is a large part of the reason why the *aggadah* has long been defined as what it is not, that part of rabbinic literature which aims at setting norms for conduct, the *halakhah*. Aggadic discourse takes many forms, scholastic and folkloristic, dryly informational and passionately moralistic, casual and sophisticated. It is too reasoned to be termed wisdom literature and too creative to be transmitted tradition. None of the literary styles of the Greco-Roman era or of other cultures that modern scholars have studied is nearly its equivalent. The problem of its nature remains.

Studying a sample of it intensively, we do not do much better with the puzzle of aggadic freedom. Aggadic statements may be deeply profound, religiously uplifting, or astonishingly trivial. They reflect a rich reverence for the Bible but may twist and turn its texts to say things at variance with their simple meaning. En masse, they are breathtakingly tolerant of diverse opinion—apparently relishing it—but they also evidence a modest drive toward individual consistency and an irresolute interest in reconciling opposing views. Again and again, rabbis give reasons for objecting to their colleagues' reasoning, but not only are these rebuttals generally not decisive, but the *aggadah* calmly transmits to later generations the assertions and the challenges and the lack of decision. Furthermore, with one exception, the data of the sample evinced little self-consciousness about what constituted acceptable or unacceptable patterns for doing aggadic inference.[205]

Clearly, the *aggadah* is an uncommonly open intellectual domain by Western religious standards and is particularly unexpected for a faith that, by its own standards, asserts that the products of this thinking are, as Oral Torah, constituent parts of God's revelation to Israel. Yet freedom surely must have its limits in rabbinic Judaism. But what reins in the free-ranging aggadic process and sets its limits remains utterly unclear. Let us see what we can learn about these two issues by extending our purview beyond the Talmudic sample to other parts of the Talmud—to the Jerusalem Talmud and to some rabbinic works probably available about the time the Talmud was completed.

Chapter 5

∞ Does Extending the Sample Alter the Findings? ∞

When the Babylonian Talmud was complete, it finalized a massive work that gradually became the intellectual foundation for all later Judaism. One of the many consequences of that process was that its manner of conducting aggadic discourse substantially set the pattern for such thinking in later generations. Yet for all its later centrality, when the Bavli essentially achieved the form in which it has come down to us, it was not the only rabbinic document of its time. Not only did the Jerusalem Talmud, the Yerushalmi, exist, but so did various early midrash collections. These documents, too, are the products of the developing rabbinic way of thinking aggadically, and they also participated somewhat in shaping later Judaism's sensibility of what constituted acceptable aggadah. Though there is considerable scholarly debate concerning which works (as we have them) existed at about the time the Talmud was completed, it seems worthwhile to take a brief look at some likely early rabbinic works, particularly with an eye to seeing how their diverse literary contexts modify our Talmud-based sense of what aggadic utterance might be. First, however, let us see what extending our vision beyond the Talmudic sample we have examined would tell us about NHD, or nonhalakhic discourse, in the Babylonian Talmud.

More on the Bavli (1): The Character and Contents of Its *Aggadah*

Ranging informally through the Talmud indicates that our study of a sample of its aggadic discourse yielded a fairly reliable indication of what is found elsewhere in that work. No radically new topics of interest or forms of argument turned up in the further investigation, though certain innovations in previously noted practices and many striking individual statements did appear. However, one emphasis, of particular interest to this investigation, deserves special attention—namely, the several statements evidencing rabbinic self-consciousness about the uncommon nature of aggadic utterance. Thus, in a passage much cited by modern writers, Abaye gave a rationale for biblical verses yielding many aggadic meanings. Said he, "For Scripture says, 'God has spoken once, twice have I heard this, that strength belongs to God' (Ps. 62:11). So the School of R. Ishmael taught, '(Is not My word like fire) And like a hammer that shatters a rock into pieces (Jer. 23:29).' As the rock splits into many fragments, so one verse may convey many meanings."[1] As we have seen, Talmudic *aggadah* celebrates the multiplication of expositions of a given verse,[2] and these are sometimes signaled by the introductory phrase *davar aḥer*, another "thought," the idiom for an additional interpretation.[3] The notorious aggadic multiplication of opinion is addressed in the recourse to heavenly opinion in the conclusion of the exegesis of Es. 5:4, which troublingly says the virtuous Esther invited the wicked Haman to a banquet. No less than fourteen different explanations of this behavior are then offered. The text then concludes with a metaphysical touch. "Rabba b. Abbuha came across Elijah [one day] and asked him, 'According to whose opinion did Esther see fit to act this way?' He replied, 'For all of the reasons given by the Tannaim [the sages of the Mishnah era] and the Amoraim [the post-Mishnaic Talmudic sages]'!"[4] A similar sensibility lies behind the aggadic discussion sparked by R. Ḥisda's exegesis of Es. 1:1. Since he had turned the three numbers involved in giving the sum of Ahashuerus's provinces into a three-step history of his empire, he was challenged to do a similar exegesis with another biblical number. He demurred, saying that the Esther verse is different, for it is "superfluous," the literal meaning having been given elsewhere. Then he calmly generalizes, "Learn from this that this text was given for exposition [and not to convey literal meaning]."[5] Statements such as these are as close as we get to deviations from what the sample illustrated. We turn now to some of the highlights of this broader view of the Talmud, beginning with a quick overview.

Wherever we turn in the Babylonian Talmud, we find *halakhah* and *aggadah* freely intermixed. Thus, an aggadic mention of *lashon hara*, "the evil tongue," the idiom for gossip, shifts into a lengthy discussion of the laws and the seriousness of this sin.[6] Other familiar aggadic patterns abound, such as extensive exegesis, deftly utilizing a hermeneutic device,[7] and unembellished counsel[8] appearing in fairly inexplicable order. Statements may be presented as single opinions or parts of differing points of view, with discussion and perhaps modification, or not.[9] Occasionally, this can lead on to a full-scale dialectical examination of the aggadic positions presented, and such passages take on something of the Bavli's typical pattern for investigating halakhic proposals: the *sugya*, the dialectical examination of diverse views on a topic.[10]

The range of subject matter remains extraordinarily broad. There are dicta on the classic religious topics but also on matters like the varieties of rainfall,[11] proper behavior during an epidemic or famine,[12] and cures for cataracts or migraine.[13] Though the utterances are frequently hyperbolic, commonsense objections can be raised, on occasion to good effect.[14] Of course, the rabbis' common sense includes a much more elastic sense of nature than ours.[15] They take for granted the efficacy of charms and spells, including the sages' ability to work wonders,[16] and the possible transformation of animals and plants into demons.[17] Their views of wonder-working and nature achieve dramatic display in the tale related without comment about Rabbah killing (literally, ritually slaughtering) R. Zeira in the course of a Purim celebration but later reviving him.[18] Tales about the sages occur frequently, very often to educate others for proper behavior.[19]

The basic form of aggadic teaching is the interpretation of a biblical verse, and this can be quite complex. A single word can trigger chains of exposition for no good reason other than the joy of the creativity involved: four different biblical uses of *adir*, "mighty"; six uses of *yedid*, "beloved"; four uses of *tov*, "good"; and, finally, four uses of *zeh*, "this."[20] The sages also often show themselves to be meticulous readers of the Bible who will reject exegeses that overlook even slight variations in the quoted texts. So a proposed substitution of Moses for Joshua is dismissed, because the Moses proof-text has *vehaish*, "and the man," whereas the text being commented on only has *ish*, "man."[21] Rava's assertion that Job was written in Moses's time because Nu. 13:20 refers to his "homeland," *utz*, is spurned, because the Numbers reference is to *etz*, "wood."[22] One teacher suggests that *malkat sheva*, the queen of Sheba, cannot be a woman, for she should then be referred to as *malkhuta desheva*.[23] The considerable discussion over who fed Elijah—the *orevim*, "ravens"—includes a rejection of their being people from a certain town, because denizens would require the term *oreviyim*.[24] Elsewhere, Rabbi's prayer is challenged for citing a text with a plural noun to refer to a single individual.[25] A teacher can find an exegetic prompt in the ubiquitous conjunction *ve*, "and," which links the adjectives describing the calf Abraham sought for his visitors (Gen. 18:7).[26] When Rav and others seek to prove God's punishment from the phrase "Hand to hand" (Prov. 16:5), the objection is raised that *miba ͑e leh* (or its variants), "it requires [the reading]," in this case "From hand to hand."[27] R. Ḥiyya b. Hinena rejected R. Hinena b. Papa's reason for the destruction of the Temple, because his proof-text reads *hamulah*, "tumult," not *milah*, "[the allegedly blasphemous] word."[28]

For all their attention to the details of the Bible text, the sages recognize that some verses, like Job's gall spilling out (Job 16:13) or the kings of Israel and Judah sitting on a threshing floor (1 K. 22:10), should not be taken literally.[29] Furthermore, they can also be quite free with biblical texts. Thus, they can specifically ask for the plain meaning, the *peshat*, of Prov. 23:2, only then to adduce the imaginative interpretation of "ruler" therein as a sage.[30] R. Jeremiah, reacting to the parallelism in Job 3:19, asks about the first part of the verse, "Don't we already know that?" to introduce another interpretation of the text.[31] Rava can even set the text aside to teach a lesson drawn from its context.[32] When R. Huna cited R. Ashi's ingenious interpretation of the names of the villages in Josh. 15:22, he was pressed to do the same with the list in Josh. 15:31. He demurred, saying that R. Ashi, who taught him the former lesson, could also do this, but he himself could not.[33] Most astonishingly, when an anonymous teacher proves his aggadic point by citing a text and it is pointed out that there is no such verse, the Talmudic text simply states, "There is a text to a similar effect...," which then grounds the lesson![34]

Exegetic freedom abounds, as one may gauge from Mar Zutra's comment that four hundred camels would be needed to carry the interpretations of even the genealogical list of Azel, 1 Chr. 8:38–9:44.[35] Words may be radically reinterpreted or broken up to make phrases. When a teacher claimed that the children Elisha had the bears eat, 2 K. 2:23, were really churlish young men, R. Joseph insisted that the word for "children" is the name of a place.[36] Radical letter rearrangements seem quite acceptable. R. Yoḥanan linked the word *ḥeshkat*, "darkness," Ps. 18:12, with its parallel term *ḥashrat*, "collection," 2 Sam. 22:12, to yield *hakhsharat*, "making fit," to bolster Mar's teaching that the clouds sweeten the salty ocean water.[37] A catalog of rabbinic dream interpretations is based on verbal similarities.[38] R. Yoḥanan clinched an exegesis by citing the Greek homophone of a Hebrew word.[39] So did Ben Azzai, proving that the "fruit of a goodly tree" must be an *etrog*, since the Hebrew word for "goodly" sounds like the Greek for "water," which is where *etrog* trees grow.[40] But many other languages might also indicate the meaning of words.[41] Words can be considered "abbreviations," *notarikon*, yielding sentences, not only read in proper order but also reversed, or they may be read as "numbers," *gematria*, and thus carry the meaning of other words with a similar numerical value.[42] In an intriguing reference to a dispute between R. Eliezer b. R. Yose and certain heretics, it is assumed that both groups accepted the aggadic "logic."[43] We gain some insight into the openness, yet not unboundedness, of acceptable aggadic discourse from R. Yehudah's hyperbolic dictum about acceptable synagogue translation into the vernacular: "One who translates a verse with literalness is a liar and one who adds [his words] to it is a reviler and blasphemer."[44]

Besides the Written Torah the rabbis could call on the Oral Torah, and occasionally they indicate that they had traditions concerning aggadic matters. That the friends of Job lived three hundred parasangs from one another is introduced by the authorizing term *utena*, "it was taught," indicating it was a recognized early rabbinic teaching.[45] More uncommonly, when the question is asked how Moses found Joseph's coffin, the answer begins *amru*, "they [prior teachers] said [about this]," but who said it or when is not specified.[46] Most unusually, R. Idit, described as an expert in rebutting heretics, responds to a challenge by saying that Jews have "a faith," *hemanuta beyadan*, that neither Metatron nor any other angel is an intermediary between them and God.[47] A more common usage for an aggadic tradition, *masoret [beyadenu meavotenu]*, "[we possess] a tradition [from our fathers that . . .]," is used by R. Levi to authorize his saying that the kings Amoz and Amaziah were brothers.[48] R. Isaac used this phrase to teach that the spies Moses sent into Canaan all had names corresponding to their (evil) deeds, though only one such name had come down to his generation.[49] But the most common term for identifying aggadic traditions is *gemara*, "a tradition," or its verb form, *gemiri*, "they taught," both used to authenticate teachings passed down to the rabbis who cited them.[50]

The Oral Torah not only provided the Talmudic masters with traditions, it authorized their power to teach on their own. Perhaps the strongest statement about the value of whatever the rabbis say is attributed to the founding Babylonian master Rav: "Where [in the Torah are we taught] that even the casual speech of the sages requires study? As it is written, 'And its leaf does not wither and all it does prospers' (Ps.

1:3)."[51] Is this why the *aggadah* contains matters that by Western standards (and already to some Talmudic masters) seem trivia of no conceivable religious interest? Consider the exegesis of Jer. 5:16, which according to one interpretation proved that the heroes referred to there produced heaps of excrement naturally and not because of illness. R. Mari demurred, insisting that one who has excess excrement suffers from bowel disease; and upon being asked why the Bible needed to teach us this, he responded that it taught that the person should then seek a cure.[52] Or does Rav mean something less grandiose—that the apparently trivial figures and statements in the Bible can yield truth when properly interpreted? (Note the aggadic reconciliation pattern here.) Thus, when Rav's identifications of certain obscure biblical personages were queried with the somewhat strong phrase generally used in halakhic contexts—*mai kamashma lan*, "what do we learn from this"?—it elicited lessons about the limits of fine ancestry and how to respond to sectarians.[53]

The Talmud has many accounts of what rabbis or biblical characters did or what happened to them, but in some places it moves from brief anecdote to longer tale or collections of thematically similar materials. Thus there is a considerable narrative telling how King Solomon got the wondrous Shamir stone from the demon Ashmodai.[54] A lengthy series of passages graphically depicts incidents connected with the fall of Jerusalem.[55] Such tales can center around sages, as in R. Joshua b. Hananiah's discussion with Caesar, a tale followed by an account of his contest of wits with sixty sages of Athens, all of whom he bests.[56] The story of Akiba's marriage and how he became an eminent scholar verges on becoming a short novella.[57] Rabbah b. Bar Hana is the chief character in a long series of tall tales about wondrous waves, animals, and journeys.[58] Only rarely is an anecdote humorous, as in the story of the scoundrel Hanan, who was fined half a *zuz* for boxing someone's ear. Finding no takers for his battered *zuz* coin, Hanan hit him on the other ear and gave him the whole *zuz*.[59] However, most stories about the sages are brief and sober, even when we yearn for more detail, as in the poignant account of R. Eliezer's excommunication after the debate over the ritual status of Achnai ovens.[60]

The sages appear to have no interest in writing fiction, but they do have a sense that some stories are not meant literally, particularly the abbreviated tale they call a *mashal*, "a parable." In the Bavli, *mashal* is often used in a general sense, as in a saying about Ezekiel's vision of the dry bones, "In truth, it was a *mashal*."[61] So, too, the book of Job is called a *mashal* and is compared to the story about the lamb that Nathan tells

David when upbraiding him over Bathsheba.[62] The plethora of detail provided about the death of Judah b. Goria for rendering legal decisions in his master's presence is justified as preventing one from saying that the account was only a *mashal*.[63] Mostly the term introduces a brief anecdote about human experience that will clarify the lesson at hand. Thus, marrying the daughter of a scholar or marrying one's daughter to a scholar are equivalent to breeding good vines with one another, rather than crossing good vines with thornbushes.[64] To explain how one can say that the righteous walk in God's ways but the wicked stumble in them (Hos. 14:10), a *mashal* compares it to two men who roast the Paschal lamb and eat it, one to fulfill the commandment and one merely to have a meal.[65] *Mashal*-like comparisons may be used in halakhic discussions to explain the law, but they themselves, only being exposition, remain *aggadah*. Thus, Akiba compares the shades of leprosy with four tumblers of milk containing varying amounts of blood.[66] A seduced woman may be presumed to consent to whatever pain she suffered, like one who says to a friend, "You may rip up my silk garment with impunity."[67] The prohibition of sexual relations in the second degree of familial relationships is like protecting a vineyard; one is more concerned with the outside than the inside.[68] A man can do with his wife whatever pleases him sexually in the same way that he buys from the butcher the meat that now appeals to him.[69]

The folk adage continues to be a subsidiary warrant for a teaching. Rava does ask Rabbah Mari for a scriptural basis for a considerable list of such adages, perhaps to lend them greater authority; but whatever the case, he thereby acknowledges their salience.[70] When Rav argued from the villain Ahab's listening to Jezebel's counsel that one who hearkens to his wife goes to Gehinnom, R. Papa's rebuttal was the maxim, "If your wife is short, bend down and let her whisper to you." This has sufficient cogency that two efforts to reconcile the divergent views follow.[71]

Central beliefs of Judaism are challenged more frequently than was the case in the sample. R. Abbahu taught that though God rules people, the *tzaddik* rules Him—by getting Him to annul His decrees.[72] God is said to wound His own children—specifically, by giving them an evil *yetzer*, "inclination"—but the charge is mitigated by indicating that He has also provided its therapy, the Torah.[73] God can act so improperly—diminishing the moon's size each month—that even He requires an atonement sacrifice.[74] God's justice is impugned by the angels, since the second verse of the Priestly benediction indicates God can sometimes be partial—and God agrees with them.[75] Such statements are noteworthy, because they go against the bulk of rabbinic opinion that we see exhibited, for example, in the concluding passages of chapter 2 of tractate *Sukkah* (29a), which explain why such troubling events as eclipses and government seizure of property are due to various sins in the community and thus illustrate God's justice.

While the rabbis are not prophetic in their stance and normally defend the honor of the people of Israel, the people can, as we have just seen, become the object of rabbinic censure. Thus, they deserved the destruction of the Temple and exile,[76] normally so decried, and the people can be characterized as so brazen that they needed the Torah to restrain them.[77] Resh Lakish's defense of Israel that had it not been for the sin of the Golden Calf other Jews would not have been born is challenged by six refutations, which themselves are rejected.[78]

On occasion, despite the rabbinic reverence for the biblical text, realism prompts the rabbis to disparage certain biblical texts. Karna calls Jacob's request to his sons to take his remains to the ancestral burial place (rather than rely on the resurrection) *devarim bego*, an obscure idiom possibly meaning "words with a hidden meaning."[79] Even more astonishingly, Resh Lakish says that "many" verses in the Torah are so nearly heretical that they deserve to be burned.[80]

The sages, usually so respected, are now and then treated quite roughly by their colleagues. Ben Azzai says that compared to him they are all as valuable as a garlic husk except Akiba, whom he calls "Baldy."[81] R. Zeira says that R. Benjamin b. Yefet is not in the same intellectual class as R. Ḥiyya b. Abba.[82] And in some classically notorious stories Ben Azzai accuses Akiba of being insolent in following his teacher into the privy, and R. Kahana is chided by Rav for hiding under the master's bed (when Rav had intercourse with his wife) and then making some coarse comments about Rav's behavior.[83]

The Bavli (2): More on Aggadic Argument and Reconciliation

As was the case with the general picture of nonhalakhic utterance, so too the modes of argument we encounter throughout the Talmud are familiar to us from the study of the sample.

The practice of dialectically juxtaposing contrary religious views remains widespread. Verses of the Bible may themselves create the contradiction,[84] or a question may be introduced to test which one will have difficulty in answering it.[85] But the clashes may be of ideas that are put forth with or without supporting verses, as with the presentation of four views of creation,[86] five descriptions of God's manner of mourning the Exile,[87] and positive and negative views of the Exile (and of God's relation to Israel).[88] Often the dialectical controversialists are named: Rava and Abaye on the religious status of sages,[89] and whether the filial relation of the Jews to God is conditional or unconditional;[90] and Rava and R. Joseph on the protective quality of study.[91] More frequently, the divergent views appear to be stated and then explored by others.[92] So a skeptical comment about the authorship of the book of Job,[93] or whether Ahashuerus, Ahab, and Nebuchadnezzar each ruled the whole world,[94] provoke vigorous dissent. This treatment is given R. Yose's view that the Israelites accepted the Torah only in order to become immortal,[95] and to R. Elazar's dictum that those doing a mitzvah do not suffer harm.[96] Any of these patterns can become quite convoluted when new texts or masters' statements are introduced to the arguments.[97]

Common sense, as the rabbinic culture understood it, often provides the reason for opposition to an *aggadah*, particularly a hyperbolic one. Thus, R. Hisda rejects R. Papa's understanding of the many sacrifices made in David's procession bringing the Ark to Jerusalem as demanding too many altars.[98] A term for such objections—*salka daatakh*, is it conceivable?—introduces an objection to R. Tanhum b. Hanilai's suggestion that, violating the belief that angelic beings do not eat, Abraham ate with his three visitors.[99]

Whatever the reason for challenges to aggadic dicta, the aggadists have many strategies for turning them aside. The simplest of these may be to reinterpret a challenged biblical verse when its exposition is challenged—say, in the case that it is said to contradict an aggadic teaching.[100] Or a teacher may respond, *im ba'et, ema*, "if you require it [by rejecting my previous textual exposition], I can say [instead] . . ." and suggest a more compelling verse for his teaching.[101] He may also adduce new data, whether his own ideas or an accepted tradition.[102] Such alternative arguments can mix text and new content in quite complex fashion.[103] Arguments can be rejected on the basis of the Bible even without citing a specific verse, as in the charge that Baba b. Buta should not have given Herod advice on how to rebuild the Temple. He should have remembered that Daniel (literally, "God has judged me") was punished for advising Nebuchadnezzar to do this, thereby being made a royal courtier (like Hatach, the chamberlain in the book of Esther). Even ignoring that, how could Baba b. Buta have forgotten that Daniel was put in the lions' den?[104] R. Judah clarifies how the Torah could call Jochebed a daughter, implying she was young, when an aggadic tradition says she was 130 when she married. He says, without giving a source, that the signs of maidenhood were restored to her.[105] R. Joseph objects to R. Naḥman's exegesis of 1 K. 22:20 proving that Ahab had as many merits as sins and bases his refutation on 1 K. 21:15. The response is that Ahab subsidized the students and sages of his time, so the Bible indicates he was forgiven half his sins.[106] Similarly, the radical suggestion that some sages bring destruction on the world draws the explanation that the malefactors are rabbis who issue rulings solely on the basis of rote learning rather than by utilizing their dialectical skill.[107] R. Eliezer's dictum that one who teaches his daughter Torah, surely a meritorious act, actually teaches her "obscenity" evokes the modification that he "really" was speaking metaphorically.[108] R. Tanḥum resolves the objection to R. Meir's counterintuitive preachment that fetuses in their mothers' wombs joined in the "Song of the Sea," Ex. 15, by suggesting that their mothers' bodies became transparent, and they, like the rest of the Hebrews, saw God's presence there.[109] The question whether the Talmudic master Samuel spoke well or disparagingly of Pelatiah (Ez. 11:13) is answered positively, since that would be "consistent," *letaameh*, with Samuel's other dicta (halakhic, in this instance).[110] When an act seems unjustifiable, as Elisha having bears eat the children who mock him, reasons can be suggested why this was, in fact, justice.[111]

A standard way of reconciling the ascription of a given act or situation to several different persons (or places) is to assert that the diverse names all refer to the same reality, as Resh Lakish does by saying that the Evil Yetzer, Satan, and the Angel of Death are one reality.[112] The opposite approach, referring clashing views to different times or situations, is another major reconciliation tactic and the more common one of this pair. Thus, whether God spoke only to Moses or to all of Israel becomes all Israel hearing God at Sinai, but God speaking to Moses alone in the tabernacle.[113] In the hereafter, will many or few people see God? Many will see God indirectly, few will do so directly; many will proceed by receiving permission, but a few will not require it.[114] Does God cry over the destruction of the Temple, or is there no sadness in God's presence? In the inner chambers God does weep, but not in the outer ones.[115] Is matchmaking as difficult as splitting the Sea of Reeds, or are marriages ordained in heaven prenatally? Second marriages are difficult, first ones destined.[116] Apparent contradictions in the dicta reported of one sage can also be disposed of by the two-situation method. Does R. Elazar believe that it is good to leave a bit of one's bread when eating, or is it idolatry? If one has a full portion, it is good to leave some, but to do so when food is limited is idolatry.[117]

Infrequently, conflicting rabbinic positions are united. R. Naḥman said that Huldah the prophetess was descended from Joshua. But R. Ena Saba pointed out that she, according to R. Judah, was one of the eight prophets born to Rahab, the harlot. R. Naḥman then suggested that Rahab converted and married Joshua, only to be faced with the tradition that Joshua had no children, a difficulty swept away by saying that he had no sons, just daughters.[118]

When all else fails, drastic measures may be employed. Resh Lakish's comment that Moses slapped Pharaoh contradicts a tradition that he said Pharaoh should be treated as a king, while R. Yoḥanan said he deserved disrespect as an evildoer. The difficulty is resolved by an anonymous comment suggesting, "Reverse it [the names in the citation]!"[119]

Despite all this virtuosity at reconciliation of difference, it must be emphasized that the reconciliations are the aggadic opinion of a given sage (named or anonymous) and not a decision that this is a normative position for aggadic interpretation. Note that the precipitating statement remains in the tradition, and no aggadic mechanism exists to insist that the resolution proposed to the problem seen in it now is the official answer of the rabbis. For, in the last analysis, despite these tendencies to create aggadic coherence, the Talmud far more frequently merely presents the contrary positions without trying to reconcile them. This strongly suggests that stating a new view, even a contrary one, is itself an aggadic value.

The evidence for this judgment is overwhelming. In addition to all that has been adduced in previous chapters and already in this one—most spectacularly in the diverse comments on Es. 5:4—here is a brief selection: R. Naḥman can prove that the *Shekhinah* is in the South, R. Abbahu that it is in the West, while three other sages prove that it is omnipresent.[120] God's relationship to Israel provides a rich ground for varied speculation, some teachers stressing Israel's deficiencies but God's compensating love, while others emphasize Israel's merits. R. Meir and Resh Lakish insist the Jews are so brazen they needed the Torah to control them,[121] and God had to coerce them into accepting it[122] or as good as bribe them to do so.[123] But R. Yoḥanan and R. Elazar b. R. Simeon say they received the Torah because of their modesty.[124] R. Avira argues that it was because of the merit of the Israelite women who outwitted the Egyptian persecutors.[125] The Jews may be understood to be God's own family, but only conditionally so, as R. Judah teaches, or unconditionally, as R. Meir asserts.[126] Converts can be seen both as the purpose of Israel's being sent into exile[127] and as undesirable as boils.[128]

Finally, a word needs to be said about the rhetoric that clothes these "logical" maneuvers. It, too, is much the same in the extended evidence as it was in the sample, a judgment attested by even a brief look at some new aggadic hyperbole. Self-consciously, the rabbinic addiction to hyperbole is justified by pointing out that such *leshon havai*, "idle talk," is only an imitation of biblical usage.[129] The rabbis exaggerate to commend a given virtue, as in the teachings that even fetuses curse flatterers, that the charitable are greater than Moses, and that the hard-hearted are like idol worshipers.[130] Nature itself mourns when great sages die, and the world and infinite heavenly host (whose numbers are geometrically amplified) were created only for Israel's sake.[131] Ocasionally, we cannot tell whether their rhetoric is inflated or we have a different sense of nature, as when R. Ḥanina defends an overstated account of population by saying that, like a deerskin, the land expands with inhabitants.[132] R. Elazar b. R. Shimon rejects R. Yehudah's claim that the waters surrounding the Jews in the Sea of Reeds were twelve *mil* high, because later, when they came down to drown the Egyptians, they would also have engulfed the Jews. Hence, he says God heaped up the waters sacklike—in fact, enabling them to reach a height of 300 *mil*![133] Sometimes, the exaggeration seems of the "tall-tale" variety, as in the report that Yoḥanan b. Narbai ate three hundred calves, drank three hundred barrels of wine and had forty measures of young birds at one meal[134] or that certain people had bellies so large that a yoke of oxen could pass under them.[135] The exaggeration in some rabbinic hyperbole bothered some rabbis enough that we find texts such as this one:

> We have learned [*Tam.* 2:2] "There was an ash heap in the middle of the altar and sometimes there were about 300 *kor* of ashes on it." Said Rava, "It is an exaggeration [*guzma*]." [Also] "They gave the daily offering [a lamb] a drink from a cup of gold." [*Tam.* 3:4] Said Rava, "It is an exaggeration." R. Ammi said, "The Torah, the [books of the] Prophets and the sages sometimes spoke in exaggerations. The sages spoke in exaggerations as noted [above]. The Torah spoke in exaggerations as in the verse, 'The cities are great and fortified up to heaven.' [Dt. 1:28] The Prophets spoke in exaggerations as in the verse 'So that the earth rent with their sound.' [1 K. 1:40]"[136]

Clearly, the rabbis of the Talmud knew that aggadic discourse created special difficulties, but they seem to have no great difficulty in living with it.

Aggadah in the Talmud of the Land of Israel

Even a cursory acquaintance with the text of the Yerushalmi, the traditional name for the Talmud of the Land of Israel, indicates that despite its similarity to the Bavli, it has a rather different character. Both are highly authoritative documents of the Oral Torah. They center on a number of Mishnaic tractates, present the views of various rabbis on them, yet go beyond these matters to include other topics; and thus—a matter of concern to us—they consist of a mix of *halakhah* and *aggadah*. However, the differences between them, in authority, length, acuity, and style, have long been noted by scholars.[137] In recent scholarship, Jacob Neusner and Jay Harris have given us helpful epitomes of the characteristic intellectual approach each Talmud displays. Neusner writes, "The Bavli is different in form; different in program; different in interpretation of the literary task; different in modes of exposition and different in manner of argument. The Yerushalmi tends to cite; the Bavli to argue; the Yerushalmi is happy to lay out possibilities; the Bavli insists on settling questions."[138] Harris specifies, "It seems, then, that the redactors of the Bavli took from earlier materials the stance that there are among the *Tannaim* no systems of exegesis exclusive to an individual or a school. All techniques are available.... While scarcely maintaining consistency throughout all tractates, the Yerushalmi often divides the earlier tannaitic materials into two schools, that of R. Aqiba and that of R. Ishmael."[139] In keeping this general framework in mind, it should be remembered that neither scholar is concerned with the issue of the universe of nonhalakhic—that is, aggadic—discourse as contrasted to halakhic material in these works. Yet for our purpose—studying the Bavli's *aggadah* to gain an understanding of what will later be seen as the classic instance of the aggadic language-game—looking at the Yerushalmi's similar yet different *aggadah* begins to give us some insight into the way in which aggadic discourse, while still recognizable, may vary in different literary-social settings.

Within its lesser bulk, there is far less aggadic material proportionately in the Yerushalmi than in the Bavli (which scholars regularly explain is due to separate Palestinian *midrash* books, a phenomenon unknown to Babylonia). Estimates of this difference vary widely. Ginzberg says that one-sixth of the Yerushalmi is *aggadah*, compared to one-third of the Bavli, but Stemberger, who accepts the former appraisal, suggests that the latter should be raised to two-thirds, a view that the passages studied for this volume do not bear out.[140] Neusner, who does not use the category *aggadah* in relation to the Yerushalmi, says that the material "independent of the interests of the Mishnah ... [is] not apt to add up to much more than 10% of the whole."[141] Some scholars have also sought to characterize the different aggadic tone of the two works. Zechariah Frankel's mid-nineteenth-century introduction to the Yerushalmi—which Stemberger calls "A Classic"[142]—indicates that while the Bavli's tales sometimes cannot be taken at face value and occasionally are bizarre, the Yerushalmi's are generally believable, though occasionally odd. While both have considerable charm, the Bavli's literary style and powerful imagination is quite superior to that of the Yerushalmi.[143] On the whole, that characterization has, with some variation of emphasis, been echoed by later writers.[144]

We can gain our own sense of this body of *aggadah* by studying the Yerushalmi tractate *yShevuot* and then comparing it with what we saw in the Bavli.[145] Within the lesser bulk of the Yerushalmi tractate, a rough comparison indicates that aggadic material occurs less frequently there than it does in the Bavli. Where *yShevuot* spreads over eighty-eight folio pages (in the Vilna, Romm edition) of which twenty-five have some *aggadah*, the Bavli tractate has ninety-six (much fuller) folio pages of which forty-five have aggadic texts. Moreover, there are only three places in *yShevuot* where lengthy aggadic passages accumulate (at *mishnah*s 3:8, 6:5, 7:2), but twice that many are found in the Bavli (15b, 16a, 18b, 31a, 35b, 39a).

Most of the extended biblical exegesis in *yShevuot* is halakhic, though, as we shall see, some is aggadic.[146] As usual, there are random, nonhalakhic comments. Twice we find the rhetorical introduction to a halakhic passage, "See here ... ,"[147] and elsewhere we have the observation that Ḥanan and R. Simeon said the same thing.[148] More substantive is the question, "Is there then such a thing as a Hebrew slave in these times?"[149] Neusner nicely renders R. Judah's comment on certain mitigated countercharges, saying he termed them "a lover's quarrel."[150] Opinions may be provided by a single sage[151] or a number of views may be adduced.[152]

There is surprisingly little hyperbole to be found in this tractate. A discussion of God's forgiveness has no statements stressing God's magnanimity or the sinner's need to repent.[153] If a text says that a fire will burn up not only the wood but also the stones of a house, that only proves the evil of a false oath.¹⁵⁴ Diocletian's retinue as he went to Egypt is put at 1,200,000, or twice the number of Jews who came out of Egypt.¹⁵⁵ And a report of the famed aggadist, Samuel b. Naḥman, that twenty-four councils in the south were wiped out because of false oath-taking, is probably more enthusiastic than historical.¹⁵⁶

The single greatest focus of the *aggadah* in this tractate is rabbi stories. We learn that a disciple should greet his master, "Peace be unto you, my Master,"¹⁵⁷ and that when Abimi, the brother of Ḥaifa, said he studied the law of vows and oaths, Ḥaifa examined him in considerable detail.¹⁵⁸ We hear of a son of the patriarch who, leading services, forgot it was the beginning of the month, yet got praised for that.¹⁵⁹ R. Jacob bar Aḥa confessed he could not remember something R. Simeon b. Lakish said on a given topic,¹⁶⁰ while R. Zeira indicated that R. Ba b. Memel never got an answer to his question of how to reconcile an opinion on complex oaths with the language of the Mishnah because it was formulated after he had died.¹⁶¹ Rabban Gamaliel thought that when he knocked out the tooth of his slave Tabi he could then emancipate him, but that turned out not to be possible.¹⁶² We have a story about Samuel nicely handling an issue of a scarf a creditor seized from his debtor in the marketplace, but it possibly should be classified as *halakhah*.¹⁶³

These accounts speak of a commonplace world we can easily recognize—of proper respect for a king,¹⁶⁴ of the various levels of government,¹⁶⁵ of importunate creditors,¹⁶⁶ of four-flushers and those who are what they seem,¹⁶⁷ and of a common paradox in the lending and collection of money.¹⁶⁸ Yet these rabbis also have a different sense of what can transpire in nature than we do. Thus, the tractate has a single reference to angels and another to a (heavenly?) voice calling out.¹⁶⁹ Three comments are made about huge snakes or about seeing other such uncommon creatures.¹⁷⁰ However, a flat assertion that nothing is square in its natural condition is vigorously challenged but defended.¹⁷¹

The pages of *yShevuot* do not contain many passages in which aggadists radically manipulate texts to yield a lesson, nor do we find much juxtaposing of contradictory rabbinic opinions to set up an aggadic teaching. Similarly, the few comments we have on theological matters have no quarrel with common rabbinic teachings but echo them. Thus, God has foreknowledge that he can use to forgive a transgression. Apparently contradictory texts on God's leniency are quickly reconciled, as is the suggestion that the All-knowing One might forget one's sins.¹⁷² The reality of freedom of the will is asserted without comment.¹⁷³

The "logic" that guides these aggadic texts is quite familiar after studying the Bavli. We find the conventional pattern of asking for the text that grounds a view.[174] Opposing texts are not permitted to challenge each other but are quickly reconciled via a theory of simultaneous revelation that is substantiated by two verses.[175] The pattern of having a gentile's assertion provoke a Jewish lesson, in this case halakhic, also occurs.[176] The exegesis is often close to the text;[177] R. Samuel b. Yudan can insist that the specific wording yields a precise message,[178] as does R. Zeira, whose teaching flows from a modifier the text does not include.[179] That is as close as this material comes to insisting on following the grammar of the biblical texts or ignoring it.

This does not mean these sages never embroider the texts, for they do that to Moses's reaction to hearing the laws regarding the sacrifices.[180] But their sense of what a verse "simply" says is quite elastic, as in the judgment that, since Satan went around continually, angels of destruction have no joints and thus cannot sit.[181] So, too, if God punishes Jews for doing vain things, that surely means uttering vain oaths.[182] No folk sayings are adduced as substantiation of aggadic lessons in this tractate. The one saying we find, "Whether you are righteous or guilty, don't get involved with an oath," seems more a cliché of the academy than of the folk.[183] We have no searching exploration of the views of various aggadists and only two examples of some mild, dialectical opposition to the teachers' dicta.[184]

In sum, Neusner's description of the bareness and conventionality of the Yerushalmi as compared to the Bavli is borne out by this limited aggadic sample. We are better prepared now to speculate about what constitutes the Bavli's characteristic aggadic discourse, a usage that should not simply be equated with the total realm of possibilities in the aggadic language-game entire. That is, one might produce a quite sedate body of *aggadah* from the Yerushalmi that the sages would recognize as such despite its radical difference from the scintillatingly exciting *aggadah* of the Bavli.[185] One qualification must, however, immediately be entered. Scholars have often indicated their belief that the paucity and plainness of the Yerushalmi's aggadic textual exegesis is related to the existence of a separate Palestinian literature devoted to the aggadic enterprise.[186] If we are to try to understand aggadic discourse generally, it behooves us to take a look at its forms in the early midrashic literature and two other aggadic works of roughly the same period.

Aggadah in Other Early Rabbinic Works

Our purview now expands to include nine works related to the two Talmuds by era of redaction and numerous similarities of personnel, theme, and style. For our purposes it will help to consider them in three subgroups: the four Tannaitic *midrashim*—*Mekhilta, Sifra, Sifre Nu.,* and *Sifre Dt.*—all works in which both *halakhah* and *aggadah* appear; *Avot* and *Avot de Rabbi Natan,* works that are entirely aggadic but not exegetic/homiletic; and the *midrash* books *Gen. R., Lev. R.,* and *Pesikta de Rav Kahana,* nonhalakhic works of which the first is essentially exegetically organized and the latter two are homiletically structured.

The Tannaitic *Midrashim*

The *aggadah* in these four collections seems, on the whole, quite familiar. It occurs in a literature interspersed with halakhic comments. It utilizes many of the technical terms familiar to us from our study of *aggadah* in the Bavli (though the Tannaitic works provide our earlier sources for such language).[187] What distinguishes these books, however, is their close connection with a book of the Torah, such as Exodus, Leviticus, Numbers, and Deuteronomy. Hammer, surveying these works as a whole, points out the considerable variations that occur in their treatment of the text.[188] However Fraade, comparing *Sifre Dt.* with the Habakkuk *pesher* of Qumran and Philo's comments on the Torah, distinguishes it from its contemporary commentaries. The three works in various ways use the deictic and dialogical form, and Philo and *Sifre Dt.* both have the concatenation of multiple interpretations, but the latter alone carries this out without "any standard hierarchical principle or plan."[189] Neusner agrees that these works are exegetical[190] but rejects the term "commentary" for them[191] and after his rhetorical, logical and topical comparative analysis of Sifra, Sifre Nu. and Sifre Dt., he uncovers the authorship's distinctive plan for each of these works.[192] Despite these issues, he would not deny that these four books constitute a group whose family resemblances set it aside from the other five works we shall consider.

Because the Tannaitic *midrashim* largely follow the Torah text, Sifra is, like the book of Leviticus, largely halakhic.[193] *Mekhilta,* which covers only twelve of the forty chapters of Exodus, largely concentrates on the legal material but also skips some significant legal material, i.e., the construction of the tabernacle.[194] The aggadic portions nonetheless reflect a full range of concerns common to *aggadah* elsewhere.[195] A number of scholars have commented that the distinction between halakhic and aggadic passages yields a valuable insight related to the vexing problem of whether these books can be attributed to R. Ishmael (*Mekhilta* and *Sifre Nu.*), or to R. Akiba (*Sifra* and *Sifre Dt.*), or their "schools." While they find some consistency in the halakhic passages, the *aggadah* in these works is largely a mixture of both literary streams.[196] Hammer finds *Sifre Dt.* a restatement of the standard themes of Tannaitic Judaism,[197] and Neusner finds the *Mekhilta*'s straightforward restatement of well-known themes so flat and expected that he creates an ingenious apology for it.[198]

A study of selected portions of these works, then, highlights their general similarity with what we have previously encountered. Perhaps that is because so much of the aggadic material of these books occurs in the Talmud—though it does so in a related form but not as a direct citation.[199] One central issue of this study—what limits the extraordinary freedom of aggadic utterance—is merely reinstantiated by this material. Thus, despite someone being rebuked for an aggadic extravagance, that troublesome utterance is transmitted alongside the rebuke.[200] Yet two subjective impressions remain. There is a certain tameness about the aggadic imagination in these books as contrasted to the range of *aggadah* met in the Talmud. The kind of aggadic dialectical cross-examination, the *sugya* variety of argument that we met in the Bavli, almost never surfaces here. So, too, the uninhibited comments about people or the Talmudic aggadic asides that may go anywhere are rare in these works. The *aggadah* of the Tannaitic *midrashim* has a sobriety that contrasts markedly with the free-flowing exuberance of Talmudic nonhalakhic discourse. Yet that impression, placed in its context, is a modest deviation from the general sense of the considerable similarity between the *aggadah* of the Tannaitic *midrashim* and that of the Talmud.

Avot and *Avot de Rabi Natan*

Two immediate impressions register when one reads the Mishnah tractate *Fathers* (Founders? Exemplars?) and what has loosely been called its "Talmudic" elaboration, the *Fathers According to Rabbi Nathan*.[201] These works are entirely aggadic,[202] and though they often exhort the reader to action, they mostly do so as a matter of wise counsel rather than as biblical interpretation or that part of Oral Torah that is binding law. They also are, in their own way, rather sober. *Fathers*, in particular, rarely exhibits that fusion of hyperbole and creativity that gives Talmudic *aggadah* its special charm. Line after line it gives good advice, often in pleasing form, but it never strays far from straightforwardly transmitting the maxims of the wise.[203] While *Fathers According to Rabbi Nathan* is far more expansive[204] and, as Neusner has shown, gives special prominence to sage stories,[205] it remains closely related to *Fathers* not only in content but in aggadic tone. One sees this most clearly in relation to exegesis of Scripture. This occurs more frequently in *Fathers According to Rabbi Nathan*, but with nothing like the prominence, imagination, or intensity we shall encounter in the early *midrashim*. Both these works are, despite all their differences, more like the Talmud than the *midrashim*.[206] Saldarini's description of the situation that gave rise to these documents is quite persuasive: "These ... documents must be seen as part of a religious and cultural tradition which was both oral and written and which remained flexible over centuries. The authors and editors of these materials preserved, rearranged, rephrased, and reinterpreted with a freedom unknown to readers of the printed book, but with a reverence and respect for the past often lacking in those familiar with print."[207]

This brief literary encounter requires us to distinguish rhetorical style from *aggadah*. That is, we now see that all aggadic utterance need not mimic the nonhalakhic discourse in the Talmud. *Aggadah* is less a specific group of ways of speaking than a broad cultural context in which initiated listeners understand the special impact (aggadic, not halakhic) of the remarks addressed to them. One may utilize unexpectedly different verbal patterns to carry on aggadic discourse, as *Fathers* and *Fathers According to Rabbi Nathan* do, presenting us with *aggadah* whose literary style is quite different from that of the Talmud. Thus, several styles of speaking can be characterized as *aggadah*, not *halakhah*.

The Early Aggadic *Midrashim*

An examination of the earliest aggadic works devoted to interpreting the Bible, what people generally mean when they say, "the Midrash"— namely, *Genesis Rabbah* (*Gen. R.*), *Leviticus Rabbah* (*Lev. R.*) and *Pesikta de Rav Kahana* (*PRK*)[208]—clearly reinforces the notion that the universe of aggadic discourse transcends any particular literary form. For example, while they all are almost entirely *aggadah*, a significantly different literary conception structures them.[209] Whereas *Gen. R.*

proceeds in commentary-like fashion, *PRK* selects the verses it will discuss based on the synagogue lectionary for the festivals and special Sabbaths (and uses a pattern of discourse directed to the public), and *Lev. R.* occupies a formal place somewhere between the two of them.

However, far more important for gaining a sense of the breadth of the aggadic realm is the tone of these works and those related to them. The nonbiblical *aggadah* of *Fathers* and *Fathers According to Rabbi Nathan* was quite sober in expression, but these *midrash* books are awash with imagination and creativity. What in the Bavli was an occasional ingenious foray into lore and only occasionally a lengthy collection of such comments, here emerges, page after page, chapter after chapter, book after book, in a riot of exegetical and expository invention. *Midrash*, the biblical exegetical (and highly creative) sector of aggadic discourse, is therefore the one branch of rabbinic literature to have engaged contemporary literary critics, particularly those of a postmodern bent, and we may leave the subtle literary questions they have raised concerning these books to them. We shall briefly examine these three classic works (with an occasional dip into *Lamentations Rabbah* and *Song of Songs Rabbah*), utilizing the three-step agenda applied to the Bavli, moving from their surface characteristics to their contents and thence to the "logic" that structures them. With one qualification, these books manifest no aggadic paths we have not seen in the Talmud, only a barely restrained exuberance in taking them.

Some Surface Characteristics of Early *Midrashim*

The *aggadah* that fills the *midrash* books rarely surprises us by a radical departure from the nonhalakhic discourse in the Talmud. However, three particular aspects of this aggadic exegesis should be noted. The first of these is the sheer energy and verve of these interpreters. One simply cannot imagine what one will find as one turns the pages of these works. They constitute a special celebration of the ingenuity and inventiveness of the human spirit.

The second impressive characteristic of this aggadic performance is the special density of interpretation these works tend to propagate. In keeping with the rabbinic belief in the polysemy of the Bible and aggadic practice, the compilers of these books often enthusiastically aggregate many teachers' views on a given text.[210] The term *davar aḥer*, another interpretation, occurs so frequently and is so apt for these works as a whole that it may almost be considered a governing theme of the *midrash* books. The one loss from this devotion to piling up expositions is that it tends to limit the number of the random, brief comments that were a significant part of the Bavli's *aggadah*.[211]

Third, the one unexpected form of biblical exposition, the *petiḥta*, seen in some of these works—*Lev. R.* and *PRK*—involves the special use given to an extraneous text that is brought to bear upon the original text being expounded. In the *midrash* books featuring this mode, the new texts are often taken from the Writings. While such pairing of texts occurs frequently in Talmudic *aggadah* (and elsewhere), it is generally done there to clarify something in the wording or meaning of the original text. In any case, the focus remains on the original text. Here the alien text, which linguistically may have little in common with the original text, now becomes the center of the exposition, and through the art of the aggadist its interpretation eventually works its way back to give the teacher's understanding of the original text. The method not only adds a certain literary grace to the search for meaning but also leads to a considerable expansion of the exegetic reach. By contrast, other devices for illuminating the lesson, like having a sage argue with a philosopher or a Roman official like Hadrian, do not produce as significant an expansion of the homiletic horizon.[212] This pattern is first encountered in some of the *midrashim* of this period of the completion of the Talmud and is unique to them. In due course it became a standard form for much of later midrashic public activity.

To return now to continuities, hyperbole remains a mainstay of this aggadic rhetoric. Often it is used simply to emphasize the point the rabbi is making, as in the lengthy list of creations that came into being only because of Israel,[213] or raising the number 24 to the sixth power to indicate the grandeur of Jerusalem,[214] or gratitude for the impostors among the poor lest the forgetfulness or inadvertance of people causing their occasional refusal to give alms doom them to punishment.[215] Sometimes it is used to gain attention, as in the delightful stories of rabbis like Akiba and Rabbi saying wildly improbable things when their introductory teaching is met with congregational drowsiness.[216] Occasionally it seems employed as something of an art form, not only in the famous number-plays of rabbinic *aggadah* but in what seem almost like competitions in exaggeration.[217] The result is assertions like: the rabbinic agreement that Behemoth daily eats the produce of a thousand mountains, but a disagreement on whether the creature can lie down on one mountain or requires a thousand mountains;[218] the cries of Jacob's sons, when Joseph throws Benjamin into jail, sounding around the world;²¹⁹ that a certain Ḥirah is identified with Hiram, making his life span variously five hundred or one thousand years;²²⁰ or, quite notoriously, when R. Abbahu said that Mordecai, one of a number of people who gave sustenance to Israel, himself suckled Esther when no wet nurse was available, causing the community to guffaw, whereupon he nonchalantly reminded them that one Tanna had ruled that male milk is ritually acceptable.²²¹ In these fantastic images, as in the ingenious exegetic practices and artistic expositions of much of nonhyperbolic *aggadah*, the observation of R. Ḥanina b. Papa about this discourse is uncannily apt:

> Another interpretation of "I am *Adonai*, your God" (Ex. 20.2). The Holy One appeared unto them with a stern face, an in-between face, an explanatory face, [and] a playful face. A stormy face for Bible, appropriate for pedagogy; a face of equanimity for Mishnah; a clarificatory face for Talmud; [and] a playful face for *Aggadah*.²²²

Panim soḥakot, a playful face—yet surely one that evokes awe and reverence—deserves to stand alongside *davar aḥer* as a classic motto for aggadic utterance.

Aspects of the Content Found in the *Midrashim*

Much of the teaching in these works draws on the common wisdom of the period, like R. Abbahu's dictum, taking off from the Genesis reference to gaining bread by the sweat of one's brow (Gen. 3:19), that perspiring is one of five things beneficial to the sick²²³ or R. Simeon b. Yoḥai's version of the kinds of inquiries a king would make of his son's tutor.²²⁴ However, the central object of these *midrash* collections is the interpretation of the Bible. The rabbis' imaginative fulfillment of this task rests on their conviction that God's book, the Torah, God's Written Law, is unique among documents in human hands and that its language contains an infinite concentration of Divinely intended meaning and significance. As R. Zeira taught, even the calligraphic letter embellishments (literally, "thorns") on the words in the Torah scrolls contain heaps of meanings (the absence of any one of which) would destroy the entire universe, as Dt. 13:17 indicates, "It will be a waste heap eternally and shall not ever be rebuilt." R. Zeira derives this from S. S. 5:11, which mentions, in the rabbinic interpretation, God's locks being in curls, *taltalim*, which can be read as "heap-heaps." So, too, R. Samuel b. Naḥman pointed out that 1 K. 5:12, imputing

3,000 parables to Solomon, was counterfactual, the Bible containing only 800 verses he authored. He resolved this contradiction by interpreting Prov. 25:12 as saying that each of Solomon's verses having come as prophecy, they could yield two or three additional parables. But other rabbis contended that Solomon had 3,000 parables for each verse and that each parable itself could yield 1,005 more parables.[225] God's revelation was that full of meaning for them.[226]

The astonishing consequence of this attitude is that this discourse permits an aggadist who detects a usage in the biblical text that clashes with his expectations (or that will allow him to give a striking exposition) to, as it were, rewrite the Bible as R. Levi does, saying, "Scripture really should have said, '(Come, My) bride, *to* Lebanon [a euphemism for Jerusalem] with Me,' " rather than *from* Lebanon, as S. S. 4:8 says.[227] Or, if a text appears to be devoid of meaning, it is, according to a dictum ascribed to R. Akiba, only because "you don't know how to expound it."[228] R. Elazar opines that the Torah is more given to generalization than to detail, a view reminiscent of Yitshak Heinemann's treatment of *midrash* as filling out the details of the text.[229] It is this sense of the overbrimming divine truth in the revealed book that also brings on rabbinic elation on hearing a fresh interpretation of a verse. So R. Simeon b. Yoḥai asked if R. Elazar knew his father's interpretation of S. S. 3:11 and then kissed him on the head, when it was told him, saying, "If I had come only to hear this, it would have been [reward] enough for me."[230]

The aggadic drive to expose new levels of meaning in Scripture probably combines with many inaccessible motivations to produce many an unexpected, even daring, theological assertion. In *Gen. R.* 9.7, R. Samuel gives a utilitarian argument to prove aggadically that even the Evil Urge is good. More radically, the Torah can, for rhetorical purposes, be accused of using language even the foulmouthed would eschew,[231] or of condemning God for allowing an avoidable injustice.[232] Since Is. 49:3 says that God will be glorified through Israel and, as one might well infer, God will not be glorified on His own, this is why Moses is understood to be urged to heap up praises on the people.[233] The anthropomorphic impulse here often cuts God down to human size. God can be depicted as fearful of discussing things with the snake, since it is evil and a master of retorts;[234] the ministering angels can accuse God of rewarding evildoers;[235] and God bewails His need to expel Adam from the Garden of Eden.[236] But it is as one who desolately weeps and wails over the destruction of the Temple, His abode, that God is most famously humanized.[237] However, the rabbinic ambivalence about such extravagant anthropomorphizing of God breaks into the open in a formula (with variant wordings) occasionally used to justify the expositor's daring, most fully: ʾilmale mikra katuv, ʾi efshar le-omro, "had Scripture not written [the precipitating word or phrase], it would not have been permissible [in rabbinic discourse] to say this...." Moshe Halbertal has made a strong case that this formula is primarily intended as a positive endorsement of the aggadist's daring in humanizing God and far less as an expression of anxiety at the potential impudence.[238]

We see another form of aggadic theological daring: the jarring juxtaposition of opinion apparently created by the transmitters or redactors of our *midrash* texts. As we find them today, the religious positions presented merely differ from one another, or present contrary interpretations, as in the several opinions we get about suffering in *Gen. R.* 92.1 (T 1136). But not infrequently the views are flatly discordant, as are the three opinions in *Lev. R.* 36.6 (M 851) on the length of time that the merit of the patriarchs had its beneficial effects, all of which are contradicted by the views expressed in the previous paragraph, *Lev. R.* 36.5 (M 849). These oppositions are not limited to events of this world but can extend into the next, as in the controversy between R. Meir and R. Yose on whether *mamzerim*, "bastards" (halakhically defined), will overcome their illegitimacy and become full Jews then.[239] The chosenness of Israel, obviously a topic dear to the rabbis, engenders a considerable split between those who say Israel was chosen for a reason and those who argue for its being an eternal condition.[240]

Aspects of the "Logical" Moves in *Midrashim*

The aggadists appear to modern readers to take such license with Scripture that one may easily forget that they are also consummate masters of the details of the biblical text. When it suits their purposes they can insist on reading the verse before them with scrupulous care. Though they often tear out of its context the detail that appeals to them, they also can offer interpretations based not only on the entirety of a given verse but on what precedes or follows it.[241] Occasionally, when a verse is built on the parallelism of its clauses, their interpretations may follow a similar balancing strategy.[242] And a teacher may follow the sweep of a story to make his point.[243]

This care extends to individual words. Should David call himself a poor man in Ps. 102:18, R. Abin, rhetorically baffled, asks, "Who can fathom David's character? Sometimes he calls himself 'a poor man' sometimes 'a king,' " which tension he resolves with his teaching.[244] When Habakkuk uses the sun and the moon to create a poetic image, a sage then uses them realistically in his message.[245] Jephthah is chided for using such sweeping language in his vow that instead of it being revocable, he had to sacrifice his daughter.[246] Where Scripture appears to be prolix, the reason must be that it means by this to teach us a special lesson.[247]

Not infrequently they meticulously examine the text, concentrating on a single aspect of it. They have formulas for this variety of exegesis, such as: *en ketiv . . . ela*, "[another possible word] was not written [here] . . . but [so the word used must yield a special lesson]"; or, *en ketiv kan*, "it is not written here"; or, more simply, *lo neemar*, "[another term] is not said [hence we learn . . .]." They can derive a lesson from the fact that a verb is in the imperfect tense or is a present participle when we might have expected the perfect tense.[248] A singular verb can suggest Israel's unity,[249] or it may daringly be used to say that God as well as Israel went into Exile.[250] Plurals also may be carefully noted to suggest unexpected teachings.[251] The use of a final letter *heh* to indicate direction may suggest that Sheol has various depths,[252] and the second-person suffix "Your God, O Israel" indicates that the strangers who joined Israel in the Exodus (Ex. 12:38) were responsible for making the Golden Calf.[253] So, too, a somewhat unusual prefix may be construed as indicating that a harp played by itself,[254] and, in a list, should a letter shift in a place-name occur twice, it will attract a comment.[255]

The belief that Scripture encodes an infinite truth strongly motivated the midrashists to use ingenious methods to elucidate them. No device encountered in these books is foreign to the Talmud, but the sheer number and creativity of them here is most impressive. Perhaps the simplest means of finding additional meaning is to give a text's consonants a new set of vowels, as when the *eikhah*, "how," of Lam. 1:1 is vocalized as *ayekah*, "where are you?" which occurs in Gen. 3:9, making possible a new theodicy related to the destruction of the First Temple.[256] Words may be split in two, even reversing their simple meaning, as when *leadam*, "to Adam," is revocalized to produce *lo adam*, "not" Adam, and thus an explanation of why Adam was not given the Torah.[257] In the operation known as *sirus*, "disarrangement," the words of the text may be put into another order even if this reverses the meaning, perhaps one reason why this method is called by a term also used for castration.[258] When the *notarikon* mode is employed, the word can be broken into bits or read as an acronym, whereas in *gematria* the Hebrew letters are read in terms of their numerical equivalents.[259]

Even leaving the words as they are, aggadic creativity is not to be impeded. Perhaps the least surprising of their acts is to read aggadic messages out of texts that are clearly halakhic.[260] More license is taken when a feminine text is said to describe a male[261] or when a plural word is taken to mean an individual.[262] We can be casually informed that, as against a given interpretation of Gen. 15:12, "there are those who reverse it."[263] While Gen. 1:26 may use the *kal* verbal form to say "God knows," the aggadist turns this into a *hiphil* so he can say "God made known. . . ."[264] Aggadic license reaches impressive heights when R. Yudan, bolstering an *aggadah* that says God will redeem Israel by means of seventy-two letters, argues that Dt. 4:34 has just this number. However, should you then count them and discover seventy-five, he suggests you simply drop out the second occurrence of the word "nation" to make the count correct.[265] One is hardly surprised, then, to discover that the rabbis frequently interpret the Bible's Hebrew words as if they were Greek,[266] a complacency that suffers in the discovery that the Hebrew can also be interpreted as if it were Egyptian.[267]

The interpretations are so varied that the occasional generalization about method arouses hope that one might discover the rules that order the aggadic universe in the *midrashim*. Occasionally familiar halakhic hermeneutic terms surface, like *kal veḥomer*,[268] a fortiori, or perhaps only its conclusion, *al aḥat kamah vekamah*,[269] "how much the more so then. . . ." *gezerah shavah*, "identical word or phrase usage," may be mentioned when two distant verses are to be linked,[270] and occasionally *binyan av*, "a general rule in such cases," is used where a comprehensive statement about interpretation has been suggested.[271] We also come across the mention and occasional use of the hermeneutic associated with Naḥum of Gimzo.[272] Less-formalized exegetic patterns also are adduced: the mention of a number can educe the *keneged*, "equivalence," strategy that applies the number to something in Jewish religious life;[273] we hear of interpretation via *mashal*, "proverb" or "parable," and *melitzah*, "figures of speech";[274] the somewhat obscure references to "establishing" a verse, *l'kayem mah sheneemar*, which can refer, at the least, to explaining a verse, as in the interchanges between R. Judah and R. Nehemiah in PRK 20.7 (M 317), or to fulfilling it, in a prophetic sense, as in *S. S. R.* 7.9.1; and there is an occasional preference for finding textual substantiation from the text at hand rather than from another text brought in to explain it.[275]

Upon closer scrutiny, however, all these generalizations, while recognized patterns utilized in the community, turn out to be more the personal choice of a given sage seeking a rhetorical device to heighten emphasis than anything as formal as our rules of grammar or proper syntax. Thus, though in *Gen. R.* 48.15 R. Simeon gives us the rule for interpreting dotted letters, other teachers prefer another procedure in expounding *Gen. R.* 51.8. The several authorities for the rule that the phrase "And it came to pass in the days of . . ." always portends trouble are corroborated by R. Samuel bar Naḥman but are later disputed by two other sages with differing views of what these words allegedly always mean.[276] R. Simon's rule that the phrase "And it came to pass after . . ." always means that things then reverted to what they were is disputed by other sages.[277] R. Lazar's insistence that the text "And God . . ." always means God and His heavenly tribunal seems unreasonable on the face of it,[278] and R. Abba's assertion that God never reversed a good statement is immediately negated by citing a contrary case.[279] Should there be any doubts that the usage *en . . . ela*, "[this] only means," is a rhetorical flourish rather than a regulative phrase, we discover that it is used by various sages in immediate sequence to refer "only" to Abraham, "only" to Isaac, and "only" to Jacob.[280]

As in the Talmud, the plethora of opinion in the homiletic *midrashim* tends to generate diverse points of view about how odors travel,[281] or whether there are seven or eight synonyms for the term "south,"[282] or the meaning of a rabbinic phrase like the saying that a certain interpretive principle "arose in the Exile."[283] Matters of faith can also evoke different positions, as did the issue of just when the *yetzer*, the inclination to practice idolatry, had been uprooted among Jews (the belief that it had not being challenged here).[284] The usual warrant for another opinion is a verse that is read as teaching something contrary,[285] and it may be adduced not for its content but because of a verbal similarity (though the term *gezerah shavah* is rarely used).[286] Even without biblical support, the sages may cite *masoret aggadah*, "an aggadic tradition," to validate their dissent.[287]

At their simplest, such juxtapositions of opinion involve two sages,[288] and the simple contrast of opinions ends this kind of exchange.[289] Yet clashes of opinion in which several divergent positions are enunciated are not uncommon.[290] However, the two-person clash can lead on to a fuller dialectic in which a position is analyzed to see how it might give a response to an inquiry that the other view's verse would find easy to answer.[291] Occasionally the *midrash* text may then take the dialectic an argumentative step further.[292] Such dialectic becomes more formal (and thus communally validated) when generally known terms are used to characterize specific stages in the discussion,[293] or to generalize about the positions of the participants.[294] Thus, direct confrontations between two opinions may be signaled by the term *hetivun* or *etivun*, "they objected," and this or its equivalent may bring on the retort *lo tavra*, "this is not a refutation," followed by a proof.[295]

Other than citing a different verse, a variety of strategies may be employed to reject a sage's argument. Though their own teachings rest on what moderns see as an imaginative view of reality, they may, to our surprise, occasionally reject a literalistic interpretation of a verse as unrealistic,[296] or as having no corroborating biblical warrant.[297] In one notable instance of empirical concern, an interpretation is negated because it depended on the word *semikhah*, spelled with the letter *sin*, and such a word designating a household implement is not to be found in the Bible even if spelled with the letter *samekh*.[298] They also may reject interpretations that fly in the face of chronology.[299] Though theological audacity is accepted and widely used in aggadic matters, rabbis will sometimes reject teachings they consider reverentially unacceptable,[300] and when all else fails, a point of view can be dismissed simply because it is utterly repugnant.[301]

This aggadic tolerance (promotion?) of divergent opinion gives rise to a steady but not dominant desire to bring greater coherence to the understanding of Scripture or Jewish faith, and this then becomes another aspect of this discourse's "thickness." At its most basic, as we have seen above, someone objects to a sage's teaching and then overcomes the difficulty by an interpretation of his own.[302] This urge moves a step further when another teacher shows there is a common thread in quite diverse views.[303] Then, too, one may ascribe a difference based on a given verse as merely construing its clauses differently,[304] or argue that two different-sounding terms have the same meaning,[305] or that two different names for one person are really identical, since they have the same numerical equivalent.[306] R. Judah b. R. Simon's view that those who have not gone to wild animal shows in this world will get to see Leviathan and Behemoth fight to the death in the next world draws the objection that this would render the meat for the messianic banquet unkosher. The unabashed response to this is that God will issue a special law to cover this case, as a biblical verse is interpreted to prove.[307]

As in the Bavli, the full-scale integration of different views is most often effected by recourse to the dimension of time. R. Ḥaninah and R. Levi differ as to why Reuben, Simeon, and Levi merited having their lineage mentioned in the book of Exodus, the one saying because they rebuked their father and the other saying because they were related to Moses and Aaron. The clash between these views is mitigated by saying that the former enabled them to accept the rebuke of their father, giving them the merit for the latter.[308] Was Nebuchadnezzar lowered from the wall alive (so R. Eliezer b. R. Nathan) or dead (so R. Simeon)? R. Joshua b. Levi settled the issue by saying he was alive when they started but, being delicate, dead when he got to the bottom.[309] Were the chambers referred to in the Song of Songs the side chambers or the upper ones? Surely, *lo pelige,* "they didn't differ," for it was the former in the rainy season and the latter when sun was expected.[310] Destiny rather than fact can be invoked to impose some unity on contrary views,[311] and, acknowledging the Torah's unique literary status, one may, to eliminate a clash of views, invoke the principle *en mukdam omeuḥar batorah,* "the Torah does not rigidly adhere to chronology."[312]

These attempts to reconcile divergent opinions are not always piously accepted. They, too, can be challenged by further opinion in what begins to look like infinite regress.[313]

A Summarizing Observation

This chapter began with a question about the reliability of the findings in the Talmudic sample for aggadic discourse in early rabbinic literature generally. All the data about nonhalakhic discourse in the two Talmuds, the halakhic *midrashim,* the *Fathers,* and the *Fathers According to R. Nathan,* as well as the early exegetical and homiletic *midrashim,* allow at least the preliminary judgment that, though nonhalakhic discourse may take somewhat different forms in given literatures, it remains, as previously indicated, astonishingly diverse in content and open in opinion.

Given that the *aggadah* is the voice in which authoritative teachings about Judaism are to be communicated and that rabbinic Judaism is a religion proudly conscious of its difference from other faiths, how can it have an official discourse that houses a near lack of discrimination in content and, in its form, so paltry an interest in noncontradiction? This matter rises to self-consciousness and response in *Git.* 6b's account of R. Abiathar and R. Jonathan's different (theoretical) views concerning the blemish that led a certain Ephraimite to suspect his concubine of infidelity (Ju. 19:2). Sometime later when R. Abiathar came across the heavenly messenger Elijah and asked him what God thought of this controversy, Elijah said that God knew both explanations. When R. Abiathar then protested, "Surely, God cannot be uncertain!" (as aggadic discourse regularly seems to imply!), Elijah responded, "Both are the words of the living God." He then reconciles the two views by conferring rabbinic authority upon the Ephraimite, saying he found the one flaw and excused it, and the other he did not. But the text does not end by giving this reconciliation of the explicit contradiction the final word and, thus, an implied acceptance. Rather, two further reconciliations are given, each based on the common device of assigning them to different situations. It is a delightfully Derridean moment. The law of noncontradiction is as good as rejected and then quickly affirmed and reaffirmed—but the rejection remains in the transmitted tradition and testifies to the logical anarchy that threateningly asserts itself in the very nature of this discourse; and by adding two additional reconciliations to the first one, the authority of all three is impugned.

We remain, then, with our two questions, the one concerning the limits of aggadic utterance, the other concerning the nature of nonhalakhic discourse as a whole, and it is to these that we must now directly turn.

Part Three

The Limits and Nature of *Aggadah*

Chapter 6

◈ Is Aggadic Discourse Self-Limiting? ◈

Most of this work has treated aggadic discourse in isolation from *halakhah*, but that ignores its Talmudic intertwining with legal discussion. Surely we could learn much about *aggadah* by comparing and contrasting it with its congenital linguistic twin. That suggestion, however, would demand a comprehensive knowledge of two realms of expression, each of which seems inexhaustible. No wonder, then, that Hayyim Nahman Bialik's evocative essay "Halakhah and Aggadah,"[1] has long been considered a classic of insight and imagination. Bialik's concern was literary: the reclamation by modern (secular) Jews of a major form of Hebraic diction, the *halakhah*, whose legal prose and casuistry seemed to many contemporary aesthetes utterly inferior to the *aggadah* with its free-flowing content and abounding self-expression. Bialik, the lover of every manifestation of the national spirit, would have none of this. "*Halakhah*," he contended, "is the crystallization, the ultimate and necessary outcome of *aggadah*. Aggadah is the molten core of the *halakhah*."[2] He saw them as "two definite forms, two different styles, which complete each other in life and in literature."[3] Our far less ambitious but more empirical study bears out the master's understanding in the literary particulars of their Talmudic usage.

The close affinity of these two realms should come as no surprise, since the traditional definition of *aggadah* is that which is not *halakhah*. Logically, then, the two are part of a greater whole, the diction of Oral Torah, though such a delineation of the parts and the whole is never made explicit in the Talmud or early *midrash*. H. Z. Hirschberg and B. Mirmelstein identified three bases for the strong connection between the two: a common source, the Bible; a common group of teachers, the rabbis; and a common theme, the life of the Jewish people.[4] They and other scholars, like Saul Lieberman, Abraham Arazi, and Eliezer Segal, illustrated some ways in which the two modes of discourse interacted in rabbinic literature.[5]

A charming tale about R. Isaac the Smith epitomizes much of this development. His students R. Ammi and R. Assi kept pestering him, the one demanding aggadic instruction, the other halakhic, neither allowing the other to proceed. R. Isaac said they reminded him of the man who had a younger and an older wife. The younger kept plucking out his gray hairs, the older the black, until he was almost bald. So R. Isaac quieted them by discussing a verse with both aggadic and halakhic significance (a not uncommon range of meaning).[6] And while his treatment of the verse is different in each case, the hermeneutic could easily have been reversed and the legal or nonlegal content could have remained the same.

In general, the rhetorical styles of the two types of discourse are quite similar; on any given page of the Talmud one cannot easily separate one sort of material from the other simply on stylistic grounds. Both use hermeneutic devices like anecdotes and parables, invent difficulties so that they may resolve them, care about the teachers whose dicta they transmit, and often try to maintain some consistency in their stated views.[7] In the Bavli, as Louis Jacobs has carefully noted, aggadic as well as halakhic topics are presented in the complex literary dialectical form called the *sugya*.[8] It comes as no surprise, then, that interpreting the biblical verse Dt. 17:8 in relation to the issue of a sage who does not accept the formal decisions of his peers, the Bavli understands a key term to refer to one with halakhic mastery, while the Yerushalmi says it refers to one competent (among other areas) in *aggadah*.[9] A far more uncommon illustration of the affinity of the two modes of teaching is provided in a discussion of the physiology of conception (relative to Levirate marriage). Sufficient weight is attached to aggadic teaching that, in Goliath's case, many fathers are said to have impregnated his mother, even though this contradicts a premise of the halakhic discussion.[10] Thus, there has long been agreement among modern scholars that, as Moritz Steinschneider had already put it in 1857, "the Halacha and Haggada were separated only by degrees."[11]

Clarifying something of the overlap between the two modes of speaking should help us determine what most significantly characterizes *aggadah*. To that end, it will be helpful to examine the several ways in which halakhic discourse displays a number of the features we have seen to be the hallmarks of *aggadah*.

Significant Traits of the *Aggadah* Found in *Halakhah*

The aggadists are notorious for the liberties they often take with the biblical text they are expounding. Something of this textual license is found in halakhic exegesis. R. Ishmael, for example, who believed the Torah should be understood in a simple, commonsense way, nonetheless read three of its commandments as *mashal*, as speaking figuratively.[12] Rava, after objecting to Abaye's transposing words to get a foundation for his view of the law of inheritance, then himself does extraordinary violence to Nu. 27:11, detaching a suffix from one word and a prefix from another to create a new word on which he then bases his own ruling.[13] A sage can suggest that one of two conflicting biblical passages dating the breach of Jerusalem's wall (and thus affecting the date of a fast day) is the result of an erroneous biblical calculation.[14] Despite the care they took about the wording of legal texts, the rabbis occasionally felt they had the freedom to alter them to provide a basis for their understanding of the law. They boldly declare, *ḥasorei miḥasera*, "[the text] clearly lacks [something] ... ," and they will then supply the missing material.[15] A more radical treatment of a tradition is signaled by forms of the verb *epukh*, "reverse it," or the fuller *[ipkha] itemar*, "[the reverse] was said," or *itemar hakhi itemar*, "[if this was] said this is what was [in fact] said," terms demanding the reversal of the views of the cited authorities or of certain legal provisions in the text.[16] A slightly softer version of the latter is *ipekha mistabra*, "reverse it to the more logical [version]."[17] Of a ruling by a colleague they will imperiously declare *beduta*, "that's fiction," thus operatively indicating the rejection of that view.[18]

The Mishnah's halakhic texts, unlike legal writing in the form of law codes, generally reflect a pluralism we commonly associate with the *aggadah*. Thus, chapter 1 of the Mishnah tractate Eduyot collects a number of issues disputed by Hillelites and Shammaiites as well as others. In Talmudic usage, such legal diversity may mimic aggadic discourse by utilizing the standard aggadic signal for the elaboration of opinion, *davar aḥer*, "another interpretation."[19] Individual authorities might adduce multiple reasons why they affirmed their halakhic stance against a challenge, as R. Isaac b. R. Joseph did, suggesting in one dictum three possible answers he could give, each introduced with the established formula *i baʿet ema*, "if you require it, I could say."[20] Aggadically and hyperbolically, we hear of sages whose reasoning was so ingenious they could supply plausible arguments that the ritually clean was unclean and vice versa. Rav is reported to have ruled that a qualification for becoming a member of the Sanhedrin was the logical agility to prove from the Torah that creeping things are ritually pure.[21] R. Meir is the most famous of these "sophists," but while his student Symmachus was satisfied to produce forty-eight reasons for each rule of ritual cleanness and uncleanness, we also hear of an acute student at Yavneh who had a hundred and fifty reasons why an unclean, dead creeping thing should be ruled ritually clean.[22]

The dialectic of halakhic opinion is so central a feature of Jewish law that we are accustomed to the continual pairing of certain halakhic antagonists, like Hillel and Shammai, R. Nehemiah and R. Yehudah, Rav and Samuel, and Rava and Abaye. This is not to belittle the more common pattern in which various masters, not infrequently including the views of "the rabbis," occur. Shaye J. D. Cohen sees this halakhic openness as

> the major contribution of Yavneh to Jewish history: the creation of a society which tolerates disputes without producing sects. For the first time Jews "agreed to disagree." The major literary monument created by the Yavneans and their successors testifies to this innovation. No previous Jewish work looks like the Mishnah because no previous Jewish work, neither biblical nor post-biblical, neither Hebrew nor Greek, neither Palestinian nor diasporan, attributes legal and exegetical opinions to named individuals who, in spite of their differences, belong to the same fraternity. The dominant ethic here is not exclusivity but elasticity.[23]

The exegetic freedom we encounter so frequently in the *aggadah* has its counterpart in the *halakhah* by virtue of the tasks that it must carry out. Stemberger specifies,

> Halakhic exegesis not only has to supply details which are missing in the Bible but which provide instructions for the application of a biblical rule; it must also resolve contradictions..., reconcile the biblical text with current practice..., find biblical support for regulations not yet envisioned in Scripture (a Scripture passage as *asmakhta*, "support," or *zekher*, "remembrance, reference"), etc.[24]

Generally this is a sober pursuit, one that provides the backdrop for R. Yoḥanan's dictum that when a group of judges must render a decision, only those whose biblical basis for the relevant law is different from that of their colleagues are entitled to a vote. Yet there are certain reminiscent liberties that halakhic exegetes may take with the biblical text, as indicated in Steinsaltz's treatment of the term *asmakhta*. He writes, "Lit[erally], (mere) support. Sometimes the Rabbis in the Talmud explicitly state that the Biblical verse cited as the basis for a law is merely an allusion to the law rather than its actual source ... in the Talmud's phrase ... 'the law is Rabbinic, and the verse is a mere *asmakhta.*' "[25] R. Ishmael can even be quoted as saying that in three places the *halakhah* "crushes the Biblical text under its heel," by which he meant that the rabbinic ruling goes far beyond what the Torah states. Lest this be considered an eccentricity on his part, R. Naḥman b. Isaac and R. Papa are later cited on the same page, adding to R. Ishmael's dictum.[26]

Nonetheless, it is just in the area of exegesis that we come across a decisive difference between the two forms of rabbinic discourse despite their many similarities. In aggadic discourse it is clearly meritorious to uncover new meanings in a single biblical text. In halakhic exegesis there is a firm principle that each verse—or smaller interpretable part of a verse—can have only one halakhic implication. The equation is reversible: each halakhic rule has only one basis in Scripture (though sages may differ on just which verse provides its scriptural foundation).[27] Certain terms operate on this basis, e.g., *behedia ketiv beh*, "this [proposed rule based on a text] was explicitly stated elsewhere [in the Torah], so it cannot be used here"; and *tzerikha*, "[this verse] is needed [as the foundation for another law]."[28] The *halakhah* has a restrictive, limiting tendency within it, as we shall shortly see in some detail, but there are two additional similarities between the two discourses that should be added to this brief survey.

Students of *midrash* have been attracted to the *aggadah* because its exegetic and anecdotal material is often highly imaginative and creative. Legal prose is generally thought of as having the drab character we associate with, say, an insurance contract, so much less attention has been given to the flights of imagination that have a secure place in halakhic literature. The theological foundation for this aspect of jurisprudence is found in R. Judah's mythic picture of God each day teaching some new aspect of *halakhah* to His *bet din*, God's own study/judicial tribunal.[29]

This Jewish belief in the inexhaustible fecundity of the *halakhah* and the virtue of participating in it grandly enhances the universal experience that it is of the essence of the law to be clear and definite, hence to split hairs and thus create new law. This concern with specifics encourages some halakhists to raise wildly improbable questions that then engender serious discussion.[30] For example: R. Jeremiah b. Abba—apparently an inveterate legal problem poser—uses the laws of hiring or borrowing an animal (as against owning it outright) to multiply the number of Temple offerings that would then be required. This ingenuity in problem creation matches the imaginative virtuosity of R. Zeira, who had demonstrated how a hirer could end up owing many cows to a borrower of his cow. Both of these suggestions then lead on to larger discussions.[31] R. Zeira raises a similarly creative question about the law concerning someone found murdered in a field, and R. Jeremiah wonders how one determines the ownership of a pigeon, one of whose feet is in and one outside a legal boundary that might establish who owns the bird. The text adds that for posing this conundrum R. Jeremiah was turned out of the Bet Midrash. (Later commentators disagree as to whether his case was considered frivolous or an implied challenge to his colleague's stated opinion.)[32] Elsewhere we hear of a certain Pelemo, who asked if someone who had two heads must put *tefilin* on both of them. He was threatened with being put under a ban, but a man then came who asked about giving priestly due for the two-headed son his wife had just delivered. A serious halakhic discussion then ensued.[33] R. Zeira once inquired whether wheat that fell from heaven might be used for Temple sacrifices. In this case, as in Pelemo's, the issue of whether such a thing is possible is raised, but it is not clear that the likelihood of an odd event is a standard limit for the halakhic imagination, for it is quite clear that the *halakhah* deals with theoretical as well as practical law.[34] On occasion a halakhic ruling by a master seems so to stretch the bounds of the probable that it is termed *guzma*, "hyperbole." While the disbelief is indicated, so is the sage's teaching.[35]

Our final similarity has to do with emotional appeal. We have often heard how the *aggadah* appeals to people and touches their hearts. The *halakhah*, too, could have this effect. "Our rabbis taught . . . before taking leave of one's companion one should not conclude with ordinary talk, or joking, or frivolity, or idle chatter but with some words of *halakhah*," thus following the example of the prophets who concluded their messages "with words of praise and comfort." While this borders on aggadic counsel, the corroborating material that then follows lends some probability to its being intended as practical law.[36]

The *Halakhah*'s Distinctive Trait: Enforceable Decision

E. P. Sanders gives us valuable insight into the issue of similarity and difference between the sister patterns of rabbinic speech when he writes,

> Positively, the collective character of the [rabbinic] literature means that there is, on certain kinds of issues, consensus if not uniformity. This has been widely recognized with regard to *haggadah*, but there is also a type of consensus—in fact, in this case, uniformity—with regard to *halakah*: while Rabbis disputed what the *halakah* on any particular point should be, they believed *without exception that there should be halakah*.[37]

In this statement Sanders takes it for granted that the implication of "there should be *halakah*" will be clear to his readers, but the matter is too important to our investigation not to be unpacked. It means, "Ideally—though not always in fact—we should have an unambiguous statement of God's law for the people of Israel." The short definition of *halakhah* given in the *Entziklopediyah Talmudit* is "The fixed decision [*keviyat hapesak*] in a situation where there is a doubt or a controversy in law, whether of Torahitic law or rabbinic [law]."[38] The article goes on to state that this identification of the term with decision-making became current in the discussions of the Talmudic masters and their legal successors.[39] Menachem Elon identifies the specific legal issue in which this was established. "Approval of pluralism in regards to theory [debate and study], and rejection of pluralism in regard to practice became an established legal principle in the law of the rebellious elder (*San.* 11:2)...."[40] That is, once the Sanhedrin has reached a majority opinion about practice, to teach that one should act differently is a capital crime in Jewish law. The Mishnah specifies, however, that there is no violation if a dissenting elder only teaches his minority view as "theoretical study," *shanah velimed*. Should he, however, teach it as "proper conduct," *hora laasot*, then he is subject to the full penalty.[41]

This pattern of the law moving to decision after debate and then enforcing such decisions as a part of the law is widely found and fits well with basic Jewish belief. Since the Jews have a corporate as well as an individual responsibility to the one God who revealed His law to them, their behavior should not be random or impetuous, but orderly. This ideal provides the background for R. Ḥisda's (retrojective) tradition that when the halakhists of Jeconiah's exile "closed a *halakhah*, it was not reopened."[42]

Something of this drive for the one law of the one God may be seen in the several accounts we have of halakhists changing their minds, often abjectly, as a result of their colleagues' arguments.[43] There is as good as no counterpart to such a concern for coherence in the *aggadah*. Though the contingencies of history and personality regularly prevented the rabbis from stating (or the Jewish people from achieving) the ideal order of God's law, the halakhic process continually strives toward it. This striving to specify what is mandatory is a fundamental characteristic of the *halakhah* and decisively distinguishes it from the *aggadah*.

This legislative-judicial function of the *halakhah* is attested by a number of halakhic terminological usages that have as good as no equivalent in the *aggadah*. Chief of these are the terms *halakha k* . . . and its Aramaic equivalent, *vehilkheta k* . . . , which, following a Talmudic discussion of alternatives, gives the decision: "and the law follows so-and-so . . ."[44] We never come across what would be its aggadic equivalent, *vehaggadah k* . . . , the *aggadah* follows so-and-so. Aggadic differences do not move toward a decision but seem rather to glory in the multiplicity and diversity of aggadic opinion (but see below). Halakhists want to know what the practical, actionable outcome of a discussion was and utilize terms like *mai havei alah*, "what came of it"? or the more common, *lemai nafka minah*, "what was the practical result"?[45]

Halakhic discussion often calls attention to the division of opinion by utilizing terms from the roots *ḥ-l-k* or *p-l-g*, "divide/disagree."[46] Similarly special verbs accentuate the decisive character of halakhic discourse: *kava*, "to fix"; *pasak*, "to give a ruling"; and, rather figuratively, *ḥatakh*, "to cut."[47] Such verbs are not used of aggadic activity. Specific wording being so critical for legal determinations, the halakhists often adduce other texts on the same matter or related to it to seek to determine an authoritative verbal formulation. So, too, they will often search for the author of an anonymous statement by asking *aliba deman?* or *man hu?* or *keman?* "according to whom"? Positively this leads to a typically hyperbolic (needless to say, aggadic) assertion, "One who repeats a statement and gives the name of the one who said it brings redemption to the world."[48] Though there is some interest in the consistency of views of a sage's aggadic views, the specific wording of his statement is not nearly as critical to aggadic reasoning as it is to halakhic debate.[49]

The Talmud also provides numerous rules to help one determine what, in fact, the *halakhah* is. But though these would seem to settle most matters, the later literature indicates how fluid decision-making remained over the centuries.[50] Furthermore, the Talmud describes an elaborate system of courts having existed in the period before the destruction of the Temple. These were, in ascending level of authority, courts of three, twenty-three, and seventy-one, the Sanhedrin, and the system not only rendered decisions but had significant sanctions available to enforce their decisions. After the destruction of the Temple there were certain local courts, but much of the power to decide and to enforce was in the hands of the individual sage.[51] In certain periods individual sages might impose substantial sanctions against those who resisted their rulings, as R. Naḥman did when he seized the home of a man who had resisted his direction to return certain jewels deposited with him.[52] Among other sanctions that the Talmud indicates were imposed on malefactors were fines, flogging, and the several bans of varying severity, *nezifah, niddui, shamta* and *ḥerem*.[53] We shall return later to this issue of sanctions.

All these terms and institutions, and certainly the sanctions, are unknown to the conduct of aggadic discourse. We may speculate that this has something to do with the rejection of individual standards implied in the strong rabbinic condemnation we find of people who comment that this *halakhah* appeals or makes sense to them.[54] And in a somewhat related tale we hear of Resh Lakish "crying like a crane" because the disciples had rejected his halakhic view for that of R. Yoḥanan, but that outburst did not move them.[55]

Despite the movement to decision that characterizes halakhic discourse, it is not unceasingly decisive but exhibits a certain openness. The chief method of developing the law seems to have first been debated between various authorities as to what constitutes the proper law; then, in Talmudic times, the colleagues met and formally voted on the matter, an apparently infrequent institutional resolution of the ongoing difference of opinion. That may be called the "ideal situation." In reality, certain matters might fall under one or another category of the law, and thus their status remained formally indeterminate, that is, *safek*, "doubtful," or *talui*, "officially undetermined."[56] It remained for the local rabbi to rule on the proper usage in that community. Moreover, there are two levels of authority within halakhic determination. The more compelling is a teaching that is *halakhah lemaaseh*, "law to be acted on," but there is also what may be called "theoretical *halakhah*," the law yielded by study and analysis but not set forth as a dictum to be acted upon. In less-certain instances, a more cautious halakhic attitude manifests itself in the Talmudic text that says *matin*, the sages "incline" in a certain direction, or, when an individual is involved, *nirin*, his teaching "appears to be" reasonable, though not a consensus opinion (and thus it may be followed in practice).[57] We have a charming example of this mix of determination and limited direction in an account of an effort to determine which of two homonyms is used in a certain halakhic ruling. Since the Judeans are reputed to be exact in their language, R. Abba suggests consulting them, with the result that the correct tradition is that the sages differ: some teach the one view while some teach the other.[58] On rare occasions, one sage categorically denies the possibility of another sage ruling as he has. When R. Adda said that R. Hananiah b. Gamaliel had defined the *halakhah* regarding which holy day sins were not judged by the earthly court but left to Heaven, R. Joseph retorted "Did someone go up to Heaven and bring back this information?"[59] Richard Kalmin has pointed to a historical development in this process. He writes, "Specifically, fifth generation Amoraim occasionally express the view that disputes between early Amoraim admit of no final decision, and both positions are valid."[60]

Not infrequently we think a matter has been settled because the Talmud declares that a certain response to a colleague's position is a *tiyuvta*, literally, "an answer," but rhetorically, "a term for a refutation," and often we are right to take it that way.[61] On other occasions, however, this sign that an issue has been determined is false, most notably when someone retorts *tiyuvta vehalakhah*, how can that refutation stand when, in fact, the law follows another sage's ruling?[62] Surely, however, the most famous indication of the openness of the halakhic system is its official determination that certain matters are *teku*, literally, "it stands," that is, the issue is presently unresolvable.[63] A medieval observation by the many-sided scholar Nahmanides summarizes uncommonly well the mix of fixity and openness in the halakhic process in Talmudic times as well as in his own:

> Any student of Talmud knows that where the commentators differ, no view can be absolutely demonstrated to be correct and, generally speaking, no counter-argument is completely unanswerable. For, in this field, there can be no proof to a certainty as in mathematics or astronomy. However, we do our best, and are satisfied if, in the balance of the arguments, we can reject one of the opinions. . . .[64]

In addition to all this substantive legal data, a word must be said about supererogation, the law's own sense that its greater purpose, particularly that of religious law, would be served best by doing more than the law requires. Perhaps the classic case is that of the porters of Rabbi b. R. Huna who negligently broke a barrel of his wine. When he seized their garments in compensation, they appealed to Rav, who, as a matter of law, not only made him return them but pay them their wages for the day, citing Prov. 2:20. That verse's admonition "to walk in the way of good men and follow the paths of the righteous" may be taken as the theme of a number of halakhic provisions that stand on the border between what the law makes enforceable and what is left to moral responsibility and religious sensibility.[65] Obviously, a legal system with a significant sense of supererogation has an inherent motive for openness.

In sum, Ze'ev Falk's suggestion that *halakhah* has a broader reference than mere law is persuasive. He identifies four connotations to the term: duty to God; nonscriptural law; the decision of a legal difference of opinion; and the product of the rabbinic academies rather than of folk custom.[66] Perhaps the net should be cast somewhat wider. Sometimes the term *halakhah* seems to mean only a rabbinic teaching rather than a strictly legal one. Thus, we read in *San.* 107a that David failed God's test with regard to adultery because a "*halakhah* was hidden from him, namely, a man has a small organ which, if he tries to satisfy it, it becomes ravenous but which, if he starves it, it is satisfied." An even broader use of the term is found in Sifre Num. 69 where R. Simeon b. Yohai asserts "It is a well-known *halakhah* that Esau hates Jacob." In some highly limited sense, to be sure, the term *halakhah* connotes rabbinic teaching generally or can be used of the whole aura of rabbinic instruction of which, to be sure, the law is the major and most significant portion.[67]

With this qualification in place, we can nonetheless responsibly assert that halakhic discourse inherently moves to decision in a manner that radically distinguishes it from the tone and interests of aggadic diction.[68]

We can substantiate this judgment from the aggadic side by a brief examination of the ways in which aggadic discourse in the Talmud operates like the *halakhah*.

To begin with, the term *shemaata*, "tradition," which Steinsaltz defines as "[a]n Amoraic Halakhic tradition, as distinct from a Baraita or an Amoraic Aggadic tradition,"[69] occasionally is used in reference to aggadic material, as in *Ber.* 33b and *San.* 69b. The halakhic style of dialectically testing the opinions of differing authorities is sometimes applied in aggadic discussions even in *midrash* books.[70] When, occasionally, the rabbis want to say that an aggadic notion came down to them by tradition, they use the more inclusive term *gemara* or the more explicit phrase *masoret beyadenu meavotenu*, "we have a tradition from our fathers."[71] On rare occasions we get some anecdotal evidence of one view being preferred to another, though it is difficult to tell the practical effect of what happened. Thus, after four exchanges of biblical verses with R. Joshua on whether the final redemption depends on Israel's action or God's alone, we are told that "R. Eliezer remained silent."[72] Rare indeed in aggadic exchanges is the instance in which R. Sheshet acknowledged that his colleague R. Ḥana b. Bizna's contrary reasoning on the issue before them seemed better than his.[73] Far more weighty is the uncommon use of the halachic term *tiyuvta*, "[that is] a refutation," as the conclusion to an aggadic discussion.[74] There are also a very few cases where the term for the ultimate determination of the law by a vote of the sages, *nimnu vegamru*, is applied to aggadic disputes, but we are given no information as to what prompted these unusual acts.[75] Aside from such uncommon references to some sort of aggadic decision-making, we do not find rules or institutions for differences of aggadic opinion as we do with halakhic disputes.[76]

For a religion of revelation, the *halakhah*, God's will for our action, exhibits remarkable openness within its fundamental concern for disciplined behavior. The *aggadah* reverses the balance so radically that it is exasperatingly difficult to determine what might constitute its disciplined core. Consider, for example, the implications of R. Ḥiyya the Elder's response to Rav's question concerning Rabbi's teaching about fit tools for ritual slaughter. He is reported to have said: "Did he tell you this as a *haggadah*, in which case he might then retract [it], or did he tell it to you as an *ulpan*, a teaching or practice, in which case he would not retract [it]?"[77] Note that R. Ḥiyya cannot tell simply from the wording whether the teaching is meant as *halakhah* or *aggadah*, and, as the texts have come down to us, teachers do not normally label their dicta as being of one mode of instruction or the other. Rav would know that by means of the tacit understanding of rabbinic communication that he gained as part of his socialization in the rabbinic master/disciple subculture. More important, however, is the different sense of authority and discipline attached to an aggadic as against a halakhic teaching. The *aggadah* may be Oral Torah, but its content apparently has little fixed normative value.

It is, however, the freedom of the *aggadah* that gives it its notoriety. Thus when R. Tarfon rebukes R. Elazar Hamodai for "piling up" words in declaring the manna came down sixteen cubits high, he responds,

"I'm only expounding (*doresh*) a verse." He then proceeds to justify his astonishing claim by the accepted aggadic "logic."[78] Similarly, we hear of R. Levi spending six months giving negative interpretations of 1 K. 21:25, "There was none who sold himself to do what was evil in the sight of the Lord like Ahab." He dreamed one night that Ahab visited him and complained that R. Levi had forgotten the last half of the verse, "whom Jezebel his wife incited." The sage then spent six months interpreting the same verse in a positive manner.[79]

According to an anecdote Leo Baeck featured in his study of old rabbinic attacks against the *aggadah*, it was utter flexibility such as this that led R. Zeira to condemn the aggadists, particularly those who utilized books of *aggadah*.[80] When defenders of such exegesis challenged R. Zeira to give them a verse and let them demonstrate the value of their craft, he listened to their interpretation of it as first referring to this world and then to the world to come. He then interpreted the verse in reverse fashion, as first referring to the world to come and only then to this world, thus providing a somewhat different, yet acceptable, Jewish teaching. One of his antagonists then showed that their exegesis could yield the same message. R. Zeira retorted, "However you twist and turn the verse, we learn [in any strong sense of that term] nothing."[81] I detect something of that same spirit in R. Sheshet's exasperation with R. Ḥana b. Bizna's interpretation of Zech. 2:3. When R. Sheshet pointed out that the following verse took an opposite position, R. Ḥana countered that the key word applied to the enemies of Israel, not their saviors, leading R. Sheshet to exclaim, "Why did I get involved with Ḥana in an aggadic matter?"[82] This can lead to the situation where we have two accounts of an exegesis in which different interpretations are given to different questioners, but the reasoning in the second version is the exact opposite of that in the former one.[83] Of course, freedom has its virtues, particularly because it might allow for a solution to an old, troubling issue that resisted resolution, as in the joy connected with R. Joshua's demonstration that Job served God not merely out of fear but also out of love.[84]

Nonetheless, the breathtaking scope of aggadic freedom may lead to extraordinarily negative teachings. We are told that a certain Menasseh b. Hezekiah (suspiciously bearing the name of the king of Israel most abominated by the rabbis)

> sat and expounded [*yoshev vedoresh*, the formal term for engaging in exegesis] *behaggadot shel dofi* [literally, "of taint,"[85] *aggadot* that were tainted, or perhaps, that cast a taint on the Torah]. Menasseh said: And did

Moses have nothing better [then] to write than [such verses as], 'And Lotan's sister was Timna,' 'And Timna was Eliphaz's concubine,' and 'During the days of the wheat harvest Reuben went and found mandrakes in the field.' [Such sacrilegious teaching caused] a Heavenly Voice, *Bat Kol*, to issue forth

and denounce him with the words of Ps. 50:20. To this is added a further reproof from Is. 5:18 as well as some eminently respectable interpretations of the allegedly superfluous verses.[86] Aggadic discourse can accommodate such insulting teaching as part of God's Oral Torah to the point of not conveniently forgetting this tradition or censoring it out from all that was deemed worthy to be passed on. To be sure, the cautionary tale becomes a proof that no verse of the Torah is superfluous,[87] but in the process it sets a most undesired role model before future generations.

For a monotheistic religion whose major emphasis is sacred deeds, to harbor an uncontrolled yet authoritative mode of religious discourse seems counterintuitive. Its freedom surely must have some limits, and it is the search for these, as difficult as they may be to discover, to which we now turn.

What Might Delimit Aggadic Freedom?

Ithamar Gruenwald, speaking of *midrash* and not all nonhalakhic discourse, clearly sets out our predicament. "An interpreter can do with the scriptural word (even the Word of God), almost anything he considers fitting and proper ... but the limits of permitted interpretation are not given."[88] David Stern, also focusing on biblical interpretation, agrees but sensitively suggests how we may move beyond this lack of explicit boundaries: "[I]nstitutional controls on interpretation ... surely must have existed. Yet ... it is difficult to say what lay behind the borders of discourse. To be certain, most institutional controls work silently through what Frank Kermode has described as 'the tacit knowledge of the permitted range of sense.' "[89] Stern then points to five aspects of the rabbis' semiconscious sense of what constitutes appropriate speech in their community: each exegetic school has its own style; there are hermeneutic rules; interpretations often reflect nuance rather than outright difference; real problems in the Biblical text attract the comments; and there is "a kind of underlying 'deep structure' " that governs the discourse.[90] All but the fifth, however, deal more with positively shaping midrashic discourse than with setting forth the boundaries it may not cross. "Deep structure" would indeed seem to be an effective guardian against the impermissible, but its silent depths seem to prevent our clarifying how the discourse is contained. Gruenwald takes us a helpful step further in his discussion of what he calls the "midrashic conditions." He specifies them as "the formal principles of exegesis (the *middot*) . . . ; social needs, new ideological and political positions, historical requirements, or any current disposition of the community. Moreover, . . . there is also the need to meet a certain consensus of opinions maintained and jealously guarded by the social group."[91] Several of these factors seem to clarify what might produce innovation rather than delimit radical deviation. Nonetheless, this shift of focus from the internal operations of the aggadic process to the social conditions in which it operated is suggestive. We turn, therefore, to the investigation of the degree to which four factors, internal and external, might work to channel aggadic freedom: sanctions, rules, rebukes, and social pressure.

CAN SPEECH LEAD TO SANCTIONS?

Jewish law gives courts and, by extension, individual masters broad powers over certain kinds of speech, but, as we have seen,[92] this almost always refers to the kind of rabbinic teaching that leads to action contrary to the stipulations of Jewish law. Thus, Menachem Elon entitles his discussion of the sanctions available in Jewish law "Methods of Enforcement of Judicial Decisions."[93] San. 10.1, however, is the notable exception to this rule. It says that all Jews will have a place in the world to come except those who "say [maintain] that resurrection is not [taught] in the Torah, or that the Torah was not from Heaven [i.e., given by God], and the Apikoros. R. Akiba said, 'Plus the one who reads "External Books." . . .' " The text then adds certain other heinous acts and the names of some classical Jewish reprobates—but that is about as much as classic Jewish law is willing to say directly about the boundaries of interpreting the Oral Torah. Shaye J. D. Cohen summarizes the situation well in saying,

> At no point in antiquity did the rabbis develop heresiology and ecclesiology, creeds and dogmas. At no point did they expel anyone from the rabbinic order or from rabbinic synagogues because of doctrinal error or because of membership in some heretical group. . . . A few rabbis—not heretics—. . . were expelled because of their refusal to accept the will of the majority. . . . [Theirs] is not the work of a sect triumphant but of a grand coalition.[94]

The stipulations of San. 10.1 do not give us much guidance for the proper conduct of aggadic teaching. Someone who does not believe in the divine revelation of the Torah, or as an Apikoros is probably vaguely related to the hedonistic nontheism of Hellenistic Epicureanism—a much disputed matter—is hardly likely to be involved in the study and interpretation of the Oral Torah. R. Akiba's individual anathema on reading "External Books" also gives us little direct help with aggadic freedom. Yet all this data—and the banning of books like Judith and Tobit—indicates that the sages believed there were intellectual limits to Judaism as they understood it and, though they generally avoided specifying them, some views that clashed so egregiously with their beliefs that they overcame their customary reticence and condemned them.

We can test this general view by the one substantial test case the *aggadah* provides: the excommunication of R. Elisha ben Abuya.[95] Jeffrey Rubenstein and Alon Goshen-Gottstein have each recently given us a detailed study of the accounts of his fall from rabbinic eminence.[96] While each in his own way is broadly concerned with the literary and hermeneutic issues in the stories about Elisha, our concern here is with the narrow issue of what they indicate about the traditions of the rabbis using sanctions to delimit aggadic freedom. To that end Elisha, whom Goshen-Gottstein calls "the rabbinic archvillain,"[97] would seem to be a promising case. I draw on both their works in what follows, though I am somewhat more indebted to Rubenstein.

At one time Elisha ben Abuya was fully worthy of the title *rav*, for even after his being excommunicated, some teachings are cited in his name, and his student, the renowned R. Meir, is not only depicted as still eager to learn Torah from him, but we are informed about the teachings of that instruction. And while his name is detached from other teachings of his, the tradition preserves an indication that they are Elisha's. He must have done something terrible to bring down upon him not only the condemnation of his colleagues but also that of heaven. Though the rabbis generally take great care to make certain that everyone knows that God's forgiveness is available directly and at all times to those who repent, the Elisha ben Abuya stories relate that a Heavenly Voice declared, "Except for *aḥer*,"—literally, "the Other," "the Alien," the derisive term commonly used to refer to him. Yet it is not clear what the sin was that turned Elisha, the great sage, into the model rabbinic outsider.[98]

Many different sins are ascribed to Elisha, a good indication that there was no single, well-known reason for his being banned, though it is conceivable that it was totally repressed. The various evil acts ascribed to him have no common theme except malfeasance. The Bavli's tale, among its other indictments of him, says that he implied the heretical notion that there may be two powers in Heaven. Nonetheless, he is not then called or treated as a *min*, a sectarian, Gnostic or otherwise. (This also throws doubt on the addendum to the Bavli account that taints him with reading heretical books, against Akiba's opinion in *San.* 10.1 that this excludes one from a portion in the world to come.) He remains a member of the Jewish people, albeit a badly sinning and therefore excommunicated one. Rubenstein notes[99] that this very story includes two linguistic mitigations of his (near) heresy: *shema*, "perhaps," and *has veshalom*, figuratively, "Heaven forfend." Moreover, in a move Alan Segal deems a sign of his reverence, the account first doubly defuses the impact of the sinfulness to follow and only then allows him to be pictured suggesting that God is not one.[100] Yehuda Liebes, by contrast, seeks to make a case that Elisha is sufficiently invested in Gnostic mystical notions that he merited excommunication under Jewish law, but Rubenstein's detailed case against Liebes's argument is well taken.[101]

What sins might Elisha have committed that merited his being put under a ban? The Yerushalmi tale accuses him of murdering promising students of the Torah, the "cutting of the shoots" of *Hag.* 15a. If we take that literally rather than hyperbolically, the civil authorities should have acted against him, and the rabbis would hardly have continued to accord his teachings the respect they gave them. Shabbat desecration is another capital crime in Jewish law, and Elisha is accused of violating it. But since he did so in a time when Jews could no longer inflict this ultimate punishment, it is conceivable that the rabbis then condemned him to excommunication. However, that is not likely, since our evidence also points to a variety of Sabbath prohibitions he violated as well as many other repugnant acts he did. Thus, he is variously accused of dissuading students from continuing their studies, of visiting a prostitute, and of having Greek songs sung in his home. At his worst, he is charged with informing the Roman authorities how to suborn the Jews into breaking Sabbath law. None of these sins would render him liable for as severe a punishment as he received. Rather, this heaping up of disrepute seems to me more likely to have been an after-the-fact justification of the tradition of his pariah status rather than a realistic indication of what brought it about.

Moreover, another motif in the Yerushalmi makes his excommunication not the result of a specific halakhic violation but of a loss of belief brought on by occurrences that clashed with the rabbinic tenet of God's pervasive justice. Even there we have different versions of the precipitating incident. The one ascribes it to witnessing a death brought on despite following the rule to take the young from a bird's nest but to let the mother go (Dt. 22:6), a duty that promises the observant long life. Its companion explanation is seeing a dog carry the bloody tongue of a notable sage, leading Elisha to deny the resurrection of the dead. (Note that this only obliquely violates *San.* 10.1, which bars from the future life those who deny that this latter doctrine is taught in the Torah's five books.) Had Elisha joined an idolatrous or dualist or atheistic group, he might well have been liable to excommunication. But the closest we come to that in this group of explanations ascribes his problem not to will but to intrauterine influence, his pregnant mother having smelled the smoke of idolatrous sacrifices, thereby infecting her fetus with its evil effects.

One further possibility demands our closer consideration. The accounts in both Talmuds begin by citing Eccl. 5:5, "Let not your mouth lead you into sin ... else God may be angered by your talk ..." This hints that there was something about Elisha's teaching that transgressed a limit. This suspicion is reinforced by the version in which a child tells Elisha that his study-verse is "And to the wicked God said, 'Who are you to recite My laws?'" (Ps. 50:16). Was Elisha then guilty of faulty teaching? If he had been teaching the *halakhah* against the established rabbinic position, he would have clearly violated rabbinic law, and all this speculation about what constituted Elisha's sin would have been unnecessary. We may well presume, then, that something in Elisha's aggadic teaching had exceeded the permissible freedom given to scholars in this realm of discourse. Unfortunately, nothing in the surrounding data provides any support for this supposition. His faulty speech is either having told students of Torah to follow other careers or the Roman authorities how to get Jews to violate the Sabbath. It is not much to justify the uncommon punishment of excommunication.[102] The case of Elisha ben Abuyah gives us little basis for suggesting that sanctions effectively served as a limit on aggadic discourse, though the knowledge that there was such punishment in their community may have had some deterrent effect on those who entertained quite uncommon ideas.

Let us then see whether rabbinic rules—the various hermeneutic "measures" that indicate how exegesis should be conducted—effectively delimit the content of aggadic utterance.

MIGHT HERMENEUTIC RULES CONTAIN AGGADIC OPENNESS?

The Mishnah (Ḥag. 2.1) gives us an explicit rule concerning what one should not teach:

> The [laws of] forbidden sexual relations must not be taught if three [or more] students are present. So, too, [one may not teach] "The Work of Creation," if two are present, or "The Chariot" to [even] one student, unless he is a scholar who can make proper inferences. Woe to the person who speculates about four things[,] for he is as good as nonexistent. [These four are] what is above, what is below, what [came] before, and what [will come] afterward. And one who does not properly honor his Maker would be better off not having been born.

This statement, after insisting on intimate groups for halakhic instruction on incest and other such forbidden sexual relations, is even more restrictive—but not utterly proscriptive—when it comes to aggadic instruction on either of the two classic topics of Jewish mysticism, The Work of Creation and (The Work of) The Chariot. It then homiletically decries simpler forms of unworldly speculation and, climactically, disrespect of God. The rhetorical shift toward the end of the passage indicates a movement from legal injunction to aggadic wisdom. No topic is censored out as unworthy of proper study, though some should be taught under special circumstances and others ought to be avoided by sensible people. That seems to be the sum of what the rabbis explicitly said in limitation of what might be taught as part of the Oral Torah. However, since much of the *gemara* on this *mishnah* (Ḥag. 11b–16a) discusses "what is above," i.e., in the Heavens, as well as the creation and even Ezekiel's description of the divine chariot, it is not clear how tightly the Mishnah text should be read.[103]

To be sure, we do occasionally come across individual sages indicating a limit they observe or commend. When R. Simlai came to R. Jonathan and asked to be instructed in *aggadah*, R. Jonathan refused. He said he did so because of a tradition in his family not to teach *aggadah* to Babylonians or southerners, and besides, Simlai was then a minor.[104] Mar b. Ravina told his son not to expound, even derogatorily, any biblical verses dealing with the individuals to whom the anathema of *San.* 10.1 denied a portion in the world to come, except for Balaam, who should be thoroughly denounced.[105] Both cases seem quite individual rather than characteristic of the system as a whole.

Far more suggestive are usages that, by their encompassing language, sound like they are general aggadic rules, two candidates being the interpretive directions *kol makom she* . . . , "everywhere that it [says X it means/implies Y]," and *en . . . ela . . .* , "[X] does not [mean] anything but [Y]." On examination, expressions such as these turn out to be rhetorical devices of emphasis rather than rules for acceptable hermeneutic. Thus, with regard to *kol makom she . . .* , we hear in *Meg.* 10b that R. Levi (others, R. Jonathan) cited, as a tradition of the Men of the Great Assembly, that in every place a text says, "And it came to pass that . . . ," trouble ensues, only to have contradictory verses cited against this view.[106] The status of *en . . . ela . . .* resolves itself more quickly, for we occasionally find it used in an identification, as in *Lev. R.* 36.6 (M 852), only to be followed by other statements specifying that the individual previously referred to by that designation is *en . . . ela . . .* , none other than someone else—in this instance, another of the patriarchs.

The closest thing we seem to have as rules for aggadic discourse are the thirty-two *middot* by means of which R. Eliezer b. R. Yose Hagalili said the Torah is aggadically expounded.[107] Most modern scholars consider Midrash Agur, the document in which R. Eleizer's list comes down to us, an early medieval document and thus beyond the purview of our investigation, but it seemed unwise to exclude it from this discussion.[108] Nearly a century ago, H. L. Strack considered them "rules, *middoth,* which one must know in order to form a correct opinion of the Talmudic exposition of Scripture,"[109] though he added that in aggadic contexts they were applied rather more freely than in halakhic discussions. Strack's view seems untenable if the normal coercive sense of the word "rules" is applied to the *middot.* As Stephen Lieberman notes, "[T]he exegetical 'measures' [*middot*] . . . are but rarely used, and references to them are encountered only on occasion. . . . [Rabbinic literature] was much freer than any study of the rabbinic 'measures' could possibly suggest."[110] Wilhelm Bacher perceptively describes them rather as one of the "generalizations" descriptive of rabbinic exposition.[111] Salo Baron judged David Daube's effort to connect the *middot* with Greek rhetorical practice as having overlooked the considerable differences between them.[112] Saul Lieberman was more judicious in his discussion of the Hellenistic influence on the *middot* but limited his discussion of those that essentially applied to the *aggadah* to the final six rules, calling particular attention to their similarity to Hellenistic guidelines for dream interpretation.[113]

Summarizing our results thus far, the *middot* do not function as rules internal to the *aggadah* that limit the range of its discourse. They apply only to the exegetical portion of *aggadah,* are not regularly applied even there, and tell us about how one might conceivably generate an acceptable interpretation rather than specifying how or what ought not be said.

A final candidate rule, however, suggests itself for our purpose, since its negative form indicates that something is being ruled out: *en mikra yotze miyede peshuto*, "no Biblical text ever loses its plain-sense meaning [despite the interpretation placed upon it]."[114] David Weiss Halivni argues that for the rabbis the *peshat* of a verse is not its plain sense as moderns understand that phrase but rather its contextually determined meaning.[115] Equally significant is Halivni's argument that the rabbis believed that their *midrash* work (generally referred to in this book as *derash*) was the proper—indeed, God-authorized—way of determining what the text meant.[116] Baruch J. Schwartz, however, suggests that this is not so much a rule as "an ad hoc interpretation, or at most... a minority or even individual opinion. If so... these words are not an expression of any ideological preference accorded by rabbinic thought to a type of exegesis."[117] Whatever historians ultimately judge to be the case, taking this as a rule would not help us with our problem of the limits to aggadic utterance. By asserting the permanence of the *peshat* of the text, regardless of what sense the *derash* derives from the language, the rule provides a charter for freely proceeding with interpretation, for regardless of the content of the *midrash*, the *peshat* of the biblical text retains its fundamental authority. Indeed, it is this assertion that distinguishes the midrashic celebration of the polysemous nature of the biblical text from the apparently similar work of the deconstructionists. The rabbinic tradition can be as free as it is with interpretation because it has a theological foundation, the God-determined, never-vitiated meaning of the Bible's words. This privileging of the Bible is precisely the kind of foundationalism that the deconstructionists decry, but then what keeps their nonfoundational deconstructing from self-destructing into relativism and moral nihilism is not clear.

If stated rules do not constrain the *aggadah*, perhaps the rebuke often offered to certain disturbing comments may function to that end.

Does Public Rebuke Police the Discourse?

From time to time in rabbinic texts we come across outbursts indicating the exasperation of a rabbi with a colleague's aggadic comment. To our sensibilities some of these have a moderate tone, though we cannot gauge how great was their impact within the rabbi/disciple subculture. Thus, R. Nahman b. R. Hisda was nudged by his father with his sandal and told (again) to stop bothering people about the implication of Ez. 1:3 that God spoke to a prophet outside the Land of Israel.[118] So, too, the text anonymously rejects an interpretation of the Joseph story by means of a folk adage about foxes by saying, "[How dare you compare Joseph to] a fox!"[119] In the name of R. Eleazar, R. Isaac cryptically, if artfully, denies that Lev. 16:30 yields the meaning ascribed to it: "He [the verse] doesn't lend himself to her [the exposition] and she doesn't lend herself to him."[120] On occasion we hear from a visitor from the Land of Israel to Babylon that various of their interpretations were "laughed at in the West."[121] R. Yohanan can even suggest that Resh Lakish's interpretations delimiting the number of Jews who have a portion in the world to come are displeasing to God.[122]

However, by anyone's standards, some rebukes are scathing. R. Jonathan would have needed a thick skin to recover easily from R. Hiyya's reprimand: "If you learned this text, you didn't review it; and if your reviewed it you didn't go over it a third time; and if you did all that, someone must never have explained it to you!"[123] R. Ishmael was no less disparaging when he said to R. Eliezer, "You tell the text 'Stay silent until I come and interpret you!'"[124] The masters can accuse others of interpretations that do violence to the texts, and they use verbs such as *megabev*, "rake up," *okef*, "override," and *meavet*, "pervert," to express their displeasure.[125] Perhaps the height of ridicule—a term the text itself applies to this event—is reached in R. Berekhiah's report that R. Abba b. Kahana said to R. Levi "You are a liar and falsifier!" for teaching that Abraham was born circumcised and did not have to undergo the pain of the operation.[126]

This disparagement of colleagues' interpretations is sufficiently well established that it results in something of a genre of put-down stories, many of which come to their climax in the derisive term *dayyecha*, literally, "sufficient for you," figuratively, "That's enough from you." The term, apparently as a free-floating generic one, is utilized by R. Levi (with the addition of the phrase *ad ko*, "to this point") in objection to R. Miasha's having drawn an analogy from Abraham to God.[127] It is also applied to R. Meir, once by an anonymous "they" and twice by R. Judah in other contexts.[128] Four of these stories, transmitted to us as a group, make R. Pappus b. Judah the butt of their derision. Considering what we have seen various rabbis do with texts and say about innocent Bible texts, his remarks do not seem exceptional. The disparity between his interpretations of texts and the slurs cast on them is heightened by the fact that his critic in the stories is R. Akiba,[129] himself a notoriously imaginative homilist and one frequently rebuked by his colleagues. Perhaps as much in sadness as in reproof, R. Yoḥanan commented that R. Akiba, in a *midrash* consigning many Jews to perdition, had forsaken his customary love of his people.[130] R. Ishmael was more direct when he told the disciples to tell R. Akiba that he was simply wrong in saying that angels eat bread.[131] Other rabbis were more derisive, like R. Yose the Galilean, who accused R. Akiba of the near heresy of robbing God of His holiness.[132] In those passages and elsewhere, R. Elazar b. Azariah, in terms which mix praise with devastating scorn, says to R. Akiba, "Why are you trying to do *aggadah*? Quit talking [in an area in which you are incompetent] and go back to [something you're expert in, the intricate *halakhah* concerning] ritual impurity and its transmission."[133] R. Judah b. Batira twice threatened R. Akiba with calling down God's punishment on him for revealing by his exegesis matters about which the Torah text is silent.[134] In another instance, though his colleagues found that his exegesis disturbingly transgressed their sense of the appropriate or permitted, they also had to admit that R. Akiba had brought them a measure of comfort they had otherwise not been able to find. In a halakhic context, R. Tarfon upbraids Akiba for an exegesis whose wordplay he considers audacious, saying, "I can't stand it!"[135] So, too, when his colleagues, walking by the destruction on the Temple mount, broke into tears, he began laughing, prompting them to say, "How long will you go on astonishing us?"[136] However, both these instances end with Akiba giving a learned justification for his apparent eccentricity, one that the rabbis then acknowledge to have given them new insight into the Torah. The implication seems irresistible: aggadic freedom may lead us into frightening new areas, but that trauma is worth risking, for it may well teach us new Torah truth.

The ironic result of this small study of rabbinic rebuke is how utterly ineffectual it is. There would not be so much of it if it made rabbis and their disciples leery of indulging their exegetic creativity. Moreover, the content of the provocative material is not hidden from later generations but included as part of the sacred texts, thereby doubling back on the rebukes and nullifying much of their impact. Some aggadic statements may be deeply disturbing to some sages, but they are not so reprehensible as to be excised from the corpus preserved and transmitted as Oral Torah.

There is, however, one form of exasperating exegesis that draws forth a flat rabbinic condemnation. One who is *megaleh panim batorah*, literally, "[one] who reveals faces [aspects of meaning] of the Torah," is flatly denied a share in the life of the world to come, the reward customarily awaiting all Jews. This flies in the face of the radical rabbinic commitment to the exposition of Scripture, an activity normally highly encouraged, since God's authorship gave the Torah many such "faces." But when exegesis goes so far as to become "revealing faces" (particular "faces"?) it becomes despicable. Thus, Rabbi denies such a miscreant the hope that the Day of Atonement rites will effect his return to God's good graces, even without his having repented.[137] The Tosefta, in its additions to an apparently traditional list of those barred from the life to come, includes this egregious interpreter, as does a separate dictum of R. Eleazar Hamodai (with a differing list of disqualifying iniquities).[138] Despite the seriousness of the issue and considerable discussion of the term, the sages cannot agree on just what acts it prohibits. *Sifre Nu.* 112.3 and one opinion in the *San.* 99b discussion connect it with the notorious Menasseh b. Hezekiah and his teaching of *aggadot shel dofi*, which disparaged the Torah (as discussed above). The Tosefta, R. Eleazar Hamodai, Rabbi, and most of the voices in the *San.* 99b analysis do not connect it with verbal exposition but with acts transgressing the emerging rabbinic *halakhah*. However, even the group with the restrictive understanding splinters over what sins come under this rubric. For our purposes, the general view we may infer from this discussion is the common one that though there are varieties of halakhic exegesis that are prohibited and punishable, the same is not true of aggadic operations. That split standard seems to be responsible for the unique qualification in R. Eleazar Hamodai's dictum that limits it to those who are *megaleh panim batorah shelo kehalakhah*—that is, those who reveal faces of the Torah that "are not in accord with the *halakhah*." No other sage mentions this condition, though it is used once in the *San.* 99b discussion of the possible meanings of the term.[139]

Thus, once again, we have not been able to discover internally stated limits to aggadic freedom. Instead, the interpretations of *megaleh panim batorah* regarding interpretation of the Bible reinforce the conclusion that the rabbinic language system divides authority between the realm of action, which it empowers with definitions and sanctions that are controlling, while endowing the concomitant realm of exposition a liberty constrained only by the acts it brings people to do. So much seems clear already regarding biblical interpretation, whether halakhic or aggadic, but it does not seem unreasonable to me to extend this generalization to early rabbinic linguistic/"logical" activity as a whole.

The Unspoken Social Sense of the Permissible

There being as good as no evidence for internal controls of aggadic utterance (that is, for a "logic" that sets bounds for intelligible discourse), let us consider how factors external to the discourse—that is, how the social group uses it—might serve to police its proper bounds. Primarily with the *midrash* books in mind, Bruns proposes that we think of the rabbinic form-of-life as authorizing and, in its own way, constraining this freewheeling language-game, while Gruenwald more functionally points to the reasonable inference that the sages realized that they had to meet "the consensus of opinions maintained and zealously guarded by the social group."[140] Much that the rabbis say about themselves and their disciples indicates that they were a self-consciously distinctive, elitist group. Anyone who wished to be in good standing among them had to conform to their special modes of eating, washing, dressing, and carrying on their religio-intellectual life. However, neither Bruns nor Gruenwald moves from the level of general observation and indicates some of the specific ways in which their uncommon pattern of behavioral-orderliness-with-astonishing-intellectual-freedom was assured. Our records tell us much about the rabbinic idealization and memories of what may have once been. But as the research of David Goodblatt (for Sasanian Babylonia) and Catherine Hezser (for Roman Palestine) have demonstrated,[141] the sages' traditions do not give us much realistic insight into how a community, much concerned to defend its strong sense of identity, lived with an authorized discourse that gloried in extraordinary freedom of religious thought.

We may, however, get some insight into the tacit restrictive influence the *rav*, "the master," "sage," exercised on his disciples, his junior colleagues, and perhaps even on his scholarly equals, by considering what the rabbis tell us about the master's status. R. Eleazar b. Shamua's dictum epitomizes the situation well: "Let the honor of your student be as dear to you as your own; the honor of your colleague as your reverence [*mora*] for your *rav*; and let your reverence for your *rav* be like your reverence for Heaven [i.e., God]."[142] (*Mora* is a term derived from the biblical root *y-r-'*, which describes the proper human relationship to God—that fear-awe-reverence which is the experiential grounding of biblical Judaism, though its texts also centrally commend and require the love of God.) In the rabbinic subculture as in many others, the religious leader has a special godlike status, and that intimacy with God endows him with special powers. With that general judgment before us as the context of what may yet be said in this regard, some further modest observations in this regard are pertinent.

Jacob Neusner has convincingly argued that the rabbis need to be considered not only as intellectual leaders and life-guides but as holy men, the magi of their community, whose leadership was essentially carried out through their charisma.[143] Self-serving though the evidence may be, the rabbis did not hesitate to emphasize the proper respect due them and to make it a significant obligation under Jewish law.[144] The *aggadah* reinforces the drive to please the *rav* by its several cautionary tales about what happens to those who cross their master. Often, the sage or sages "set their eyes" on the malefactor, and he is turned into a heap of bones. Perhaps this phrase became an idiom for this kind of punishment, for it is used even of R. Sheshet, who was blind, as the anecdote about him and a provocative Sadducee pointedly reminds us.[145] But there is at least one tale where an obnoxious inquirer of Rabbi then simply takes a drink, and his stomach bursts.[146] Most of these stories seem to be about aggadic matters,[147] but others appear to involve matters of *halakhah*.[148] Even if the masters did not frequently go about using their special powers to rebuke those who exceeded the proper limits of teaching, the fact that the *rav* had such power must surely have had a chilling effect on the temptation to aggadic excess.

Yet this social approach to the problem of aggadic limits does not take us very far. Even in the face of group disdain, as we have seen above, some people will say something that seems outrageous and the rabbis will consider it significant enough Torah that they record it in their sacred texts. We have an inkling of this in a discussion between R. Eleazar and R. Yoḥanan. The former interprets a verse to restrict the number of Jews who gain the world to come and, despite R. Yoḥanan's statement of displeasure, maintains his view. Seeing that R. Yoḥanan remains troubled by his teaching, he finds another verse that implies R. Yoḥanan's position. Note that despite a double indication of distaste, R. Eleazar does not abandon his disturbing view, and R. Yoḥanan does not threaten him with banning or blast him with his special rabbinic powers. All that R. Eleazar was willing to do was to suggest that there is a different teaching in another text.[149]

Bruns, who takes a philosophical approach to understanding the non-Hellenic structuring of the *midrash* process and its resulting collections, utilizes the Wittgensteinian notion of diverse universes of discourse arising from different social "forms-of-life."[150]

> There is... no conflict of authority in midrash because in midrash authority is social rather than methodological... the whole dialogue... — rabbinic practice—is authoritative, and what counts is conformity with this practice rather than correspondence to some external rule or theory.[151]... [One understands an individual *midrash* by remembering that] Context... is social rather than logical... as in a conversation where no statement is likely to make much sense when taken in isolation from the whole, even though the whole itself is not an internally coherent system superior to its parts but a chaotic system in perpetual transition back-and-forth between order and turbulence. In such a system... the conversation itself is the true author of all that is said in it.[152]

Bruns properly calls our attention to the manner in which a socially constituted discourse powerfully affects what is said in it. Wittgenstein may be read as overstating the logical features of such group-authorized discourse when he termed them "language-games," thereby intimating their rule-structured nature. But we need to take this term as a useful figure for the widespread phenomena of different jargons having their own appropriate "logic" and of the inevitable arguments about what the rules of the game really mean. The less-technical and formal a linguistic system, the more tacit and even intuitive its deep standards are, and one must become socialized to them to participate in the system. These "rules" not only define what is comprehensible but thereby also set limits for what is, in this "language," non-sense. *Midrash* may, of course, be either put to halakhic or aggadic purposes, and the rabbis clearly believe there are limits to the former activity but are as good as uncommunicative about those that apply to the latter. These shaping and delimiting notions have for centuries been communicated to even immature young minds subliminally. Nonetheless, this has made *midrash* understandable and even pleasurable to many of them rather than a "chaotic" discourse. It is these largely unstated structures of aggadic cogency that disappear in Bruns's momentary hyperbole, and it is just they that must yet concern us.

Rethinking What Limits *Aggadah*

What emerges from this investigation is the futility of seeking stated or easily inferred limits for the *aggadah* from the *aggadah* as if it were an independent domain of discourse. When, however, we recall that *aggadah* is classically defined in terms of *halakhah*—that in rabbinic literature which is not *halakhah*—it seems most appropriate to conceptualize *aggadah* as one sector of a two-domain religious language-game.[153] In rabbinic Judaism it is the *halakhah*, the laws governing living and the process of legal determination, that Jews are expected to obey. All other rabbinic teaching—the *aggadah*—is offered without stated sanctions for unacceptable imaginative form or institutional limits to too-daring content (though one might conceivably go beyond the limits of the rabbis' exceptional religious openness). Despite this odd constitution, the *aggadah* is fully a partner in the Oral Torah, and its teaching in diverse ways influences and reinforces the *halakhah*. Nonetheless, two levels of authority coexist in rabbinic discourse, and it is the *halakhah*, the realm of mandated behavior, that may therefore be said to provide the critical framework that aggadic instruction transgresses at its peril. While the following text in the Bavli is not explicit about this division in rabbinic discourse, its sense of the interplay between the fixed and the movable in rabbinic teaching is applicable to the dialectic of *halakhah* and *aggadah*:

> Why are the words of the Torah likened to "goads" (Eccl. 12:11)? To teach you that just as the goad directs the heifer along its furrows so as to bring life into the world, so the words of the Torah direct those who study them from the paths of death to those of life. But [should you think that] just as the goad is movable so are the words of the Torah, the text therefore (also) says "nails." And [should you think that] just as the nail is fixed and does not increase, so too the words of the Torah are fixed and do not increase, therefore the text says "well planted"; just as a plant grows and increases[,] so the words of the Torah grow and increase. "Masters of assemblies," these are the disciples of the wise who sit in manifold assemblies and occupy themselves with Torah. Some pronounce [items] unclean and others [declare them] clean, some prohibit and others permit, certain [witnesses some rabbis] disqualify while others [of them] declare [them] fit. Should a man [then] say: "How in these circumstances shall I learn Torah?" Therefore the text continues, "All of them are given by one shepherd." One God gave them, one leader [Moses] spoke them from the mouth of the Creator, blessed be He, as it is written, "And God spoke all these words" (Ex. 20:1).[154]

I find it difficult not to read into this text a religious charter for the total rabbinic language-game with its bipartite authority structure of halakhic requirement indirectly setting the limits for, while simultaneously validating, aggadic freedom. Speculatively, I suggest that this unique system of constraining the robust freedom of spiritual imagination had its roots in the rabbis' fundamental religious experience; they felt more certain of what God wanted them to do than of how they ought to think about Jewish truth. That is not all that needs to be said, but it is an important first insight.

On the basis of our aggadic evidence it seems reasonable to think of rabbinic discourse in terms of a genetic metaphor. Its two modes of exposition are more alike literarily than different from one another, like congenital but not identical twins. The only thing that fully differentiates them is the different authority vested in each of them, a matter to which we shall return once we have studied all our data. But even at this stage of our investigation, we can say something useful about this uncommon, possibly unique, religious language-game. The bipartite structure of Judaism's official religious language is—from the human side—the rabbis' ingenious linguistic creation, allowing its teachers in a time after revelation to speak with near-biblical authority in demanding obedience to the continuing elaboration of God's law while allowing extraordinary latitude to those speaking of Jewish religious belief. That is a religious phenomenon worth anyone's attention. But those of us devoted to understanding and interpreting Jewish belief today need to study the classical Jewish manner of working at this task so that we might better envision how today's aggadic discourse should be fashioned so as to fulfill this subsidiary but critical aspect of Jewish scholarly responsibility to God under the Covenant.

Chapter 7

◈ Positively, What Is *Aggadah*? ◈

Aggadic discourse encourages imaginative freedom and is not explicitly self-policing. Rather, its bounds are set by halakhic discourse, its congenital linguistic realm, and the norms of *halakhah* resulting from its drive to decision and mandate. How then might we positively characterize this subordinate domain, one known as early as is the *halakhah*, and already then considered sufficiently distinct from it as to deserve its own name, *aggadah*? The question immediately precipitates a religio-cultural difficulty. While we can, with qualification, reasonably use the Western secular category "law" to convey the nature of the *halakhah*, no similarly applicable taxonomic term fits the content and method of the *aggadah*. Prudence and utility regularly lead scholars confronting this holistic issue to shun the positive approach and utilize the standard negative, if empty, Jewish identification: it is all that which is not *halakhah*. Joseph Heinemann clarifies:

> [I]t is difficult to define precisely the nature of the Aggadah. In terms of content, it includes wise sayings, expressions of faith, expositions and elaborations of Scripture, stories, and so on. Its formal patterns include epigrams, anecdotes, examples of wit and humor, terse explanations of a single word in Scripture and stories of almost epic length. Since the Middle Ages it has been customary to define the Aggadah by what it is not.... to this day no more precise formulation has been found than to define Aggadah as that multifaceted type of material found in talmudic-midrashic literature which does not fall into the category of Jewish law.... The chief defect of this negative form of definition is, of course, that it conveys no positive information about the nature and character of what it seeks to define.[1]

To the extent that modern students of nonhalakhic discourse have tried to work positively with this issue, they have pursued what may, heuristically, be divided into two modes of proceeding: the far more popular mode, the literary-historical approach; and the other mode, only rarely employed, which may be termed philosophic. Each has much to commend it, but each also comes with special difficulties. The literary-historical has the difficulty for our purposes that its advocates generally limit their analyses to a given aspect of the *aggadah* and signal this by attaching adjectives like "narrative," "exegetical," or "theological" to the term *aggadah,* or they specify that they are studying *midrash* (generally meaning expository rather than halakhic *midrash*). *Aggadah* and *midrash* both being notoriously polysemous and overlapping in shifting ways,[2] one may nonetheless infer from their work that all nonhalakhic discourse is being characterized rather than one of its parts. To keep our holistic goal here clear, I shall, despite its crudity, employ the acronym NHD (Non-Halakhic Discourse) in this chapter to remind us of the full range of aggadic discourse being studied here.

The philosophic approach seeks to expose the logic—that is, the structuring principles—that renders this apparently disorderly discourse coherent when employed in its appropriate area of use. Though this might lead to a positive, comprehensive view of NHD, it can only establish its validity by showing its applicability to specific, diverse aggadic operations. The literature on these two approaches is vast, so we must limit our exploration of them in what follows.

The Literary-Historical Approach

All modern study in this field (like most other Jewish academic disciplines) has modeled itself after Leopold Zunz's pioneering study *Die Gottesdienstlichen Vorträge der Juden, Historisch Entwickelt.*[3] To answer the Prussian government's question concerning the legitimacy of Jewish preaching in the vernacular, Zunz identified the *midrash* literature as the relevant source of the data he needed for an appropriate response. Then, though he had no Jewish precedent for doing so, he boldly applied the critical methods of academic philologists and historians to determine when the texts likely came into being. The resulting chronological insight was so enlightening that for more than a century the critical historical study of Jewish literature was the chief concern of Jewish scholarship. (We shall later see a telling example of the commitment to the historical method when we discuss the dismissal of a philosophic, Hegelian analysis of rabbinic thinking that appeared shortly after Zunz's pathbreaking work.) A major result of this focus was the collection and publication of early manuscripts of many aggadic works, occasionally resulting in critical editions of a particular *midrash* book, an activity still in progress.

For about a century, the Zunzian approach to *midrash* and *aggadah* was mainly concerned with determining what data they might yield about Jewish history with particular concern for the literary history of its texts. But as the twentieth century moved along, a stronger interest in the literary aspects of these materials (in terms of their sociohistorical situation) became the dominant interest.[4] Thus, while the discovery and publication of the Dead Sea Scrolls added some new information about the history of the prerabbinic period, they have been far more useful in helping us understand the development of Jewish thought and literature, but not, unfortunately, *midrash,* since the Qumran *pesharim* are quite distinct from later rabbinic textual exegesis.[5]

The main stream of this development has sought to interpret the *aggadah* in terms of its Greco-Roman social and literary setting (and, more recently, reading the Bavli's *aggadah* in terms of its Sasanian setting). Yitshak Heinemann's *Darkhe Ha-aggadah* gave this method pathbreaking, academic exposition in his treatment of the literary devices found in rabbinic exegetic *aggadah* with frequent comparisons to Greek parallels.[6] The Greco-Roman influence on rabbinic literature was more directly treated by Saul Lieberman, with special attention to vocabulary and to some hermeneutic rules;[7] by David Daube, who was concerned with these rules as well as story treatment;[8] by E. E. Halevi, who indefatigably identified verbally similar motifs in the two literatures;[9] by Martin Hengel, who argued for a pervasive Hellenization of Palestinian Judaism;[10] and by Henry Fischel, who showed substantial similarities between rabbinic usage and the literary modes favored by various Hellenistic movements (most notably, the Cynic *chria*).[11] Some of these writers made plain their reservations about the extent of the Greco-Roman influence on rabbinic literature generally,[12] leaving more recent writers like Sandra Shimoff, Adam Kamesar, and Martin Jaffee[13] to test whether in their areas of interest the influence appears to have been great or limited. Now, too, Stephen J. Lieberman has supplied a mass of evidence demonstrating that two aggadic hermeneutic "rules" were known in cuneiform hermeneutic long before they are attested in either Greco-Roman or rabbinic literature.[14]

Useful as these findings are for appreciating certain aspects of NHD, it remains clear that, on the whole, these remain two independent kinds of literary materials. From a theological perspective, the differences between rabbinic and Greco-Roman writing are unsurprising. The rabbis believe that the ultimate voice of the text, oral or written, is the one God of the universe, while the various Hellenistic writers know the traditions they deal with deserve a certain mythic respect, but remain essentially human creations. That divergence of belief does not, however, divide rabbinic and Christian exegetes and homilists (again, only an aspect, though an important one, of NHD). The recent work of Marc Hirshman and Burton Visotzky on the intercultural transactions of later centuries investigates this possibility.[15] Hirshman contrasts the relative restriction of the rabbis to the genre of *midrash* with what he finds to be the far more impressive breadth of form and appealing personal liveliness of patristic writing; Visotzky's more painstaking, methodologically sensitive analysis of texts yields only the positive conclusion that the direct concern of the rabbis for Christian argument was relatively rare, with some fathers more interested in Jewish teaching than any rabbis seem to have been in Christianity. Both agree that the two intellectual streams begin with a similar reverence for the Bible and express it in their distinctive ways in terms of a common background sensibility that grows from their immersion in Greco-Roman culture. As Visotzky puts it, "To say it bluntly, the rabbis were Hellenists, much as were the Church fathers"[16]—but that does not take us very far toward our positive goal.

This survey of the influence of Hellenistic literary styles on early rabbinic literature has demonstrated that the Hellenistic background of some areas of aggadic discourse is a necessary ingredient of understanding NHD. Yet, the Greco-Roman influence cannot on its own serve as a sufficient basis for the specific nature of aggadic discourse as a whole. The fact is that there simply is no linguistic realm in Hellenistic culture in which we can find a bifurcated religious discourse like that of the Oral Torah. If anything, it is precisely by the literary standards of Greco-Roman culture that undergird those of modernity that the literature of rabbinic discourse seems shapeless.

We do not get much additional help in our quest by focusing our analysis on sociocultural factors. Richard Kalmin, for example, shows how this can explain the differences between the stories portraying rabbis as social agents in the Yerushalmi and the Bavli.[17] He finds the Yerushalmi outgoing and positive toward involvement with nonrabbis while the Bavli's accounts are more insular and assertive of rabbinic leadership. This substantive difference can be understood as deriving from the different social orders in which these communities functioned. The Yerushalmi reflects the cosmopolitan tone of a community that, while insisting on its distinctiveness, shared something of the openness of the Greco-Roman ethos. The Bavli, by contrast, is part of a far more restrictive and hierarchical culture, and thus depicts its communal notables as a relatively inner-directed group.[18] Were further research to indicate that many such differences in substantive aggadic themes could be explained in a similar fashion, we would gain considerable insight into the literary concerns of the two Talmuds but not much help in understanding why they jointly employ a unique two-level discourse, the more puzzling systemic part of which is NHD.

This disappointment only intensifies with contemporary scholarship's conclusion that it cannot tell us very much about the rabbis' *Sitz am Leben*; their "schools" of interpretation; their "academies" for study; how one became, stayed, and eventually graduated from being a disciple; how their homilies, transformed for transmission in midrashic anthologies, are related to the public lectures they gave; or in what social situations their various kinds of nonhalakhic statements arose. Richard Sarason concluded, "While all scholars agree that the early rabbinic halakhic literature ... is an 'in-group' literature, compiled by rabbis for rabbis talking about matters of interest to rabbis, the exact institutional context of rabbinic study-activity before the Arab conquest is notably difficult to reconstruct from the texts themselves."[19] David Goodblatt's work on the rabbis in Sasanian Babylonia is one foundation of Sarason's observation. Goodblatt concludes:

> [D]oes the existence of the *kallah* imply the existence of some other institution of which it was a part? Since I found no BT [Babylonian Talmud] evidence for any such "parent institution," I prefer not to hypothecate one.... Rabbinic instruction in Babylonia thus was carried out mainly in disciple circles and by means of apprenticeship. In addition there were various kinds of non-permanent academic assemblies ... [T]he evidence of this study suggests that the rabbis were not as institutionally advanced as other elements in late antiquity ... [U]p to the end of the Amoraic period we do not find the same degree of institutional sophistication that we find in both the West and in Mesopotamia.[20]

More recently, Catherine Hezser has massively demonstrated that something similar is true of the earlier centuries of rabbinic life in Roman Palestine: "The boundaries of the rabbinic movement in Roman Palestine were not clear-cut but blurred." More specifically she indicates, "In sociological terms, the rabbinic set was not a corporate group but a loose network.... People can at most have followed the advice of one particular rabbi, thereby transgressing the [halakhic] rules of other rabbis who differed with that particular view.... The editors' efforts to [create a dialectic of unanimity and pluralism] . . . may be seen as attempts to cope with the existing diversity."[21] This being her view of the best we can find out about halakhic conformity, a matter of prime importance to the rabbis, it seems unlikely that we shall learn much about aggadic discourse as a whole from what we can learn about the specific social dynamics of the rabbinic group.

These findings are indicative of a considerable move to modesty in historical claims about the rabbinic period being set before us. Goodblatt describes it this way:

> During the final third of the 20th century a revolution occurred in the study of rabbinic literature. Up to that time a majority of scholars believed in the historicity of the stories and anecdotes about the talmudic masters of the first five centuries C.E. They assumed that these narratives contained reliable information, or at least a "kernel of truth," about their *dramatis personae*. Today there is a new consensus. . . . [Its theme is that] rabbinic sources did not intend to record contemporary history. Instead they sought to interpret earlier texts (including the Bible), to teach moral and religious lessons, and to discuss legal opinions. Nevertheless, these sources can still provide the historian with valuable information.[22]

This perspective has helped persuade scholars that, as Sarason put it, "the most fruitful course for future scholarship on these materials must be to get *back onto* the page."[23] This limited usefulness of the older historic methodology was balanced by the growing commitment to a new hermeneutic openness among secular literary critics. Thus, the preponderance of studies of *aggadah* and *midrash* have treated them as varieties of imaginative discourse, ones strongly influenced by their historic and cultural settings, and it is to the various analytic paths taken from this general perspective that we now turn.

Literary Approaches: Orality and Folklore

Zipporah Kagan concisely sets forth the program of this many-branched approach to aggadic discourse when she says, "Aggadah is literature and should be treated as such. Its significance lies in the meaning that it bestows upon the human situation contained in it; in the answer it gives to the problems it raises. All this is given within a literary framework, hence the necessity to examine both the conceptual and artistic aspects of the Aggadah."[24] To illustrate the variety of approaches to *aggadah* and *midrash* as literature, we will artificially distinguish between four centers of literary concern: orality, folklore, criticism, and deconstruction, the latter two of which substantially overlap.

The analysis of rabbinic literature from the standpoint of its oral character may, for our purposes, be epitomized in the progress from Birger Gerhardsson's 1961 book *Memory and Manuscript: Oral Transmission in Rabbinic Judaism and Early Christianity*,[25] to Martin Jaffee's 2001 book *Torah in the Mouth: Writing and Oral Tradition in Palestinian Judaism, 200 BCE–400 CE*.[26] In the forty years between these two magisterial works scholars increasingly recognized that though students of rabbinics in recent centuries always encountered texts in written (i.e., printed) form, they were, as they frequently indicate, conceived and shaped for oral learning and transmission. Gerhardsson essentially opened up this line of study by applying to rabbinica what had been learned from research into Scandinavian oral traditions. This and the evidence from a number of other cultures clarified how the early oral transmission of these materials—the sagas, for example—left its impress on the form of the later written versions of early folk history. Gerhardsson's close study of the copious data on rabbinic speech and the high value the scholar-community placed upon it clarified, as little else had, why, for example, rabbinic texts often are puzzlingly concise and exhibit a certain choppiness in their flow, as compared to documents that originated in writing. Many scholars of rabbinic literature have since employed this general approach, as Martin Jaffee's generous bibliography indicates.[27]

Jaffee's own contribution centers on the analysis of the rabbinic ideology of orality, what he terms "Torah in the mouth," his evocative translation of an axial term of rabbinic ideology, *Torah shebeal peh*, whose dialectical partner is *Torah shebikhetav*, "written Torah" (i.e., the Pentateuch).[28] Jaffee seeks to understand this concept and thus the literature that celebrates it, by comparison and contrast to Greco-Roman rhetorical models and literature, as well as by utilizing the cultural-anthropological and philosophic notion of performative language—that is, discourse whose full significance is given it only as it is articulated in appropriate social settings. He clarifies carefully the limited but definite role that written texts played "in discipleship training among Galilean Amoraic masters" but subordinates these to the rabbinic ideal of Torah as an oral performance by a master or a disciple.[29] Richard Kalmin and Yaakov Elman have applied such insights to the comparative study of the Bavli and Yerushalmi. The former, studying how these works depict the figure of the sage, argues that the Bavli has a greater commitment to orality (and thus a somewhat more open verbal style), whereas the Yerushalmi exhibits some of the signs of written patterns of formulation. These he traces back to the differences between the more orally oriented Sasanian environment of the Bavli and the more document-influenced Greco-Roman ethos.[30] Elman's broader scope shares this view, though he helpfully calls attention to the mention and actual use of documents in both societies, indicating how this occurred in Babylonia (though it was to a lesser extent than in Palestine). The Bavli's "long period of oral transmission and composition took place against a background of what I shall term 'pervasive orality' in Babylonia, as contrasted with the greater prevalence of written transmission in the Greco-Roman cultural sphere."[31]

None of these scholars suggests that orality is a means of distinguishing *aggadah* from *halakhah* or vice versa; they are speaking of rabbinic discourse as a whole. Only Elman has the dual nature of rabbinic utterance in mind, and he suggests that "anecdotal and narrative material... [was] handled with much greater freedom [for writing than legal material or Talmudic dialectic]."[32] Understanding rabbinic texts as having largely been shaped by their oral origins and performance (as well as their anthological redaction) gives us considerable insight into their choppy, even jumpy, flow, in contrast to the relatively unbroken, cumulative flow that characterizes so many Greco-Roman texts and thus our continuing expectation of ancient literature.

Dan Ben-Amos points directly to what is involved in this transformation, though with his folklorist's agenda in mind: "The shift from orality to literacy involves thematic, stylistic, and poetic modifications, and although in their new state the [folk]tales have a relatively higher degree of stability, they can offer us glimpses into their performance history."[33] His statement indicates the affinity of orality studies to that of folklore, and so we now inquire what that discipline may teach us about the distinctiveness of aggadic discourse. Even a cursory acquaintance with rabbinic literature indicates that it abounds with folktales and folk sayings, the wisdom drawn from people's everyday life and not just from the scholars' self-conscious activity.[34] Moreover, these materials are strongly associated with aggadic rather than halakhic discourse, a distinction directly relevant to our concern.

In recent years, the application of an academic folkloristic perspective to the study of the Talmud and *midrash* books is closely associated with the work of Dov Noy and his students at Hebrew University. His pioneering *Motif Index of Talmudic and Midrashic Literature* (1954) brought the structural insights of the international study of folklore to bear upon rabbinic literature. While his expansive interests embraced the entire range of Jewish folklore, he wrote a number of studies on folklore in rabbinic writings and sought to distinguish folk materials from that of the scholar class. Thus, in his study of animal-language tales he suggested that "[a] storyteller who used all the five associated 'leads' and [based] his story ... thereon ... is more of a creative artist than a narrator who uses the same verse, but develops it in only one or two directions.... On the other hand, a preacher who, unlike the folk-narrator, has a definite didactic goal, will move directly to his destination, concentrating on a single associative element, and will not attempt to entertain his public by additional associations, however tempting they may be."[35]

Recognizing the signs of folk creativity in NHD would thus explain why a literature reflecting God's revelation through the work of a sophisticated scholar class contains tall tales, legends, fables, folk remedies, maxims about everyday life, and odd bits of information. Dan Ben-Amos has suggested that we must read this literature "with the realization that the rabbis lived in a society in which orality and literacy did not exclude but were interdependent upon each other. Learning did not contrast with orality but was simply one of its dimensions."[36] Continuing the taxonomic interests of his teacher, Dov Noy, Ben-Amos has diagrammed the "traditional genres" of the Oral Torah based on the common terms for them and the extensive breadth of learning associated with R. Yoḥanan ben Zakkai.[37] He has identified the differentiating characteristics of folklore as "traditionality, irrationality, and rurality; anonymity, communality and universality; primacy and oral circulation..." adding that what makes folklore "a culturally unique mode of communication, and [gives it] its distinctiveness is formal, thematic and performative." And it is the correlation between these latter three levels of communication by which the speakers of folklore are distinguished in a society, but "it is the sole property of neither peasants nor primitives."[38] His studies and those of others interpreting aspects of rabbinic literature in terms of international folklore scholarship have helped clarify how much of what prior generations had taken to be the solitary creation of the Hebraic spirit is, in fact, not infrequently a local version of a global human activity.

Galit Hasan-Rokem has expanded the horizon of what constitutes folklore beyond that of Ben-Amos, her teacher, and given it book-length exposition in her study *Web of Life: Folklore and Midrash in Rabbinic*

Literature.³⁹ While paying careful attention to the general scholarly literature on folklore and respectful of her Jewish predecessors, she indicates that her "approach views folk narratives as woven into the very fabric of rabbinic Aggadah and rabbinic literature in general and not merely as an amusing digression providing relief from heavier and more important matters.... The assumption here, then, is that the rabbis were concerned with comprehensive ethnographic recording of their culture...."⁴⁰ Her assumption about the rabbis' interest in "ethnographic recording" and her identification of folk literature with the social concerns of all the subgroups among the folk seem to me an overextension of the reach of her hermeneutic, otherwise evident in the insights of her investigation and the variety of materials she analyzes. Whatever the judgment of subsequent scholarship on these issues, fokloristic approaches can only be of limited, if valuable, help in seeking a systemic view of NHD. Thus far they have clarified neither why the variegated forms of folklore become a unity called *aggadah* nor why so much of aggadic literature shows the creative shaping of a sophisticated class of authors. To some extent, it is this sense of high artistry in much of the *aggadah* that has led scholars to favor more formal literary approaches to it.

Literary Approaches: The Standard Critical Mode

No mode of studying the *aggadah* has generated more academic interest than that which studies it as literature and treats it with the accepted canons of literary criticism.⁴¹ But the very desire to expose its literary features has led scholars to concentrate on those aspects of NHD which are most amenable to this hermeneutic, and thus a repetition of our prior stricture about equating studies of *midrash* or *aggadah* as equivalent to NHD is warranted. Literary studies on *midrash,* for example, tend to sidestep halakhic *midrash* so as to concentrate on the homiletic or expository *midrash* books and the tales of the Talmud. So, too, literary studies of *aggadah* do not always signal their selectivity by using an adjective like "narrative" to characterize their limited area of interest. With that reminder in mind, we can nonetheless learn much about a major feature of NHD by looking at some of its literary admirers.

Written early in the twentieth century, Hayyim Nahman Bialik's essay "Halakhah and Aggadah" gave a poet and author's appreciation of aggadic literature. It remained for Yitshak Heinemann at midcentury to apply the methods of high literary criticism to the *aggadah* in his pioneering, magisterial volume *Darkhe Ha-agadah* ([The Conceptual] Ways of the Aggadah). His very first sentence announces, "The purpose of this book is to describe and clarify the methods utilized by the rabbinic sages in the most difficult and characteristic portions of the *aggadah*."[42] Heinemann's mission is apologetic: to demonstrate to the denigrators of the rabbinic imagination, whether cultural, historical, or philosophic, the intrinsic artistic and intellectual worth of aggadic literature. In doing so by the highest standards of Western literary scholarship, he would further validate, at least to readers of Hebrew, the place of Jewish culture in modern civilization.

Heinemann's pathbreaking accomplishment is most impressive. He is sensitive to the various influences that later scholars have pursued: the Greco-Roman setting, orality, folklore, artistic patterns, and intellectual structures. Bringing to bear his prior scholarship in the fields of ancient philosophy and writing, he analyzes with uncommon depth the relation of *aggadah* to Hellenistic literature, the parallels with Philo being particularly suggestive. His broadscale division of aggadic activity into "creative historiography" and "creative philology" has not, however, been utilized as much by later writers as has his concern with the specific rhetorical techniques—he simply calls them "methods"—utilized by the aggadists. After his detailed exposition of these artistic and intellectual devices, only the uninformed can call this literature shapeless and nearly primitive. (He even provides a special index of these "methods.")[43] His work clearly stands behind all subsequent modern study of aggadic literature.

Four decades later, Yonah Frenkel published his monumental two-volume work, *Darkhe Ha-agadah veha-midrash*, and the similarity to Heinemann's title is quite intentional, as the plan and the emphases of the volumes indicate.[44] In the light of later literary studies and with proportionately less concern for the similarities with contemporaneous writing in Greek, Frenkel brings an extraordinary range of learning to bear on a similar concern: the high artistry often to be found in early aggadic and midrashic literature. In this he continues Heinemann's apologetic bent, with Frenkel seeking to redeem *aggadah* from the low esteem it has long had among students of the Talmud. He lays the foundation for this in part 1 of his study by arguing for the study-house of the scholars and not the synagogue of the people or its folk culture as the vivifying and generating situation of aggadic-midrashic discourse. Specifically, this material continually exhibits, under his analysis, the application of sophisticated rhetorical skill rather than only the occasional artistry found in preaching to the untutored public or the raw wisdom that makes folklore attractive.

Frenkel seeks to clinch his case (as did Heinemann) by illustrating the many artistic devices embedded in this literature.[45] He is freshest, however, in his careful study of three major aspects of aggadic creativity: rabbinic tales, parables, and maxims.[46] His strength as a literary critic is regularly displayed as he closely reads the stories told by the rabbis, opening up layers of meaning in them that prior acquaintance with them had not made evident. One may not always be convinced by his particular interpretation—a common problem with reading literary criticism, but one reminiscent of the polyvalence of aggadic discourse itself, and thus a fitting method with which to explore this subject matter. His admirable critical sensitivity is matched by his breadth of interest, as witnessed by his critical treatment of rabbinic maxims or epigrams.[47] One is hard-pressed to think of other scholars who have found this material worthy of major artistic analysis. Frenkel's elucidation of the literary patterns found in these brief statements breaks fresh critical ground and gives us new insight into why many generations have found these maxims memorable.

Frenkel's approach to literary criticism has a classical tone to it. He utilizes Aristotle's discussion of the necessary framework for drama and tale as a framework for his own standards of judging the aesthetic and intellectual accomplishment of a given rabbinic tale or parable. Though he is informed by modern literary concerns, he tends to assimilate these to the traditional criteria by which high culture has judged the artistic merit of literature. Thus, critics who operate from another hermeneutic base, and certainly those who have a substantially different one, will disagree about the adequacy of his findings.[48] This issue is of particular interest here, since Frenkel presents his case for the study-house provenance of this material as, in effect, a general theory of *aggadah* and *midrash*. In agreement with other of his critics, it seems to me that Frenkel has overstated the centrality of advanced literary construction to these rabbinic traditions, for it cannot readily accommodate the considerable amount of conflicting data—rabbis preaching in synagogues, or often otherwise speaking the language of the folk, or the strong signs of independent folklore in these texts, for example. The problem of NHD arose partially because of its disturbing diversity, and it continues to plague us today because modern study of this literature continues to expand our sense of what is to be found there.

Less-global claims for the formal literary character of much aggadic material have continued to demonstrate their hermeneutic merit. David

Stern's study of the *mashal* form, *Parables in Midrash*,[49] may be said to have set new standards of detail and horizon for the application of the notion of literary structure to early rabbinic literature.[50] His sense of the importance of form is brought out in his terming the *mashal*'s structure "normative" and referring to it as its "regularized form" attained through a process he terms "regularization."[51] With the object of his investigation now clearly in focus, he then demonstrates how much is learned by applying to it the classic analytic tools of rhetoric and poetics, modes of analysis that have also been employed by others taking the literary critical approach.[52]

The Talmudic story has also recently received scrutiny in works by Jeffrey L. Rubenstein and Alon Goshen-Gottstein.[53] Since both have discussed at length the Elisha ben Abuyah tales, we gain a sense of the variety of literary interpretations possible by even a brief comparison of their approaches. Both focus on the fictional, creative character of these records, and both feel that whatever historically may be said about the man must be subordinated to the sense we can get of how the stories evolved and what this may say about the rabbinic circumstances that produced them. Rubenstein tends to be more concerned with a close reading of the texts and the depth and nuance of meaning it yields, ending with a general theory of how this tale (and the five others he studies) came to its final form. Goshen-Gottstein's close reading seems to me somewhat more intuitive and speculative, responsive to details that lead in directions other than what a more straightforward, if attentive, reader might find significant. Thus, he concludes this section of his book with a final "contraversion" (the title of the series in which this volume appeared), suggesting the admittedly bare possibility that Elisha was, like Akiba, a martyr but that the creative force of rabbinic transmission-creation turned him into an archheretic. Goshen-Gottstein's reading has, of course, the great virtue of demonstrating something of the dynamic rabbinic artistic intelligence he finds in the texts.

The Documentary Approach

Though Jacob Neusner takes a literary approach to early rabbinic literature[54] and practices form-criticism, his carefully delineated focus is on broad literary structures with a concern for the conceptual traits these indicate. Judith Hauptman has characterized it this way:

> His holistic approach to the examination of rabbinic texts dictates looking at each work as a whole, evaluating its worldview, program, and

religious, social, and political agenda. New research directions generated by this perspective include searching a text for the editor's imprint, trying to understand how he reworked earlier materials in order to fashion a message of his own; and comparing two works from the same period, noting their similarities and differences in order to appreciate the variety of approaches to life and law that existed at the time. In particular, Neusner warns against forcing the entire mass of rabbinic material into a seamless whole, as has been the case for so long.[55]

This shapes his unique method and largely identifies what he means when he uses the term *aggadah*—the extended passages that are found either in essentially nonaggadic books or in the *midrash* books that are essentially *aggadah*. That is, in keeping with his understanding of cogent interpretation in this literature, he concentrates on how extended passages of non-normative material interact (or do not) with the halakhic discourse whose integrity requires "dominating the task of [rabbinic] discourse"[56] rather than on the messier multitude of discrete, variegated utterances and processes that one would seek to embrace if one thought of *aggadah* as the entirety of NHD.[57]

Before elucidating what I take to be the two foundational concerns of his work,[58] I must indicate some limits of my ability to do so. I cannot claim to have assimilated the vast breadth of Neusner's writing over the years. This is particularly significant because he has not only changed his mind about a number of matters about which he once appeared certain, but the presently available volumes are only a part of a larger project presently only partially completed and perhaps only partially envisaged.[59] Moreover, two aspects of Neusner's work with *aggadah* puzzle me. The first of these is what moved him, after his decades of unconcern with the *aggadah*, to unexpectedly turn his attention to this material, even adopting the usage of rabbinic writings having a dual-discourse. As late as 1995, in his magisterial *Introduction to Rabbinic Literature* (for the Anchor Bible Reference Library), there is hardly any mention of the *aggadah*, an unconcern presaged in his prior works on the Bavli, the Yerushalmi, and the Mishnah (as well as much else).[60] In the near-dozen works now available, the *aggadah* suddenly appears as a distinctive, major mode of rabbinic thinking, though a subordinate one. The second aspect is that, though he considers *aggadah* a literary category very much like *midrash* (which he also occasionally calls these materials), he largely limits the examples he gives of it in his recent aggadic studies to extended theological-exegetical-narrative texts.[61] As he indicates, he is particularly concerned with expressions of what he terms Israel's religious exteriority, its concern with and relation to the world and to non-Jews.[62] But this already involves us in his substantive statements, and I now return to them.

Neusner's understanding of his intellectual task begins from a global view of what constitutes a cultural system of a social order, "a set of cogent ideas that proposes coherently to describe, analyze and interpret how things are within a determinate social—or even world—order, whether real or imagined."[63] Thus, the Pentateuch has its religious system and so, too, the Qur'an and the *halakhah* of early rabbinic Judaism. Such a system is established by means of native categories and native category-formations.[64] These notions are given more detailed exposition at the conclusion of the first volume of his study of this activity.[65] There he indicates that native categories are the persons, places, things, or reified ideas that bear a fixed meaning and impart determinate sense where they occur—what linguists call a head-noun. A category-formation is the rules that govern the making of connections, the building of constructions, models of analysis, and such—what linguists broadly connect with syntax. In short, Neusner wishes to study the *aggadah* as well as the *halakhah* in terms of his understanding of them as individual yet related modes of creating this kind of system for a social order.

The results of his various projects thus far leave one with considerable respect for the intellectual substance of the *aggadah*. While it does not have equality with the *halakhah*[66] in rabbinic literature's determination of its desired system of social order, yet its concern with exteriority (found in its category formations) complements the focus on interiority discovered in its halakhic category formations. Thus, at the end of his volume *Dual Discourse, Single Judaism: The Category-Formations of the Halakhah and of the Aggadah Defined, Compared and Contrasted*, Neusner can say,

> The single Judaism yielded by the dual discourse of the Halakhah and the Aggadah presents no puzzle ... both modes of discourse recapitulate the story of Scripture, each in its own manner. ... In the Halakhic framework it is to translate the laws into jurisprudence ... by treating the cases of Scripture as rules sustaining abstraction and generalization. In the Aggadic framework the purpose is to do the same, that is, to treat a case as exemplary. ... The Halakhah generalizes, organizes, and rationalizes the laws, forming of them a coherent design for the social order. The Aggadah weaves of the parts a single fabric, finding the whole in a detail or linking one whole part to another to underscore the unity of the divine narrative.[67]

Neusner makes no claim that this description encompasses every halakhic and rabbinic utterance, and he openly indicates that this or that material is anomalous to his categories or is not relevant to his purposes.[68] But having set forth his view of what is involved in a system of social-order building, he is convinced that he has carried through the central intellectual task of understanding the abstract substantive achievement of rabbinic discourse. The investigation carried on in this book, despite its more cultural and less rationalistic approach to rabbinic discourse, is further advanced by Neusner's highlighting of the intellectuality at work in a significant portion of NHD.[69]

Literary Approaches: The Poststructuralist Mode

"To assimilate or interpret something is to bring it within the modes of order which culture makes available, and this is usually done by talking about it in a mode of discourse which a culture takes as natural."[70] This astute observation of Jonathan Culler helps us understand the transition that took place in literary criticism in the decades somewhat after the middle of the twentieth century largely due to our culture's altered sense of what was "natural." As epitomized in the title of a recent book on the history of science and ideas in this period, *From Certainty to Uncertainty*,[71] it involved a change in our general expectation of things. Specifically, the philosophic work of Hans-Georg Gadamer, which made hermeneutic central to understanding generally, the literary-philosophical analyses of Jacques Derrida and Roland Barthes, which fostered a body of antilogocentric and postfoundational criticism, and the feminist argument for the influence of gender and the postcolonialist argument about race upon the allegedly universal quality of male reasoning—all radically reoriented our views of reality and language. There was a new self-consciousness about how our "reading" of whatever we studied necessarily shaped our thought. In this cultural environment, the study of *midrash* encountered the new literary currents of structuralism and poststructuralism, semiotics, deconstruction, cultural studies, "indeed all the modes of postmodernism as they have come into fashion and gone out of it . . . [and] has gone through a virtual sea change."[72]

Susan Handelman, in her learned volume, *The Slayers of Moses*,[73] called on scholars of early rabbinic literature to replace their overly historicistic, philological, and formalist hermeneutic concerns by what she argued was the protopostmodernism of classical *midrash*. This issue soon became a cause célèbre as a result of a number of critical reviews, particularly David Stern's lengthy, appreciative, but searchingly troubled response to the book, Handelman's far-ranging rejoinder, and Stern's concluding response.[74] What remains clear nearly two decades later is that they do not fundamentally disagree on the importance of what Stern there called "the not inconsiderable body of literature, Continental and American, that has done so much to revolutionize literary criticism in the past several decades," and its relevance to the study of *midrash*. Indeed, near the beginning of his review he commends Handelman "for attempting to join the gains made in the new philosophically oriented hermeneutical criticism with the study of ancient literary criticism and interpretation."[75] Many students of rabbinic literature found deconstructionist literary theory particularly appealing because it made "natural," in Culler's sense, a new literary sensibility. The midrashic blurring of the distinction between text and commentary, the "polysemy" (Stern's persuasive substitute term for the more commonly used "indeterminacy") seen in texts, the celebration of deconstructing texts, and the openness to clashing opinion—matters that had previously rendered *midrash* alien to Western literary critics—now became admirable. "Critics and theorists from the general literary world ... found themselves fascinated by the same wayward, antic features of midrashic interpretation that had often been considered scandalous in the past."[76] Yale University Press introduced its volume *Midrash and Literature* this way:

> Midrash, or the rabbinical exegesis of Old Testament writings, is kindling a special degree of interest among today's literary theorists. It has been recognized ... that many of the various kinds of hermeneutical narrative that make up so large a part of textuality in our civilization are in significant ways the offspring of midrash. Moreover, in recent years, contemporary criticism has become aware of striking resemblances between its own pursuit of meaning and the midrashic grasp of the open character of the text.[77]

The heady promise of this volume, arranged under the leadership of the eminent critic of English literature Geoffrey Hartman and with the participation of a number of other well-known figures in the world of literary criticism as well as that of many of the most prestigious scholars of rabbinic and associated literature, was not followed by much further interest on the part of the generalists. Stern summarizes the cooling of the relationship by commenting:

> Students of midrash ... early on ... found that midrashic literature resisted many of the categories and phenomena that post-structuralist

> theory had initially seemed to open up to them.... Still, the vantage point that theory offered from which to view midrash with its value as a lexicon of critical terminology and conceptual categories was revolutionary ... [e.g.,] narratology, rhetorical criticism, and semiotics ... intertextuality ... and methodologies drawn more eclectically from both philosophical and theological hermeneutics. ...[78]

He concludes, "The moment of interdisciplinary excitement ... has now largely passed.... Yet whatever its fate in the larger literary theoretical world, the midrash-theory connection has had a lasting impact on the study of midrash."[79] Thus, it influences most recent writers dealing with this literature even if it is not the shaping principle of their studies, as in the case of the works by Rubenstein, Goshen-Gottstein, and Cohen discussed previously. Yet the continuing influence of the poststructuralist approach can be illuminated by attention to three instances where it has resulted in significant insight into the special nature of *midrash*.

A few years after his exchange with Susan Handelman, Stern published an article entitled "Midrash and Indeterminacy."[80] Its title testifies to postmodernism's effect on his agenda, though he proposed exploring the similarities of the extraordinary freedom of the *midrash* with the deconstructionists' radical rejection of a stable textual meaning in order to identify the ultimate difference between them. If, as the new hermeneutic emphasized, texts, despite purporting to convey a single message—their logocentricity—necessarily contained more meaning than interpretation could make plain, then the exegetic freedom of the *midrash* was not odd but exemplary. Nonetheless, Stern argued, simple self-respect demanded recognition of the differences that also existed between the two modes of reading text. "What differentiates midrash from indeterminacy is not its style but rather the latter's formal resistance to closure.... In contrast midrashic polysemy is predicated precisely upon the existence of such a perspective, the divine presence from which all contradictory interpretations derive."[81] Thus, while we can now hardly read *midrash* as we did before deconstructionism, we also cannot read it as if the rabbis were merely its early practitioners.

In Steven Fraade's work on the *Sifre to Deuteronomy*[82] we see another significant influence of the postmodern perspective on the study of *midrash*—namely, the concern with the reader who, as a decidedly active partner, turns an inert text into meaning. We contemporary readers cannot exempt ourselves from that scrutiny by claiming that, in some objectively neutral way, we are merely identifying the presumed reader for whom a given text was intended; all such judgments are our creative reading of the text. In the *Sifre to Deuteronomy* we are immediately struck by what we perceive as the cryptic nature of its ongoing commentary—that is, its characteristic practice of leaving out all sorts of connections and developments that we anticipate finding in expository literature. Fraade suggests,

> What is most striking in the end is the way in which the commentary engages the attentive student as a participant in a timely yet timeless network. Through the textured fabric of that work biblical writ (and the event of its revelation), inherited tradition (in all its fluidity), and historical time (including its messianic reversals) are all made transformatively *present* in the social world of its *performative* study.[83]

Gary Porton applauds Fraade's insight and frames it this way:

> By transforming the received material, the redactor produced a polyphonic text, one that contains multiple interpretations of the same passage, and an incomplete text, one which leaves gaps in the exegesis. This draws the audience into the text and necessitates their interaction with it in order to understand both Sifre and the Bible.... [Thus] the ideal rabbinic sage [or his disciple] is the desired reader of Sifre.[84]

Once again, what once seemed "unnatural" to the modern reader is, within a newly extended horizon of literary appreciation, "natural," even something of a creative accomplishment. It should also be pointed out that the text whose aggadic materials Fraade was dealing with was far more a halakhic *midrash* than an aggadic one. Rabbinic literature as a whole has a discourse congenial to its performative goal, one growing out of the sociocultural practice of rabbinic life. Though this is a striking example of the effect of postmodernism on the study of rabbinic texts, it must be noted that it has only a tangential bearing on our specific inquiry, the special nature of NHD.

Concerning Daniel Boyarin's *Intertextuality and the Reading of Midrash*[85] (and his further exemplification of his theory in *Carnal Israel*),[86] our third example, a not-uncritical reviewer wrote, "This is undoubtedly a major contribution to midrashic studies.... This study signals the moment at which a distinctively hermeneutical program of midrashic literary research begins to define its field."[87] Boyarin's statement of his position takes place against a detailed analysis of the prior great literary analysts of the *midrash*, Yitshak Heinemann and the unrelated Joseph Heinemann (both set against the background of Maimonides' attitude toward the *aggadah*).[88] Against their acceptance of the modern view that "we know what reading is" and its driving issue, "Why does midrash deviate from it?" (an attitude he associates with their logocentric sense of reality), Boyarin asks, "[S]eeing how midrash reads, what theoretical concepts are useful for understanding it?"[89]—an approach eclectically derived from our sense that we are always creatively "reading" reality.

In this work Boyarin demonstrates how the recent literary notion of intertextuality enriches our understanding of what transpires in the midrashic text.[90] Again, it is the incompleteness, the oddness in construction that regularly characterizes these midrashic works that attracts his attention. He compels us to see that the biblical text, the focus of midrashic commentary, is itself a series of texts in which similar challenges to understanding abound and evoke comment by other biblical texts. It has become a commonplace in modern studies of the Bible to make reference to the "midrash" already present there as later writers respond to what they perceive as lacunae in the biblical text. Very often the rabbinic *midrash* introduces another biblical text—one often from a quite different biblical genre—to imaginatively fill in what troubled the midrashist in the exegetic target. Boyarin wants us to recognize that the rabbis are, in their way, carrying forward the biblical pattern of text commenting on text, with text and commentary not rigidly distanced from each other. Thus, the proper concern of contemporary scholars of *midrash* needs to be textual practice and not the historical interest or classical literary forms which so engaged the students of prior modern generations.

Acknowledging that the term "intertextuality" is used in a number of different ways, Boyarin gives the three senses that are important in his work. They are a fine introduction to the manner in which poststructuralists approach texts.

> The first is that the text is always made up of a mosaic of conscious and unconscious citation of earlier discourse. The second is that texts may be dialogical in nature—contesting their own assertions as an essential part of the structure of their discourse—and that the Bible is a preeminent example of such a text. The third is that there are cultural codes, again either conscious or unconscious, which both constrain and allow the production (not creation) of new texts within the culture: these codes may be identified with the ideology of the culture, which are made up of the assumptions that people in the culture automatically make about what may or may not be true and possible, about what is natural in nature and in history.[91]

Had Boyarin left matters at this level, one might think that, for all the concern with culture as providing tools for our understanding, the commitment to intertextuality in literary studies would engender a hermetic, verbalistically regimented manner of reading. Boyarin, among the other accomplishments of his successor volume, *Carnal Israel*, demonstrated how this way of approaching texts might yet be of help in yielding some indication of what actually transpired in the society in which the rabbis lived. Thus, he now called his hermeneutic "cultural poetics, a practice that respects the literariness of literary texts ... while attempting at the same time to understand how they function within a larger socio-cultural system of practices."[92] His treatment, for example, of the indeterminacy of aggadic passages concerning women's sexuality, a major concern of this volume, allows him to listen to the "oppositional voices" encoded in the text and argue that they "are intimations of the social conflict outside the text."[93] Here the clashing voices of midrashic opinion, previously such an impediment to those hoping to find them significantly instructive, become newly precious. In the tradition's preservation of diverse opinions, we may discover stands previously not allowed to shape common practice but obviously significant enough to be transmitted to later generations. In fact, Boyarin gives a striking example of how the midrashic literature, read with cultural poetics, can today speak to those facing new troubles or opportunities, in this case ones related to embodiment, gender, and feminism.

With all the accomplishments of the poststructuralist approach to *midrash*, it can only be of limited help in clarifying the specific nature of nonhalakhic discourse. As noted above, much of its wisdom applies to rabbinic literature generally, the halakhic as well as the aggadic. And only part of NHD is exegetic; much of the rest of it may, at best, have unconscious reference to other texts, but a determined intertextuality puts us on a quite slippery slope of subjectivity. For all the partial insight the literary approach to NHD has given us, we must turn elsewhere to round out our view of this uncommon discourse.

Might Feminism or Comparative Religion Better Elucidate NHD?

Though literary analyses of NHD remain the most productive means of clarifying its uncommon character, two nonliterary modes of doing so might substantially increase our reach in this regard.

The first of these is feminism. Any rule that bifurcates a given realm of activity and makes the one superior to the other, all the while asserting the intimate relationship of the two, suggests the possibility that this is another example of patriarchy's subtle controlling power. One might then argue that the imaginative, free-flowing, value-sensitive nature of *aggadah* expresses the femininity inherent in all human beings, while the rule-oriented, detail-obsessed, dialectic logicality of the *halakhah* stems from the masculine in all of us.[94] This suggestion, however, needs to be made more as an imaginative insight than a rigid distinction in response to the widespread feminist rejection of "essentialism," the notion that gender creates definite character types. We must look to the work of feminist scholars of rabbinic texts to determine what, if anything, might be made of this possibility.

At present, feminist scholars of rabbinic literature have moved in other directions, one well described by Judith Hauptman. "It is important to apply the same high-powered analytic techniques currently being used in rabbinic research to texts dealing with women and marriage [so as to achieve both] new insight into rabbinic texts and a deeper understanding of rabbinic attitudes toward women.... The key question is, In what direction was the rabbinic system as a whole headed?"[95] Her subsequent paragraph about Midrash Halakhah and Midrash Aggadah stays within the focus she has delineated and does not consider the possibility that the classic Jewish distinction between halakhic and aggadic discourse might itself benefit from a feminist analysis.[96] The agenda Hauptman outlines is, with modifications, admirably exemplified in recent volumes by Charlotte Fonrobert and Judith Baskin, the former dealing essentially with halakhic texts, the latter with midrashic texts.[97] Baskin, in the course of explaining (justifying?) her concentration on aggadic depictions of women (against the contemporary echoes of the long-term deprecation of the *aggadah*) suggests that there may be something about this realm of discourse that is particularly attuned to discussing women. Her discussion of the context within which rabbinic literature needs to be read has several allusive comments about the nature of *midrash* and comes to a climax thus:

> While *halakhah* is characterized by carefully framed and exhaustively debated legal mandates, both proscriptive and prescriptive, the more variegated *aggadah* offers occasional glimpses into contemporary circumstances and daily practice, illuminating the outlines of lived experience in all of its good and bad intentions and improvisational disarray. As I argue in this book, aggadic literature frequently preserves a more nuanced

and complex view of women and their activities than the impersonal dictates of halakhic discourse.... Often the *aggadah* seems more reflective of the complexities of actual human relationships as they are lived, while the *halakhah* appears to point toward an ideal, but not yet achieved, condition of order.[98]

I am suggesting that it may be but a reasonable feminist step from these substantive observations to the more global question of whether the very nature of the twin discourses may be significantly shaped by gender. But the value of this suggestion must be left to feminist scholars to evaluate.[99]

A second promising hermeneutic might arise from the field of comparative religion. Two large and venerable faiths formally recognize such a system of divided status in their central sacred literature: the family of Hindu faiths (poorly denominated "Hinduism") and Islam.

In Hinduism[100] a "basic distinction between Sruti and Smriti writings is generally accepted. Sruti is the original, primary scripture and authority, whose truths were directly revealed to or intuited by early seers or risis. They are accepted as sacred, infallible and God-made. Smriti literature is derivative or takes its authority from the Sruti. The Smriti books are of human, not divine origin, and were written to explain the Sruti and make them understandable and meaningful to the masses. Prabhavananda as cited by Donald H. Bishop writes that... 'They comprise, in short, the daily duties, usages, and customs to be observed by the several castes and by people in different stages of life.'"[101] V. Madhusudan Reddy makes the superiority of the one set of sacred texts over the other unmistakable through this citation from Shananenda's *The Cultural Heritage of India*: "It is a recognized rule of procedure that whenever there seems to be a difference between the Sruti (the Vedas) and the Smriti, the Sruti has to be upheld as the supreme authority and the Smriti has to be interpreted in consonance with it."[102] William Cenlauer suggests that the Oral Law in Judaism "resembles the oral tradition in India," pointing out that "The *Tanna*, reciter, in Rabbinic Judaism is much like the *pandit* in Sanskritic Hinduism."[103] But this would make the Sruti/Smriti duality helpful in delineating the particular character of the Oral Law as a whole but not of NHD, which is but one of its parts and yet has an identity of its own for which we seek adequate description.

A somewhat similar situation confronts us when we look at the relationship of Qur'an to hadith in the teaching of Islam. "Since the lifetime of the Prophet himself the Muslims called reports which spoke of his actions and sayings 'the best *hadith*,' and, in due course the word became increasingly confined to such reports,"[104] says Siddiqi. He continues, "It would not be an exaggeration to state that the Qur'an and *hadith* provided the bedrock for all the intellectual and academic enterprises of the Arabs."[105] While many of the hadith were written down quite early, many others were first transmitted orally and later written down.[106] The legal importance of the hadith literature is, with some qualification, "accepted by all the important Sunni jurists as the second source of Islamic law, after the Qur'an," a subordination of authority then illustrated by noting that "Acceptance of *hadith* as a source of Islamic law is advocated in the Qur'an" and the subsequent citation of the appropriate text.[107] Robson specifies that "*Hadith* was given a kind of secondary inspiration. Though not the eternal word of God, like the Kur'an it represented divine guidance."[108]

It should be noted that hadith is regularly spoken of as a legal genre, as indicating what a faithful Moslem is required to do. Rather than think of it then as some kind of list of rules, it will be helpful to give some indication of the breadth of its styles. Reuven Firestone provides this overview:

> The Hadith par excellence, as known today, represents the *sunna*, "the beaten track"—the custom and practice of the prophet Muhammad. The *sunna* refers to Muhammad's acts and statements, which are considered authoritative for the determination of proper Muslim behavior. These prophetic acts and teachings were remembered in the form of short narratives and anecdotes (*hadith*s) preserved in the minds of Muhammad's surviving contemporaries and their descendants and students.[109]

It is also significant for our comparative purposes to note that Moslem scholarship and recent Western academic study of this literature have been much concerned with the clashing teachings of some later collections of hadith with one another.

Despite the clear hierarchy of authority between the Qu'ran and the hadith, a preliminary judgment suggests that we are unlikely to gain much help from this instance of a sacred dual discourse in regard to our effort to understand NHD synoptically. The Moslem usage seems far closer to the rabbinic legal distinction between *deoraita*, "scriptural rulings," and *derabbanan*, "those made by the sages." Both carry legal authority, though the prior group has a greater stringency. In the classic distinction between *halakhah* and *aggadah*, the former is clearly legal while the latter is only highly commended.

But a deeper investigation by scholars at home in this literature as well as in the works of the rabbis may both circumvent the charges of "orientalism" visited on much Western scholarship and find a more fruitful ground in Islamic teaching for this comparative purpose.[110] Perhaps, too, scholars of world religion can point to another religion in which the widespread Scripture/Tradition duality is supplemented by a bifurcated understanding of Tradition and that would be a comparative companion to rabbinic Judaism's *halakhah/aggadah* understanding of Tradition.

Philosophic Constructions of *Aggadah* (1): H. S. Hirschfeld, the Forgotten Hegelian

There have been two major efforts to provide a philosophic analysis of the underlying system by which aggadic discourse persuades or convinces its hearers.[111] The work of the mid-twentieth-century thinker Max Kadushin is familiar to all scholars in this field and will be discussed shortly. The pioneering work of his mid-nineteenth-century philosophical predecessor, H. S. [Hirsch S.] Hirschfeld (1812–84) has, by contrast, been unjustly forgotten and demands special attention here.[112] The reason for this, it seems to me, is quite clear, and it is instructive about the modern study of *midrash*. The work of Leopold Zunz in the first third of the nineteenth century, climaxed by his magisterial 1832 volume on the sources and history of Jewish preaching, convinced almost all thoughtful Jewish modernizers that critical history, textually and philologically pursued, was the indispensable medium for the needed interface. But as early as 1840, Hirschfeld, though similarly passionate about *Wissenschaft*, "scientific study," utilized a philosophical hermeneutic in the first of his two planned volumes on rabbinic thinking, a treatment of halakhic exposition.[113] Two significant reviews of this work appeared, which Ismar Schorsch characterizes as follows: "[D]espite grudging respect for his learning and ingenuity, Levi Herzfeld and [Abraham] Geiger dismissed [it] . . . with its unhistorical method and excessive Hegelian framework as falling short of the standards of *Wissenschaft*."[114] Herzfeld's negative critique of the work came after a lengthy compilation of every instance he could dig up of Hirschfeld's injudicious interpretation. Geiger treats Hirschfeld in the course of a paper on the proper historical way of treating the rabbis so as to indicate the commonalities of German and Hebrew intellect. After a word of praise, he dismisses Hirschfeld's work in a phrase, scorning him for "clothing [his argument] in an entirely inappropriate philosophical garment," and in a later footnote anathematizes him: "Hirschfeld not having done this [properly] thereby directly caused his book to miss the 'wissenschaftliches Moment' [the present call for science]."[115] Stigmatizing Hirschfeld for not being a historian had the effect of excluding his work from the consideration of serious Jewish scholars. That may explain why I was unable to find any review of his second, 1847 volume, the one on aggadic exegesis, or, initially, even a copy of it in two of our most extensive North American Jewish libraries.[116]

Hirschfeld was undeterred by this early criticism, as his continuing pursuit of his philosophic plan indicates. He probably persisted in this course because, as his physician said in a memoir concerning him, "Of course, he was a Hegelian, as were all philosophically inclined young people of that period."[117] He simply had a different idea of what the time required and made his philosophic loyalties clear by making the initial words of each of his titles "Der Geist der ... ," "The Spirit of ... ," for first the halakhic and then the aggadic exegesis of the Bible. The term *Geist*, which lies at the heart of Hegelian thinking, may here be understood to mean something like the collective human mentality in its dynamic emergence. Spirit is more than logical thinking, for it encompasses every aspect of human consciousness at its best. Moreover, Absolute Spirit progressively unfolds itself through history, so even the keenest individual reasoning is not purely personal but reflects a complex human inheritance. Hirschfeld wanted to demonstrate how *Geist* had made itself manifest in the two classical Jewish forms of ratiocination, *halakhah* and *aggadah*. Thus, though he regularly speaks of the importance of *Wissenschaft*, "science," and of *Geschichte*, "history," he proposed manifesting these intellectual desiderata through a Hegelian historical-rational interpretation of these Talmudic modes of thinking.[118]

Cultural reasons probably led him to focus his treatment of *halakhah* and *aggadah* in terms of their exegesis of the Bible, since in his staunchly Lutheran environment this was the central religious concern. (It must be noted, however, that both his volumes extend beyond exegesis and the literature specified in their titles.) Moreover, since the German ethos was also highly prejudiced against Judaism and featured polemics against its legalism and lack of love, Hirschfeld's effort to show how universal *Geist* manifested itself in rabbinic thinking likely added to his agenda.

Hirschfeld's 1847 book does not lend itself to concise exposition. That is partially due to its verbosity and length—546 pages (though small in size), organized into two major sections, namely, aggadic exegesis in general and aggadic exegesis (in practice). The first section has three divisions—three, two, and three chapters, respectively—and the whole (including the introduction and overviews for each chapter) contains 100 titled subsections ("ss." in citation). The second section has four divisions—five, five, three, and two chapters, respectively—and the whole, including overviews to each division, contains 138 titled subsections. It does not help in utilizing the volume that the contents pages give only the major headings and subsection numbers but not the pages on which they begin. However, the greater barrier placed before today's reader is the deductive approach of its Hegelian argument, which, contrary to the inductive approach the modern reader in this field takes for granted, expounds the theory first and then shows how the details of practice instantiate it.

Before saying more about that, fairness requires the comment that the very Hegelianism that placed this stumbling block in the present-day reader's path is also the source of the book's amazing breadth and the author's remarkable insight. He writes from an encompassing perspective—so rare in recent times—one that enables him to recognize that *aggadah* and *halakhah* are two parts of one discourse, a familial closeness that makes it imperative to sort out the differences between them. He does this searchingly and with great sensitivity in the first seven subsections of the introduction to the book. Bialik's justly famed essay on this topic half a century later is clearly more artistic in insight and execution, but substantively he says little that Hirschfeld, whom he undoubtedly did not know, had not long before pointed to. There is hardly an issue touched upon in contemporary studies of *aggadah* (feminist approaches being the notable exception) which Hirschfeld did not treat a century and a half ago, often in a manner foreshadowing our contemporary interest.

To return now to the deductive program of the book: its manner of argument is made plain by his refusal to provide a relatively brief announcement of his thesis and then a speedy passage to the bulk of the work, an analysis of the relevant data that finally climaxes by demonstrating how it cumulatively validates the book's thesis. It seems that Hirschfeld will satisfy this expectation, for he announces already in subsection 3, "Halakhic and Aggadic Exegesis: The Difference, Poesy and Prose," what will later be his summary insight that *aggadah* is

Geist in its Hebraic aesthetic mode. But what follows then is not the textual proof for that assertion; instead, he spends the entire first half of the book on "aggadic exegesis in general," a transition whose first division is a section on "the Idea and the *Geist* of the *Aggadah*." It is not a historical-textual approach most of us are comfortable with today, but it lends its own depth to Hirschfeld's argument. Thus, his Hegelian sense of the historicity of *Geist* leads him to devote the first three subsections of the overview to this first section of the book to the relation of aggadic exegesis to biblical prophecy's experience of proclaiming God's will to the people. This then allows him to explicate, in his own terminology, the passage from firsthand to secondhand interpretive teaching, that is, from God's direct revelation to what is, at its core, commentary.

Moreover, this Hegelian drive for comprehensiveness leads Hirschfeld to a comparativist approach to exegesis. In the second major section of the book, when he finally examines the data on exegesis, he devotes the first of its three divisions to hermeneutic, by which he means other, nonrabbinic, interpretations of the Bible. Here he first studies how *Geist* manifests itself in the Jewish exegesis seen in translation-paraphrases like the Targums, the Septuagint, and the Peshitta. He then moves on to the allegoristic interpretations of Philo, to the Apocrypha, and to other Greco-Judaic works. And then he considers the interpretive practice of other religions—for example, in paganism in general and Egypt in particular, in Gnosticism (to which he relates the *Zohar*, some of whose exegesis he considers ancient), and in the New Testament and various church fathers. As impressive as that is, it is in the second and third chapters of the next division of this section, that on Pharisaic commentary, that I find the culmination of his study insofar as it relates to our investigation here of NHD as a whole.[119] It is to this material that I now turn.

The prelude to his examination of the accepted forms of rabbinic exegesis discusses whether there are rules to the work as the book, *Midrash Agur, or The Thirty-two Middot of R. Eliezer*, suggests. He rejects this notion,[120] notes that there were certain aggadic traditions (p. 323), that Zunz had already indicated that there was "*midrash*" in the Pentateuch (p. 324 n. 3), and that various terms give testimony to these traditions (p. 325); but he concludes that the work ascribed to R. Eliezer really is a takeoff on rules employed in halakhic exegesis but not a realistic description of how aggadic exegesis was to be done (p. 326). This is the first of many observations that, in due course, compel him

Positively, What Is *Aggadah*? 173

to inquire about what restricts the freedom of aggadic exegesis. He picks up the (rabbinic and) Zunzian hint and discusses how the imaginative activity of *aggadah* is the offspring of the Bible's own evocation of fantasy in its sense of wonders, miracles, myths, and legends. (He will later, pp. 350–53, add to these examples the Bible's own exaggeration, irony, pithiness, mysteriousness, and such.) Here *Geist* presents itself as poesy, giving aggadic exegesis its special color and tone, and even its content (pp. 341–44). One can also point to certain axioms that ground this work: the biblical text is holy, and hence accurate and full of meanings; thus, what derives from it is also holy. Moreover, no other people has any revelation like it, hence it is the only statement of knowledge one needs (pp. 346–49).

Having prepared us for the limits of any general observations, he begins the work of examining rabbinic exegetic practice with a discussion of how grammar often is the basis of rabbinic interpretation, only to observe that it is precisely the ungrammatical reading that is made the basis of a teaching (pp. 353–55). This leads to his conclusion, "Thus, grammar does not limit the *aggadah*'s exegetic activity" (pp. 355–56). The same is true of lexicography, where faithfulness to the meaning of words is also often subverted by splitting a word, reading it as one of its homonyms or making a pun on it, substituting other words for it, or reading it as a term from another language (pp. 356–62). He concludes, "The principles by which all these derivations and other explanations of words are considered authoritative, do not permit themselves to be specified and designated; they lie in the *Geist* of the *Aggadah*. The way is given and one follows it without self consciousness . . ." (p. 362). The same may be said of the use of etymologies as the basis of rabbinic exegesis, whereby the ambiguities of Hebrew words and the imprecision of its grammar work to increase the range of interpretation (p. 362f.). Similarly, the punctuation of the text, its division into verses, its separation of words, and the order of letters in a given word do not restrict the exegete when he chooses to go in another direction (pp. 363–67). We find the rabbis using sound plays, substitutions (*temurah*), letter look-alikes, ciphers, number substitution (*gematria*), or acronyms (*notarikon*), all in radical distinction from halakhic exegesis, which shows great respect for the biblical text (pp. 367–74). Here, in aggadic exegesis, one must recognize the importance of aesthetic considerations, which can be triggered by even a slight hint in the text (p. 376). This amplification of aggadic freedom leads back to the discussion of rules for the process and a considerations of several patterns suggested in rabbinic texts (pp. 380–82) as well as, once again, the "measures" in R. Eliezer's list (pp. 382–90). But the conclusion is unavoidable: "The 32 rules ... have no real place in the *aggadah*, or at the least a very rare application.... Bringing them together does give us some insight into the method of aggadic exegesis and characterizes its direction for us" (p. 390).

While the next few pages (subsections 173–74) continue in this vein, the inexorable progress of this exposition of aggadic freedom leads on to a climactic subsection, 175. There Hirschfeld seeks to provide his understanding of the rationality behind this system. He contends that while there were certain rules and practices to aggadic exegesis, ultimately it was individual genius that determined what led to exceptional interpretations, and each of the over two hundred rabbis mentioned in these books had his personal effect on the whole (pp. 397–98). Which word in a sentence will be seized upon for aggadic instruction has no rule, but "The hint will be where it wills to be" (p. 399). What then controls "such an eccentric method that it does not go far afield and ... turn the text against the *Geist* of the whole ... ?" In part, the sense of the text does that, but it is clear that most of the usual rules for the simple sense of the text do not hold (ibid., p. 401). While in theory "one might make anything out of anything.... There had to be something vital, winning, capturing, pleasing, witty, meaningful, substantial and contentful which called forth the characteristic and individual talent, whose origin cannot be described[,] for it arises as a free creation of poesy which, by the power of *Geist*[,] creates out of nothingness" (p. 402). Put in other terms, "Truth and poesy accompany the living activity which comes to attention in aggadic enlightenment." Thus, the heart of aggadic exegesis is allowing *Geist* to seek truth, to express itself poetically in response to life, to find a basis for all this in the biblical text, and to give it midrashic form (p. 403).

Hirschfeld continues his discussion for another hundred-and-twenty-plus pages, some reaching out to other aspects of midrashic activity, some returning to matters he has previously treated, but after subsection 175 he says nothing new about the fundamental issues of aggadic creativity. He does not need to, for his accomplishment in this work, for all its faults, is extraordinary. It is regrettable that for over a century the Jewish scholarly establishment insisted that only history, critically and philologically pursued, was the proper way of studying classical Jewish texts, and thus it obscured Hirschfeld's achievement. Most of us not being Hegelians, there will be limits to how far we can follow him. But how he envisioned rabbinic thought in its entirety, and the attention he gave to *aggadah* as well as *halakhah* should evoke the admiration of all who bring even a slight philosophical interest to their study to Judaism.

Philosophical Constructions of *Aggadah* (2): Max Kadushin, the Innovative Theorist

Almost a century after Hirschfeld's initial volume, the scholar-rabbi Max Kadushin published the first of several books creatively explicating rabbinic discourse in American terms.[121] Like Hirschfeld, Kadushin wished to explain the "logic" guiding a literature that Western sensibilities deprecated as incoherent, and whose intellectual content had been poorly served by the twentieth-century scholars who sought to set it forth.[122] This strong apologetic intent may perhaps explain why Hirschfeld had devoted separate major works to *halakhah* and later *aggadah*, while Kadushin concentrated on what unified rabbinic thought as a whole and only occasionally focused on why the rabbis utilized two related but different modes of discourse for expressing what Jewish belief meant and demanded of them.[123] We must therefore first sketch in Kadushin's understanding of the general structure of rabbinic thinking before turning to his specific interpretation of the *aggadah*.

To appreciate Kadushin's innovative approach to and uncommon descriptive language for the abstract factors structuring rabbinic teaching, we need to keep his stated purpose in mind. "Our work may well be characterized as a psychological study of rabbinic Judaism. Such a study, however, cannot be based on the studies already made in the field of religious psychology. The phenomena of Rabbinic Judaism call for an entirely different approach."[124] By identifying his work as "psychology" he apparently wanted to qualify his work as near-scientific, that is, unlike the inward kind of speculation practiced by philosophers. He claimed to base his theories on observation, perhaps of the sort that allows those doing therapy to speak of general patterns they see underlying an individual's self-understanding, the theoretical discipline called metapsychology. As it were, Kadushin sought to provide a "meta" level to rabbinic thinking. Moreover, following the practice of sophisticated researchers generally, he wished to adapt a method utilized in other humanistic fields to the peculiar nature of the phenomena he sought to analyze, in his case the axial era of a community's discourse. This led him to break radically with his predecessors' presumption that one must seek to explicate the nature of rabbinic thinking in linear terms (Euclidean geometry long serving as the ideal structure for Western rationality). Instead, he famously argued that this group's discourse was best understood by analogy to organic[125] structuring, that is, as "an entity whose parts cannot be understood except by reference to their contribution to the whole entity."[126]

Kadushin identified the fundamental principles of rabbinic thinking with value-concepts as distinguished from cognitive-concepts.[127] Whereas the latter are primarily denotative, value-concepts are primarily connotative—that is, incapable of precise definition, known best in the living usage of a community, and thus dynamically expanding and contracting their implications over time. Unlike cognitive-concepts, value-concepts have a "drive to actualization," the special property that, when one accepts them, one feels urged to express them in one's behavior.[128] Kadushin claims four such value-concepts lie at the heart of all rabbinic thought— God's justice, God's love, Torah, and Israel— each one generating many subsidiary concepts. Many statements of rabbinic thought reflect the actualization of only one or several of these or their satellite concepts, while some statements bring all four root themes into full play.

While it is this embracing vision that drives most of Kadushin's work, he does, from time to time, discuss the way in which value-concepts are differently expressed in halakhic and in aggadic teaching.[129] While both forms manifest the drive to actualization, the *halakhah* seeks to concretize value-concepts in the actions of every day life; it therefore tends to specificity and precision,[130] making it the more important rabbinic mode of value actualization.[131] Despite this, the rabbis had a positive attitude toward the *aggadah*, as indicated by their numerous statements proclaiming the need to acquire this great sector of Torah learning.[132] Its special function was to make the value-concepts as vivid to ordinary people as were the cognitive concepts that lay behind community discourse. The *aggadah* served to bolster and invigorate this aspect of the everyday speech of the folk. The primary means of achieving this—and the basis for Kadushin's understanding of its linguistic function—was the sermons and lectures that, as the great compendia of aggadic literature testify, the rabbis took every opportunity to give. This practice linked the rabbis and the folk closely together by virtue of their sharing these common values.[133] Popular instruction being its function, one understands why the aggadic mode of Torah teaching, though part of God's oral revelation, employs commonplace devices such as parables, folktales, maxims, and the like to convey its deeply significant message.

Kadushin does not point to the *aggadah*'s vivifying function to explain its surprising freedom of expression and near license in exegetic activity, though he might well have found some justification for it there. He does, however, contrast aggadic exegetic liberality with halakhic sobriety in textual interpretation. Whereas the early *halakhah* is derived by patterns that can be described by a tradition of hermeneutic rules, Kadushin denies that the *aggadah* is at all shaped this way. Whereas halakhic texts are respectful of the *pshat* (the straightforward meaning of a text) and thus their halakhic *derash* (their interpretation of it) is normally quite circumspect, the aggadic texts glory in freeing the *derash* from the *pshat*, and providing ever-new readings of even familiar texts.[134] While the fourfold value affirmations of both modes of discourse necessarily engender a certain diversity of opinion in each style, this is radically more pronounced in the *aggadah* than in the *halakhah*.[135] This aggadic proclivity to openness becomes most evident in its glorifying the process of giving new and different interpretations to a given text, in contrast to the firm halakhic rule that a given text may be utilized by a rabbi to validate only one halakhic injunction.[136]

Kadushin contends that there is a further literary-logical difference between halakhic and aggadic dicta. The former have an implicit nexus, an internal interconnectedness with other halakhic statements, allowing them to be categorized and thus seen in their class significance. True, this is only somewhat visible in the Mishnaic period, but it comes into fuller view in the various Talmudic analyses of given laws.[137] By contrast, aggadic statements are all independent units, without any internal agglomerative intent. Were it not for the imposition of certain literary forms, the larger units of aggadic teaching would not have come into being.[138] This is a further factor making for the openness we associate with aggadic utterance and is the foundation of its inhospitality to hierarchical rankings of its various statements.

Kadushin's understanding of rabbinic thought met with less antipathy than that of Hirschfeld, but while it remains of some interest as an approach to rabbinic theology, it has no place in the contemporary study of *midrash* and *aggadah* and no academic followers.[139] For our purposes, Kadushin's work on the *aggadah* deals with only part of the more embracing domain of NHD. Nonetheless, by insisting on asking the philosophic question about this uncommon intellectuality, by seeking a fresh hermeneutic to do justice to its uncommon character, and by daring to break with the notion that rational explanation was necessarily linear, he remains a significant model for anyone interested in understanding the intellectual aspect of rabbinic discourse.

Chapter 8

∽ Reconstruing
the *Aggadah* Problem ∾

Though we have already learned much about various aspects of aggadic discourse, we can, I believe, gain greater insight into its nature as a whole by modifying our current understanding of it in three related ways. First, we need to rethink the status and stringency of the accepted definition of *aggadah*. Second, we require a more complex reality than we have hitherto utilized to serve as the analogic base for conceptualizing this non-Hellenic universe of discourse. Third, each rabbi's thought was shaped by and contributed to the special religious ethos of the elitist scholarly community that dominated his life. This involved an intense devotion to the inherited religious tradition that the rabbis understood God to have initiated at Sinai in the twin forms of Written and Oral Torah. Thus, their individual expressions of belief need to be parsed in terms of the many-valued logic created by the rabbis' simultaneous foundational commitment to God-Torah-Israel (and, to a much lesser extent, the individual rabbi's participation in that relationship). Let me explain each of these proposals in turn.

Three Insights into NHD, (1): Deconstructing the Definition

The classic Jewish definition of *aggadah* as NHD has been utilized so long and so widely that one simply assumes that it has an ancient rabbinic basis. But, as we have noted, when one seeks to find its origin in early rabbinic literature one cannot.[1] Only in the post-Gaonic era, the second millenium CE, do we find this definition set forth in a significant rabbinic treatise. Appropriately enough, it is given to us in the series of definitions which open the *Introduction to the Talmud* of

Samuel the Nagid, a text of such high regard later that it was regularly published as an appendix to printings of the Talmud from the nineteenth century on. Until recently most scholars have assumed that the author was the famous poet-statesman Samuel the Nagid, who lived in Spain in the latter half of the tenth century and the first half of the eleventh. Recent scholarship has, however, accepted the claim of a seventeenth-century Egyptian halakhist who identified the author as "Samuel ibn Ḥananiah Hanagid, the head of the *yeshivah* in Egypt," who lived more than a century later than the more famous Spaniard of the same name and similar position.[2] Yet even this Samuel's definition is not as logically decisive as the commonly utilized later one.

> And [the term] *haggadah* [refers to] every interpretation given in the Talmud on any matter which is not *mitzvah*; that is *haggadah* and you are not required to accept its teaching except as it seems sensible to you. And you should know that everything the Sages established as *halakhah* in a matter of *mitzvah* [*beinyan mitzvah*] is from the mouth of Moses our Rabbi who received it from the mouth of God. You are not permitted to add to it or to subtract from it. However, textual interpretations of an individual in terms of what occurs to them or they imagined, what seems sensible in such textual interpretations one accepts and to the rest one does not grant authority.[3]

At least three ambiguities arise from this paragraph. In the second part of the statement, he seems to equate *haggadah* with textual interpretation, thereby leaving out all that aspect of NHD which is not exegetic. Moreover, while he identifies *halakhah* with the Sinaitic revelation, he does not do the same for *aggadah*, despite Talmudic testimony to that effect (perhaps because, like many moderns, he has difficulty in associating God's revelation with a conditionally authoritative realm of discourse). Most surprising, however, is that he does not contrast *haggadah* to *halakhah*, as we would expect, but to the more inclusive and ambiguous term, *mitzvah*. In the Talmud *mitzvah* is used not only to refer to a commanded action but also to one that, while meritorious, is not necessarily required.[4] Curiously enough, in his opening paragraph Samuel does refer to Talmudic material that is "not *halakhah*," but that unique usage is not in reference to aggadic discourse. Rather, he uses it in explaining why Judah the Nasi included matters in the Mishnah that are not *halakhah*—namely, that he and other rabbis had been taught these legal opinions by their teachers and now continue that tradition, so the Talmud includes matters that are *halakhah* and non-*halakhah*, that is, statements that are not what the sages consider the authoritative law.[5] That Samuel's definition was not quickly accorded authoritative status is circumstantially attested by the fact that at the Disputation of Barcelona in 1263, Nahmanides, who sought to rebut the binding authority of aggadic statements in the Talmud, did not cite Samuel's treatise with its statements to that effect. The history of how "*aggadah* is that which is not *mitzvah*" became "*aggadah* is that which is not *halakhah*" remains to be written.

This ongoing communal indecision about the nature of *aggadah* should not be surprising when we recall the indeterminate results of our efforts in chapter 1 to determine what the word *aggadah* (in its several forms) meant in the Talmud and related documents. Insofar as one can say anything positive and yet inclusive about the Talmudic sense of the term, then, it was a body of learning of the Oral Torah that a scholar had to know, one that had some indefinite relation to Bible meanings and interpretation, one that often functioned in public, popular discourse and had special appeal there, but, though it was highly praised by some sages, others disparaged it.[6] Even with an expansive interpretation, this broad statement fails to encompass the diverse and often surprising material that our intensive study of NHD turned up. How did the Bible-focused rabbinic realm of *aggadah* become the conglomerate NHD?

To understand this development best, I think we must think as pragmatists who believe that creative rationality follows rather than precedes human action. A problem in current activity engenders an intellectual problem—e.g., Kuhn's "cognitive dissonance"—leading, if all goes well, to a new understanding of things. Applied to conversation, that means that new second-level, abstract "rules" about the discourse arise from the effort to bring greater clarity and less perplexity to the operation of a grammatical/syntactical system that has previously served people reasonably well. In the case of rabbinic discourse, I can venture a surmise as to the stages by which *aggadah* evolved into NHD. To begin with, the lists in the Talmud and related works in which the term does and doesn't occur indicate that *aggadah* was then only one of a number of imprecisely denominated bodies of study-teaching materials of the Oral Torah but clearly not yet NHD. However, already then one finds a budding consciousness of the need for stated guidance concerning appropriate and inappropriate procedures in rabbinic discourse. Mostly this occurs as Talmudic statements seeking to delimit what should not be done. For example, there are several *en lemedin* rules. These deal with impermissible types of argument or deduction. Specifically, they say that "one does not learn [derive authoritative dicta from] . . . [various bodies of material, including the *aggadah*]."[7] But at this stage such sayings do not yet appear to function as a community consensus but only as the valued observations of certain masters. In the Gaonic period (when authority began to be institutionalized) we find a significant number of statements from the leading authorities delimiting the authority of aggadic utterances, but just what their character was or how authoritative the Gaonic statements actually were is not clear. It seems reasonable to speculate that this rising consciousness of the need for guidance with regard to the *aggadah* is connected with a similar increase of Gaonic generalization about proper halakhic procedures, probably in response to sectarian or philosophical challenges. Then, some centuries later, this evolved into the kind of statement claiming general acceptance that we find in Samuel the Nagid's *Introduction to the Talmud*. The last stage involved transforming "not *mitzvah*" into "not *halakhah*" and having this statement of things become axiomatic in Jewish writing-thinking. When that happened, it was assumed that, like all good Jewish teaching, it was an early rabbinic tradition, even though no one could explicitly find it there.

It should be noted that there have always been objectors to this definition with its implication that aggadic discourse, for all that it is Oral Torah but not mandatory, is thereby an inferior form of divine revelation. While protagonists of the need to accept aggadic teaching as one does the halakhic have been few, their cause has been indirectly bolstered by the many commentators on the Talmud who have struggled mightily to make its aggadic portions more literally compelling. Nonetheless, *aggadah* as NHD has become our accepted usage despite the secondary status it assigns to this much-beloved mode of discourse.

This view of the emergence of the present definition suggests the special manner in which it should be utilized. It clearly does not have the formality required of a definition in logic, that is, one that conforms to the logical law of the excluded middle, whereby statements must be either *a* or non-*a*. We cannot be that precise about "*aggadah* is what is not *halakhah*," for neither of its Hebrew terms can be defined with any precision, and even what is included in the "not" is murky. Nonetheless, despite its Euclidean imprecision, thinking of rabbinic discourse this way made sense to its practitioners, to the community that learned from them, and to the scholarly community that applied its special standards to studying aspects of this material. In sum, despite its phrasing like a logical pronouncement—all that x which is not y—our definition is more precisely seen as an effective community convention, one that generations have found enables them to deal well with the agglomeration of materials that surround the heart of rabbinic teaching, the *halakhah*. The closest, then, that our investigation allows us to come to a positive definition of *aggadah* is something like: it is our community "rule of thumb" for the statements in the Talmud and other rabbinic works that are commended but optional.

Three Insights into NHD, (2): Network as Paradigm

The historical record explains something of the odd nature of NHD: it just evolved that way. But if this development resulted from a complex interaction between scholars and the community as a whole, it cannot have been altogether mindless, though it was likely more semiconscious than openly thought through. On some level, it must have made sense to have the term *aggadah* mean NHD, though that meant forcing the glories and the irritants of the discourse to have equal claim on the term. But what could that sense have been? The question arises from a cross-cultural cognitive dissonance felt in Western culture—which drives our sense-making inquiry—because it does not possess similarly honored kinds of intellection. Thus, following the preferred Hellenic model, we try to convert *aggadah*-as-NHD into a linear structure of thinking. But as we have seen with the various genre patterns studied in the previous chapter, they clash too badly with one another to produce a reasonably intelligible whole by Western cultural standards.

Max Kadushin had the genius to recognize that rabbinic discourse could never properly be explained in the linear terms that most philosophy and science cherished. He therefore sought an explanatory model that did not seek to replicate the wonder of geometry or its inductive counterparts. Rather, following the hints given by other thinkers who recognized the limitations of linearity, he moved to a conceptual model in which the whole is as great a factor in shaping the entity as are its parts. Kadushin found his new paradigm in biology, with its special concern for the organic whole. He then showed how rabbinic thinking—mainly the aggadic but also the halakhic—was organized in organic fashion with the interaction between four master concepts and their many subconcepts generating the dynamics of rabbinic diction.

As far as the *aggadah* is concerned, this model was at its best in explaining the high intellectuality of the rabbis, but beyond that it does not illuminate NHD as a whole. I suggest that we now possess a better, though still quite rough, model to pursue a nonlinear approach to explaining the nature of aggadic discourse—namely, network organization.

In the late 1990s Western science on many fronts reached a new insight into the principles of organization that structure "small worlds" of the most varied kinds.[8] The same structuring patterns describe not only the World Wide Web but also "Hollywood [actors' associations], the metabolic network within the cell, [scholarly] citation networks, economic webs, and the network behind language" so that the study of networking "became important for many scientific fields."[9] "Networks that have grown up under different conditions to meet markedly different needs turn out to be almost identical in their architecture."[10] Particularly since there are many diverse areas that confusingly manifest a certain limited randomness as well as a certain limited orderliness—a description that sounds most applicable to NHD—the further investigation of the common structuring patterns for such "small worlds" is proceeding avidly.

To be sure, it is quite a jump from the ties among things or persons to those among ideas and thoughts, the realm of NHD. No one has yet studied whether the intellectual notions of thinkers who operate in a common fashion function as a network that demonstrates the mathematical patterns that scientists have discerned so widely elsewhere. The difficulties in the way of such research are daunting—for example, how do we determine the precise contents of a given idea? or what constitutes a proper connection between one idea and another? Nonetheless, if we remember that the common Jewish understanding of *aggadah* as NHD is a loose but workable one, that "most theoretical studies of real phenomena are studies of approximations,"[11] and that a certain measure of aggadic license would not seem inappropriate in describing aggadic discourse as a whole, let us see what clearer insight into NHD we may gain by thinking of it by analogy to a network. Barabasi appears to approve of such extrapolation when he says, "One of the most fascinating aspects of the birth of a new science is the new language it creates, allowing us to casually converse about ideas and issues we were struggling to describe before."[12] Let us then see what thinking of NHD by analogy to common network structure might help us see.

Networks are not hierarchical or otherwise centrally organized.[13] They manage to function as wholes without these common features of many other organized entities. NHD is, for a major instrument of religious expression, spectacularly free of institutional, theological, literary, or other instruments of constraint, and that is one reason it is normally seen as a chaotic realm. Despite this uncommon holism, one that embraces even statements by its practitioners that drew strong criticism from their colleagues, it functions well as a means for communicating, analyzing, and refining religious insights.

Networks have an uncommonly tolerant variety of organization, one neither featuring what its constituent elements have in common (totalizing them) nor glorying in their difference from one another (their distinctiveness). Rather, they operate with a remarkably democratic structure that allows difference and sameness to exist in harmony. So many odd opinions, methods, and points of view pop up in NHD that most scholars have abandoned hope of positively characterizing what unifies it in its wealth of difference, and prefer instead to deal with one or another of its individual styles.

One cannot usually ascertain the nature of a network merely from understanding its parts particularly, because as wholes they often manifest a character quite different from that of their constituent parts.[14] Similarly, there is a long record of learned wonder that the *aggadah*, with its odds and ends of folk medicine, intemperate comments by sages about their students or colleagues, tales so wondrous that they caused even rabbinic eyebrows to be raised, and other such curiosities, is the accepted medium for explicit theoretical Jewish discourse about the most significant Jewish religious beliefs and musings. Yet there is a counterbalancing record of Jewish satisfaction with NHD in this role, perhaps because thanks to the triumph of the whole over the parts, it allowed for the creation of new modes of aggadic expression, such as works of philosophical, mystic, or other nonlegal content.

With no node or group of nodes as the organizing basis of the network as a whole, the failure of a single part, or even of a large part of the whole, will not necessarily cause the network to fail. Thus one great virtue of a network's special pattern of organization is that, after trauma, the remaining sectors often are able to take over the functions of the defunct nodes. Through the ages there have been parts of NHD that have disturbed caring Jews. Yet once we think of aggadic discourse in network terms, it becomes a major value of its uncommon form of unity that one can disregard parts of the received aggadic tradition without having to give up the system as a whole with its many deeply appealing teachings.[15]

Networks are not brought into being by identity of outlook or content, but by the linkage of the nodes regardless of their diversity. If anything, this hospitality to individuality makes possible their exceptional flexibility and their capacity for unexpected outcomes. In NHD, acceptance of individuality rises to the level of extraordinary tolerance (some would say encouragement) of contradictory and clashing opinion, and that not only between contesting sages but occasionally even between the traditions connected with a single rabbi. Yet it is just such openness that has provided the flexibility that has enabled Jewish thinking to meet the challenges that history has continually thrown up.

Networks are not static realities that are established at a given time and that remain the same, or basically the same with some modest changes. Rather, the linkage form of network organization provides a continual opening for new nodes to join the network and for the possibility of new links being established between previously unconnected nodes.[16] NHD is notorious for its openness to what might find a place in it. This characteristic, so much the opposite of what we normally think of as organized thinking, opens rabbinic thinking not only to individual forms of expression or concern but also to that ongoing exploration of the spirit that a static form of discourse might well inhibit.

Networks are not impervious to what history or chance might do to them. That is, the exigencies of time may play an important role in their evolution, but while the changes time initiates may be unpredictable, the form the happenstance has induced will be shaped by the universal patterns of network organization.[17] Judaism has been so intimately concerned with faithful survival until the messianic time that one would surely expect that historical change would find a congenial place in its religious thinking and expression. NHD's networklike nature provides just that critical capacity.

Theoreticians posit that growth (and, I take it, a certain decay) is a normal element in network existence. New nodes are continually being added or new links are continually being established.[18] One often has the sense as one reads a lengthy aggadic passage that one has stepped into the middle of an ongoing discussion. And turning the pages of an aggadic work with its regular surprises makes one feel one has momentarily eavesdropped on an ongoing exchange of ideas and impressions. Though the hand of the redactor of these traditions may be evident to the critical reader, the flow of NHD opinion simply includes it as another node in these lively exchanges. Something like this flow of creativity continued from the early rabbinic period until shortly past the first millennium CE. Since that time we have come to NHD, despite our own efforts at aggadic creativity, as inheritors of a tradition whose classical period is past but that evidences the ongoing growth characteristic of a functioning network.

Finally, with all this emphasis on freedom, so characteristic of NHD, it should also be noted that aggadic discourse can function this way because it knows itself to be part of the greater network of Oral Torah that links it closely to the *halakhah* with its special trait of authoritative fixity. Whereas Jewish religious law can find its otherwise unstated foundation (its *Grundnorm*) in the belief adumbrated in the *aggadah*, the latter, in turn, depends upon its unstated links to the *halakhah* to give it the stability and structure it cannot give itself. Thus, in multiple ways, the network paradigm enables the Western mind to grasp more clearly than heretofore how the rabbis thought aggadically.

Three Insights into NHD, (3): Thinking Situationally

How does all this shape the content of an individual rabbi's reflection about Jewish religious belief, the specific area of NHD that primarily concerns me? A vast cultural divide separates the sages' way of thinking from contemporary modes of doing theology and philosophy, a distance that makes creating an interface between them and us notoriously difficult. Thus, the rabbis of the Talmud did not consider doubt an indispensable beginning for serious reflection; they began with the assurance we call faith. They did not think their judgment about the adequacy of ideas the final measure of truth and value; they began as the grateful recipients of God's revelation to their people. They did not want to be philosophers (as they knew them) but believing, practicing students and teachers of the Torah tradition by which their people had lived for over a thousand years. No wonder they showed little concern for self-assertive creativity but expressed their individuality as part of a scholarly guild studying and reflecting on Torah, God's revelation to Israel, and offering leadership to the Jewish people in living out its historical relationship with the one God of the universe. However, to moderns their NHD intellectual practice is quite off-putting in at least two principal respects: their community effort seems more committed to arguing than to reaching a conclusion about the substance of their religion, and their hospitable attitude toward contradiction can be dizzying.

We may hope to create an interface between these diverse perspectives by replacing our predilection to look for understanding through linear explanations with what philosophers today call a many-valued logic. Let us examine a relevant instance of such a shift. Early modern Jewish philosophers envisaged Judaism in terms of the rational idea of God and such derivative concepts (in relation to God) as unity/uniqueness and ethical/holiness as well as (in relation to people) commandment and social responsibility. When they studied or cited early rabbinic literature, they delighted in showing that, underneath all the aggadic gamesmanship, the rabbis were ethical monotheists.

Rather than reading the rabbis as protomoderns, we seek today an insight into the rabbinic mind that is more faithful to what they said they believed. In making this shift we ought not gainsay the scholarly accomplishment of these pioneering master-teachers or the social usefulness of their evocation of the universal teaching of a community long segregated and now under attack for its clannishness. Empathetically projecting ourselves into the rabbinic mind-set (as best we can), ethical monotheism might be seen as a reasonable contemporary statement of the ideal faith of all humankind—that of the Covenant with the Children of Noah—but it is quite inadequate for the complex reality and demands of the Covenant with the Children of Israel. One might perhaps retort that God is clearly the grounding element of this later Covenant faith, since neither the Jewish people nor the Torah can call God into being. Yet, neither biblical nor rabbinic thinkers believed their people learned about God from their own ratiocination; they believed they learned it from the Torah, the divinely revealed account of God's doing with the people of Israel. This divine instruction also taught them—and observation long reinforced—that they alone of all the nations on earth were its recipients. I am proposing that we will understand rabbinic Jewish thinking more adequately if, in our terms, we envision it developing not from a single premise but from several equally primary beliefs—what is meant by a many-valued logic. It may be encapsulated in the complex Talmudic truth that the one and only God gave the Torah to the people of Israel.

The complexity of each of these three fundamental notions deserves some amplification. God, for example, is so far beyond our ability to describe that the multiplication of symbolic terms for God is a major characteristic of rabbinic thought. With God's judgment critical to much rabbinic thinking, it is clear why Kadushin wanted to give this aspect of Divinity special prominence, leading him, so as to avoid the stigma of Judaism-as-legalism, to immediately offset it by equal emphasis on God's mercy. But as halakhic prescription makes plain, it is God's transcendent unity, not God as Judge or Merciful One, that is most critical to rabbinic Judaism. Of course, the incomparable One may now be spoken of as judging or as forgiving, but not ultimately as either—only as the unity in which their apparent contradiction is overcome. So it is theologically preferably and functionally simpler to set aside Kadushin's bifurcated God-talk and to speak in as integral a fashion as possible of God.

In similar fashion, the distinguishing characteristic of the sages' belief about Torah is that it must be understood not only as religious texts (Written Torah) but as the oral traditions and procedures God ordained to accompany and extend them (Oral Torah). And while the people of Israel plainly refers to that ethnic group which is bound by the legendary 613 commandments of the Sinaitic Covenant, it is not the only group with which God has a relationship. Israel's Torah teaches it that God has a Covenant with humankind, the Noachides, who are commanded to fulfill seven commandments, and that it was their collective failure to do this that was the stimulus for God's calling Israel into being. The uncommon style of rabbinic cognition grows from the many-leveled significance of these interrelated primary realities.

In this contemporary aggadic construction of the rabbinic mentality, I am acutely conscious of speaking from the modern side of the interface and reflecting its conviction that meaning is substantially generated by the systemic wholes of language and culture that generate them. The rabbis themselves are largely unconcerned about this issue, apparently because they know God's Torah to be the ground and guarantee of their thinking. We never come across an authoritative, *halakhah*-like rabbinic statement of the comprehensive character of Jewish belief, only aggadic statements of individual opinion (such as mine here); rabbinic Judaism is not a creedal faith. The aggadists overwhelmingly present their thinking in what we would call atomistic fashion, and it is this self-limitation of horizon that, as I see it, leads to the continual contradictoriness that so characterizes rabbinic thought.

We may brashly schematize the lines of thought open to a rabbinic thinker mathematically. At its simplest, there are three, and they stem from the dichotomy basic to the notion of the Covenant: that God, the One of unique perfections, is intimately tied to Israel, a historical, limited, error-prone folk. So an aggadist might frame a given teaching focusing on God's role, or that of the people of Israel, or on their kind of partnering. Let one sage speak of God's omnipresence and another, concerned for God's closeness to Israel, may with equal religious validity emphasize God's localized presence, even God's suffering, with Israel, while a third may seek to show how both are simultaneously true. Again, one teacher may legitimately anathematize those who suggest that another Power exists alongside God, while another, zealous for the close connection between Israel and God, may with equal rabbinic validity daringly assert that, as it were, when Israel does not bear witness to God it diminishes God's reality. Is it God, acting alone, who will bring the Messiah, or the people of Israel by their observance, or some joint action of theirs? And should the theme be one that also concerns Torah or humankind as a whole (often "the nations"), the rabbinically acceptable perspectives multiply accordingly.[19]

By contrast, when one seeks to construe rabbinic theology as a static grid, rabbinic contrariness and inconsistency connote a chaotic, undeveloped mentality. But construed as a many-valued way of thinking, one carried on in faithfulness to their complex belief and within the dynamics of network linkage, a more positive view emerges. In this light, rabbinic religious cognition, rabbinic theology as an integral aspect of NHD, appears as a creative religious response to what the teachers of this faith knew was the best way to verbalize their reflection on their people's uncommon, yet ongoing, involvement with Ultimate Reality. They may be said to have realized that human thought and language in a time after God's direct revelation was necessarily inadequate to the transcendent-yet-significantly-known truth of God's reality and relationship with them. Because the Oral Torah taught them to cherish reason's role in clarifying what God wanted of them, they created a linguistic system with one way for speaking about duty and balanced it with a companion system for speaking of everything else, including belief. In their pairing of *halakhah* and *aggadah* they fashioned a dual-discourse system appropriate to their faith, which was as uncommon in other religions as was the content of their Jewish belief.

∞ Afterwords ∞

Can We Theologize as the Rabbis Did?

In his 1923 essay "Apologetic Thinking," a review-response to books by Max Brod and Leo Baeck, Franz Rosenzweig praised Brod for building his case for Judaism on Talmudic data, treating aggadic passages "seriously, even one might say, halakhically."[1] The comment, for all its self-consciousness, reflects Rosenzweig's insistence in his essay that if one must undertake the apologetic task, it ought to be done with proper emphasis on "the Law" as Judaism's central concern. Ever since that time, it has been the dream of the few who have ventured into the field of Jewish theology to find a way to speak of Jewish faith on the basis of the authority of the *halakhah*. But it remains an unrealized ideal. In the perspective of this investigation it may be said that Jewish theology remains an aggadic enterprise.

Perhaps the best example of this is found in the writing of Rabbi Joseph Baer Soloveitchik. The Rav, as he was respectfully referred to by his host of Orthodox disciples, brought immense halakhic erudition and authority to his abstract papers about Jewish belief. Yet even when it came to as practical an issue as the advisability of interreligious theological dialogue, he presented his case not on the basis of the halakhic considerations but as the necessary consequences of the utter inwardness and ineffability of human faith, surely an aggadic approach to the matter, if a highly subtle and sophisticated one.[2] That his disciples to this day have accepted his teaching as normative says much about the possible practical effects of aggadic teaching, particularly when, as in this case, its cogency is matched by the halakhic stature of the teacher setting it forth.

There is one major difference, however, between the way the rabbis carried on their aggadic discourse and that of the Rav. The Talmudic masters took it for granted that those they were addressing largely shared their religious convictions, and while they might be speaking to a question that had arisen within that faith, their discourse largely bespeaks a world of common belief. Hence their discourse substantially rests on the interpretation of biblical texts or reference to common verities. The Rav's *aggadeta* is initially directed to the many disciples who, of course, believe. But they must reinterpret his thought to the modernized American Jewish community, which has made of even caring Jews believers with reservations, or questions, or doubts. Thus the Rav presents his ideas not as exegesis but as philosophically nuanced formulations that can speak to those whose sense of reality is substantially shaped by the irreverent broader culture in which they live. He seeks, by erudition, penetration, and example, to show how the Torah's truth can speak cogently to every variety of contemporary intellectual yearning. This unique diction (though it, like that of the rabbis, grows from participation in the community of classical Jewish observance and scholarship), gives the claims of Western culture far more prominence in his teaching than the Talmudic sages did.[3] It is this alien aggadic idiom, I surmise, that explains in large part why the Orthodox Far Right holds him in less than the highest esteem.

If the community of the most classically observant and knowledgeable Jews—with its strong claim to an unbroken tradition stretching back to the rabbis—does not see even the Rav's teaching as authentically modeled on the rabbis, their judgment on the host of academics who do not come to their study with his bona fides will be clear. The rabbis of the Talmud did not interpret the Written Torah and Oral Torah in terms of their historical development, their ethical or aesthetic inner concerns, or with a hermeneutic of suspicion, not infrequently growing out of secular or agnostic attitudes toward God and a rejection of even liberalized notions of revelation and Jewish religious duty. We may feel—and I include myself in this group, though as part of its believing, moderately traditionalizing camp—that some or another of these essentially nineteenh-century insights are so true that they must now shape how we see the world and people (and God and Torah, for those of us who are religiously concerned). Of necessity, this stance leads us, in varying ways, to embrace Western academic study methods and reasoning, and, for my minority, how we seek to explain the continuing truth of Jewish belief. This Western/Jewish academic understanding demands that we strive, as best we can, to allow our texts to speak to us in as great a measure of their integrity as our intellectuality allows us to, all the while trying to be conscious of the preconceptions we bring to them. The judgment seems inescapable to me: no, with our altered sense of truth and halakhic practice, we cannot today say we are working out or presenting our *aggadah* pretty much as the rabbis did. We create our Oral Torah with far too much innovation for that, despite all our insistence and argument in defense of the continuity of our teaching.

All that being granted, it is also true—remarkably so, in my eyes—that the contemporary academic effort to express the nature of Jewish belief is carried on in ways that emulate the activity of the Talmudic sages. We know our work to be aggadic, not halakhic, and will take all strong assertions about this or that being a necessary part of Jewish faith as the rhetoric of personal conviction, not the establishment of Jewish dogmatics. We expect any work after the announcement of a new intellectual program to be grounded directly or indirectly on a solid knowledge of classical Jewish texts, one reason many initially promising positions have not gone on to fulfill their promise. We proffer our work for consideration to the diverse community of contemporary Jewish academic sages, generally not expecting (though perhaps dreaming) that in a day of clashing methodologies they will agree with us but hoping that they will find our work instructive enough to be worthy of attention and criticism. And though at present the adulation of radicaler-than-thou intellectual positions has faded, any new stance seeking a place amid the jostle of competing Jewish theologies will be judged in substantial part by its quasi-halakhic consequences: what would this make of Jewish religious practice? and, in part, how is it evidenced in the Jewish life of its protagonist? Though the content of Jewish theologizing has in this growing sector of the Jewish academic community significantly changed from that of the rabbis, much of the form of their theologizing has reasserted itself among us.

Will later generations of learned Jews, the arbiters of such issues in Jewish history, judge this modernized NHD an authentic link in the chain of Jewish tradition? We cannot know, but its protagonists, believing that this new aggadic idiom is their best method for eliciting and expressing God's continuing Torah truth today, will study and speak in this new/old Jewish voice.

On Concluding

Some thirty years ago a student's sudden need for local summer work spurred me to begin the reading and research that turned a peripheral notion of my doctoral studies into an initial bit of scholarly investigation. On and off over the years since, as the press of my primary agenda allowed, the work became, in turn, my *torah lishmah*, my study-for-its-own-sake, then the deep textual ground without which I did not believe Jewish theology ought to be articulated,[4] and finally a writing project that might one day become a book. As I now conclude this long textual love affair, I am mindful of a comment by Shai Agnon. The Israeli Nobelist was ruminating over the custom of medieval Jewish writers to conclude their books with the phrase *tam venishlam* (followed by some expression of thanks to God). The first verb means "finished" or "made whole," but the second verb, related to the noun *shalom*, has the sense of "fulfilled" or "perfected." But, he said, he could not claim to have given full expression to his vision of the book, so he would conclude it *tam aval lo nishlam*, "finished but not perfectly realized." Everyone who writes, I believe, knows that feeling yet also knows that a time comes when a work is *tam* and needs, as the Hebrew idiom for publishing puts it, *latzet le'or*, "to go forth to the light." And in that spirit I say *shalom* to my old study-companion with the medieval formula

תושלב"ע

Tam Venishlam, Shevaḥ Le'el, Bore Olam
Finished and Completed, Praise to God, Creator of the Universe

Notes

The following abbreviations are used in the notes and the bibliography:

AdRN	*Avot de-Rabi Natan*
AJS Review	*Association for Jewish Studies Review*
CCAR Journal	*Central Conference of American Rabbis Journal*
HUCA	*Hebrew Union College Annual*
HTR	*Harvard Theological Review*
JAAR	*Journal of the American Academy of Religion*
JBL	*Journal of Biblical Literature*
JJS	*Journal of Jewish Studies*
JJTP	*Journal of Jewish Thought & Philosophy*
JQR	*Jewish Quarterly Review*
JS	*Jewish Studies*
JSJ	*Journal for the Study of Judaism in the Persian, Hellenistic and Roman Period*
JSQ	*Jewish Studies Quarterly*
LBIYB	*Leo Baeck Institute Year Book*
PAAJR	*Proceedings of the American Academy of Jewish Research*
RSR	*Religious Studies Review*

Introduction to a Religious Puzzle

1. See the recently published volume *Textual Reasonings, Jewish Philosophy and Text Study at the End of the Twentieth Century*, ed. P. Ochs and N. Levene (Grand Rapids, MI: Eerdmans, 2002).

2. I believe it was in the spring of 1957 that I took the course that was taught by the famous John Herman Randall. A firm believer in the power of the human mind and therefore a polemic secularist, he did not much care for my paper. Its survival is due to my happy experience some years after Vatican Council II, when for two summers I taught at the Trinity College Bible Institute.

When Sr. Miriam Ward, who organized and led that program, later wanted to publish a volume honoring ten years of the institute, I found my old paper and, after revision, it was published as "What Knowledge Does Judaism Think It Possesses?" in *Biblical Studies in Contemporary Thought*, ed. Miriam Ward (Burlington, VT: Trinity College Bible Institute, 1975), listed as no. 164 in *A Life in Covenant: The Complete Works of Eugene B. Borowitz, 1944–1999*. A bibliography by Amy W. Helfman (New York: The Ilona Samek Institute of the HUC-JIR, 1999).

3. I had no idea how to go about doing this but made some fumbling efforts to educate myself in the content of rabbinic religious thinking by doing my rabbinic thesis on "The Rabbinic Doctrine of Torah" (1948), and my doctoral dissertation, entitled "Universalism and Particularism in the Tannaitic Midrashim" (Hebrew Union College-Jewish Institute of Religion, 1952).

Chapter 1. What Is the *Aggadah* Problem?

1. Wilhelm Bacher, "The Origin of the Word 'Haggada'," *JQR*, o.s., 4 (1892): 406–29. For a contemporary review of this process and an argument for thinking of *aggadah* in terms of its origins in synagogue lectures, a popular contemporary stance, see Joseph Heinemann, *Aggadot Vetoldotehen* (Jerusalem: Keter, 1974).

2. The procedure is derived from Lev. 5:1 and associated with Dt. 17:9 in *ySan.* 3.9. In a discussion about bills of divorce it is used in relation to authenticating the legal opinion of R. Judah the Nasi, *yGit.* 4.2. Further uses of the term are found in *yShev.* 4.1, *y.San.* 11.3, *Yoma* 74a, *Ket.* 21b, *Shev.* 35a, and *San.* 30b.

3. Three times each in *Pes.* 115b and 116b, with a shift from the Hebrew to the Aramaic in the latter case.

4. Many of the technical terms used in early rabbinic literature have no simple English equivalents and often convey several levels of meaning we think it better to specify separately. They operated with what often seems to us a "fuzzy logic." But our contemporary speech shows similar patterns and we, like the rabbis, assume that familiarity and common usage will communicate our meaning to others. Works like this one are means of bringing Western-trained minds into the circle of rabbinic meanings. In 1933 when Herbert Danby published his monumental English translation of the Mishnah, he thought it desirable, despite his extraordinary accomplishment in translating ancient religio-legal provisions into English, to include an appendix entitled "Glossary of Untranslated Hebrew Terms." In it he listed and sought to define forty-nine terms that would not yield even to his powers of translation. Herbert Danby, *The Mishnah* (London: Oxford University Press, 1933), pp. 793–97.

5. *Y. Ḥag.* 1.8. This idea provides the background for R. Judah the Nasi's interpretation of Ex. 19:8 and 19:9 that Moses first reported the penalties of

not following the laws set for being at Sinai and then, responding to another verb, he revealed the rewards, "words which touch the heart like an *aggadah*" (*Shab.* 87a).

6. *Sifre Dt.* 49 (F 115). There has been some speculation as to who the *Dorshe Haggadah* are, but we do not have much direct evidence to enable us to say anything reliable.

7. *Sifre Dt.* 48 (F 113).

8. *San.* 100a.

9. *Sifre Dt.* 306 (F 339).

10. *Ḥul.* 89a.

11. *Y. Pes.* 5.3. What appears to be another version of this anecdote is found in *Pes.* 62b. There the issue is studying a certain otherwise obscure *Book of Genealogies* (apparently not a halakhic treatise). In this case R. Yoḥanan is finally talked into doing the teaching but when Simlai then insists on completing it in three months, R. Yoḥanan throws a clod at him and berates him by saying, "If Beruriah, who could learn 300 *halakhot* from 300 masters in one day, couldn't fulfill her responsibility in three years [where do you get the nerve] to say [you'll do it] in three months?"

12. *B. K.* 60b.

13. *Sot.* 49a. On this and other matters relative to the laws pertaining to the *aggadah*, see the *Entziklopediah Talmudit* (Jerusalem: Talmudic Encyclopedia Publishing, 1947), 1:60ff. (original pagination), s.v. "aggadah."

14. *M. K.* 21a and 23a.

15. *Taan.* 30a.

16. *Yoma* 75a, where the Torah's comparison of the wilderness manna to the grain *gad* suggests the *aggadah* and its wide appeal. Cf. *Mek. Vayasa* 6 (H 170).

17. *Sifre Dt.* 317 (F 359).

18. *Mek Vayasa* 1 (H 157).

19. *Ḥag.* 3a.

20. *Y. Hor.* 3.4.

21. *B. B.* 9b–10a and cf. 145b.

22. *Lev. R.* 1.2 (M 6).

23. *B. B.* 145b.

24. *Taan.* 7a.

25. *Y. Yev.* 12.6, cf. *Gen. R.* 81.2 (T 969). Here, as in other such stories, the main point is why the otherwise richly competent student couldn't answer. Levi confessed that once he mounted the high platform and was addressed, his spirit became "exalted" and he couldn't answer. For the tribulations of R. Joshua b. Ḥananiah with the questions put to him by the Alexandrians, see note 45, below.

26. *Y. Ket.* 12.3. A similarly subtle put-down of aggadic expertise comes in a comment on Dt. 17:8, "If a matter arises ... which is too difficult for you to judge...." The words "for you" refer to someone competent to make decisions

on matters of the calendar, while the words "a matter" refer to a (mere) *baal aggadah* (*ySan.* 11.3).

27. *PRK* 28.25 (M 223).

28. *Sot.* 40a. In *yHor.* 3.5 R. Samuel b. R. Yose b. R. Bun expounds Prov. 28:11, comparing an aggadist to a master of *talmud*. The latter may come to a city with bars of gold but cannot convert them into ready cash, whereas the one who comes with small change—the aggadist—will readily be able to sustain himself.

29. *PRK* 12.3 (M 205).

30. *San.* 99b.

31. *Y. Hor.* 3.5. The context of this exegesis is a lengthy discussion of aspects of authority and priority in the Written Torah and Oral Torah. While some things may appear settled by the way in which this compilation is arranged, I am left with a sense of how fundamentally undetermined were many of the major issues at stake here. A good example of the problems involved is found in Samuel's dictum, transmitted by R. Zeira, that "We do not 'learn' [required duty] from *halakhot*, nor from *haggadot*, nor from *toseftot*, but from *talmud*" (*yPeah* 2.6 = *yḤag.* 1.8). This is not a direct attack on the *aggadah* but merely its inclusion in a list of Oral Torah sources that should not be the basis of reaching a halakhic determination, including *halakhot* (here apparently understood as something like lists of rules without the dialectic that led to the decision that they were mandatory). A similar instance of the derogation of *aggadah* is found in *tSan.* 7.7, which gives us the sages' rule for priority in their discussions: thus, what was done takes precedence over the hypothetical, *halakhah* takes precedence over *midrash*, *midrash* takes precedence over *haggadah*, and the latter then simply drops out of the continuing discussion of such priorities.

32. Leo Baeck's "Der alte Widerspruch gegen die Haggada," in *Aus drei Jahrtausenden* (Berlin: Schocken Verlag-Juedischer Buchverlag, 1938) treats this topic at a time and in a place that is itself extraordinary. That he had more confidence in the scholar's ability to make this connection of methodological freedom and lack of authority—see ibid., pp. 171–72—is not only a tribute to his scholarship but to his spirit. I am indebted to him in this discussion for his emphasis on R. Zeira's central role on this issue.

33. Yonah Frenkel, *Darkhe Ha-aggadah veha-midrash* ([Israel] Masadah: Yad la-Talmud, c. 1991), pp. 492–95.

34. Raphael Patai, "Ethnohistory and Inner History: The Jewish Case," *JQR* 7, no. 1 (July 1976): 5. We read something similar in Marvin Fox, "The Rav [Joseph B. Soloveitchik] as Maspid [Eulogist]," *Tradition* 30, no. 4 (Summer 1996). Fox comments about the Rabbi Gold who was the subject of Rabbi Soloveitchik's eulogy, "Anyone who has learned in a typical yeshiva is aware that mastery of the aggadic portions of the Talmud was not required. In fact, excessive preoccupation with this material serves to call into question one's seriousness. It is, then, not surprising that Rabbi Gold [who devoted himself

to mastery of the *aggadah*] was not recognized as a member in good standing of the elite fraternity of great and creative Torah scholars." One sees something similar among academic scholars of rabbinics. George Foote Moore can speak of "mere midrash." *Judaism in the First Centuries of the Christian Era: The Age of the Tannaim* (Cambridge, MA: Harvard University Press, 1927), 2:249. H. Freedman, translating the tractate *Zevaḥim* in the Soncino Talmud, 1948, speaks in a note of an interpretation as "merely aggadic," p. 584 n. 4, *The Babylonian Talmud, Seder Kodashim,* ed. I. Epstein. Zevaḥim, tr. H. Freedman (London: The Soncino Press, 1948). W. D. Davies, *Torah in the Messsianic Age and/or the Age to Come* (Philadelphia: Society of Biblical Literature, 1952), p. 86, reminds his readers that he has cited "haggadic passages ... so that they must lack a certain seriousness which more halakic passages would afford"; and, more recently, David Stern, *"Aggadah," in Contemporary Jewish Religious Thought,* ed. Arthur A. Cohen and Paul Mendes-Flohr (New York: Scribner's, 1987), p. 9, says "Although midrash and aggadah have always been considered part of sacred tradition, as part of oral Law, in historical fact the two have been the neglected stepchildren of rabbinic literature, ignored and disparaged in favor of more serious and practical rigors of the halakhah and the Talmud."

35. David Stern, *Midrash and Theory: Ancient Jewish Exegesis and Contemporary Literary Studies* (Evanston, IL: Northwestern University Press, 1996), p. 7. I am grateful to Richard Sarason for clarifying the details of this development.

36. One such discussion is found in *Tem.* 14b.

37. So already the experience of Hermann L. Strack, *Introduction to the Talmud and Midrash,* 5th ed. (Philadelphia: Jewish Publication Society, 1931), p. 90 n. 1. Gunter Stemberger's recent valuable revision of this work says nothing different.

38. In addition to previously mentioned material of this sort, see *yHor.* 3.5, where a master of *talmud* is contrasted to a master of *aggadah*. The halakhic discussion of the laws for teaching on the day following a nocturnal emission is in *yShab.* 1.4, and the brief reference to question asking is in *yNed.* 10.8. I can attach no special significance to the fact that the bulk of this data is found in the Jerusalem Talmud.

39. The *mishnah, talmud,* and *aggadah* lists occur in *yMeg.* 4.1; *Gen R.* 40.7 (T 388) and 66.3 (T 748); *Lev. R.* 9.3 (M 177), 13.5 (M 282), 15.1 (M 322), 21.5 (M 481), and 36.1 (M 839); and *PRK* 12.25 (M 223). The *midrash, halakhot ve-aggadot* lists occur in *Ned.* 4.3, *yShek.* 5.1, *Taan.* 16a, and *Sifre Dt.* 48 (F 113; and see the commentary by Stephen Fraade, *From Tradition to Commentary* [Albany: SUNY Press, 1991], pp. 115–16), and *AdRN B,* 18 (four times), 45 (four times).

40. For example, *San.* 99b, *Ḥul.* 92a, *Sifre Nu.* 112 (F 120), and *Sifre Dt.* 49 (F 115).

41. Louis Finkelstein, "Midrash, Halakhot and Haggadot" (in Hebrew), in *The Jubilee Volume for Isaac Baer,* ed. S. Ettinger et al. (Jerusalem: Israeli Historical Society, 1961). He states the basis of his case on pp. 28–29 and summarizes his argument on pp. 46–47. In the summary, the cogency of his case is under-

cut by the uncommon definitions he assigns to certain key terms. In this account of Finkelstein's position I have not presented what seems to me his untenable assertion that the formula, as he reads it, is simply axiomatic, requiring no substantiation. I have instead presented what to me a more tenable statement of his position. Judah Goldin begins his paper "The Freedom and Restraint of Haggadah," in *Midrash and Literature*, ed. Geoffrey H. Hartman and Sanford Budick (New Haven, CT: Yale University Press, 1986), pp. 59–60, by reiterating the Finkelstein position, but neither refutes the critics of the position nor gives additional substantiation for it.

42. The *mishnah, midrash* lists occur in *Lev. R.* 3.7 (M 74 and note the questionable status of the text) and the remainder in *AdRN* 8, 18 and 40. The *mishnah, talmud* lists occur in *yHag.* 1.8 (plus "even what a veteran student will in the future teach before his master was already said to Moses at Sinai"), *yB. K.* 4.3 (the tale about the Roman officers sent to study Jewish law), *Kid.* 30a, *M. K.* 15a (a halakhic passage permitting various ritually defiled persons to study these areas but not those who had a nocturnal emission), *B. B.* 8a and *Hag.* 14a (both framed in terms of "masters" of these areas), and *Sifre* 306 (F 39, Fraade, *Tradition*, pp. 96–97).

43. *Gen. R.* 16.4 (T 147); *Lev. R.* 22.1 (M 497) and 30.2 (M 692); and *PRK* 27.2 (M 405).

44. *Ber.* 22a, a different version of the *M. K.* 15a passage cited above.

45. *AdRN* 28. An entirely different kind of list of four may be found in the twelve questions that the Alexandrians asked of R. Joshua b Hananiah—three concerning "wisdom," three concerning *aggadah* (about complex biblical texts), three asking impudent questions, and three about proper behavior (*Nid.* 69b and 70a).

46. *Taan.* 30a.

47. *San.* 101a.

48. *AdRN B* 12. There is a question about whether *aggadot* occurred in this text.

49. *Sifre Dt.* 317 (F 359).

50. *B. B.* 134a, cf. *Suk.* 28a. A shortened version is found in *AdRN B* 28.

51. *Y. Meg.* 3.1.

52. *Er.* 54b; *San.* 100b; *B. M.* 33b deals with the conflict over the priority of these studies but limits itself to the two of them; in *Shab.* 120a *mishnah* is paired with *gemara*; in the three lists of *Sot.* 44a the *mishnah gemara* of the initial list is then supplemented in the next two with *maasim tovim* "good deeds"; *tSot* 7.20–21 (Z 309) has two lists, the first containing *mishnah* and *midrash*, the second, *halakhot* and "a good deed," plus "interpret and receive a reward"; *Sifre Dt.* 161 adds *targum* to Bible and "deed" to *mishnah* and *talmud*. Four variant lists without *aggadah* are found in *Ber.* 47b, which calls for serving as a disciple to the sages in addition to knowing Bible and the oral tradition; in *AdRN* 29, which is satisfied with a combination of *midrash* and *halakhot*; in *Sifre Dt.* 58 (F 124), which adds to *mishnah*, "deed," *midrashot*, and

dinim, "laws"; and in *Sifre Dt.* 313, which says that when God revealed the complete Torah at Sinai, that meant that the Israelites then knew how much *midrash, halakhah,* "inferences from minor to major and analogical reasoning," were contained in it.

53. *Y. B. B.* 6.3.
54. *Lev. R.* 18.2 (M 205).
55. *PRK* 3.13 (M 50–51).
56. *PRK* 7.8 (M 129).
57. R. Shimi b. Ukva (others say Mar Ukva) had this role for R. Joshua b. Levi (*Ber.* 10a). Ravina had a disciple doing this (*Yoma* 38b), as did R. Ḥisda (*Er.* 21b, cf. *Suk.* 53a).
58. The varying concerns of certain subcommunities of Jews are noted in *PRK* appendix 2 (M 457) as masters of Bible, of *mishnah,* of *talmud,* of *aggadah,* of *mitzvot,* and of good deeds.
59. *M. K.* 28b, where R. Tarfon warns the colleagues who are going to comfort him in his mourning not to speak too glibly.
60. *B. K.* 54b–55a where, astonishingly, two sages are not certain about the text of the Decalogue.
61. In *yMaas.* 1.2 R. Jonah suggests that perhaps one opinion concerning a biblical verb used in a halakhic discussion might have been learned from such a source, but it is unclear to me whether that would diminish its relevance or not. In *yYev.* 4.2 these masters are invoked to support the derogation of Goliath as having been sired by 100 fathers, a good instance of what we shall later see as the aggadists' affinity for hyperbole. In both instances the term is used anonymously.
62. *Pes.* 114a.
63. *Shab.* 89a.
64. *Shab.* 55b, *Meg.* 15b, *B. B.* 10b, and *Ḥul.* 92a.
65. *Gen. R.* 94.5 (T 1174f.).
66. *Ḥul* 60b.
67. *San.* 57b.
68. *Y. Shab.* 16.1, and see the negative attitude expressed in what follows this story.
69. *Git.* 60b.
70. *Ber.* 23a–b. There is then some question about the desirability of having these aggadic volumes, unlike the merit clearly associated with the rabbinic rule to wear phylacteries.
71. *B. M.* 116a, *B. B.* 52a, and *Shev.* 46b.
72. In collecting the data on R. Samuel b. Naḥman the following conventions were observed: though his father's name is variously given as Naḥman or Naḥmani, all are elided to the former name; no passages in which he reports the words of others, or where his being the source of a statement was questioned, or where he spoke in a halakhic mode were included, but where others reported his words, such passages were included. The four accounts of

his being addressed in this manner are found as follows. R. Simon b. Yehotzedek's inquiry is given in three places: *Gen. R.* 3.4 (T 19–20); *Lev. R.* 31.7 (M 725), and *PRK* 21.5 (M 323); R. Judah the Nasi II's is in *Gen. R.* 12.10 (T 108); R. Ami's is in *Lev. R.* 31.1 (M 714) and *Lam. R.* 1.41; and R. Ḥelbo's is in *Lam. R.* 3.43. There are some slight verbal variations for the repeated stories and an occasional change of literary context.

73. The reply to R. Ḥelbo does not have a culminating text. As we shall see later in our study, the preferred form, the material warranting the lesson, is to give a proof-text.

74. *Gen. R.* 12.10 (T 108).

75. Respectively, *Lev. R.* 31 1 (M 714–15); *Lam. R.* 3.43; and *Gen. R.* 12.10 (T 108).

76. Thus, with regard to the source of creation's light, we have a contrary view that the light came from the Temple at *Gen. R.* 3.4 (T 19–20), *Lev. R.* 31.7 (M 726), and *PRK* 21.5 (M 324). So, with regard to the gates of heaven ever being closed to prayer, R. Anan insists that such a thing never happens and gives biblical proof for his view (*Lam. R.* 3.43).

77. *Shab.* 113b in reference to Ruth 2:14.

78. *Er.* 54b in reference to Prov. 5:19.

79. *Ket.* 50b in reference to Ps. 106:3.

80. *B. B.* 75a in reference to Is. 54:12. Its meaning is still debated. Other such interpretations by R. Samuel b. Naḥman are found in *Ber.* 34b on Is. 64:3; *Ber.* 62b on 1 Chr. 21:15; *Shab.* 55a on Ez. 9:4; *Shab.* 113b on Is. 10:16; *Taan.* 8b on Job 37:6; *Meg.* 10b on Is. 55:13; *Ḥag.* 5b on Jer. 13:7; *B. B.* 16b on Jer. 18:22; *B. B.* 123b on Gen. 30:25; *San.* 96b on Jer. 21:9; and *A. Z.* 24b on the special use of Ps. 93.

81. *Meg.* 14a in reference to 1 Sam. 1:1.

82. *Sot.* 10a in reference to Gen. 38:13 and Jud. 14:1.

83. *San.* 93b in reference to Dan. 1:6.

84. *Taan.* 20a in reference to Dt. 2:25 and Josh. 10:12, a rare aggadic *gezerah shavah*, "argument by verbal analogy," in this material.

85. *Ber.* 63a.

86. *Sot.* 11b.

87. *B. K.* 16b.

88. *Ber.* 63b, the sort of reversal of biblical meaning that, as we saw earlier, caused R. Zeira to belittle aggadic freedom.

89. *Sot.* 12b.

90. *San.* 100a.

91. *Taan.* 8b.

92. *Sot.* 12a–b.

93. *Sot.* 13b.

94. *San.* 22a.

95. *A. Z.* 25a.

96. *B. B.* 123a. A verse is cited before this with reference to Reuben and, in a following passage, in the name of R. Jonathan, R. Samuel b. Naḥman's teacher, it is applied to attest to the merit of Rachel and how Leah stalemated this. But that takes us into issues of the editing of this material that go beyond this study.

97. *Ḥul.* 91a. This opinion is based on the counsel of *A. Z.* 25b to always try to keep a heathen on your right so as to be able to defend yourself against a sudden attack.

98. *Taan.* 27b. As it stands, the explanation is as mysterious as the custom.

99. *Sot.* 22a.

100. *Zev.* 62a.

101. Specifically, there are twenty nonexegetic verse comments plus more passages duplicating some of these. Two deserve special mention: the unusually lengthy and rhetorically disputatious colloquy between R. Samuel b. Naḥman and his disciples (*yBer.* 9.2), and his absolute inversion of the psalmist's humble recognition of his inability to adequately praise God at Ps. 106:2 into praise for the capacity of his disciples and him to pray (*yBer.* 9.1). The latter passage reinforces the problem of the limits of aggadic freedom.

102. There are twelve passages with a climactic verse, plus four others duplicating some of these, and twelve without a verse, plus one duplicate. The substantial number of passages in the latter category reinforces the problem of how *aggadah* shifted from a largely biblical category to one that included every sort of rabbinic utterance that was not *halakhah*.

103. The numerical data is nineteen of eight-one total texts in *Gen. R.* and eight of thirty-nine in *Lev. R*, but only one of eight in *Lam. R.* The specific contexts involved are relevant. *Gen. R.* is more than twice the bulk of *Lev. R.* and is an exegetical *midrash* book covering Genesis, whereas *Lev. R.* is homiletically oriented and interprets selected Leviticus texts primarily by means of other biblical texts. *Lam. R.* is much smaller than even *Lev. R.*, being an exegetical treatment of a biblical book that has only five chapters.

104. *Lam. R.* Proem 24.

105. *Gen. R.* 41.2 (T 400ff.) and *Lev. R.* 11.7 (M 234f., who says this is R. Ishmael). A shorter version of the objection-response device is found in *Lev. R.* 27.6 (M 633f.), where God's harsh interest in bring Israel into debate (over their behavior) is gleefully greeted by the nations, causing God to change His mind and favor Israel. But in each of those cases the nations point out that the favorable texts are ambivalent, a most unusual note of skepticism for the aggadic material we have examined and one barely mitigated by its being voiced by the nations.

106. *Gen. R.* 84.6 (T 1006f.).

107. *Lam. R.* 3.10.

108. *Gen. R.* 9.5 (T 70).

109. *Gen. R.* 81.5 (T 976f.).

110. *Gen. R.* 44.8 (T 431). Another potentially helpful but unsatisfying use of *haggadah* occurs in *tEdu.* 1.14–15. There R. Akiba is reported to have expounded the five matters with which the *mishnah Ed.* 2.9 reports he believed fathers endowed their sons *kemin haggadah*, "in the manner of a *haggadah*." One wonders why this unique comment is introduced, since the passage, for all its occurring in the Mishnah and the Tosefta is, by our standards, nonlegal and therefore aggadic to begin with. If, however, the comment means to call our attention to the fact that R. Akiba and the sages then argue the theme of inherited characteristics by citing and interpreting various biblical texts, that is not so different from occasional other passages in this material (some of it halakhic) where reference is had to diverse biblical texts and their interpretation.

Chapter 2. The Surface Characteristics

1. *Shevuot* seemed to be a fine candidate for investigation, because much of it deals with how people lived then and thus might have been expected to contain many aggadic comments treating of the interplay between law and reality. In fact, this entire tractate yielded as small a proportion of aggadic material as did the least productive chapters in the remainder of the sample.

2. An excellent discussion of this problem is found in E. P. Sanders "Did the Pharisees Have Oral Law?" in *Jewish Law from Jesus to the Mishnah: Five Studies* (London: SCM Press, 1990), esp. pp. 104ff., 117–20.

3. Other such difficulties abound, e.g., while the rationale for a given legal ruling is generally not itself considered binding, one may ask if that is also true of one for not doing something, such as R. Abbahu's teaching concerning why all the poems of Balaam were not included in the daily liturgy (*Ber.* 12b).

4. For example, R. Joshua b. Levi urges his children to be careful about cutting through jugular veins when slaughtering meat, and R. Judah urges people to respect old people who have lost their knowledge of Torah (*Ber.* 8b). I judge this to be aggadic material.

5. In *Ber.* 4b R. Joshua b. Levi says it is a "commandment" to say the Shema, "Hear O Israel," before going to sleep even if one has recited the evening service that contains it. Is he speaking literally or figuratively? Some similarly problematic statements are Abba Benjamin on praying "before" his bed (*Ber.* 5b); the dialogue between R. Isaac and R. Naḥman (*Ber.* 7b); and the two passages in which R. Huna b. Judah cites R. Ammi (*Ber.* 8a).

6. *M. K.* 17a.

7. *San.* 75a.

8. *Er.* 18a–19b.

9. *Ned.* 3.11; *Shev.* 20b; *Ḥul.* 77b; *Nid.* 43a.

10. Thus, the cautionary conclusion to the halakhic incident concerning R. Simeon b. Shetaḥ, *Shev.* 34a. See, too, the comments concerning the punishment of the wicked and of the righteous in *Shev.* 39a–b.

11. Ulla (*Shev.* 36a); and the accounts of Justinia and, later, of the woman who came before R. Akiba (*Nid.* 45a), though these might well be considered in the category of halakhic tales, since they have a legal effect.

12. In *Er.* 18b R. Naḥman explores the implications for the behavior of Adam and Eve of the ruling that a man should never walk behind his wife. In *Shev.* 35b R. Joshua provides an exegesis to support his view of God's providence, the underlying ground for his dispute with R. Eliezer concerning the sanctity of the names of God given in the story of Gibeah of Benjamin (Ju. 20:18–28).

13. *Ned.* 22a–b.

14. Halakhically, R. Ḥisda supplies some imaginative exegesis to explain the ruling on oaths of Rabbi (Judah the Nasi) and R. Simeon b. Elazar (*Nid.* 45b). Aggadically, R. Abba twice provides verse bases, in the latter instance giving a fine lesson (*Ned.* 22a); R. Yoḥanan explains the name of the archangel Michael (*Ber.* 4b); and Mar Zutra provides the full scriptural basis of R. Isaac's teaching about the protection offered by bedtime prayers (*Ber.* 5a). In the latter two cases, the extension of the aggadic teaching hoped to clear up an ambiguity in the preceding exegesis.

15. *Ḥul.* 68b, 71a, 77a; *Nid.* 46b.

16. A discussion on a specific case of what may be done with an injured animal yields the comment, "The Torah does not squander the money of the Jewish people" (*Ḥul.* 77a).

17. The area of a building's court educes a reference to a royal court and then another to Isaiah being in Hezekiah's inner court and finally an inquiry as to his purpose there (*Er.* 26a). So, too, a discussion of the number of watches in a night produces a citation from the Psalms, which introduces a lengthy aggadic passage discussing King David's sleep habits as they affected his religious diligence (*Ber.* 3b).

18. *Ned.* 22a, beginning with R. Samuel b. Naḥman's citation of R. Jonathan.

19. *Shev.* 18b, R. Ḥiyya b. Abba citing R. Yoḥanan twice. Here the same verses are utilized, and in each case another teacher's exegesis is offered, again utilizing the same texts. In *Shev.* 47b, however, two teachings of Simeon b. Tarfon are given that have no textual or thematic relation to each other. On *Ned.* 32a–b, five statements of R. Ammi b. Abba occur in a row. The third and fifth of these are not thematically related, while the others deal with aspects of the Abraham story. The second, third, and fourth are hermeneutically related, all utilizing *gematria* and thus providing a numerical basis for the interpretation. This device can supply much of the structure of lengthy aggadic passages, as we shall see below in the discussion of *Ber.* 4b–8b, the largest continuous aggadic passage in the sample.

20. Twice R. Isaac's citation of a verse to make his point results in another sage's linking the same verse to a different one and ultimately to R. Yoḥanan's rejection of the last one given as too childishly simple, thus eliciting his own preferred verse and exegesis (*Ber.* 5a).

21. In *Er.* 19a, a discussion of punishment leads to a mention of Gehenna, and thence to statements concerning its operation, the location of its entries, its names, and, finally, its location. Were this a continual feature of Talmudic *aggadah*, its thematic study would be far simpler than it is, for while such excursuses do appear, they are exceptions to the customary intellectual fragmentariness of the discourse.

22. All the reservations about method mentioned earlier in this chapter should be kept in mind when evaluating these judgments. In addition, special problems arose when trying to determine whether passages closely linked in theme but without the citation of the text in subsequent comments were isolated ones—that is, complete though nontextual units—or ones that relied on the verse though not specifying it (as is often done).

23. Further difficulties beset these judgments. Where an unnamed "voice" seemed to be citing a tradition it knew, I deemed such a passage anonymous, though the tradition was given in the name of a sage. Where I thought that such an introduction might as likely have come from the person named, I counted the passage with those that were named.

24. Thus, following the comment of R. Yoḥanan in *Ber.* 4a. An associated phenomenon is the use of "and it is also written" as an introduction to Ps. 55:19 after the statement of R. Yoḥanan in the name of R. Simeon b. Yoḥai at the beginning of *Ber.* 8a. A similar sort of difficulty occurs when a second authority makes a pronouncement obviously dependent upon a verse mentioned in a prior teacher's dictum but not mentioned in his own statement. The two statements are now closely integrated but appear to have been independent teachings. Thus, R. Ḥisda's comment following that of R. Aḥa b. R. Ḥanina (*Ber.* 8a).

25. See the comment on Ps. 119:47 (*Ber.* 3b); the material following Abba Benjamin's statement on *Ber.* 5b; and that of R. Ḥelbo citing R. Huna (*Ber.* 6b). And does the discussion between R. Aḥa b. Rava and R. Ashi extend to the second exchange, or is that the addition of another teacher (*Ber.* 6a–b)?

26. The material following R. Yoḥanan citing R. Yose on Ps. 56:7 is a good case in point. His exegesis is followed by questions and answers concerning it, some passages with the citation of other texts, others without such expansion, direct challenges, or the introduction of other material, even a story and the statement of conflicting opinions (*Ber.* 7a).

27. *Ḥul.* 76b identifies Arioch as Samuel.

28. R. Naḥman (*Er.* 18b), and, slightly more developed, R. Jeremiah b. Elazar there. So, too, the ethical treatment of a verse on leprosy at Lev. 13:45 (*Ḥul.* 78a). Clause by clause, R. Kahana (*Er.* 19a); R. Ammi b. Abba (*Ned.* 32b).

29. The story of Justinia is presented briefly (*Nid.* 45a). At greater length we hear accounts of R. Akiba in prison (*Er.* 21b), and of R. Yoḥanan's visit to the ill R. Elazar (*Ber.* 5b). Both tales are largely dialogue with little action indeed. An apparently constructed dialogue, explaining why Moses said just what he did at Dt. 29:13, becomes quite lengthy (*Shev.* 29a).

30. R. Ḥisda responds to R. Simeon's challenge by citing Resh Lakish (*Nid.* 45b).

31. *Shev.* 39b.

32. Rav and Samuel on Gen. 2:22 (*Er.* 18a).

33. This occurs quite frequently, e.g., *Ber.* 5a (Rava), 7a (R. Yoḥanan citing R. Yose), 10a (R. Yoḥanan citing R. Simeon); *Ned.* 32b (R. Zechariah relying on R. Ishmael); and *Shev.* 18b (R.Yoḥanan citing R. Simeon, followed by three items that utilize the same exegetic form).

34. The textual basis for differing positions may be sought (*Ned.* 22a and *Shev.* 15b). An exchange may lead to the citation of a verse (*Shev.* 6b [Rava]); or a rejection of another position may lead to exegesis and interpretation (*Ned.* 31b–32a [R. Yose opposing R. Joshua b. Karḥa]); or unsuitable interpretations are proposed and rejected, leading to the one the rabbi approves of (*Er.* 21a [R. Ḥisda citing Mari b. Mar]); or the passage probes the implications of the verse used by one master in the system of another who has taken a differing stand (*Er.* 18a [see the complicated exegesis that follows the initial interpretation of Gen. 2:22]).

35. Surprise will be evident in a number of aggadic passages yet to be considered in this chapter. For some further examples, see the data adduced below. In this vein, R. Yoḥanan utilizes three statements with a progression between them to make his point (*Er.* 18b), and note the wordplay involved; R. Jeremiah b. Elazar creates a threefold emphasis to drive home the difference of our relationship to God (*Er.* 19a); David, Job, and Ezekiel all failed to explain Ps. 119:96, but Zechariah finally did, according to R. Ḥisda's citation of Mari b. Mar (*Er.* 21a); R. Levi b. Ḥama gives four increasingly powerful strategies to use against the Evil Urge (*Ber.* 5a).

36. *Ber.* 5b.

37. The somewhat extended story of R. Akiba in prison stresses his obedience to the stated will of his colleagues (*Er.* 21b). In the account of R. Meir and the bandits, he not only learns proper behavior toward sinners but is instructed by a woman, his wife, Beruriah (*Ber.* 10a). R. Huna not only accepts the gentle reproof of his colleagues and amends his behavior (toward a tenant farmer) but is then rewarded by having his sour wine become valuable (*Ber.* 5b). In the case of R. Joshua, who had sought to curse a vexatious Sadducee, the moralizing is explicit: "From this we learn that it is not proper to act this way" (*Ber.* 7a).

38. *Ber.* 5b. The wonders extend to the natural area, as when we hear of a serpent that ate thirteen hides filled with straw (*Shev.* 29b; cf. *Ned.* 25a). They may extend to what we would call the supernatural area, as when Elijah comes (from heaven) and engages a sinner in conversation, finally killing him (*Ber.* 6b).

39. *Ber.* 5b, and note the retrojection there, for not only is David described as acting like an ideal rabbinic scholar, but his counselors naturally consult with the Sanhedrin.

40. Though the story of Justinia is short, it creates and then relieves its inner tension (*Nid.* 45a).

41. R. Zeira teaches God's generosity (*Ber.* 5a); R. Simeon b. Pazzi, God's unique creativity (*Ber.* 10a); and though the term *mashal* is not directly used by R. Jeremiah b. Elazar, his argument about comparative human-human and human-divine relationships misses only the term to be clearly a parable (*Er.* 19a).

42. This emerges most clearly when one scholar makes a personal, derogatory reference to another one during an exchange—hardly the sort of material that those who passed on the tradition would be likely to place into the mouth of a sage. See the discussion in the next chapter on this aspect of aggadic discourse.

43. The dialogue between R. Akiba and the woman who had intercourse as an infant, followed by the exchange with the students, seems shaped by the hands of tradents despite its disclosing an apparent blunder of R. Akiba, for that is immediately explained (*Nid.* 45a). The inventiveness of the rabbis is most evident when they report long, private conversations between biblical characters, as in the passage following R. Hamnuna's exegesis (*Ber.* 10a–b). The stories of the sages reported above feature more talk than action, and all seem more formulated than direct accounts.

44. In the Mishnah, *Ned.* 3.11, the opprobrium and glory of circumcision are demonstrated entirely by contrast. Not infrequently the rabbis will specify what is a better course of conduct: so the school of R. Ishmael on atonement (*Shev.* 14a). Or we are told what people prefer: bringing an offering to being beaten (*Shev.* 37a). Note how Rava's contrast between the prescriptions of the sages and those of the Torah raises the issue of their importance precisely because they are not part of the Written Torah (*Er.* 21b).

45. Resh Lakish (*Er.* 19a). Here one of the classic hermeneutic rules is explicitly utilized. In the *aggadah* of the sample I did not find these rules utilized.

46. "Bitter as olive, sweet as honey" (*Er.* 18b). The *mashal* form occurs frequently with or without the term: R. Joseph (*Ber.* 13a); R. Simeon (*Ber.* 7b); R. Akiba (*Nid.* 45a). The haste of the Hebrews to leave Egypt, despite the gains that might come from the despoiling of the Egyptians, is nicely caught in a parable of a prisoner who does not want to wait for a reward but only wants freedom (*Ber.* 9b).

47. Almost every page of the Talmud yields examples: *Ber.* 7b–8a; *Er.* 18a and 21a; *Ned.* 22b; *Shev.* 35b.

48. R. Jeremiah b. Elazar easily puts words into Noah's dove's mouth and then draws a human lesson from the animal (*Er.* 18b).

49. Abba Benjamin describes prayer as a written petition that can be torn up (*Ber.* 5b).

50. Rava, expounding S. S. 7:14 (*Er.* 21b); the woman describing infant intercourse to R. Akiba (*Nid.* 45a).

51. "If you steal from a thief, you have a taste of it" (*Ber.* 5b); "Pray for peace even to the last clod of earth [thrown on your grave]" (*Ber.* 8a); "Of a camel, [even] the ear [is valuable—and thus a tiny part of anything valuable]" (*Shev.* 11b).

52. *Er.* 18a.

53. R. Simeon b. Pazzi (*Er.* 18a). We shall see further examples in chapter 5.

54. R. Yoḥanan uses "Behind a . . . but not behind a . . ." three times, with mounting intensity, to make his point about where one ought not walk (*Er.* 18b). "An utterance the mouth can't say, the ear can't hear" (*Shev.* 20b). We find the rare instance of two paragraphs being linked this way, with contrasting parallel formulations—"I am not a dog that I . . . ," "I am not a king that I . . . ,"— in *Ned.* 24a. Sometimes the artfulness is the redactor's, as in the sevenfold list of statements, "The merit of the . . . is in the . . . " (*Ber.* 6b). Both the statements of R. Akiba and R. Gamaliel in *Ber.* 8b exhibit this verbal parallelism.

55. We find two such statements side by side in *Shev.* 47b: "Touch the oily and be oily," and "A king's servant is like a king." "The righteous promise little, do much" (*Ned.* 21b).

56. The *shekhinah* is variously proved to be present with ten, three, or two persons, or even one (*Ber.* 6a); "Hezekiah did six things, of three they approved, of three they did not . . ." (*Ber.* 10b); R. Akiba and R. Gamaliel both introduce teachings with "For three things I like . . ." (*Ber.* 8b).

57. *Ber.* 7b.

58. *Ber.* 7a.

59. R. Ammi and R. Assi (*Ber.* 6b); *Er.* 19a, where the logic assumes that a Jew who had intercourse with an idolatress would have had surgery to hide his circumcision.

60. Abaye (*Ber.* 6b).

61. *Ber.* 5a. Note that another dictum of R. Isaac on this theme occurs shortly thereafter without the "as if," though it is equally imaginative.

62. *Ber.* 6b.

63. *Ber.* 8a.

64. *Ned.* 32a.

65. *Ber.* 4a.

66. *Er.* 21b.

67. *Er.* 21b.

68. *Er.* 19a. In a somewhat similar vein is the statement of Ulla cited by R. Ḥiyya b. Ammi that, since the destruction of the Temple, God has nothing in this world but the "four cubits of the *halakhah*" (*Ber.* 8a).

69. *Ber.* 6b.

70. *Ber.* 6a. The language used here, and often when the rabbis wish to stress the point they are making, involves a blanket negative and an exception: no/ never . . . but/except. I do not recall ever having come across one that could be taken literally. Hence this form, ʾ*en* . . . ʾ*ela*, may be taken as a signal of hyperbolic usage.

71. *Ber.* 5b.
72. *Ber.* 6b.
73. *Ber.* 10b.
74. *Ber.* 6b.
75. *Ber.* 12b.
76. *Er.* 19a.
77. *Er.* 21a.
78. *Er.* 21b–22a.
79. *Er.* 18b.
80. *Er.* 21b.
81. *Er.* 22a.
82. *Er.* 21b.
83. *Er.* 21b.
84. *Ber.* 4b.
85. *Er.* 18b.
86. *Er.* 18b.
87. *Er.* 18b.
88. *Ber.* 4b.
89. *Ber.* 4b.
90. *Er.* 18b.

Chapter 3. The Substantive Concerns

1. *Ber.* 3a.
2. *Ber.* 7a.
3. *Ber.* 3b.
4. *Ber.* 7a.
5. *Er.* 18a.
6. *Ned.* 32a.
7. *Ber.* 5a.
8. *Ber.* 9b.
9. *Ned.* 32a.
10. *Ned.* 32a.
11. *Ber.* 4b.
12. *Er.* 21b.
13. The first three teachings he derives from Psalm 82 and the last one from Mal. 3:16 (*Ber.* 6a).
14. *Ned.* 32b.
15. *Ber.* 7a.
16. *Ber.* 9b.
17. *Ber.* 7a.
18. *Shev.* 35b as one of many, many examples that could be cited.
19. *Ned.* 22a.

20. *Er.* 22a.
21. *Shev.* 18b.
22. *Ber.* 5b.
23. *Ber.* 8a.
24. *Ber.* 5b.
25. *Ned.* 31b.
26. E.g., *Ber.* 6b.
27. *Ber.* 5a–b.
28. *Ber.* 8a–b.
29. *Ber.* 9b, and note the realistic rejoinder that is explained away by a piety that cannot abide the contrary experience.
30. *Ber.* 5a.
31. *Ber.* 7b.
32. *Ber.* 6b.
33. *Ber.* 4b. The idea is a mainstay of rabbinic thinking and a continually recurring theme in their negative as well as their positive preaching.
34. *Ber.* 5a.
35. *Shev.* 39b.
36. *Shev.* 8a.
37. *Ned.* 32a.
38. *Ber.* 5b.
39. *Ned.* 31b.
40. *Shev.* 8a.
41. *Er.* 21b. R. Papa's comment is not only hyperbolic, but also probably refers to an eschatological punishment in Gehinnom.
42. *Ned.* 32a. The rabbis frequently take this quite literally, seeking verbal similarity (in biblical texts, to be sure) between the sin and the punishment.
43. *Ber.* 4a.
44. *Ber.* 6b, 8a.
45. *Ber.* 6b.
46. *Ber.* 8b. One typical form of the warning is "Be careful of . . ."
47. *Er.* 18b.
48. *Ned.* 22a, where idolatry is used as the comparison. In *Ber.* 7b the results of an act are said to be worse than the wars of Gog and Magog.
49. *Er.* 18b, *am haaretz*, which may roughly be translated as "peasant" but whose connotations of ignorance and impiety are a high insult in Talmudic and post-Talmudic literature; cf. *Ber.* 6b where "wicked one" is so used, and *Ber.* 8a, which speaks of an "evil neighbor."
50. In *Ber.* 8b R. Papa's act does not lead to trouble, but only because of his foresight in avoiding the proscribed act. An angel comes to execute a sinner in the story in *Ber.* 6b.
51. *Ber.* 5b.
52. *Ber.* 8a.
53. *Er.* 21b.

54. *Er.* 18b, *Ber.* 10a, and so quite frequently.

55. *Er.* 21b, a statement that is too much for Rava, who proceeds to give another interpretation.

56. *Er.* 22a.

57. *Ber.* 7a.

58. *Er.* 19a.

59. *Shev.* 39a.

60. *Ned.* 32a.

61. *Ber.* 7b.

62. *Ber.* 5a. This page and the following provide a number of references to this theme.

63. *Ber.* 5b.

64. *Ber.* 7b.

65. *Ber.* 8b.

66. *Er.* 19a.

67. *Ber.* 5a.

68. *Er.* 21b.

69. *Ber.* 5a.

70. *Ber.* 8a.

71. *Ned.* 22b.

72. *Ber.* 5a.

73. *Ber.* 8a, but this, like so many other aggadic generalizations, regardless of their sweeping language, is not universally valid. The rabbis never see empirical data refuting biblical data, but they often are sufficiently impressed with the disparity suggested that they reinterpret what seems to be the plain sense of the biblical text to accommodate the facts learned elsewhere.

74. *Er.* 21b.

75. *Ber.* 7a.

76. *Ber.* 9b.

77. *Ber.* 4a.

78. *Ber.* 3b.

79. *Er.* 21b.

80. *Er.* 21b.

81. *Er.* 18b.

82. *Er.* 21b. R. Ḥisda is here reporting the words of Mar Ukba.

83. *Nid.* 41a and *Ḥul.* 77a. These statements occur in the course of halakhic discussions and are used to reach halakhic conclusions. They provide good illustrations of the difficulty of categorizing statements that, though they require action, are themselves not specifications of religious duty but may, or may not, be accepted as applicable in a given halakhic dispute.

84. Yitshak Heinemann, *Darkhe Ha-agadah*, 2nd ed. (Jerusalem: Magnes Press, 1955).

85. *Er.* 18a, and note how the difference of opinion between Rav and Samuel as to the bodily part from which Eve was created gives rise to an unusually lengthy series of aggadic comments on their implications.

86. *Ned.* 32a–b.
87. *Ned.* 32b.
88. *Ber.* 7b.
89. *Ned.* 32a.
90. *Ber.* 13a.
91. *Ned.* 32a.
92. *Ber.* 13a.
93. *Ber.* 7b.
94. *Ber.* 7a in the context of a discussion about God's anger.
95. So Ulla (*Shev.* 36a).
96. *Er.* 18b, where there is some defense of Manoah lest the proof that implicates him be extended to Elkanah and Elisha. A rebuttal of this is given, and R. Ashi notes that he did not even have the sense of Rebecca and her damsels as described in Gen. 24:61.
97. *Ber.* 12b.
98. *Ber.* 10a.
99. *Ber.* 7b.
100. *Er.* 21b.
101. *Ber.* 9b.
102. *Ber.* 4b.
103. *Ber.* 10b.
104. *Ber.* 10b, but this passage precedes the prior citations.
105. *Ber.* 4a.
106. *Ber.* 8a.
107. *Ber.* 8a. The first view precedes Ulla's statement; the latter two follow it. The passage continues with some extraordinary examples of the disciples' willingness to endure poverty—and impose it on their families—so that they might study.
108. *Ber.* 8a. Note the admiring comment that if this is how he acted in old age with its frailty, one can imagine how much more zealous he was in his youth with its vigor.
109. *Ber.* 7a.
110. *Ber.* 6a.
111. *Shev.* 41b.
112. *Er.* 21b–22a.
113. *Ber.* 4a.
114. *Ned.* 32a.
115. *Ned.* 32b.
116. *Ber.* 5a.
117. *Ber.* 12b.
118. *Er.* 26a.
119. *Er.* 22a.
120. *Er.* 18b.
121. *Ber.* 5a.
122. *Er.* 21b–22a.

123. *Ber.* 4a.
124. *Ber.* 5b.
125. *Er.* 18b.
126. *Er.* 21b.
127. *Shev.* 36b.
128. *Shev.* 26a. Ben Azzai was reported to be sad that he did not study with R. Ishmael when he heard the proper interpretation of a given text from one of his students (*Ḥul.* 71a).
129. *Er.* 21b.
130. *Shev.* 11b.
131. *Ber.* 9a.
132. *Ḥul.* 68b.
133. *Ḥul.* 77a.
134. *Shev.* 7a.
135. *Ber.* 5a.
136. *Shev.* 6b.
137. *Shev.* 10b.
138. *Er.* 25b.
139. *Shev.* 18b.
140. *Ber.* 5a.
141. *Ber.* 6b.
142. *Ber.* 5b.
143. *Ber.* 5b.
144. *Ber.* 8a.
145. *Ber.* 5b.
146. *Ber.* 6b.
147. *Ber.* 9b.
148. *Ber.* 5b.
149. *Ber.* 5b.
150. *Ber.* 7a.
151. *Ber.* 8a.
152. *Ber.* 7b.
153. *Ber.* 10b.
154. *Ned.* 23a.
155. *Ber.* 6b.
156. *Ber.* 8a.
157. *Ber.* 8a.
158. *Ber.* 6b.
159. *Ber.* 6b.
160. *Ber.* 8a.
161. *Ber.* 10b.
162. *Ḥul.* 78a.
163. *Ber.* 6b. R. Ḥelbo in the name of R. Huna, followed by R. Elazar, R. Abba b. Kahana, and R. Simeon b. Azzai, all of whom vie to see who can more grandly make this point.

164. *Ber.* 5b, cf. 6a.
165. *Shev.* 15a.
166. *Ned.* 22b.
167. *Ned.* 21b.
168. *Shev.* 47b.
169. *Ber.* 7a.
170. *Ber.* 7b. This is part of an extended passage on anger.
171. *Ber.* 7a.
172. *Ber.* 10b.
173. *Shev.* 35b.
174. *Er.* 18b.
175. *Ber.* 6b.
176. *Ber.* 10a–b.
177. *Ber.* 10a–b.
178. *Ned.* 24a.
179. *Ned.* 22a.
180. *Ned.* 22a–b.
181. *Ned.* 32a.
182. *Er.* 18b.
183. *Ber.* 10a–b.
184. *Ber.* 12b.
185. *Ber.* 7a.
186. *Shev.* 39a–b.
187. *Ned.* 32a.
188. *Er.* 19a.
189. *Shev.* 6b.
190. *Ber.* 8b.
191. *Er.* 18b.
192. *Er.* 22a.
193. *Shev.* 18b.
194. *Er.* 18b.
195. *Ned.* 32b.
196. *Er.* 18b.
197. *Nid.* 45b.
198. *Ber.* 10b.
199. *Ned.* 32a.
200. *Ber.* 10a. For syntactical reasons, I have rearranged the order of the characteristics; I did not think its original form would sufficiently convey its message in the context of our discussion.
201. *Ned.* 26b.
202. *Shev.* 18b.
203. *Nid.* 44b. Note the analogy to a lizard tail, indicating not only the rabbis' occasional attention to empirical evidence but also their sense of the continuity of human beings with the rest of the animals God created.
204. *Ber.* 7b.

205. *Ber.* 6b.
206. *Ber.* 10a.
207. *Ber.* 7b.
208. *Ned.* 24a.
209. *Er.* 18b.
210. *Ber.* 6b.
211. *Ber.* 5b.
212. *Er.* 21b.
213. *Ber.* 6b.
214. *Ned.* 32b, where several passages deal with this general theme.
215. *Ber.* 5a.
216. *Ber.* 5a and note the delightful metaphors that form the basis of this creative exegesis.
217. *Ber.* 5a. He epitomizes much of the rabbinic attitude in this statement. Note that in the previously cited passage, it is "wisdom"—which for the rabbis is Torah—that delivers the imperiled city from its attackers.
218. *Ber.* 7a.
219. *Ḥul.* 76b.
220. *Ḥul.* 77b.
221. *Ned.* 25a.
222. *Shev.* 29b.
223. This story is duplicated in the sources cited in the two preceding notes.
224. *Ned.* 26b.
225. *Ḥul.* 78a.
226. *Shev.* 23a.
227. *Ber.* 10a–b.
228. *Ber.* 3b.
229. *Ber.* 10b.
230. *Er.* 18b.
231. *Er.* 24b.
232. *Nid.* 47b.
233. *Ned.* 25a.
234. *Ber.* 5b.
235. *Ned.* 32a.
236. *Ned.* 32a.
237. *Ned.* 32a.
238. *Er.* 18b.
239. *Er.* 18b.
240. *Ber.* 6a.
241. *Er.* 26a.
242. *Ber.* 4b. Elsewhere in aggadic literature we hear of ministering angels.
243. *Ber.* 6b.

244. *Ber.* 13a.
245. *Ber.* 12b.
246. *Er.* 19a.
247. *Er.* 21a–b.
248. *Er.* 19a.
249. *Ber.* 4a.
250. *Nid.* 34a.
251. *Nid.* 45a.
252. *Er.* 18b.
253. *Er.* 19a.
254. *Ber.* 8b, where R. Gamaliel is describing Persians.
255. *Er.* 21b.
256. *Shev.* 6b, and note the disdain with which R. Papa treats Rava for being so naive about gentile politics.

Chapter 4. The "Logic"

1. Though the Mishnah (whose text is the basis of the dialectic analysis that fills the Talmud) is imprecisely thought of as a legal compendium, our sample contains a *mishnah* (*Ned.* 3.11) that is not only aggadic but exemplifies the variety of appeals that can be applied to a single theme (in this case, circumcision): R. Elazar b. Azariah said, "Repulsive is the foreskin, for that is what the wicked are called, as it is written, 'For all the nations are uncircumcised.' " (A textual appeal with heavy rhetorical overtones.) R. Ishmael said, "Great is circumcision since thirteen covenants were made by it." (Inference from presumed biblical knowledge.) R. Yose said, "Great is circumcision for it takes precedence over the Sabbath and its severity." (Inference from law.) R. Joshua b. Korḥa said, "Great is circumcision, for Moses's [punishment in neglecting it] was not suspended for a single hour." (Biblical example with hyperbole.) R. Nehemiah said, "Great is circumcision, for it takes precedence over [the laws of] leprosy." (Inference from law.) Rabbi said, "Great is circumcision, for despite all the commandments that Abraham fulfilled he was not called whole until he circumcised himself, as it is written, 'Walk before Me and be whole.' " Another comment: "Great is circumcision, since, but for it, the Holy One, blessed be He, would not have created the universe, as it is written, 'But for my covenant by day and night, I would not have set the ordinances of heaven and earth.' " (Hyperbolic inference from an interpreted biblical verse.) See Jer. 9:26 for the first comment. Herbert Danby gives a succinct commentary on the various statements, in *The Mishnah* (London: Oxford University Press, 1933), p. 268.

2. The two common terms used to introduce a proof-text indicate their purpose. The Hebrew one is *shene-emar*; the Aramaic one is *kidikhtiv*. Both mean "as it is written," implying that there is something about this writing

that commands attention and action. The rabbinic view of the simple meaning of the text is far broader than ours, and attempts to characterize it have not proved generally satisfying; a current favorite is "contextual." For an illustration of the problem, note the intent of R. Ḥisda's rebuke to his disciple (*Er.* 21b).

My citation practice here, as often in this volume, is to give a very limited number of examples, though many more could be adduced, since most aggadic passages illustrate many different matters worthy of comment. I have tried to compensate for this parsimony of citation by otherwise citing widely from the sample to indicate how the aggadic mode functions in various legal contexts. I trust that the reader who examines the various texts will recognize how, taken together, they provide cumulative evidence of points modestly annotated elsewhere.

3. R. Ḥaggai carefully interpreting the dual form (*Er.* 22a). Somewhat more loosely, R. Yoḥanan on Is. 6:6 and Dan. 10:13 (*Ber.* 4b). Beruriah famously instructs her husband, the great R. Meir, on the proper reading of Ps. 104:35 which requires him to change his practice with regard to the brigands that troubled him (*Ber.* 10a). Rabbi is challenged for reading *lo'* as if it were a possessive and not the negative "no," though an anonymous voice turns that into another message (*Ned.* 32a).

4. Resh Lakish on Is. 66:24 (*Er.* 19a).

5. R. Jeremiah b. Elazar (*Er.* 18a).

6. *Ber.* 3b, *Ber.* 4b, *Ned.* 3.11, and so quite frequently, enabling one verse to serve as the commentary on another.

7. Though something is added to the texts that we might not see, note how simply R. Ishmael, according to R. Zechariah, reads the Genesis 14 story of Melchizedek and Abraham (*Ned.* 32b). When R. Aḥa b. Ulla reads Eccl. 12:12 and changes its meaning, Rava objects (*Ned.* 21b).

8. R. Ḥelbo citing Hos. 6:3 to prove his point (*Ber.* 6b), and so often, as at *Ber.* 7a and *Ber.* 8a.

9. Rava cites Dan. 7:23 to substantiate governmental hierarchy (*Shev.* 6b).

10. R. Judah in Rav's name (*Ned.* 32a), and, since this is quite a common thing, see also *Shev.* 18b, *Ḥul.* 78a, *Nid.* 45b.

11. Job 3:17 is adduced as a parallel to Dt. 23:23 (*Ned.* 22a).

12. Ps. 37:8, Is. 27:4, and Dt. 9:19 expand the strange tale of the circumcision of Moses's sons (*Ned.* 32a). For another example, see *Ḥul.* 78a.

13. R. Yoḥanan, citing R. Yose's use of Is. 56:7 to this effect (*Ber.* 7a).

14. R. Yoḥanan, citing R. Simeon b. Yoḥai's contrast of Ps. 2:1 to Ps. 3:1–2 (*Ber.* 7b).

15. Rabin b. R. Adda, citing R. Isaac, who answers his own questions with proof-texts loosely connected to his topics (*Ber.* 6a). The practice is widespread; so *Er.* 18a.

16. *Ber.* 7b and *Ber.* 12a. The rabbis often indicate this procedure by the word *veod*, "and more."

17. Note how the several biblical interpretations on *Er.* 21b cannot leave the text to stand as it is.

18. Particularly for the halakhic use of these modes of reading, see David Weiss Halivni, *Peshat and Derash: Plain and Applied Meaning in Rabbinic Exegesis* (New York: Oxford University Press, 1991). In his appendix 2, pp. 161–62 one will find a brief, insightful statement about *aggadah*.

19. In our sample, the term is used to offer two other versions of Rabbi's teaching on circumcision (*Ned.* 32a), and on *Er.* 18a in relation to R. Ḥisda's reading of Gen. 2:22. In that case, the preceding discussion of Rav and Samuel over the creation of woman is an exercise in amplification of a text, though without the use of this term. A term of similar import, though generally used to supply other views of a topic or versions of a teaching, rather than additional textual comments, is *ika deʾamri*, "others say" (*Er.* 18a and a number of times elsewhere in our sample).

20. In three different passages on *Ber.* 7b and previously on folios 3a and 4b.

21. For example, the two *yud*s used in the verb of Gen. 2:7 to describe the fashioning of Adam lead R. Simeon b. Pazzi to a comment about the conflicted nature of humans (*Er.* 18a).

22. The verb of Job 5:7 can be linked to that of Prov. 23:5, perhaps by their somewhat similar sounds, to infer that Torah study on one's bed dispels demons (*Ber.* 5a), but it is very much a stretch for a Western reader.

23. *Shev.* 9a for the strange spelling, and *Ber.* 4a, where the dots over *lule* are instructive.

24. Ex. 15:16 poetically says "pass over" twice; hence, one was Mosaic and the other under Ezra (*Ber.* 4a). So, too, Elijah's "Hear me, O Lord, hear me" (1 K. 18:37) produces two meanings (*Ber.* 9b).

25. Ps. 104:35 has "sinners" and then the "wicked," which indicates another event (*Ber.* 9b).

26. "Baca" in Ps. 84:7 sounds too much like the word for weeping not to yield a teaching (*Er.* 19a), and so, too, the exegesis of the names "Kereti" and "Peleti," as well as "Mephiboshet" and "Kileab" later at *Ber.* 4a, as well as "Ruth" at *Ber.* 7b.

27. R. Ammi b. Abba says the shift from Abram to Abraham showed he got mastery over five additional body organs, those related to temptation (*Ned.* 32b).

28. So Ps. 84:7 becomes a warning to transgressors (*Er.* 19a), and see the treatment of Lev. 19:15 at *Shev.* 30a. The concrete becomes abstract, as when the law of the salting of sacrifices (Lev. 2:13) becomes a teaching about the efficacy of sufferings (*Ber.* 5a).

29. The passions of Is. 27:4 and Dt. 9:19 become named angels at *Ned.* 32a, and a poetic figure is turned into a description of the human psyche at *Ned.* 32b.

30. There are numerous such exchanges at *Ber.* 10b. Rava turns the love song of S. S. 7:12f. into a dialog with God (*Er.* 21b).

31. R. Yose b. R. Ḥanina reads 2 K. 4:27 in such a way that Gehazi's effort to push away the Shunamite woman, *lehodfah*, is understood as split and transformed into *hod yofyah*, "the glory of her beauty," a euphemism for her breasts, thus making him a contrast to his holy master, Elijah (*Ber.* 10b).

32. R. Judah b. Menasiah and then R. Simeon b. Pazzi read two verbs in altered form to get two teachings about God (*Ber.* 10b).

33. *Shev.* 47b.

34. R. Illa turns the condemnation of the wicked of Dt. 7:10 into a theodicy for the righteous (*Er.* 22a). Gen. 14:14, which is about arming servants, is understood as Abraham forcing scholars into his household service (*Ned.* 32a).

35. Though Amos 5:2 says Israel has fallen and will not rise, two interpretations follow that reverse that negative sentiment (*Ber.* 4b).

36. For example, R. Jeremiah b. Elazar turns the simple statement about Adam producing a son at Gen. 5:3 into a proof he begot demons and shades (*Er.* 18b).

37. *Er.* 22a; this sentiment is regularly stated explicitly.

38. So R. Meir, not citing any biblical support (*Er.* 18b). Thus, Abraham becomes an eschatological savior (*Er.* 19a).

39. Eccl. 12:13, which reads "all having been heard," becomes "everything is heard" to make R. Elazar's point (*Ber.* 6b). Elsewhere this pattern may be signaled by the phrase *al tikri ... ela ...*, "do not read it [the consonantal text] as ... but as ..."

40. Rabbi construes *banah*, "built," as *binah*, "understanding," to get this message (*Nid.* 45b).

41. Ps. 68:21 speaks of the "issues" of death, and since the numerical equivalent of that term is 903, an anonymous comment teaches that there are that many manners of dying (*Ber.* 8a). Abraham's age at the time he acknowledged God is mathematically deduced from the use of the word *ekev*, "because." And see the message derived from the numbers of Satan's name that follows at *Ned.* 32a–b. Mari b. Mar eventually proves that the entire universe is $1/_{3200}$ of the extent of the Torah (*Er.* 21a).

42. Mar Zutra interprets praising God in the "time of finding" at Ps. 32:6 to refer to a privy (*Ber.* 8a).

43. R. Yoḥanan's question about one part of the Tanna's recitation (*Ber.* 5b). See page 74 in the discussion of acceptable challenges to assertions.

44. R. Eliezer hyperbolically denounces those who hold their penis when urinating, but Rava, who is not fearful of this bringing about a second ejaculation, opines that it is unusual to get aroused again so quickly (*Nid.* 43a).

45. *Ber.* 4a.

46. *Nid.* 46b.

47. *Ḥul.* 76b, where we also learn that R. Mattena said of Rava's legal acuity, "His knife is sharp."

48. *Er.* 19a, and see the following comments about Abaye and Rava's praise of the fruit of certain places.

49. *Ber.* 5b.

50. *Shev.* 31a.
51. *Ber.* 10b.
52. *Ber.* 6b.
53. *Ber.* 12b.
54. *Ber.* 5b.

55. A certain Justinia appears before rabbis discussing the age at which a girl may conceive and tells of her giving birth at age seven (*Nid.* 45a).

56. *Shev.* 40a.
57. *Ber.* 4a, 5b, 9b.
58. *Ber.* 8a, 10b.
59. *Ber.* 4b.

60. This is already to be found in the Mishnah at *Ned.* 3.11, which heaps up glorification of circumcision. In the *gemara* of our sample it was found at *Ber.* 3a, 4b, 5b, and 6a, *Shev.* 39a, and *Ned.* 22a, occasionally with the term *vehatanya*, "And thus, too, there is an authoritative teaching ..."

61. *Shev.* 18b, and note the use of the technical term *kidetani*, "as was taught." So, frequently, terms from the root *t-n-h* are used to indicate authenticated traditions.

62. There is hardly a page in the sample where this does not occur.

63. Ps. 107:10 has an allusion to sitting in the shadow of death, leading to an anonymous comment that the name "Netherworld" for this place is *gemara*, "a tradition" (*Er.* 19a).

64. Rava is exasperated that R. Papa doesn't know whether Rome or Parthia is the greater (*Shev.* 6b).

65. Twice it is said that the only way certain prayer practices do not clash with rabbinic teaching is if one broadens the sense of the disruptive prayers (*Ber.* 4b).

66. R. Naḥman b. Isaac, dealing with male precedence in walking with his wife (*Er.* 18b).

67. Again and again, the absolution of vows is permitted based on the sense of common behavior (*Ned.* 21b).

68. The sons of R. Ḥiyya were simultaneously conceived, which shows that this is possible (*Nid.* 40a).

69. Ravina discusses whiteness from experience with garments old and new (*Shev.* 6b). R. Eliezer gives three signs of the night watches: when the ass brays, when the dog barks and the babe suckles, and when a wife talks with her husband (*Ber.* 7a). Sages speak of 903 varieties of dying, from "the kiss" to the horrendous "croup" (*Ber.* 8b). But such empirical evidence can also be swept aside (*Er.* 19a).

70. The possibility that one might have to do all three of the worst sins to bring punishment upon the earth as well as upon himself is dismissed as implausible (*Shev.* 39a).

71. R. Kahana cites a popular proverb to resolve a dialectic difficulty (*Shev.* 11b).

72. As Justinia's having borne a child at age seven (*Nid.* 45a).

73. R. Zeira changed his practice due to a colleague's teaching, and a man who stood incorrectly in prayer was slain by Elijah for that (*Ber.* 6b).

74. In the account of the circumcision of Moses's sons, the term *ḥatan*, "groom," is used, for, we are told, that is what the child undergoing the circumcision is called (*Ned.* 32a). The elaborate exegeses of certain Torah texts are justified by citing the principle (not universally accepted) that the Torah speaks in human language (*Nid.* 44a).

75. God compares Himself both to a king and father in relation to the people of Israel (*Ber.* 3a). Gen. 2:22 is interpreted to see God as a groomsman for the primal couple, and a direct comparison is drawn for human behavior (*Er.* 18b). Also on that folio, R. Naḥman b. Isaac holds up Elkanah and Elisha as exemplary figures. On folio 22a, Rava describes (I hope hyperbolically) the ideal of family sacrifice proper for a disciple of the wise. And then we are presented with the figure of R. Adda b. Mattenah, who wants his family to eat reeds and such so he can study.

76. In dealing with vows, the issue of reciprocity comes up in comparisons with dogs and kings (*Ned.* 24a). A more hortatory use of comparison involves equating the act being stressed with one of very high religious merit. Feasting before fasting is given that treatment at *Ber.* 8b, and hospitality to scholars at *Ber.* 10b.

77. Painting ailing trees red is interpreted as a means of eliciting people's prayers, and this is analogous to the leper's cry (*Ḥul.* 78a).

78. *Ber.* 5a, on emotions on giving things; *Er.* 21b has Rava saying the people of Israel contrasts itself with God to its own praise; *Shev.* 35b cites a statement of Rav's contrasting the merit of receiving wayfarers with the lesser value of receiving the Shekhinah. Sometimes comparisons and contrasts are juxtaposed, and a most impressive aggadic creation emerges, as at *Ber.* 10a, on the similarities and differences between God's and people's artistry.

79. The classic example in the sample is Mari b. Mar's proof that the whole universe is teeny compared to the extent of the Torah (*Er.* 21a).

80. The trope "how much the more so" is utilized at *Ber.* 5a with regard to the feasting that might precede fasting, and at *Er.* 21b, where it is used to praise R. Akiba based on the tale of his collegial concern when in prison.

81. *Ber.* 9a–b.

82. *Ber.* 4b. The rabbinic perplexity sometimes seems rhetorical, but it can also be quite genuine, as with the rare word *kerum* in Ps. 12:9, on which NJPS comments, "meaning of the Hebrew uncertain."

83. R. Simeon b. Lakish on Ex. 24:12 (*Ber.* 4b).

84. *Ber.* 5a.

85. *Ber.* 6a.

86. The interpretation of Dan. 9:17 (*Ber.* 7b).

87. *Er.* 21b, where Rava's explanation that one ought to treat the words of the rabbis with even greater seriousness than those of the Bible seems to give the text a meaning directly opposed to its words.

88. At *Ber.* 7a, the apparent preference for R. Jonathan's version of Moses's requests of God rather than that of R. Yose. At *Ber.* 6a R. Eliezer the Great points out that R. Isaac's textual proof that God's *tefilin* support Israel really only means the one for the head.

89. At *Ber.* 5b, Abba Benjamin wanted his prayer to be literally "before his bed," but why not rather understand that phrase as "near [the time of getting out of] bed?"

90. *Ned.* 32a.

91. R. Jacob b. Iddi (*Ber.* 4a).

92. *Ber.* 12b–13a, where the concluding comments support Ben Zoma. In some such juxtapositions, a rabbi's view may be invoked as a teaching but minus any supporting text. *Er.* 18b has a conflict between R. Naḥman and R. Naḥman b. Isaac concerning Manoah when R. Naḥman b. Isaac cites a text concerning Elkanah, Samuel's father, which is not in our texts of the Bible.

93. *Ber.* 12b–13b the same teacher using an identical form of presentation, a not uncommon pattern in our sample.

94. *Shev.* 39a, the discussion beginning with "holding guiltless" versus "not holding guiltless."

95. The usual form is "Such and such a question would be simple to answer for the one who interprets the verse this way, but how would the other interpreter respond to it?" A similar test is then made of the previously "safe" verse by a question that the second interpretation would find easy to answer. Such dialectical challenges can continue back and forth several times, leading to a comparatively lengthy and involved exposition. *Ber.* 10b and *Nid.* 45b are simple examples, but in *Er.* 18a–b the development becomes extensive.

96. *Ber.* 6a.
97. *Er.* 22a.
98. *Er.* 21b.
99. *Ber.* 5a.
100. *Ber.* 4b.
101. *Ber.* 7b.
102. *Ned.* 32b.
103. *Ned.* 32a.
104. *Ber.* 9b.
105. *Ber.* 3b and then 4a.
106. *Ber.* 7a.
107. *Ber.* 8b.
108. *Ber.* 9b.
109. *Er.* 18b, it being the rabbinic rule that a man should never walk behind a woman.

110. *Ber.* 8a. The responses are picturesque: the departure of the soul is, variously, like pulling a thorn backward out of a ball of wool, or a hawser through a ship's loopholes.

111. *Shev.* 35b.
112. *Shev.* 39a–b.
113. *Ber.* 8a.
114. R. Yohanan does not want to mention Israel's fall, so he speaks of "Israel's enemies" (*Ber.* 4b).
115. For the specification of sins which may cause leprosy, see *Shev.* 8a.
116. R. Yohanan's *minayin* query to the Tanna (*Ber.* 5b), and, in a different context, on *Ber.* 7a. R. Isaac makes a *may kera* inquiry on *Ber.* 4a.
117. *Ned.* 22b.
118. *Hul.* 77b–78a. Jews are, of course, forbidden to adopt pagan practices.
119. *Ber.* 6a–b.
120. *Ber.* 9b.
121. *Ber.* 9b, elsewhere on the page.
122. *Ber.* 5b.
123. *Ber.* 7a and *Ned.* 25a (repeated at *Shev.* 29b).
124. At *Er.* 19a R. Joshua b. Levi's view that sinners repent at the gate to Gehinnom is challenged because it clashes with the view of R. Simeon b. Lakish, who said they keep rebelling there. On that folio, too, R. Jeremiah b. Elazar's assertion that there are three gates to Gehinnom, which he specifies, is troubling, for R. Meryon cited his teacher who said there is a gate in another spot.
125. *Ber.* 8a.
126. So the need to keep Resh Lakish consistent with himself (*Er.* 19a).
127. *Ned.* 22a.
128. *Ber.* 7b.
129. *Er.* 19a.
130. *Er.* 18b. The objection here is raised with the common term *metive*, "he objected." Another term used to raise an objection is *ini? vehaamar...*, "Indeed! But did so and so not say..." So the introduction to the comment by R. Isaac (*Ber.* 7b).
131. *Ber.* 7a.
132. *Ber.* 7a, elsewhere on the folio.
133. *Ber.* 3b
134. *Ber.* 9b.
135. *Ber.* 4a.
136. *Ber.* 7b.
137. *Shev.* 35b.
138. *Ber.* 7a.
139. *Ber.* 8b.
140. *Ber.* 8a.
141. *Er.* 19a.
142. *Er.* 18b.
143. See, for example, R. Elazar's reconciliation of the contradictory verses saying God does and does not hold certain transgressors guiltless (*Shev.* 39a).

The Bible's sweeping statements on God's justice clearly clash with rabbinic experience, so they frequently resort to this form of theodicy.

144. *Ned.* 32a, though the resolution of a difficulty is not involved in this passage.

145. *Ber.* 6b.

146. *Ber.* 3b.

147. *Ber.* 7b.

148. *Er.* 19a.

149. *Er.* 18a. In a similar defense, we are suddenly told in *Ned.* 32a that there are two angels named Ḥemah.

150. *Ber.* 9b, where the first and second psalms are linked.

151. *Ber.* 6a, where Dt. 4:7 and 8 are linked, as are Dt. 33:29 and 1 Chr. 17:21.

152. *Ber.* 3b, where verses are adduced defending this position. In *Ber.* 5a Mar Zutra validates an exegesis because the verse preceding the one under challenge rounds out the meaning placed upon the original.

153. *Ber.* 6a, and see also the comment by R. Naḥman b. Isaac.

154. *Ber.* 12b.

155. *Ber.* 5a, where it takes Rabbi two verses to make his point against R. Simeon b. Lakish.

156. *Ber.* 10a.

157. *Ber.* 5a. See also *Ned.* 32a, where Rabbi's exegesis must be understood in terms of a shift of consonants allowed to an aggadist.

158. *Ber.* 5b, where, in the following pages, there is a lengthy discussion of retribution and other such resolutions. Cf. the next two citations.

159. *Ber.* 7a.

160. *Ber.* 7b, where there is an extensive analysis of this problem and numerous resolutions are presented.

161. *Ber.* 8a.

162. *Er.* 19a, which is also an uncommonly lengthy discussion and analysis.

163. *Er.* 18a.

164. *Ber.* 6b.

165. *Ber.* 7b, as part of a lengthy give-and-take on this issue.

166. *Ber.* 9a, and see the ensuing discussion about when "the haste" of their departure actually occurred.

167. *Er.* 18b.

168. *Er.* 19a.

169. *Ber.* 5b, part of a lengthy debate.

170. *Ber.* 5b, as part of the same dialectical exchange.

171. *Shev.* 35b.

172. *Ned.* 32a. Even more than three conflicting opinions on a given topic can stand side by side in one place, not to mention what one might find if one combed the entire literature.

173. *Ned.* 31b–32a.

174. *Shev.* 15b.

175. *Er.* 22a. Thus, theological matters of some significance as well as exegetical details may remain unresolved.

176. *Ned.* 32a.

177. *Nid.* 45b.

178. *Shev.* 30a.

179. *Ber.* 5a.

180. *Ber.* 3b.

181. The obscure term *neshef* at Ps. 119:147 draws several such inquiries (*Ber.* 3b). On the next folio, *Ber.* 4a, the names "Kereti" and "Peleti" draw a question as to their meaning, which is only the beginning of the queries that arise on other matters there.

182. *Nid.* 45a.

183. *Ned.* 22a.

184. *Ber.* 12b.

185. *Ber.* 8a.

186. *Er.* 19a. R. Simeon b. Lakish disagrees concerning the repentance of the wicked, precipitating an effort to harmonize the clashing opinions.

187. *Er.* 21b.

188. *Er.* 22a.

189. *Ber.* 4a.

190. *Er.* 18b.

191. *Er.* 18b, another passage.

192. *Er.* 18b, another passage.

193. *Ber.* 3b.

194. *Ber.* 8a.

195. *Er.* 21b, and note that they consider his wisdom was, like theirs, Oral Torah.

196. *Er.* 26a.

197. *Ber.* 7a.

198. *Ber.* 7a.

199. *Ber.* 6a.

200. *Ber.* 3a

201. *Shev.* 9a.

202. *Ber.* 8a.

203. *Er.* 22a. R. Joshua b. Levi utilizes the term in relation to the divine image seen in the human face. The term is more commonly used in direct statements about God.

204. *Ber.* 4a.

205. One statement defended the Jewish hermeneutic of interpreting texts by their juxtaposition (*semukhin*), to the derision of certain sectarians (*Ber.* 10a).

Chapter 5. Does Extending the Sample Alter the Findings?

1. *San.* 34a.

2. *Ḥul.* 92a. The verse involved is Gen. 40:10, and the five diverse interpretations stand peaceably side by side, though the last one has a differing view alongside it.

3. *Ḥul.* 60b. The comment is prompted by the obscure term *avvim* (Josh. 13:3).

4. *Meg.* 15b.

5. *Meg.* 11a. The challenge to R. Ḥisda is direct—*may darasht beh*, "How would you interpret that?" R. Ḥisda's response is founded on the reasoning that the text is *yetera*, "superfluous"; hence he inquires, *lamah li?* "What does it [then mean] to me?" He then answers his rhetorical question, *shema mineh, lidrashah*, "a formal indication of a teacher's lesson," in this case that the verse was given to be expounded.

6. *Ar.* 15a–16b.

7. In *Men.* 53a *midah keneged midah*, "measure for measure," is used quite literally. R. Ḥisda (*Er.* 51a) utilizes *gezerah shavah*, "verbal comparison," to explain Nu. 35:5, and there is a comment about this device. Es. 5:11 becomes the basis of several rabbis topping each other with the number of Haman's children. Rabbah delightfully revocalizes Job 40:30 to make God the host at a messianic banquet of Leviathan's flesh. R. Elazar expands his exegesis of Ex. 32:10 to daringly suggest that Moses, as it were, grabbed God by the lapels, so fervent was his appeal. But the exegesis can be quite straightforward, as in the anonymous statement of *R. H.* 3b explaining that Cyrus, Darius, and Artaxerxes are the same person, resolving the chronological problem of Ez. 7:8.

8. *B. M.* 59a. Rav said, "One should always be careful of being overbearing toward one's wife because, since her tears come easily, she is easily wronged." In *San.* 86a R. Yoḥanan identifies the authors of the anonymous statements in four classic books and in *Meg.* 15a says Malachi was really Ezra. Rava, in the course of discussing the seven Noachide laws (*San.* 56b), informs us of an otherwise unknown school of Menasseh that identified two of the laws differently than the rabbis generally did. In *Pes.* 3a a discussion of the pre-Passover search for leaven is rather unaccountably turned into a discussion of the virtue of speaking euphemistically.

9. *B. B.* 164b–65a. So in *Ber.* 35b we have the differing views of R. Ishmael and R. Simeon b. Yoḥai on how to balance the need to study with the need to earn a livelihood; it is followed by the later views of Abbaye and Rava variously siding with R. Ishmael.

10. *Av. Z.* 5a. The debate may have been provoked by Resh Lakish's shocking statement that we should be grateful that our forebears sinned or we would not have come into being.

11. *Taan.* 3b.

12. *B. K.* 60b. Note that the first opinions are supported by biblical verses, but the last ones are not—and without prejudice to their significance. Note, too, that the aggadic material is introduced with the weightiest formula of authentic transmission—*tanu rabbanan*, "our masters taught."

13. *Git.* 68b–70b, a good example also of an extended aggadic passage.

14. *Meg.* 15a. R. Isaac's promise of instant orgasm is rejected as not working, and he says he meant something else. Common sense is also the basis for exegesis when a verse cannot be taken literally, e.g. *R. H.* 25b, on Dt. 17:9.

15. *Ket.* 111b–12a has a lengthy description of quite unusual natural phenomena encountered by various rabbis and indicates why one should not marvel at the eschatological promise of natural abundance such as that inferred from Dt. 32:14. Gamaliel follows a similar strategy in *Shab.* 30b. A falling egg of the Bar Yochnai inundates sixty villages (*Bekh.* 57b). Wine for the messianic banquet will be from the grapes of the six days of creation (*Ber.* 34b). Some rabbis teach that there is a good reason for natural nuisances. Some also feel there are "secrets of the universe," and a mystifying list of these is found after Rav Judah reveals some to R. Zeira (all in *Shab.* 77b). It also seems quite "natural" to them that various biblical figures should know of others that came long after them, as David and Ezekiel (*B. K.* 60b) allegedly did, or of the Torah texts relevant to them, as with Phineas (*San.* 82a).

16. Two sages make a calf for their Sabbath meal, and Rav, Zeiri, and Yannai are involved in episodes of wonder-working (*San.* 67b). In the famous oven of Akhnai controversy (*B. M.* 59b), R. Eliezer causes several natural patterns to reverse themselves. R. Ḥanina b. Dosa, a famous rainmaker, can even do so to ease his travel (*Taan.* 24b), and while lizard bites are normally fatal, any lizard that bit him itself risked death (*Ber.* 33a). Pinḥas b. Yair, on a journey to redeem exiles, gets an obstructing river to part for him (*Ḥul.* 7a). R. Isaac said that though each stone at Beth El wanted to be the righteous Jacob's pillow, they were all merged into one for his sake (*Ḥul.* 91b).

17. *B. K.* 16a. Here the passage is introduced with a second-level term authenticating the *tanya*, "transmission," a teacher taught. A story related in *Ber.* 18b takes for granted the conversation of the spirits of the dead in a cemetery.

18. *Meg.* 7b. In rejecting Rabbah's invitation to spend another Purim with him, R. Zeira does call the act a "miracle." But such miracles were more natural to them than to us.

19. *Ḥul.* 105b.

20. *Men.* 53a–b. Note the latitude in these expositions. Not only are plurals parallel to singular usages, but the feminine *zo* is considered the equivalent of the masculine *zeh*.

21. *Yoma* 75b–76a. The operative verb here is *dan*, "to reason by analogy," not the more usual *darash*, "to expound."

22. *B. B.* 15a. So, too, the story of Joab's partial fulfillment of the commandment to annihilate Amalek is said to hinge on a faulty vocalization he was taught (*B. B.* 21a–b).

23. *B. B.* 15b, and see the consequent discussion of Solomon's marriage to her.

24. *Ḥul.* 5a.

25. *Ket.* 104a.

26. *B. M.* 86b. The reconciliation is the familiar one of referring the two texts to different times.

27. *Sot.* 4b–5a. The difficulty is introduced by the technical phrase *kushya hi le* . . . , "it creates a problem for [the view that] . . ."

28. *Men.* 53b.

29. *Ḥul.* 43a and 5a.

30. *Ḥul.* 6a. Other examples are in *Ḥul.* 133b, *Ket.* 111b, and *Kid.* 80b.

31. *B. M.* 85b.

32. *Ar.* 30b.

33. *Git.* 7a. In halakhic exegesis an obvious meaning of a verse can be rejected with the term *peshita*, "that's self-evident," and so another explanation is called for. However, the term did not occur here or in any other aggadic context studied.

34. *B. K.* 81b. Note that the initial alleged textual reference is introduced with the technical phrase, *alav hakatuv omer*, "Scripture says about this . . ."

35. *Pes.* 62b.

36. *Sot.* 46b, and note the ethical impulse behind these readings. Letters, or their shapes, or their fit with other letters—all can suggest lessons (*Shab.* 104a). Breaking words into phrases can be found on *Pes.* 117a (R. Meir), *B. B.* 78b (on Nu. 21:30), *Men.* 66b (with a letter reversal), and *Ned.* 51a (where Rabbi's shenanigans at a banquet enrage a wealthy guest).

37. *Taan.* 10a. Not only are the *resh* and *khaf* now placed in one word, but the *ḥet* of both words is replaced by a *heh*.

38. *Ber.* 56b–57a. One senses here that the dream visions are being treated as quasi-revelatory and are thus treated in the manner an aggadist might bring to a biblical text.

39. *Shab.* 31b.

40. *Suk.* 35a. The reverse also occurs. A Greek loanword for "a will" can be broken into an Aramaic phrase in *B. M.* 19a.

41. A list is given in *R. H.* 26a, beginning with the interpretation of *yovel* from an Arabian locale.

42. *Shab.* 55b. R. Jose b. Zimra even proved that *notarikon* occurs in the Torah (*Shab.* 105a). *Gematria* is explicitly utilized in *Yoma* 20a and *Mak.* 23b–24a, but without being identified in R. Yoḥanan's exegesis of Lamentations.

43. *San.* 90b. The Soncino translation, p. 606 nn. 1 and 2, indicates why these may be Samaritans.

44. *Kid.* 49a
45. *B. B.* 16b.
46. *Sot.* 13a.
47. *San.* 38b. After a series of exegeses he makes his final point from Ex. 33:15.
48. *Sot.* 10b. Wilhelm Bacher, *Erkhe Midrash Amoraim*, trans. A. Z. Rabinowitz (Jerusalem: Carmiel, 1970) 2:227, says *masoret* is fundamentally a Tannaitic term, one that is used by Amoraim only in relation to *aggadah*.
49. *Sot.* 34b. The phrase is used in *Meg.* 10b as the basis of the statement that the Ark of the Covenant really took up no room in the Tabernacle.
50. E.g., *San.* 37a—that women do not conceive standing up; *San.* 44a—that demons and other such creatures do not take God's name in vain; *San.* 92b—that six miracles occurred on the day of the fiery furnace; *San.* 95b—that Nebuzaradan survived when the Assyrian host died overnight; *Shab.* 55b—that four men (Benjamin, Amram, Jesse, and Caleb) died because of the serpent (but not because of their own sins); *Az. Z.* 9a—that Abraham was fifty-two when he was in Haran; *Mak* 23b—a most interesting passage, where Rava's assertion that certain conclusions were tradition seems to carry more weight than the prior aggadic reasoning. Of special interest is the report that one cause of Aḥer's apostasy from Judaism was a vision he had that contradicted what the rabbis "had taught," *gemiri*. Bacher, *Erkh Midrash Amoraim* (see n. 48), p. 165, says the term is mostly nonhalakhic.
51. *A. Z.* 19b.
52. *Sot.* 42b.
53. *B. B.* 91a. It is not immediately evident how he arrived at his second teaching.
54. *Git.* 68a–b. Not only is this lengthy, but it also seems an integrated whole, which is most uncommon.
55. *Git.* 55b–58a. Nearly four folio sides are devoted to this topic, a most unusually extended treatment.
56. *Bekh.* 8b–9a.
57. *Ned.* 50a.
58. *B. B.* 73a–74b. One can see in this material the problem of taking the *aggadah* as part of God's revelation.
59. *B. K.* 37a.
60. *B. M.* 59b.
61. *San.* 92b. Several named authorities discuss this view. Particularly noteworthy is R. Nehemiah's retort to R. Judah, who had said, "It was true; it [also] was a *mashal*." (This can also be read as "It was a true *mashal*.") R. Nehemiah said, "If it is true [really happened?], why [call it] a *mashal*? And if it is a *mashal*, why [call it] true?" The passage concludes by restating R. Judah's language with a slight shift of emphasis: "But in truth, it was a *mashal*." Lovers of deconstruction should find this fascinating. I believe we can explain Joseph Heinemann's assertion, extending the view of Wilhelm Bacher, that

there is little use of *mashal* in the Bavli if we recall that his primary sense of *aggadah* is of the expository or homiletic sort of interpretation given in the classic *midrash* books of the Land of Israel. Heinemann, *Aggadah and Its Development* (in Hebrew) (Jerusalem: Keter Publishing, 1974), p. 163. The standard work on this literary form is now David Stern, *Parables in Midrash: Narrative and Exegesis in Rabbinic Literature* (Cambridge, MA: Harvard University Press, 1991). Note the specification of concern in the subtitle. Of *midrash* Stern said a few years after that book, "Rather than possessing a hermeneutics, a systematic base for interpretation, midrash may be said to have been impelled by a narrative of interpretation." David Stern, *Midrash and Theory* (Evanston, IL: Northwestern University Press, 1996), p. 53, reprinting an essay of 1993 in *The Midrashic Imagination*, ed. Michael Fishbane (Albany: State University of New York Press, 1993). In *Midrash and Theory*, Stern epitomizes the *mashal* in this way: "Neither a secret tale with a hidden meaning nor a transparent story with a clear-cut moral, the mashal is a narrative that actively elicits from its audience the application of its message—or what we would call its interpretation" (p. 44), and see the general discussion there. We shall return to this matter in the course of chapter 7.

62. *B. B.* 15a. The rabbis apparently see themselves only as continuing the biblical tradition, though *mashal* is generally used in the Bible to refer to an adage.

63. *Er.* 63a.

64. *Pes.* 49a.

65. *Naz.* 23a. See the two examples that follow there. The *mashal* is sometimes not clear to us. See, for example, *R. H.* 17b, which has a story of a loan made before the king, purporting thereby to explain when God is and isn't partial in judgment.

66. *Shev.* 6a. So *Zev.* 82a provides another example of an attempt to explain complex laws by means of a homey example.

67. *Ket.* 39b.

68. *Yev.* 21a.

69. *Ned.* 20b.

70. *B. K.* 92a–93a, a rather extensive aggadic passage.

71. *B. M.* 59a. The term that commonly introduces adages is used here, *veha imre inshe*, "and behold, people say . . ."

72. *M. K.* 16b.

73. *Kid.* 30b. R. Elazar says Elijah insolently charged God with causing His children to sin, and God agreed with him (*Ber.* 31b–32a).

74. R. Simon b. Pazzi provides the delightful dialogue leading up to this (*Ḥul.* 60b).

75. *Ber.* 20b.

76. *Men.* 53a.

77. *Betz.* 25b.

78. *Av. Z.* 5a.

79. *Ket.* 111a. Their meaning must be hidden, otherwise he shouldn't have said them.

80. *R. H.* 17b. The operative phrase is "Were the text not written, it would not be permitted to say this." It also occurs, with some stories repeating, in *Ber.* 32b, *Meg.* 21a, *B. B.* 10a and 16a, *San.* 95b, and *Ḥul.* 91a. Resh Lakish's more daring view is at *Ḥul.* 60b.

81. *Bekh.* 58a.

82. *Ber.* 38b.

83. *Ber.* 62a, and note that the Akiba story is then told about Ben Azzai.

84. So on the staves of the ark (*Yoma* 54a).

85. *Taan.* 9b. Other technical terms occur here: *keman azla ha dikhetiv*, "according to which position is this text ..."; *uma ani mekayem ... ela ...*, "how then shall I understand ... but [understand it this way] ..."; *bishlama leman deamar ... ela leman deamar*, "that accords well with the position that said ... but [how may it be understood by] the position that said ..."

86. *Ḥag.* 12a.

87. *Ber.* 59a.

88. *Pes.* 87a–b.

89. *Ber.* 61b.

90. *Kid.* 36a.

91. *Sot.* 21a.

92. At *Git.* 60a, the two classic antagonists, R. Yoḥanan and Resh Lakish; and at *B. K.* 16b, R. Elazar and R. Samuel b. Naḥman interpreting Jer. 18:22.

93. *B. B.* 15a–b, including the intriguing ideas that Job never lived or that he was a gentile.

94. *Meg.* 11a–b.

95. *A. Z.* 5a. A different sort of examination, less directly dialectical, is given R. Ḥanina b. Agil's query about why the Deuteronomic but not the Sinaitic Decalogue has a statement about the reward for honoring parents (*B. K.* 54b–55a).

96. *Pes.* 8a–b.

97. *Sot.* 35b–36a, R. Judah and R. Simeon. Certain technical terms of such further investigation of views are utilized here: *mai taama d ...*, "what is the reasoning of ..."; *keman azla hadetanya*, "according to whose position is the teaching that ..."; *keman ... keman ...*, "according to which position ... [and, reciprocally] according to which position ..."

98. *Sot.* 35b. The disputed verse is 1 Chr. 15:26.

99. *B. M.* 86b. The solution offered is that they appeared to do so (most likely to teach us good manners).

100. *Ned.* 39b.

101. *San.* 26b, the discussion of Ps. 11:3. Here, as elsewhere, the first two words of the phrase are elided as *iba'et*.

102. *Zev.* 102a, a discussion of the promise of kingship in perpetuity to Saul and his family. Note the typical responses: a slight case of fulfillment, where

the monarchy was passed on to one of Saul's sons, Ishbosheth; Saul's case was different (an exception to the general rule); and finally, the promise was for a specific set of circumstances, but these changed.

103. *Av. Z.* 3b, discussing what God does—which, perhaps because of its "mythological" character, leads to many alternatives being offered.

104. *B. B.* 4a.

105. *Sot.* 12a. The unity of the Oral Torah and Written Torah are assumed here to such an extent that the explicit statement of the text is reinterpreted on the basis of an aggadic teaching. In such moves one senses the sporadic concern of the sages to make all the written and oral traditions cohere.

106. *San.* 102b. Here the objection is introduced by another term of argument, *matkif le*, "he disagreed with him." The rabbis naturally wish to encourage lay support of scholars.

107. *Sot.* 22a. What is at stake is a halakhic procedure, but the denigration of it here is *aggadah*.

108. *Sot.* 21b. Even the reconciliation contains sufficient sexist bias to cause problems to the ethically minded today.

109. *Sot.* 30b–31a.

110. *Kid.* 72b. This is a fine example of the integrity of halakhic and aggadic discourse.

111. *Sot.* 46b.

112. *B. B.* 16a. One occasionally finds a list of views on a given theme, such as about the Evil Yetzer in *Kid.* 30b, where the views do not particularly differ with one another yet are somewhat different, and this may be another expression of the interest in coherence.

113. *Yoma* 4b. The formal term for raising an objection, *metive*, "he responded," is used here.

114. *Suk.* 45b. Here the objection that a contrary opinion exists is introduced by the term *vehaamar*, "but it has been said [by ...] that ..."

115. All this develops from R. Samuel b. Inia's insistence God has a secret place for His crying (*Ḥag.* 5b), and see the final insistence that on the day the Temple was destroyed the angels did cry in the outer chambers.

116. *San.* 22a. The objection is raised here with the simple term *ini*, "really"? The resolution is signaled with *la kashya*, "no problem [because] ..."

117. *San.* 92a, again using the terms *vehaamar* and *la kashya*, as in the prior citation from the same tractate.

118. *Meg.* 14b. In his response, R. Naḥman calls his antagonist, Ena Saba, by name, perhaps meaning to disparage him by calling attention to its meaning, "old eye"—the text notes the variant interpretation, "black bowl."

119. *Zev.* 102a—and though this is not unprecedented in Talmudic discourse, one should understand the statement in terms of the great value the rabbis placed on the precise wording of their teachers' and colleagues' statements, and the great value they therefore attached to repeating them exactly as received.

120. *B. B.* 25a.
121. *Betz.* 25b.
122. *Shab.* 88a. A mediating view is also given here.
123. *Av. Z.* 5a.
124. *Ḥul.* 89a.
125. *Sot.* 11b.
126. *Kid.* 36a.
127. *Pes.* 87b.

128. *Yev.* 77a. Cf. *Yev.* 109b, where a mediating position is enunciated, and *Kid.* 70b.

129. *Tam.* 29a–b, where a rather lengthy discussion of hyperbolic usage occurs. In that passage and in *Ar.* 11a, where the famous loud-sounding Temple musical instrument is discussed, there is no hesitation in characterizing rabbinic statements the same way.

130. Respectively, *Sot.* 41b; R. Elazar Hagadol at *B. B.* 9b; and R. Joshua b. Korha, at *B. B.* 10a. R. Ḥiyya bar Abba insists proper Sabbath observance atones even for idolatry (Shab. 118b), and R. Joshua ben Levi says that teaching one's grandson Torah is like receiving it on Sinai oneself (*Kid.* 30a). Condemnations can be flagrant. R. Meir avers that false witnesses cannot properly do anything in the Torah (*San.* 27a); Rava charges that it would have been better not to be born than to do insincere acts of repentance or good deeds (*Ber.* 17a); R. Samuel b. Naḥman says that one who does not finish a (religious?) deed he has begun will bury his wife and sons (*Sot.* 13b); R. Judah b. Masparta declares that the sinner Achan, at Josh. 7:18, transgressed the whole five books of the Torah (and is otherwise disparaged) (*San.* 44a); and see the sins ascribed to Ahaz and Menasseh, who are denied entry into the world to come (*San.* 103b).

131. *M. K.* 25b. Some further references: for the sake of R. Ḥanina b. Dosa's trip, a much-needed rain was halted, suggesting that even the prayers of the High Priest were not as efficacious as his (*Yoma* 53b); Rabbah b. Naḥmani had twelve thousand attendees at his semiannual *kallah* lectures, causing a tax collection problem (*B. B.* 86a); R. Ḥiyya and his sons were capable of bringing the Messiah (*B. M.* 85b); Akiba's wife was incredibly sacrificial for him, leading to his later enormous success and wealth (*Ned.* 50a). On Israel's significance, the rabbis can assert that the world could not exist without Israel (*Taan.* 3b); that only the prayers of Jews are efficacious (*Git.* 57b); that gentiles receive blessings and their ships sail the sea only for Israel's sake (*Yev.* 63a); that to strike a Jew is like striking God (*San.* 58b); and that the great Jewish archenemy, the gentile prophet Balaam, had intercourse with his donkey (*A. Z.* 4b). Another variety of these stories is the wonders God did for the patriarchs, like gathering all the land of Israel for Jacob to lie upon when he slept at Beth El so that the Israelites would later have a claim to the land (*Ḥul.* 91b).

132. *Git.* 57a, a response to a heretic, apparently expected to be convincing.

133. *Sot.* 34a, so that what begins as a commonsensical reaction produces, in turn, an even more outrageous suggestion. Note, too, how R. Yoḥanan and Rabbi stress how densely packed was the audience of their respective teachers (*Er.* 53a).

134. *Pes.* 57a, so that as long as he was around nothing ever remained of the daily priestly dues in the Temple.

135. *B. M.* 84a.

136. *Ḥul.* 90b. The cited precis is often the "cities fortified to heaven." Cf. the account of the great "pipe" in the Temple and the extraordinary range of sounds it was supposed to have made, an account about which R. Naḥman b. Isaac said, "It was an exaggeration" (*Ar.* 10b–11a).

137. Moses Mielziner at the beginning of the twentieth century noted the differences in language, style, content, treatment of the material, and its very arrangement in his *Introduction to the Talmud*, 3rd ed. (New York: Bloch, 1925), p. 61. A more detailed discussion is provided by H. L. Strack and G. Stemberger, *Introduction to the Talmud and Midrash* (Minneapolis: Fortress Press, 1992), p. 210. Specifically in regard to the *aggadah* in the two Talmuds, see J. Heinemann, *Aggadah and Its Development* (see n. 61), chap. 11, where p. 163 states his major emphasis: that aggadic discourse is less typical of the Babylonian sages than of the sages of the Land of Israel. For the views of Richard Kalmin and Yaakov Elman on the influence of the Greco-Roman provenance of the Yerushalmi as opposed to the Sasanian environment of the Bavli (particularly concerning the balance between the written and oral transmission of texts), see the discussion on orality in chapter 7 of this volume.

138. Jacob Neusner, *The Bavli's Unique Voice: A Systematic Comparison of the Talmud of Babylonia and the Talmud of the Land of Israel*, vol. 1 (Atlanta: Scholars Press, 1993), p. 300. In the seventh, summary volume of this work, his description and disparagement of the Yerushalmi reach a climax beginning in chapter 7 and may quickly be accessed at pp. 214f., 221 (a particularly devastating judgment), 229, 260, and 270. In less-judgmental tones and with a different attention to detail and demonstration, David Kraemer devotes major attention to the differences between the Bavli and the Yerushalmi in his *The Mind of the Talmud: An Intellectual History of the Bavli* (New York: Oxford University Press, 1990). Though neither Neusner nor he specifically treats the issue of the distinctive nature of aggadic—that is, all nonhalakhic discourse—in the Yerushalmi, I found Kraemer's treatment of general discourse in the two Talmuds particularly enlightening, e.g., pp. 16–20, 94–98, and 124–27. (But see the questions Catherine Hezser raises about some of his conclusions in her *The Social Structure of the Rabbinic Movement in Roman Palestine* [Tübingen: Mohr Siebeck, 1997], p. 243.) Neusner continued his line of demonstration and argument in the more recent *Are the Two Talmuds Interchangeable? Christine Hayes's Blunder* (Atlanta: Scholars Press, 1995). She has given a persuasive restatement of her position in "Response to Jacob Neusner," *Journal for the Study of Judaism* 27, no. 3 (August, 1996).

139. Jay Harris, *How Do We Know This?* (Albany: State University of New York Press, 1995), p. 72.

140. Louis Ginzberg, *The Palestinian Talmud* (New York: Jewish Theological Seminary of America, 1941), p. xxxiii. Louis Rabinowitz repeats this figure in "Talmud, Jerusalem," *Encyclopedia Judaica*, vol. 15 (Jerusalem: Keter Publishing, 1974), col. 775. Strack and Stemberger, *Introduction* (see n. 137) p. 210.

141. Jacob Neusner, *Introduction: Taxonomy*, vol. 35 of *The Talmud of the Land of Israel* (Chicago: University of Chicago Press, 1982), pp. 65 (where the context is of interest) and 88. Of course, one should keep in mind that a significant minority of the Mishnah passages are aggadic.

142. Strack and Stemberger, *Introduction* (see n. 137), p. 182.

143. Zecharias Frankel, Mevo ha-Yerushalmi (1870; reprint Jerusalem: 1967), p. 49b.

144. Mielziner, *Introduction* (see n. 137), p. 61: "The Agada in the Palestinian Gemara includes more reliable and valuable historical records and references, and is, on the whole, more rational and sober, though less attractive than the Babylonian Agada[,] which generally appeals more to the heart and the imagination. But the latter, on many occasions, indulges too much in gross exaggerations, and its popular sayings, especially those evidently interpolated by later hands, have often an admixture of superstitious views borrowed from the Persian surroundings." Compare Ginzberg, *Palestinian Talmud* (see n. 140), p. xxxiii ff., who indicates the difficulty of making such broad judgments yet goes on to indict the Bavli for its material on angels, demons, and magic. (But see Rabinowitz, "Talmud Jerusalem" [see n. 140], col. 775.) He blames all this not on the authors but on the folklore that was added to their material. In our time, Eliezer Segal has given a more institutionally based treatment of the differing styles of the two classics, but he seems to limit his understanding of aggadic discourse to the more formally literary passages rather than seeking to understand all nonhalakhic discourse. See his *The Babylonian Esther Midrash* (Atlanta: Scholars Press, 1994), 1:4–7, 1:12, 2:226–29.

145. We do not get much help on any of these topics from Samuel Jaffe Ashkenazi's aggadic anthology of the Yerushalmi, *Sefer Yefeh Mareh* (ca. 1590), for he gives no indication in his preface to the work as to his criteria for selecting material for inclusion and comment. He only provides two exegetic passages, one (with a halakhic prelude) from 1:5, 6b, II.A–C (citations are by *mishnah*, Romm edition page and Neusner numbering) and a second from 6:5, 31a–b, III.A–M, on both of which, see 6.5, 31a–b, III. A–M. For my treatment of 1:5, 6b, II. A–C see the material in this chapter at endnote 180. For my treatment of 6:5, 31a–b, III. A–M see the material at endnote 169.

146. 2:2, 10b, I.A–F clarifies some rules regarding purchasing the land for the Temple but concludes with an aggadic historical interpretation.

147. 5:2, 24b, II.G; 26a, III.E.

148. 7:7, 38b, VI.A, introduced by the words, "One discovers that . . ."

149. 7:8, 39a, II.C, data with considerable legal effect.

150. 7:3, 36a, I.A.
151. 3:9, 18a, III.D and again at H, in both instances anonymously.
152. Three versions of a political analogy to hierarchy are provided in 1.1, 3a, III.R, S, T. Five aspects of God's way of graciously but not undemandingly bestowing forgiveness are gathered in 1:6, 7b, IV.U–Y. Six instances of the simultaneous revelation of contradictory verses plus an explanation are set forth in 3:8, 17b, IV.A–G. But a dozen different voices are heard in the discussion of the punishment for swearing falsely at 6:5, 31a–b, III.A–M.
153. 1.6, 7b, IV.W.
154. 6:5, 31a, III.H.
155. 3:8, 17b, I.B, D.
156. 3.8, 18a, VII.C.
157. 2:3, 11a, IV.C.
158. 3:7, 16b, II.F–G and the following halakhic passages.
159. 1:4, 6a, V.L.
160. 1:3, 4b, I.D.
161. 3:4, 14a, I.H.
162. 5:6, 27b, II.C.
163. 6:8, 32b, I.F. If Bar Ziza was a sage, though he is not included in any lists I consulted, there is a nice comment about his relation to his sharecropper at 7:2, 36a, III.C–H.
164. 1:6, 7a, III.H.
165. 1:1, 3a, III.R–T.
166. 6:8, 32b, I.F.
167. 7:2, 36a, III.C and G.
168. 6:2, 29a, I.A.
169. 6:5, 31b, III.D and L.
170. 3:8, 17b, II.B–D.
171. 3:8, 17a–b, II.K–P.
172. 1:6, 7b, IV.U, V, Y.
173. 3:5, 15b, I.E.
174. 6:5, 31a, III.B, E.
175. 3:8, 17b, IV.A–G.
176. 7:7, 38b, VI.A. The stock figure here is Alexander the Great.
177. 3:8, 17b, IV.C.
178. 2:2, 10b, I.F.
179. 1:6, 7b, IV.X.
180. 1:5, 6b, II.B–C.
181. 6:5, 31a, III.F.
182. 3:8, 18a, VII.C.
183. 6:5, 31b, III.M. The rhetorically cryptic remark attributed to R. Yoḥanan in 7:7, 38b,VII.D, might possibly be a saying he applied here or his own nice coinage.
184. 1:6, 7b, IV.U–Y and 3:8, 17a–b, II.A–K, M–P. Joseph Heinemann suggests that the aggadic *sugya* in the Bavli may contrast one aggadic passage

with another, but the Yerushalmi usage in *yShevuot* is to argue about only one specific interpretation. J. Heinemann, *Aggadah* (see n. 61), p. 169.

185. Despite this difference in style, Martin Jaffe has argued that the basic agenda of the two Talmuds is quite close, the Bavli apparently depending upon the Yerushalmi. While Jaffe has mostly been concerned with the historical-literary relationship between the two works, he has made some suggestive comments on aggadic discourse in the last pages of his paper "The Babylonian Appropriation of the Talmud Yerushalmi: Redactional Studies in the Horayot Tractates," in *The Literature of Early Rabbinic Judaism: Issues in Talmudic Redaction and Interpretation*, ed. Alan J. Avery-Peck (Lanham, MD: University Press of America, 1989), 4:21–22. I am indebted to Dr. Alyssa Gray for this reference.

186. See Frankel, *Mevo ha-Yerushalmi* (see n. 143), 53bff., who expresses this in terms of the textual connectedness of the two literatures. Bacher, in "Talmud," *Jewish Encyclopedia*, vol. 12 (reprint), New York: KTAV, n. d.), p. 7a, follows this literary line. Rabinowitz, "Talmud, Jerusalem," (see no. 140), vol. 15, col. 775, is quite explicit on this topic, while Strack and Stemberger, *Introduction* (see n. 137), pp. 197 and 210, is more circumspect. Joseph Heinemann argues that the sages of the Bavli have less interest and "feel" for aggadic discourse than those of the Land of Israel. Heinemann, *Aggadah and Its Development* (see n. 61), p. 163.

187. For example, Towner's substantial list of structuring terms in the *Mekhilta* is substantially familiar from Talmudic usage. Wayne Sibley Towner, *The Rabbinic "Enumeration of Scriptural Examples"* (Leiden: Brill, 1973), app., p. 251ff.

188. Reuven Hammer, trans. *Sifre, a Tannaitic Commentary to the Book of Deuteronomy* (New Haven, CT: Yale University Press, 1986), pp. 2f.

189. Steven D. Fraade, *From Tradition to Commentary* (Albany: State University of New York Press, 1991), p. 13.

190. Jacob Neusner, *Sifre to Deuteronomy* (Atlanta: Scholar's Press, 1987), p. 85.

191. Ibid., p. 108.

192. Ibid., pp. 161–71, 181–182.

193. Strack and Stemberger, *Introduction* (see n. 137), p. 284.

194. Ibid., p. 276.

195. Hammer, *Sifre* (see n. 189), p. 4.

196. Strack and Stemberger, *Introduction* (see n. 137), p. 272, and cf. p. 297. Hammer, *Sifre* (see n. 189), p. 6. Towner, *Rabbinic "Enumeration,"* (see n. 187), pp. 48–49, where note 1 discusses Finkelstein's concurrent opinion in this regard.

197. Hammer, *Sifre* (see n. 189), p. 20.

198. Jacob Neusner, *Mekhilta According to Rabbi Ishmael: An Introduction to Judaism's First Scriptural Encyclopedia* (Atlanta: Scholars Press, 1988), pp. 219–27.

199. Strack and Stemberger, *Introduction* (see n. 137), pp. 272, 273.

200. Four instances are given of R. Akiba rebuking Pappos at *Mekh. Vayetze* 6 (112.4f.); Elazar Hamodai is chided for his hyperbole about the manna at *Mekh. Vayasa* 3 (166.6); Yose b. Betera says Akiba will have to pay in the next life for his exegesis maligning Zelophehad at *Sif. Nu.* 113 (122); and Yose b. Dormaskit rebukes Judah Berabi for perverting a text at *Sif. Dt.* 1 (6–7).

201. So Jacob Neusner, *The Fathers According to Rabbi Nathan* (Atlanta: Scholars Press, 1986), p. ix, a characterization repeated in *Judaism as Story* (Chicago: University of Chicago Press, 1992), p. 28. Judah Goldin prefers to see the elaboration more as a parallel to what *midrash* does to Scripture and finally calls it "a Tosefta" to *Fathers*. Judah Goldin, *The Fathers According to Rabbi Nathan* (New Haven, CT: Yale University Press, 1955), pp. xviii–xx. Here he follows prior scholars as clarified by Strack and Stemberger, *Introduction* (see n. 137), p. 246.

202. Goldin, *Fathers* (see n. 201), p. xviif.; Strack and Stemberger, *Introduction* (see n. 137), p. 246. Only R. Travers Herford dissents from this common opinion, saying that "there is neither Halachah nor Haggadah in "both," apparently using the latter term in the sense of "narrative" or "exegesis." R. Travers Herford, *Pirke Aboth* (New York: Jewish Institute of Religion, 1945), p. 8. Because of its exclusive aggadic content, *Fathers* is an oddity in the Mishnah, and this has given rise to the problem of the time it was added to the Mishnah and its placement in it. On the time, see Neusner, *Sifra in Context* (see n. 190), p. 222. On its relation to the Mishnah, see Anthony J. Saldarini, *Scholastic Rabbinism* (Chico, CA: Scholars Press, 1982), pp. 9 and 22; and Strack and Stemberger, *Introduction* (see n. 137), p. 136.

203. Herford, *Pirke Aboth* (see n. 202), p. 1; Goldin, *Fathers* (see n. 201), p. xvii; Neusner candidly says, "The document as a whole is formally simple and repetitive...." Neusner, *Story* (see n. 201), p. 19.

204. Careful analyses of the contents of *Fathers According to Rabbi Nathan* (with particular attention to what appear to be its several parts) have been carried out by Goldin (see n. 201) and Saldarini (see n. 202), and more recently and extensively, in a different manner, by Neusner in *Story* (see n. 201).

205. This is the main point of *Story* (see n. 201), and some significant points in its development may be found on pp. xii, xv, xix–xxi, 27–29, 31, 37, 46, 60, 78, 111f., 117, 137, and 145f.

206. Neusner, *Story* (see n. 201), p. xviii and, more fully, p. 136. But Saldarini asserts that both he and Schechter cite many more parallels (to ARN) in the midrash than in the Talmuds, *Scholastic Rabbinism* (see n. 202), p. 124.

207. Soldarini, *Scholastic Rabbinism* (see n. 202), p. 2, and see the fuller statement on p. 131.

208. See Jacob Neusner, *Introduction to Rabbinic Literature* (New York: Doubleday, 1994), p. 355, for the time and sequence. For the problem of why these arose in the Land of Israel and not Babylonia, see Strack and Stemberger, *Introduction* (see n. 137), p. 262, and see, too, his comments on the relation

between *Gen. R.* and the Yerushalmi (p. 303), and between *Lev. R.* and *Gen. R.* and *PRK* (p. 316).

209. See Neusner, *Sifre to Deuteronomy* (see n. 90), pp. 88–91 for a useful comparison of the interests. For a concise summary of his view of the focus of these works, see his *Introduction to Rabbinic Literature* (see n. 208), pp. 356, 360–61, 383, 385, 388–89, and 414–15.

210. The juxtaposition of several teachers with divergent views occurs so often it may be taken as a literary staple. We find three views in *Gen. R.* 1.15 (T 15) and 99.3 (T 1275); four views in *PRK* 20.6 (M 313); *S. S. R.* 5.14.1 features a playful competition to see who can give the most commandments on the tablets of the Ten Commandments! There are five views in *Gen. R.* 6.2 (T 41) and *Lam. R.* Proem 30; six views in *Lev. R.* 27.1 (Margulies, M 713); eight views of Job's date in *Gen. R.* 57.4 (T 614); and nine views of the word "Moriah" in *Gen. R.* 55.7 (T 590). Occasionally a sage will indicate that a given verse can be read in different ways. So R. Ḥama berabi Ḥaninah suggests six meaning of the text in *Gen. R.* 70.8 (T 805), and when Issi b. Yehudah claims there are five Torah verses whose meanings cannot be given with certainty, R. Tanḥuma is then cited as adding another at *Gen. R.* 80.7 (T 957). Teachers may take rather different views on the meaning of a text, as we see from the exegeses of Eccl. 7:18 given in *Gen. R.* 34.5 (T 324), 39.4 (T 367), and 39.7 (T 369). So a verse may be taken as referring to three different people of three different eras, as in *Lam. R.* 3.90.

211. Such asides do occur. When R. Levi rejects R. Abba's interpretation of Abraham's pain at his circumcision and insists (on a textual basis) he was born circumcised, we are told R. Abba called him a liar by two different terms (*Gen. R.* 47.9, T 476). So, too, R. Ḥelbo, incensed at R. Berekhiah's rejection of his view (again citing a textual basis), calls the latter a "strangler seeking to strangle" him (*Lam. R.* 3.21.8). They can be positive, as when R. Zeorah inquired of R. Zeira about "the jewel" of an interpretation that R. Huna had given of Prov. 14:34 (*PRK*, 2.5, Mandelbaum, M 23).

212. Respectively, *Gen. R.* 1.9 (T 8) and *Gen. R.* 10.3 (T 75).

213. *Lev. R.* 36.4 (M 846).

214. *Lam. R.* 1.1.2.

215. *Lev. R.* 34.10 (M 793).

216. Respectively, *Gen. R.* 58.3 (T 621) and *S. S. R.* 1.15.3.

217. Thus in *S. S. R.* 1.1.5 several sages can suggest that a previous explanation is hardly worthy of surprise, since another feature of the text yields something far more astonishing.

218. *Lev. R.* 22.10 (M 524).

219. *Gen. R.* 93.7 (T 1161).

220. *Gen. R.* 85.4 (T 1035).

221. *Gen. R.* 30.8 (T 275), and see the parallel accounts listed there.

222. *PRK* 12.25 (M 223f.).

223. *Gen. R.* 20.10 (T 194).

224. *PRK* 2.7 (M 29).

225. *PRK* 4.3 (M 62). While less expansive, a similar indication of the multiple layers of meaning in a text is given us in *Gen. R.*, where the reference to Nimrod as a "hero" (Gen. 10:8) draws the comment that this word is used in the Bible five times for praise and five times to denote evil (*Gen. R.* 37.3, T 345).

226. For another example, see *Lev. R.* 19.2 (M 419).

227. *S. S. R.* 4.8.1. His "critical" attitude toward the text is validated by his being able to elucidate another meaning in it.

228. *Gen. R.* 53.15 (T 574), and so in other places. Note how in *Gen. R.* 82.14 (T 992) Simeon b. Yoḥai is said to wonder how to interpret the inconsequential verse "And Timnah was the concubine of Eliphaz" (Gen. 36:12)—a verse Menasseh had sneered was too empty to be worthy of God (*San.* 99b)—but nonetheless manages to come up with a positive connection to Abraham.

229. *Gen. R.* 60.15 (T 656). Yitshak Heinemann, *Darkhe Ha-agadah* (Jerusalem: Magnes Press, 1954), p. 27ff., where his discussion of *ibui* occurs.

230. *PRK* 1.3 (M 7).

231. R. Aibu in *Gen. R.* 70.18 (T 817).

232. R. Simeon ben Yoḥai in *Gen. R.* 22.9 (T 216) admits that "it is difficult to say this and impossible for a mouth to say it explicitly," but the text of Gen. 4:9 says that Abel's blood is crying out "against Me," though this involves a change of consonants and vowels.

233. *Lev. R.* 2.5 (M 44).

234. *Gen. R.* 20.2 (T 183).

235. *Gen. R.* 53.14 (T 572).

236. *Gen. R.* 21.4 (T 200).

237. *Lam. R.* Pet. 24, and so not infrequently.

238. Moshe Halbertal, "Ilmale Mikra Katuv ʾI Efshar Le-omro," *Tarbiz* 68, no. 1 (1999): 40–59. Of particular interest are his survey of the occurrences of the phrase and its variants at p. 40 n. 2, the interesting equivalent in *Gen. R.* 22.9 (T216) at p. 43, and his transition remarks from the minority (negative) emphasis to the majority (positive) usage at p. 45. His discussion of the phrase as expressing a recognition that the expositors know their theological daring is, as it is put today, "pushing the envelope" (p. 53). It seems to me that the ambivalence evident in the expression might perhaps more easily be understood as another equivalent of the postmodern understanding of human literature, here evidenced in its frequent "doubling" back upon itself to negate its prior assertions.

239. *Lev. R.* 32.7 (M 753).

240. Since God seeks the persecuted, Israel is one of the entities that appealed to God (*Lev. R.* 27.5 [M 632]); Israel was chosen because it alone of the nations would accept the proffered Torah (*Lam. R.* 3.1.1). Others deny there was any contingency about this (*Lev. R.* 2.2 [M 37]); or say that Israel was one of six premundane entities but also one of those left in God's mind—with a

later voice insisting that God foresaw that Israel would accept the Torah (*Gen. R.* 1.4 [T 6]). The unconditionalists are somewhat abetted by those who assert that Israel lives on forever while the other nations eventually die out (*Gen.* 41.9 [T 396]).

241. *Lev. R.* 25.8 (M 583), a series of such comments, artfully put together.

242. *Lam R.* 1.22.57, another graceful compilation.

243. *Gen. R.* 41.3 (T 390) and *Lam. R.* Proem 34.

244. *Lev. R.* 30.3 (M 695).

245. *Lev. R.* 31.9 (M 729).

246. *Gen. R.* 60.3 (T 642).

247. *Gen. R.* 33.7 (T 313).

248. *PRK* 16.10 (M 278), and so *Lam. R.* 3.5.2; *PRK* 7.5 (M 127).

249. *PRK* 12.14 (M 215) and a similar exegesis in *Lam. R.* Proem 20. The same theme is enunciated from another usage in *Lam R.* Proem 25.

250. *Lam. R.* Proem 15.

251. *PRK* 13.4 (M 228), speaking of Jeremiah, and 22.1 (M 326), which turns Sarah into a wet nurse of gentile children, while the illogic of having several graves allows for an explanation of a difficult reference to lots of blood (*Lam R.* 4.1).

252. *Gen. R.* 50.3 (T 518).

253. *Lev. R.* 27.8 (M 541).

254. *PRK* 7.4 (M 124).

255. *Gen. R.* 37.1 (T 344).

256. *Gen. R.* 19.9 (T 179).

257. *Gen. R.* 24.5 (T 235). This technique helps with obscure Hebrew words, like *almut* in Ps. 45:15, which Aquilas, the targumist, rendered as if it were *al mavet*, "beyond death," itself involving a shift of consonants (*Lev. R.* 11.9 [M 241]).

258. *PRK* 9.1 (M 147). See Marcus Jastrow *Dictionary of the Targumim . . .* (New York: Title Publishing, 1943), s.v. "*s-r-s*," by Poel, p. 1029, for a helpful, brief discussion.

259. In *Gen. R.* 46.7 (T 464) four rabbis prove that *notarikon* was directly authorized by the Torah in Gen. 17:4 but their demonstration is, on the surface, unconvincing even by aggadic standards. Rav's *notarikon* treats the word *anokhi* in Ex. 20:2 as an acronym, which he then turns into a *gematria*, proving that much of the Torah is contained in it (*PRK* 12.24 [M 222]). A somewhat similar combination of the two patterns may be found in Ben Azzai's treatment of *eikhah* in Lam. 1:1 (*Lam. R.* 1.1.1). Bar Kappara provides the more common form of *gematria* in utilizing the numerical value of Eliezer's name to identify him with the leader of Abraham's troops (*Gen. R.* 44.9 [T 432]).

260. A sacrifical animal becomes the people of Israel in *PRK* 4.10 (M 76); the word for sheep suggests "launderers," in this case of the people of Israel's sins (*PRK* 6.4 [M 120]); the leper is transformed into the Temple defiled by Israel's sins (*Lam. R.* Pet. 21.8).

Notes to Chapter 5

261. The "woman of valor" becomes Moses in *PRK* 12.1 (M 204).
262. The "wicked" are identified as Esau in *Gen. R.* 75.8 (T 884).
263. *Gen. R.* 44.17 (T 440).
264. *Gen. R.* 8.4 (T 60).
265. *Gen. R.* 44.19 (T 442).
266. Examples are to be found in every book examined: *Gen. R.* 12.12 (T 111); *Lev. R.* 27.7 (M 639); *Lam. R.* Pet. 31.16 and 4.18.29; and *PRK* 3.1 (M 40) and 9.6 (M 156). The Hebrew word *efes*, "nothing," receives two different Greek interpretations at *Gen. R.* 40.4 (T 384) and *PRK* 17.1 (M 282).
267. *PRK* 12.24 (M 223).
268. E.g., *PRK* 1.8 (M 15), 16.1 (M 265), and 16.8 (M 272). In *Gen. R.* 92.7 (T 1145), R. Ishmael contends that there are already ten examples of *kal vehomer* in the Torah proper.
269. *Gen. R.* 48.14 (T 491), 82.2 (T 979), and *PRK* 19.5 (M 307).
270. *Gen. R.* 49.5 (T 503) and 52.13 (T 554).
271. *Gen. R.* 48.6 (T 480) and *PRK* 15.10 (M 262).
272. *Gen. R.* 53.15 (T 574), where Akiba is challenged to fulfill his master's teaching, and *PRK* 7.10 (M 130), where, without attribution, Naḥum's rule of *miut*, "minimalization," is applied.
273. *PRK* 1.7 (M 11), where a biblical "six" is taken to refer to the orders of the Mishnah or the six matriarchs (the two concubines included).
274. In *S. S. R.* 1.1.6 these are each used, together with a biblical verse, to demonstrate some practical situations.
275. *PRK* 1.5 (M 10).
276. *Gen. R.* 42.3 (T 399).
277. *Gen. R.* 62.4 (T 675).
278. *Gen. R.* 51.2 (T 533).
279. *Lam. R.* 2.1.3.
280. *Lev. R.* 36.6 (M 852).
281. *Gen. R.* 51.3 (T 534).
282. *Gen. R.* 52.4 (T 543). Sober observation also occurs, as in commenting that the word *hu*, "he," can be used either of praiseworthy or sinful people (though this does highlight the erudition of the expositor) (*Gen. R.* 37.3 [T 345]).
283. *Gen. R.* 42.3 (T 399), where the discussion is rather extensive.
284. *S. S. R.* 7.8.1.
285. *Gen. R.* 30.4 (T 271) and *Lev. R.* 34.1 (M 771), where the phrase *al daateh* is not used to introduce a theoretical position but the fact that this verse applies here.
286. *Gen. R.* 55.6 (T 589).
287. *PRK* 3.13 (M 50) and 7.8 (M 129). The reference may only be *masoret hi*, "it is a tradition," as in *Gen. R.* 73.7 (T 851). On one occasion we hear of a group of rabbis troubled by an aggadic verse who seek help from a passing *mara deshemaata*, "a master of traditions" (though *shemaata* is generally used of halakhic traditions) (*Gen. R.* 62.5 [T 676]).

288. E.g., *Gen. R.* 65.15 (T 726).

289. *Gen. R.* 38.12 (T 361), *PRK* 20.7 (M 317).

290. As in *Gen. R.* 38.8 (T 357) and 50.11 (T 528).

291. *Gen. R.* 61.4 (T 661), *PRK* 42.6 (M 125) and 42.8 (M 129), and *Lam. R.* Proem 5.

292. In *PRK* 3.7 (M 46) this happens with two disputants and in *S. S. R.* 1.2.1 each of the four differing views is followed by that additional step.

293. Thus, in *Gen. R.* 42.7 we read that one view can well accommodate the opponent's position, *neha*, but the opposed position now has a problem, *kashya*: can it accommodate the other verse in its exposition?

294. In the previous source, this was referred to as *daateh*, "his point of view." In *PRK*. 1.3 (M 6) the term is *taameh*, "his manner of reasoning." But a sage can extend the discussion by reasoning according to the general position of another teacher, as in *S. S. R.* 2.14.6.

295. E.g., *Gen. R.* 30.8 (T 273), and *Gen. R.* 30.4 and 5.

296. In *Lev. R.* 21.9 (M 487) it is unthinkable that Lev. 16:3 can be interpreted as saying that Aaron would live 412 years. In *Lam R.* Proem 8, the text of Jer. 9:18 must be interpreted figuratively, since wood and stones do not weep. In *S. S. R.* 1.1.5 the text of Dan. 6:18 implies that a stone flew from the land of Israel to seal the lions' cave, since there are no stones in Babylonia.

297. *PRK* 1.3 (M 7).

298. *Lev. R.* 23.10 (M 542).

299. In *Gen. R.* 58.5 (T 623), R. Yose rejects R. Levi linking Terah's death to the eulogizing of Sarah, since two years separated them. In *Lam. R.* 1.1.1, when R. Judah wants to link the book of Lamentations to Yehoiakim, R. Nehemiah retorts that one does not bewail people who haven't yet died.

300. When a verbal similarity suggests that Ps. 109:14 might be Esau's complaint against his father, this is rejected as contrary to fact (*PRK* 3.1 [M 37]). Despite Lam. 2:6, God simply cannot be imagined as forgetting the sacred calendar even in disaster (*Lam. R.* 2.6.10). And though 1 Chr. 29:23 says Solomon sat on God's throne, R. Isaac argues that is unthinkable, God being described as a consuming flame in Dt. 4:24 (*S. S. R.* 1.1.10).

301. *Lev. R.* 35.7 (M 826), where two sages take this tack.

302. *Lev. R.* 20.10 (M 467), for example.

303. Five rabbis may have different views about how many people survived God's attack on the Assyrian force besieging Jerusalem (2 K. 19:35), but the text continues that all agreed that Nebuchadnezzar was one of them (*Lam. R.* Proem 30).

304. *Lev. R.* 20.2 (M 446).

305. *S. S. R.* 3.4.2.

306. *Lam. R.* 1.16.51.

307. *Lev. R.* 13.3 (M 278).

308. *S. S. R.* 4.7.1.

309. *Lev. R.* 19.6 (M 433).

310. *S. S. R.* 1.16.2.
311. *Gen. R.* 30.8 (T 273).
312. *S. S. R.* 1.2.2.
313. In *S. S. R.* 1.1.10, R. Samuel b. Naḥman tries to settle the issue of whether Solomon had three or seven names by saying that the three were his primary names—but what then may be another voice indicates that he admitted the other four names were used of him and that these deserve interpretation. Resh Lakish settles the numerous views about Job's era by saying that he never existed and never will (*Gen. R.* 57.4 [T 614f.]).

Chapter 6. Is Aggadic Discourse Self-Limiting?

1. Hayyim Nahman Bialik, *Kol Kitve Bialik* (Tel Aviv: Devir, 1947), p. 207ff.
2. Ibid., p. 207.
3. Ibid., p. 212.
4. H. Z. Hirschberg and B. Mirmelstein, *Yachas Haaggadah Lehalakhah* (Vienna: Kohut Memorial Foundation, 1929), 1. The study indicates how halakhic matters continually find a place in the early works *Genesis Rabbah* and *Leviticus Rabbah*.
5. Lieberman showed how a passage in *Gen. R.* might clarify the meaning of a complex *halakhah* and suggested that this pattern of using *midrash* to clarify law might prove more generally fruitful. Saul Liebermann, "Meaggadah Lehalakhah," *Sinai* 4 (1939). A similar strategy is pursued by Arazi, who suggests that "the *aggadah* and the *halakhah* complete one another." Cryptic laws are explained by aggadic statements and clear ones are given new meaning by them but his numerous examples are not likely to be accepted by the critical mind. Abraham Arazi, "Shiluv Aggadah Bahalakhah," in *Sefer Hayovel Lerabi Chanokh Albek* (Jerusalem: Mosad Harav Kuk, 1963), pp. 41ff. Segal takes another tack, demonstrating the "use of halakhic quotations as a means of underscoring motifs in aggadic contexts." Eliezer Segal, "Law as Allegory? An Unnoticed Literary Device in Talmudic Narratives," *Prooftexts* 8, no. 2 (1988): 245.
6. *B. K.* 30b.
7. For a particularly perceptive account of the use of, *maaseh*, "anecdote," in halakhic reasoning, one that inadvertently highlights its many similarities to aggadic usage, see E. Z. Melamed, "Ha'maaseh' Bemishnah Kimekor Lehalakhah," in *Torah Shebeal Peh* (Jerusalem: Mosad Harav Kuk, 1963).
8. Louis Jacobs, *Studies in Talmudic Logic and Methodology* (London: Valentine, Mitchell, 1961), esp. pp. 99ff. More recently, in his "The Sugya on Sufferings in B. Berakhot 5a, b," he has argued, "Although the *sugya* is aggadic, it consistently utilises Halakhic-type argumentation. . . . I would maintain that a careful examination of other aggadic passages in the Babylonian Talmud exhibit similar forms, so that the style of presentation of Aggadah, as distinct from its

content, differs little from that which is to be seen in the purely halakhic *sugyot.*" Louis Jacobs, *Studies in Aggadah, Targum and Jewish Liturgy in Memory of Joseph Heinemann* (Jerusalem: Magnes Press, 1981), p. 43. Reuven Hammer comes to a rather similar conclusion in his "Complex Forms of Aggadah and Their Influence on Content," *PAAJR* 48 (1981): 200.

9. *San.* 87a and *ySan.* 11.3.

10. *Y. Yeb.* 4.2. *Aggadah* can occasionally ground a *halakhah,* but, as Menachem Elon puts it, in speaking about Alfasi, "[H]e undertook the arduous and difficult task of distinguishing between Aggadah that has only speculative or anecdotal significance and Aggadah that serves as a basis for halakhic rules governing practical conduct." *Jewish Law,* trans. Bernard Auerbach and Melvin J. Sykes (Philadelphia: Jewish Publication Society, 1994), 3: 1170–71. Note too his comment about the survival of this relationship in the later responsa literature, particularly in the geonic period. Ibid., p. 1464.

11. Moritz Steinschneider, *Jewish Literature* (London: Longman, Brown, Green, Longmans, and Roberts, 1857), p. 29. Salo Baron, having somewhat derogated *aggadah* on p. 298 of his text, then adds in his footnote to that passage, "Needless to say that this dichotomy between Halakhah and Aggadah never seemed so sharp to an ancient talmudist.... In view of the unity of the human mind, moreover, the two disciplines often indistinguishably blended in the mind of the preacher and teacher. That is why some may learn many legally relevant data from the rabbinic homilies, too." Salo Beron, *A Social and Religious History of the Jews* (Philadelphia: Jewish Publication Society, 1952), 2: 429, n. 7. Thirty-plus years later, Gunter Stemberger says, "The differences between halakhic and haggadic exegesis, at any rate, are due less to matters of principle than to different orientation." H. L. Strack and G. Stemberger, *Introduction to the Talmud and Midrash* (Minneapolis: Fortress, 1992), p. 259.

12. *Ber.* 31b, e.g., cites Ishmael's common adage, "The Torah speaks as people speak." For his three interpretations reading legal texts figuratively, see *Sif. Dt.* 237 (F 269f.).

13. *B. B.* 111b where the issue involved is whether a man may inherit from his wife.

14. *Y. Taan.* 4.5.

15. E.g., *Betz.* 24a and *Hor.* 11b. See Adin Steinsaltz, *The Talmud: A Reference Guide* (New York: Random House, 1989), p. 116.

16. Versions of the former term occur frequently in the Bavli, e.g., *Ber.* 25b and 44a, *Shab.* 59a, *Er.* 37b and *Git.* 46b. The latter term is also widely used, e.g., *Shab.* 41b and 92a, *Er.* 88b, *Pes.* 82b, *Ket.* 79b. For a helpful description of the terms see Steinsaltz, *Talmud* (see n. 15), p. 102.

17. E.g., *Ber.* 45b, *Shab.* 20a, *Git.* 23b, *B. M.* 58b, and see Steinsaltz, *Talmud* (see n. 15).

18. For numerous examples see Wilhelm Bacher, *Erkhe Midrash,* trans. A. Z. Rabinowitz (Jerusalem: Carmiel, 1970) 2:157, art. *"beduta."* Cf. Steinsaltz, *Talmud* (see n. 15), p. 106 and note the cross reference to *burkha,* an absurdity.

19. The term is already used this way in the Mishnah, *Ned.* 3.11, where after six halakhic opinions a seventh is suddenly introduced by this term. Cf. *Yoma* 67b for a similarly intrusive occurrence. The more general utilization is found, for example, in *Yev.* 85b. In *Shev.* 30a, for all the halakhic context, the term seems to reflect the common midrashic appearance of the term and introduces an aggadic opinion. The mathematical data provided by Stephen Fraade of the phrase in *Sifre Deuteronomy* indicates that it is more than two and a half times more frequent in the aggadic sections of the book than in those that are halakhic. However, since aggadic materials sometimes occur in largely halakhic passages, I cannot judge to what extent *davar aher* is used to introduce halakhic as against aggadic opinion. Stelphen Fraade, *From Tradition to Commentary* (Albany: State University of New York Press, 1991).

20. *Sot.* 4b.

21. *San.* 17a.

22. *Er.* 13b. *Gen. R.* 26.2 records R. Levi's view that in King David's time sinless children could regularly give forty-nine proofs from the Torah either for the cleanness or the uncleanness of a given item. The champion, however, seems to have been a certain Jonathan ben Harkinas, who had three hundred reasons to prove why the *halakhah* was correct in a complicated case of the permissibility of marrying with someone who had not performed the duty of a levir though the prophet Haggai had ruled that this was impermissible (*Yev.* 16a). The process extends far beyond the rules of ritual purity. Note how the sense of forty-nine ways of construing texts is adduced in reference to property cases in *ySan.* 4.2 (N 135). While *Nu. R.* is much later than the rest of the material studied here, it may help to note that this tradition was not only carried on but expanded in its insistence that there are seventy proper modes of interpreting the Torah (*Nu. R.* 13.15–16). Gerald L. Bruns nicely explores the issue of exegetic and legal freedom in his paper "The Hermeneutics of Midrash," in *The Book and the Text: The Bible and Literary Theory*, ed. Regina M. Schwartz (London: Basil Blackwell, 1990), see esp. pp. 189–97.

23. Shaye J. D. Cohen, "The Significance of Yavneh," *HUCA* 55 (1984): 29.

24. Strack and Stemberger, *Introduction* (see n. 11), p. 259. Abraham Kariv suggests that the notorious freedom the sages allowed themselves in providing *asmakhtot* for halakhic practices is the equivalent of the license the aggadists often took with texts they were interpreting Abraham Kariv, "Beyn Pshat Lidrash Be-aggadat Hazal," *Leshonenu Laam* 20, no. 9–10 (1969): 233ff. One should also keep in mind that the rabbis acknowledge that certain areas of the law are like "mountains hanging by a thread," as *Hag.* 1.8 puts it.

25. Steinsaltz, *Talmud* (see n. 15), p. 149.

26. *Sot.* 16a. *San* 4a provides some wonderful examples of halakhic exegesis as the rabbis range over issues of *sukkot*, boiling a kid in its mother's milk, and phylacteries. A number of these center on details of the plene or defective forms of terms in the relevant texts. But Akiba's textual proof that the head phylactery has four compartments is drawn from the odd word *totafot*, which

he understands as two words, *tot* and *fot*, each meaning "two," in their respective languages, Katpi and Africa.

27. See the discussion of this usage by Chanokh Albeck, "Hahalakhot Vehadrashot," in *Sefer Hayovel Likhvod Aleksander Marks* (New York: JTSA, 1950), p. 3 and note as well his remarks on the practice of *asmakhta*. On the rabbinic mix of polysemy and determinacy in biblical verses, see David Stern, *Midrash and Theory* (Evanston, IL: Northwestern University Press, 1996), pp. 17–21, a topic to which we shall return in the next chapter.

28. For the former term, see *Kid.* 21a–b, where it is used twice in a discussion. The latter term is more widely used, e.g. *San.* 24b. It can also be used positively, as to why a given textual explanation for a law was needed in this reasoning.

29. *Gen. R.* 64.4 (T 704).

30. See *Ket.* 104a, where Abaye tells R. Joseph that, as unreasonable as this seems, "all the rules of the sages have this form [of raising and responding to legal posers]." Haim H. Cohen, who seeks to display the humaneness of Jewish jurisprudence, is clearly uncomfortable with such legal rigidity. Haim H. Cohen, *Jewish Law in Ancient and Modern Israel* (New York: KTAV, 1971), p. xxi.

31. *B. M.* 35b, *Sot.* 44a, and *San.* 51b and 71a are examples of the common notion that God rewards exegesis carried on for its own sake.

32. *B. B.* 23b. For a discussion of this passage as well as R. Jeremiah's penchant for asking far-fetched halakhic questions, see Louis Jacobs, *Teyku: The Unsolved Problem in the Babylonian Talmud* (London: Cornwall Books, 1981), pp. 298–301 and his fine summary there of the place of imaginative, hypothetical reasoning in the Talmud's halakhic analyses.

33. *Men.* 37a.

34. *Men.* 69b. The classic example of theoretical law is the case of the "stubborn and rebellious son" of whom it is said that "There never was and never will be one," but even here one sage testifies that he saw such a person and "sat on his grave" (*San.* 71a). To us it seems imaginative that a demon should be brought into a halakhic discussion, but they were part of the rabbis' sense of the world. See *Yev.* 122a.

35. E.g., *Er.* 2b, *Betz.* 4a, *Ḥul.* 98a.

36. *Ber.* 31a.

37. E. P. Sanders, *Paul and Palestinian Judaism* (Philadelphia: Fortress Press, 1977), p. 71f.

38. *Entziklopediyah Talmudit* (Jerusalem: Talmudic Encyclopedia Publishing, 1959) vol. 9, col. 241, s.v. "Halakhah."

39. Ibid., col. 242.

40. Menachem Elon, *Jewish Law* (see n. 10), 3:1067 n. 128.

41. *San.* 11.2. Ben Azzai reinforces the halakhic desire for agreement on law when he chides Akiba: "We already grieve over those things about which the sages differ. Now you come and raise questions about that on which they agree!" *B. B.* 9.10.

42. *San.* 38a. The reality in his time was quite different.

43. So R. Rabbah bar Rav Huna in *Git.* 43a and Rabbi in *Nid.* 53b. *Ed.* 1.12–14 reports three instances in which the Hillelites changed their minds and accepted the Shammaite position.

44. The terms are commonplaces of rabbinic halakhic usage, e.g., *Ber.* 12b, where the law follows Rabbah's ruling. Steinsaltz, *Talmud* (see n. 15), p. 114.

45. See Steinsaltz, *Talmud* (see n. 15), pp. 126–27.

46. See usage no. 4 in the Jastrow discussion of the root *ḥ-l-k*. Marcus Jastrow, *A Dictionary of the Targumim, the Talmud Babli and Yerushalmi, and the Midrashic Literature* (New York: Title Publishing, 1943), 1: 473. For two uses of the root *p-l-g* see Steinsaltz, *Talmud* (see n. 15), p. 137. The Talmud, largely dominated by halakhic matter, occasionally applies its normally legal terminology to aggadic discussions. So a rabinic aggadic difference is called a *pelugta* in *Sot.* 37a–b.

47. Michael Guttmann, *Zur Einleitung in die Halacha* (Budapest: Budapest Seminary Jahresberichte, 1909), p. 46. He says there, "In defining the *halakhah* we have now touched its most significant activity, decision. The activity of deciding dominates the entire domain of the *halakhah* and determines its further development." An easily accessible example of how this was done is Rav Papa's resolution of the several forms of the *modim* prayer, "So let us say them all" (*Sot.* 40a), and cf. a similar resolution of his in *Meg.* 21b. Related to this is the halakhic "tendency to classify laws into categories of 'principal' and 'derivative,' which pervades all realms of Halakhah." So Moshe Silberg, *Talmudic Law and the Modern State* (New York: Burning Bush Press, 1973), p. 156 n. 13. Jacob Neusner has given close attention to this process in a number of his works on rabbinic Judaism. The meaning of "fixing" (specifying) the law is well brought out in R. Simeon b. Eliakim's comment about a proposed ruling by R. Eliezer. R. Simeon suggests that R. Eliezer intends his dictum as an act of mercy, but he, R. Simeon, worries lest the disciples see this practice and "fix it as the *halakhah* for later generations" (*Ket.* 50b).

48. *Ḥul.* 104b, which alone provides the textual support, *Es.* 2:22, and *Nid.* 19, both of which, ironically enough, do not tell us what sage originated this teaching. *Meg.* 15a, however, indicates that R. Elazar said it in the name of R. Ḥanina.

49. "The Talmud ... seeks in countless ways to discover the author of a given statement. This is not merely a kind of academic investigation but is a method by which the legislation of Rabbi is revised or criticized." Alexander Guttmann, "The Problem of the Anonymous Mishna," *HUCA* 16 (1941): 138. The authority behind a given ruling is often sought to clarify its specific application, as in *B. K.* 13a.

50. To give one example of such rules: "When an individual stand differs with that of the many [sages], the *halakhah* is according to the many" (*Ber.* 9a). However, the fluidity of these rules in Talmudic times is well attested. See, for example, *Ket.* 51a, where it is noted that although the *halakhah* follows Rabbi

where his ruling differs from that of his colleagues, in the specific case under discussion there the law, in fact, follows the opinion of R. Simon b. Elazar. Adin Steinsaltz's section, "Rules Governing Halakhic Decision-Making," in *Talmud* (see n. 15), pp. 295ff. is the best summary of this topic in English. See, however, Stemberger in Strack and Stemberger, *Introduction* (see n. 11), p. 234 who indicates how the Gaon Samuel ben Ḥofni found the need to write about this issue in his introduction to the Talmud, as have many other sages since. In the *Entziklopediyah Talmudit*'s article on "Halakhah" (in Hebrew), sec. 13 is entitled "General Rules about Halakhah among Tannaim," and the literature cited in the footnotes (see particularly n. 508 giving the Talmudic base and the mitigations of later generations in nn. 509 and 510) gives a good sense of the continuing liveliness of this topic. *Entziklopediyah Talmudit* (see n. 38), vol. 9, cols. 278ff, s.v. "Halakhah."

51. See the *Encyclopedia Judaica* (Jerusalem: Keter Publishing House, 1971), vol. 4, cols. 719ff. s.v. "Bet Din and Judges."

52. *B. M.* 35a.

53. See the *Encyclopedia Judaica* (see n. 51), vol. 6, cols. 1348f., s.v. "Flogging," and vol. 8, cols. 350ff, s.v. "Ḥerem."

54. Note the censure of R. Naḥman, which he accepts, for such remarks (*Er.* 64a). R. Yoḥanan b. Dahabai denies the world to come to anyone making such a judgment (*AdRN* 27). But in *Er.* 32b Rabbi says, without censure, that he prefers his own halakhic ruling to that of his father.

55. *Kid.* 44a.

56. The entry in Jastrow, *Dictionary* (see n. 46), p. 1016, provides numerous examples for *s-f-k*, but confines its instances of *t-l-y* (p. 1670), to the first chapter of *Mishnah Pesaḥim*.

57. For the practical/theoretical distinction, see, e.g., *B. B.* 130b and note 41 and its context in this chapter. For the terms regarding inclination rather than decision, see, e.g., *Ber.* 33b and the discussion about the correct number of blessings in the daily and festival Tefilah, the cluster of silent petitions at the heart of Jewish worship. The terms are explained by Steinsaltz, *Talmud* (see n. 15), pp. 129 and 135, respectively. For an early modern discussion of these issues, see Guttmann, "Problem" (see n. 49), second part, pp. 80–81.

58. *Er.* 53b.

59. *Mak.* 23b. Abaye then adduces a dictum of R. Joshua b. Levi to show that we do occasionally have heavenly sanction for our rulings, though in the usual case, as here, we learn the proper rule by the interpretation of texts. An even more imperious dismissal of a sage's ruling is found in *B. B.* 111a, where R. Naḥman calls a certain R. Zechariah "a nothing" and otherwise demeans those who would follow his ruling.

60. Richard Kalmin, "Changing Amoraic Attitudes Toward the Authority of the Halakhah" *HUCA* 63 (1992): 90.

61. For example, see the rejection of Rav's views with this term in *Men.* 29b.

62. Bacher treats this term and gives numerous examples in *Erkhe Midrash* (see n. 18), pt. 2, p. 313. See also the briefer treatment in Steinsaltz, *Talmud* (see n. 15), p. 142. Sometimes the rejections are stated without special terminology, as in *San.* 48b: "Maremar said, 'The *halakhah* follows Abaye.' The rabbis said, 'The *halakhah* follows Rava.' And the *halakhah* does follow Rava."

63. There is a book-length study of the term and its use in Jacobs, *Teyku* (see n. 32). On Elijah as eschatological controversy resolver see *Men.* 45a.

64. From the introduction to *Milḥamot Hashem*, as cited by Menachem Elon in Elon, *Jewish Law* (see n. 10), 3:1174–74.

65. In 1929 Isaac Herzog provided a classic overview in "Moral Rights and Duties in Jewish Law" and it was helpfully reprinted as the appendix to his *Main Institutions of Jewish Law* vol. 1 (London: Soncino Press, 1965). His survey makes no claim to be complete, and other items of rabbinic teaching could be added to his list, e.g., *en ruaḥ ḥakhamim noḥah hemenu* "a deed which carries no legal sanction but the rabbis are not at ease about it."

66. Ze'ev Falk, *Introduction to Jewish Law of the Second Commonwealth* (Leiden: E. J. Brill, 1972), 11.

67. Eliav Shochetman, in his article, "Halakhah She-eno Halakhah," *Sinai*, 120 (Av 5757), struggles mightily to deny that these instances, which he discusses in detail, show that the word *halakhah* can be used concerning material that is *aggadah*. But he must either declare the texts corrupt or stretch the meaning of *halakhah* to encompass nonlegal categories yet not call them, as the definition requires, *aggadah*. (See Israel Rosenson's letter in *Sinai* 121 [Shevat 5758] on this issue.) Jacob Neusner translates *halakhah* in the *Sifre* passage as "As a matter of fact," a clearly nonlegal reading of the term. Jacob Neusner, *Sifre to Numbers* (Atlanta: Scholars Press, 1986), 2:32.

68. An incidental observation may help strengthen the generalization about the difference between the two realms. In the twelfth century the halakhic process had evolved to the point where compendia and a full-scale code of law could be issued and, variously, accepted. There has never been an aggadic code. Instead, in the same period, aggadic discourse begins to take a new, comprehensive form: the *yalkut*, "the anthology." This celebrates difference rather than its reduction through official decision.

69. Steinsaltz, *Talmud* (see n. 15), p. 141.

70. For example, *Gen. R.* 42.7 (T 421f.).

71. For the former term, see *Mak.* 23b or *San.* 95b; and for the latter phrase, see *Meg.* 10b.

72. *San.* 97b–98a.

73. *Suk.* 52b. Note that R. Sheshet's view was a direct refutation of R. Ḥana's homiletic exegesis, one characterized by the term *matkif*, "he objected," often used to reject another's logic. Cf. Steinsaltz, *Talmud* (see n. 15), p. 134.

74. See *Meg.* 15a, where R. Naḥman's view that Malachi was the same as Mordecai is rejected (only later to face the suggestion that Malachi was the

same as Ezra). In *Yoma* 54a a discussion of the whereabouts of the ark after the destruction of the Temple is similarly ended. But a supposed *tiyuvta* to Rabbi is scathingly rejected in *Yoma* 10a.

75. *Er.* 13b describes the famous dispute between Bet Hillel and Bet Shammai on whether it is good for people to have been brought into being, ending in the compromise that it probably is not to their benefit but, since they were created, they should live responsibly. The debate over whether study or deed is more important, recounted in *S. S. R.* 2.14, 5, proclaimed study more important—but because it leads to deeds!

76. Solomon Simon has (in the aggadic spirit?) sought to argue for "Stringent Aggadah—Lenient Halachah," *Judaism* 12 (1963): 296–306. He points out that the aggadic teaching often makes heavy ideal demands upon people, whereas the *halakhah*, having to reckon with what most people can be expected to do, compromises. But though he speaks of "aggadic law" he recognizes that his "stringent *aggadah*" is "teachings ... intended to guide the conduct of the pious elite ... the chosen few who seek a higher state of grace" (p. 299). Rina Lapidus, "Halakhah and Haggadah: Two Opposing Approaches to Fulfilling the Religious Law," *JJS* 45, no. 1 (Spring 1993), argues that in Talmudic times, the two modes of treating Jewish duty had about equal authority, the superior weight of the *halakhah* having not yet been established. Her reading of four Talmudic instances does not persuade me that the classic distinction between the two discourses was not reasonably well in place already in Tannaitic times.

77. *Gen. R.* 56.6 (T 601f.).

78. *Yoma* 76a.

79. *Y. San.* 10.2.

80. "Der alte Widerspruch gegen die Haggadah," reprinted in *Aus drei Jahrtausenden* (Tübingen: J. C. B. Mohr, 1958), pp. 176–85. See the similar views of Jose Faur in "The Character of Classical Jewish Literature," *JJS* 28, no. 1 (Spring 1977), esp. p. 43.

81. *Y. Maas.* 3.10. The next comment directs his son to return to his halakhic query about a certain use of a pruning shear, but the verb used is to "sharpen" it. May we not read into this a cryptic praise of halakhic inquiry in which minds are truly "sharpened"?

82. *Suk.* 52b.

83. *Ḥul.* 27b on *Gen.* 1.20 and 2.19.

84. *Sot.* 5.5.

85. I have followed Jastrow's treatment of this term, so cryptic in this context. Jastrow, *Dictionary* (see n. 46) 287.

86. *San.* 99b.

87. The positive example is R. Simeon b. Lakish, who admits that "there are many biblical verses which look like they ought to be burned [as one does to heretical books]," but he insists that they are essential parts of the Torah and proves this by showing the significance of several such texts (*Ḥul.* 60b).

88. Ithamar Gruenwald, "Midrash and the 'Midrashic Condition,' " in *The Midrashic Imagination*, ed. Michael Fishbane (Albany: State University of New York Press, 1993), p. 11. Judah Goldin's mannered essay "The Freedom and Restraint of Haggadah" is not of much direct help in our discussion, as he ranges far beyond the early post-Talmudic period, but see below. Judah Goldin, "The Freedom and Restraint of Haggadah," in *Midrash and Literature*, ed. Geoffrey H. Hartman and Sanford Budick (New Haven, CT: Yale University Press, 1986).

89. Stern, *Midrash and Theory* (see n. 27), p. 25.

90. Ibid., p. 26.

91. Gruenwald, "Midrash" (see n. 88), p. 12.

92. Cf. n. 40 and its context, which gives a plausible interpretation of the rise of rabbinic discipline.

93. Elon, *Jewish Law* (see n. 10), 1:10ff.

94. Shaye J. D. Cohen, "The Significance of Yavneh," *HUCA* 55 (1984): 47–50.

95. A tale with similar overtones is told about R. Judah, who banned the students of R. Meir from coming into his academy because they overwhelmed their opponents with their dialectical prowess. When Symmachus forced his way in and did just this, R. Judah felt vindicated. But note that this is a halakhic discussion and that Symmachus's question is transmitted to us; and see the disclaimer of R. Yose, which follows it (*Kid.* 53a). On the story of Akabya ben Mehalaleel, see Anthony J. Saldarini, "The Adoption of a Dissident: Akabya ben Mehalaleel in Rabbinic Tradition," *JJS* 33 (1982): 547–56. In thinking about the effect of all these stories on aggadic discourse, it may help to keep in mind a historical judgment on them. Searching for reliable evidence for excommunication in rabbinic circles of Roman Palestine (and essentially concerned with halakhic issues and not aggadic freedom), Catherine Hezser concludes the section (in her chapter 1) on expulsion from rabbinic circles, "Neither the individual traditions nor their usage by the editors suggest that the ban was used—literarily or historically—to control the boundaries of rabbinic movement or to protect *halakhah* in the sense of normative rabbinic rules." Catherine Hezser, *The Structure of the Rabbinic Movement in Roman Palestine* (Tübingen: Mohr Siebeck, 1997), p. 149.

96. Jeffrey L. Rubenstein, "Elisha ben Abuya: Torah and the Sinful Sage," *JJTP* 7, no. 2 (1997): 139–225. Alon Goshen-Gottstein, *The Sinner and the Amnesiac: The Rabbinic Invention of Elisha Ben Abuya and Eleazar Ben Arach* (Stanford, CA: Stanford University Press, 2000).

97. Goshen-Gottstein, *Sinner and the Amnesiac* (see n. 96), p. 7.

98. Goshen-Gottstein is persuasive in calling our attention to the way the Bavli and Yerushalmi differ in their images of Elisha, the former being concerned about his role as one of the Jewish people, the latter of him as a teacher of Torah. Ibid., pp. 200ff.

99. Rubenstein, "Elisha ben Abuya" (see no. 96), p. 184.

100. As cited by ibid., p. 184 n. 104.

101. Ibid., app. 1, "The Sin of Elisha, by Yehuda Liebes," pp. 211–22. Liebes seeks to validate the charge against Elisha in the famous Tosefta story (tḤag. 2.3–4) of the four who entered Pardes, the realm of theosophical speculation. It indicates that Aḥer "cut the shoots"—a cryptic phrase inviting eisegesis—and since the Talmudic tales take off from this, Liebes interprets them by ranging far afield to demonstrate Elisha's transgression arose from impermissible mystic pronouncements. Goshen-Gottstein, who regularly summarizes prior scholarship on the many issues involved in these stories, is somewhat more sympathetic to Liebes. Goshen-Gottstein, *Sinner and the Amnesiac* (see n. 96), pp. 31f.

102. Goshen-Gottstein early in his study spotlights Henry Fischel's observation that "his heresy remains an enigma. . . . Modern scholarship has offered a wide range of solutions, all more or less unsatisfactory." Goshen-Gottstein, *Sinner and the Amnesiac* (see n. 96), p. 23 n. 3. Somewhat later he then extends this by noting the inner contradictions among the sins Elisha is accused of in these various accounts (p. 34).

103. Another anomaly should be noted. In at least two places, the book of Ben Sira—an "outside," i.e., noncanonical, book—is cited as the textual source for limiting one's study to this-worldly matters at *Ḥag.* 13a and *Gen. R.* 8.2 (T 57f.). *Eccl. R.* 12.1 explicitly forbids bringing Ben Sira into one's home.

104. *Y. Pes.* 5.3, II A–D . In the parallel story in *Pes.* 62b, R. Simlai asks to be instructed in the *Book of Genealogies*, and the rejection is not founded on family tradition but on a rule not to teach this to people from his hometown.

105. *San.* 106b.

106. In *Gen. R.* 33.3 (T 304f.), a similar statement that the tetragrammaton implies God's grace, whereas the term *elohim* indicates God's judgment, causes some nimble exegesis in order to explain verses that plainly say the opposite. The *kol makom* phrase seems a general rabbinic usage, since we often find it in halakhic contexts as sages specify the meaning they attach to certain terms (*Er.* 66a, 81b, 85b, etc.).

107. Stemberger provides us with a well-rounded statement of the scholarship on the thirty-two *middot*, both as a *baraita* on its own and its more common form as the expanded work *Mishnat R. Eliezer* or, more commonly, *Midrash Agur*. Strack and Stemberger, *Introduction* (see n. 11), pp. 25–34. For some classic Jewish sources on this theme, see Israel Shepansky, "Hamiddot Shehatorah Nidreshet Bahen," *Or Hamizrach* 42, no. 2 (153).

108. The *Encyclopedia Judaica* article, "Midrashim, Smaller" devotes its first paragraph to *Midrash Agur* and offers a succinct summary of the reasons for the dating. *Encyclopedia Judaica* (see n. 51), 16: 1515, s.v. "Midrashim, Smaller."

109. Hermann L. Strack, *Introduction to the Talmud and Midrash*, 5th ed. (Philadelphia: Jewish Publication Society, 1931), p. 93.

110. Stephen J. Lieberman, "A Mesopotamian Background for the So-called Aggadic 'Measures' of Biblical Hermeneutics," *HUCA* 58 (1987): 222, and see its n. 308.

111. Bacher, *Erkhe Midrash* (see n. 18), 1:69, art. "middah."
112. Baron, *Social and Religious History of the Jews* (see n. 11), 2: 427, n. 4.
113. Saul Lieberman, *Hellenism in Jewish Palestine* (New York: Jewish Theological Seminary, 1950), pp. 68–71. Norman Solomon, "Extensive and Restrictive Interpretation," in *Jewish Law and Current Legal Problems,* ed. Nahum Rakover (Jerusalem: Library of Jewish Law, 1984), p. 37f., makes some perceptive comments on Daube and Lieberman, though his concern with the *middot* is essentially concerned with *halakhah.* Bruns, "Hermeneutics of Midrash" (see n. 22) p. 190 and supporting n. 5, says, "It is certainly not clear that *midrash* [sic] is made up of what we call methods, rules, strategies or techniques." His discussion of the relevant literature is highly persuasive.
114. For examples of this usage see *Yev.* 11b and 24a. See the article under this phrase in *Entziklopediyah Talmudit* (see n. 38), 1:315 for the usual comprehensive discussion, most of which deals with post-Talmudic developments. Steinsaltz, *Talmud* (see n. 15), p. 149 translates *peshuto* as "its literal meaning" and then interprets the rule to mean that "the literal meaning is also considered [sic] a viable approach to interpreting the Torah," which seems to me to understate the weight the rule gives to the Torah text.
115. David Weiss Halivni, *Peshat and Derash* (New York: Oxford University Press, 1991), pp. 18, 63ff. and passim. On this rule generally, see the index of Halivni's book, p. 246, under the rubric "No text can be deprived of its peshat."
116. Ibid., p. 14, and so often.
117. In an extended review of Halivni's book in *Prooftexts* 14 (1994): 71–84.
118. *M. K.* 25a. Others say this happened to R. Ḥanan b. R. Ḥisda.
119. *Meg.* 16b.
120. *Gen. R.* 65.15 (T 727f.).
121. E.g., *B. B.* 16b, *San.* 109a, and elsewhere.
122. The formula is used four times in *Meg.* 16b and occurs elsewhere, as in R. Yoḥanan's similar rebuke to R. Eleazar in *Shev.* 111b. More bitingly, R. Joseph said of R. Hillel's dictum that the Messiah had come in the days of King Hezekiah, "May God forgive him for saying so" (*San.* 99a).
123. *Ber.* 18a.
124. *Sifra Tazria* 13.2. The context here is halakhic, another example of halakhic exposition sometimes showing the same traits as *aggadah.*
125. Respectively, R. Tarfon to R. Elazar Hamodai at *Yoma* 76a; R. Nehemiah b. Rabbi to R. Judah at *Lev. R.* 32.1 (M 734); R. Yose b. Dormaskit to R. Judah three times in *Sif. Dt.* 1 (F 6–8).
126. *Gen. R.* 47.9 (T 476f.). On this text see Goldin, "Freedom and Restraint" (see n. 88), p. 64.
127. *Gen. R.* 55.8 (T 594).
128. Respectively, *Gen. R.* 36.1 (T 334) and *S. S. R.* 1.12.1 and to a different verse in 2.4.1 in both of which R. Judah cites an *ʾen . . . ʾela . . .* "rule" that the Song of Songs is not to be interpreted negatively but only with a positive meaning.

129. The longer version of these stories is found in *S. S. R.* 9.1–4. A shorter version is in *Mek. Beshallah* 6 (H 112–13) with a parallel to one of the stories in *Gen. R.* 21.5 (T 200). Arthur Marmorstein felt that some sort of communal religious tension lies behind these rebuke stories. Arthur Marmerstein, *The Doctrine of Merits in Old Rabbinical Literature* (New York: KTAV reprint, 1968), p. 43. The general tone of rabbinic discussion being what it is, I am not persuaded by this speculative effort to make the rebuke stories exceptional.

130. *San.* 110b.

131. *Yoma* 75b.

132. *Hag.* 14a, cf. *San.* 38b.

133. The latter phrase is literally "leprosy signs and tents." The same wording is twice used in relation to another verse, *San.* 67b.

134. *Shab.* 96b–97a.

135. *Sifre. Num.* 75 (H 70) and note R. Tarfon's use of the derogatory verb *megabev*, to which reference was made above.

136. *Lam. R.* 5.18, where another eccentric teaching behavior is noted.

137. *Y. Shev.* 1.6, 5.A–I, cf. *yYoma* 8.7, 3.A–I, and *Ker.* 7a.

138. *T. San.* 12.9, echoed in *yPeah* 1.1, 21.F–J, *yPes.* 6.2, 4.B, *San.* 49a, and in the context of the anathemas of *San.* 10.1, on which, see the considerable Talmudic discussion of the phrase at *San.* 99a. R. Eleazar Hamodai's dictum is in *P. A.* 3.12

139. We have again and again come across this situation, one to which I shall return later. Our texts appear to have put us into the midst of a lively, apparently effective, subculture's language-style, one characterized more by its open, emergent manner than by well-established formalities.

140. Bruns, applying Wittgenstein, says, "Context, in other words, is social and not logical." Bruns, "Hermeneutics and Midrash" (see n. 22), p. 199 and see the discussion there. We shall return to this philosophic suggestion in the next chapter. For Gruenwald, see nn. 88 and 91 above.

141. The older work is David M. Goodblatt, *Rabbinic Instruction in Sasanian Babylonia* (Leiden: E. J. Brill, 1975). Specific citations from this work and that of Hezser are reserved for the following chapter. The more recent book is that of Catherine Hezser, which (see n. 95) overwhelmingly details a similar conclusion with regard to the rabbinic social order in Roman Palestine.

142. *P. A.* 4.15.

143. Jacob Neusner, *A History of the Jews in Babylonia*, vol. 2, *The Early Sasanian Period* (Leiden: E. J. Brill, 1966).

144. See, for example, the many anecdotes related in *San.* 99b–100a where the rabbis convert the anathema for an *apikoros*, apparently someone influenced by Epicurean thought, to one for those who do not pay proper respect to the masters.

145. *Ber.* 58a.

146. *Shab.* 30b.

147. So *San.* 100a, *Shab.* 30b, 33b–34a, and *yShevi.* 9.1, A–V.

148. Thus the R. Sheshet story (*Ber.* 58a) and that about R. Papa and R. Huna (*Ber.* 58b) are about proper blessings.

149. *Ket.* 111b.

150. On his philosophical perspective, see Bruns, "Hermeneutics of Midrash" (see n. 22), p. 203. The citations that will follow below are taken from some earlier pages in Brun's paper, pp. 198ff.

151. He then cites *Sifre Dt.* 96 (F 158) on Dt. 14:1 and its reading of the law against cutting oneself, yielding, via Amos 9:6, a prohibition against Jewish factionalism, and hence a reinforcement of his view of the importance of the social situatedness of this discourse.

152. Bruns, "Hermeneutics of Midrash" (see n. 22), p. 199.

153. Goldin, "The Freedom and Restraint" (see n. 88) prefers to see the two "voices" as antagonists. Thus, "They are an articulation of the fundamental, universal, interminable combat of obedience and individual conceit" (p. 69). Here I believe his literary sensibilities have obscured the greater unity that a structural sensibility easily finds binding these two languages into a greater whole.

154. *Ḥag.* 3b. This text is the pivot of Bruns's insightful essay "Hermeneutics of Midrash" (see n. 22).

Chapter 7. Positively, What Is *Aggadah*?

1. Joseph Heinemann, "The Nature of the Aggadah," in *Midrash and Literature*, ed. Geoffrey H. Hartman and Sanford Budick (New Haven, CT: Yale University Press, 1986), p. 42.

2. I fully agree with the concern of Lieve Teugels in her careful, detailed, polemical analysis of the widespread, almost indiscriminate use of the term "midrash" in our time—one reason I regularly italicize the term in these pages. Teugels, "Midrash in the Bible or Midrash on the Bible? Critical Remarks about the Use of a Term," in *Bibel und Midrasch: Zur Bedeutung der rabbinischen Exegese für die Bibelwissenschaft,* Forschungen zum Alten Testament 22 (Tübingen: Mohr Siebeck, 1998). Authors in many fields use the term to refer to any writer's interpretation of some aspect of reality, but these days scholars of Hebrew or Christian Scripture are particularly apt to use it rather indiscriminately; see Teugels's p. 44 in particular but passim. While Teugels has a clear sense of the distinction between *midrash* and *aggadah* (p. 54), she limits the latter term, as we shall see some other scholars do, to "Jewish *narrative* material in general without taking into consideration the literary form in which it appears" (p. 54 [emphasis in the original; a definition probably derived from the meaning of the Hebrew root]). But, as the prior data of this study have indicated, there is quite a difference between this sense of *aggadah* and NHD's. I would extend Teugel's epitome, "If it is correct to say that midrash is often aggadic, the opposite is certainly not the case" (p. 54); to say the same

about Teugel's limited sense of *aggadah*: it is correct to say that narrative *aggadah* is part of NHD (the classic Jewish self-understanding of the term *aggadah*) but the opposite is certainly not the case. I shall briefly return to this issue below in discussing literary approaches to NHD.

3. The second Gorman edition of 1892 was the basis for the Hebrew translation by M. A. Zak, with updates by Hanokh Albeck in *Haderashot Beyisrael ve-Hishtalshalutan Hahistorit* (Jerusalem: Mosad Bialik, 1947).

4. A critical indicator of this shift to a different sense of the historical imperative in studying this area is found in Chaim Milikowsky's assertion, "Few scholarly editions of rabbinic works are being produced these days. . . . Although in other fields of the humanities it seems that textual work and scholarly editing are more common now than was the case in previous decades. . . ." Chaim Milikowsky, "Further on Editing Rabbinic Texts," *JQR* 90, nos. 1–2 (July–October, 1999): 137, and see the literature cited there. Geza Vermes in his *Scripture and Tradition in Judaism* (Leiden: E. J. Brill, 1961), after surveying the current scholarship and praising highly the researches of Renée Bloch, calls for emulation of her work, which shifted attention to the history of exegetical themes (pp. 1–10); and see his summary of six findings in the study of the connotations of the term "Lebanon" (pp. 38–39). For a critique of the Bloch-Vermes use of the term *midrash* see Teugels, "Midrash" (see n. 2), pp. 53–56. A decade plus after Vermes, Ben Zion Wacholder could write, "There was a time not long ago when the term 'midrash' referred to a clearly defined body of literature. . . . As such the term reflected a clearly defined genre of literature, with its own language, terminology and hermeneutics. Recently, however, 'midrash' has been used increasingly to embrace different genres of writings which are in many ways only remotely related to the type of exegesis developed by the early Rabbis." Wacholder, *Messianism and Mishnah: Time and Place in the Early Halakhah* (Cincinnati: Hebrew Union College Press, 1979), p. 43. A few years later, Richard Sarason published a study featuring a detailed, careful analysis of the current literature, which was entitled "Toward a New Agendum for the Study of Rabbinic Midrashic Literature" in *Studies in Aggadah, Targum and Jewish Liturgy in Memory of Joseph Heinemann*, ed. Jakob J. Petuchowski and Ezra Fleischer (Jerusalem: Magnes Press, 1981). Sarason's desideratum "is a kind of 'phenomenological' analysis, a close reading of the texts—document by document—which would be informed by questions out of literary criticism, history of religions and cultural anthropology" (p. 69 and see n. 33).

5. Maurya P. Horgan concludes her detailed study of this issue by saying "the term 'midrash' is neither a useful or informative term by which to characterize the pesharim." Horgan, *Pesharim: Qumran Interpretations of Biblical Books* (Washington, DC: Catholic Biblical Association of America, 1979), p. 252. At about the same time, Ben Zion Wacholder held a similar opinion in *Messianism and Mishnah* (see n. 4), pp. 43–46. Later scholarship has confirmed these judgments.

6. Yitshak Heinemann, *Darkhe Ha-aggadah*, 2nd ed. (1954).

7. Saul Lieberman's major works are *Greek in Jewish Palestine* (New York: Jewish Theological Seminary of America, 1942) and *Hellenism in Jewish Palestine* (New York: Jewish Theological Seminary of America, 1950). On Lieberman and Daube, see the discussion in Gary Porton, "Rabbinic Midrash," in *Judaism in Late Antiquity*, ed. Jacob Neusner (Leiden: E. J. Brill, 1995), pp. 225f.

8. See particularly David Daube's influential paper, "Rabbinic Methods of Interpretation and Hellenistic Rhetoric," *HUCA* 22 (1949). His strong case is "that rabbinic methods of interpretation derive from Hellenistic rhetoric. Hellenistic rhetoric is at the bottom both of fundamental ideas, presuppositions from which the Rabbis proceeded and of the major details of application, the manner in which these ideas were translated into practice" (p. 240), but in an accompanying footnote he withdraws somewhat and cites his "provisional observations" in several articles. See also his book *Alexandrian Methods of Interpretation and the Rabbis* (Basel: Helbing & Lichtenhahn, 1953).

9. All in Hebrew are E. E. Halevi, *Shaarei Ha-aggadah: Ha-agadah le-or mekorot yevaniyim* (Tel Aviv: s. n., 1963); idem, *Olamah shel ha-agadah* (Tel Aviv: Dvir, 1972); idem. *Ha-aggadah ha-historit-biografit* (Tel Aviv: Tel Aviv University, 1975); idem. *Parashiyot ba-agadah le-or mekorot Yevaniyim* (Haifa: Haifa University, 1973), and numerous articles on associated themes. For a critical review of his work, see Adam Kamesar, "The Narrative Aggada as Seen from the Graeco-Latin Perspective," *JJS* 45, no. 1 (Spring 1994).

10. Martin Hengel, *Judaism and Hellenism: Studies in Their Encounter in Palestine in the Early Hellenistic Period* (Philadelphia: Fortress, 1974). Louis Feldman subjected Hengel's findings to a sustained, detailed, and, to me, persuasive critique, ascribing some of the dubious conclusions to Hengel's theological agenda. Feldman, "Hengel's Judaism and Hellenism in Retrospect," *JBL* 96, no. 3 (1977).

11. Many of Henry Fischel's studies are presented in *Rabbinic Literature and Greco-Roman Philosophy* (Leiden: E. J. Brill, 1973). The special motivation he gave to the Hellenistic influence on form in rabbinic *aggadah* may be traced to his paper "Studies in Cynicism and the Ancient Near East: The Transformation of a *Chria*," in *Religions in Antiquity: Essays in Memory of Erwin Ramsdall Goodenough* (Leiden: E. J. Brill, 1973). A striking illustration of the possibilities of this approach to rabbinic documents is found in Martin Jaffee's paper "The Oral Cultural Context of the Talmud Yerushalmi: Greco Roman Rhetorical Paideia, Discipleship, and the Concept of Oral Torah," in *Transmitting Jewish Traditions: Orality, Textuality, and Cultural Diffusion*, ed. Yaakov Elman and Israel Gershoni (New Haven, CT: Yale University Press, 2000).

12. Thus, although Lieberman wrote that there is no evidence "that the rabbis borrowed their rules of interpretation from the Greeks," he felt that they did when dealing with "formulation terms, categories and systematization of these rules. . . . Although the rabbis cannot be definitely said to have adopted a certain method from the Greeks, they may nevertheless have learned

from them the application of that method to a particular question." Lieberman, *Hellenism in Jewish Palestine* (see n. 7), pp. 78–79. Some years later, seeking to answer the question "How Much Greek in Jewish Palestine?" he summarized "We do not know exactly how much Greek the Rabbis knew. They probably did not read Plato and certainly not the pre-Socratic philosophers. Their main interest was centered in Gentile legal studies and their methods of rhetoric. But the Rabbis knew enough Greek to keep them from telling stories about Greek principles and their civil laws. Jewish opinion on the non-Jewish world was the product of knowledge, not ignorance, and this knowledge was undoubtedly a great asset." Saul Lieberman, *Biblical and Other Studies*, ed. Alexander Altmann (Cambridge, MA: Harvard University Press, 1963). Fischel, introducing Liberman's book, advocates some significant Greek influence, but not only limits his claims to the specific items he will be discussing but also summarizes his position on generalizing by indicating that the rabbinic reuse and adaptation of Greek materials and forms made the task "of recognizing and reconstructing an originally Greco-Roman item quite precarious." Fischel, *Rabbinic Literature* (see n. 11), pp. ix–xi. I do not know, therefore, what David Stern means when he writes "classical Judaism ... was itself (as scholars over the last century have definitively established) *a fusion* [emphasis added] that derived from the confrontation between native Israelite tradition and Hellenism.... That is to say, Rabbinic Judaism is already a mixture, a mingling of Israelite, or biblical, and Greco-Roman elements." Stern, *Midrash and Theory: Ancient Jewish Exegesis and Contemporary Literary Studies* (Evanston, IL: Northwestern University Press, 1996), pp. 5–6. "Fusion" seems to me to imply a strong blending (perhaps to the point of producing a new unity), whereas "mixture" and "mingling" diminish the integration. The more commonly used term, "borrowing," suggests even less, while the scholars' qualifications of their work given above certainly suggest the influence was real but not heavy.

13. Sandra Shimoff analyzed the midrashic biographies of David and Solomon in "Hellenization among the Rabbis: Some Evidence from the Early Aggadot Concerning David and Solomon," *JSJ* 18, no. 2 (1987) and concluded that "The present analysis suggests that many of the Rabbis not only adopted Hellenistic values, but actively encouraged such practices through their aggadot" (p. 186). Kamesar, "Narrative Aggada" (see n. 9), p. 54, examining "narrative aggada (= expansion and elaboration of the Biblical text in narrative form)," explores it in terms of the literalist approach of Greek writers to similar material and concludes, in extension of a thesis of Yitshak Heinemann, that "Greek exegesis is to be distinguished from aggada because it involved clear separation of 'scientific' and artistic/poetic inquiry," which aggada did not (p. 61). However, a further study of a thoroughly Hellenized Jew like Philo indicates that (as Kamesar notes Samuel Sandmel had previously indicated) Philo treats such material differently than do the rabbis, not engaging in the rabbis' extensive embellishment of the story. Adam Kamesar, "Philo,

Grammatike and the Narrative Aggada," in *Pursuing the Text: Studies in Honor of Ben Zion Wacholder on the Occasion of His Seventieth Birthday*, ed. John C. Reeves and John Kampen (Sheffield: Sheffield Academic Press, 1994). Jaffee, working with the rabbinic "homiletical" literature (his consistent translation of the term "aggadah" as he is using it in his study of orality in the shaping of rabbinic tradition), finds substantial likenesses between Greco-Roman rhetorical manuals and rabbinic oral-aural practice. Martin S. Jaffee, *Torah in the Mouth: Writing and Oral Tradition in Palestinian Judaism, 200 BCE–400 CE* (New York: Oxford University Press, 2001), pp. 128ff.

14. Stephen J. Lieberman, "A Mesopotamian Background for the So-Called Aggadic 'Measures' of Biblical Hermeneutics?" *HUCA* 58 (1988).

15. Marc Hirshman, *A Rivalry of Genius: Jewish and Christian Biblical Interpretation in Late Antiquity* (Albany: State University of New York Press, 1996). Burton L. Visotzky, *Fathers of the World: Essays in Rabbinic and Patristic Literatures* (Tübingen: J. C. B. Mohr; Philadelphia: Coronet Books, 1995). Judith Baskin provides a fine review of both books in "Rabbinic-Patristic Exegetical Contacts: Some New Perspectives," *RSR* 24, no. 2 (April 1998).

16. Visotzky, *Fathers of the World* (see n. 15), p. 2.

17. Richard Kalmin, *The Sage in Jewish Society of Late Antiquity* (New York, Routledge, 1999).

18. So the thesis, admittedly more generalized than his book, of Kalmin's paper "Kings, Priests and Sages in Rabbinic Literature in Late Antiquity," delivered at the 2000 meeting of the Association for Jewish Studies.

19. Sarason, "Toward a New Agendum" (see n. 4), p. 65 n. 26, and his continuing remarks there.

20. David Goodblatt, *Rabbinic Instruction in Sasanian Babylonia* (Leiden: E. J. Brill, 1975), 281–82, 284f. See also his discussion of the role of small groups (pp. 252 and 267), and of the influence of the image of the Sanhedrin on the gaonic *kallah* (p. 259).

21. Catherine Hezser, *The Social Structure of the Rabbinic Movement in Roman Palesine* (Tübingen: Mohr Siebeck, 1997). Of particular interest are part 2, "Relationships amongst Rabbis," specifically, sections 2, "Was the Rabbinic Movement Institutionalized?" and section 3, "An Informal Network of Relationships" as well as section 1 of her summary, "The Boundaries of the Rabbinic Movement," whose opening statement is the first citation. She foreshadowed the findings of her book in her article "Social Fragmentation, Plurality of Opinion, and Nonobservance of Halakhah: Rabbis and Community in Late Roman Palestine," *JSQ* 1 (1993/94); the second citation is from that work (p. 235). Hayim Lapin criticizes Hezser's book as being insufficiently critical of the network theory she resolutely employs and suggests various ways in which her already lengthy study might have been extended (*etmaha!* as the rabbis might have said) in his review in *AJS Review* 24, no. 2 (1999): 378ff. Martin Jaffee, however, pays her (and Goodblatt's) work indirect tribute by entitling the summary chapter of his *Torah in the Mouth* (see n. 13),

"Torah in the Mouth in Galilean Discipleship Communities," rather than utilizing a more traditional model such as "academy."

22. These ideas introduce Goodblatt's review of Kalmin's *The Sage in Jewish Society of Late Antiquity* in *JQR* 90, nos. 3–4 (January–April, 2000): 46.

23. Sarason, "Toward a New Agendum" (see n. 4), p. 67f. He has since extended this perspective in his paper "Interpreting Rabbinic Biblical Interpretation: The Problem of Midrash Again," in *Hesed Ve-emet: Studies in Honor of Ernest S. Frerichs*, ed. Jodi Magness and Seymour Gitin (Atlanta: Scholars Press, 1998). See particularly his discussion of the "overdetermination" in midrashic literature and the usefulness of noting its eisegetical (ideological), exegetical, and performative aspects while rigorously keeping in mind that these distinctions say more about our interests than about the *midrash*, which is best understood holistically (pp. 136ff.).

24. Zipporah Kagan, "Divergent Tendencies and Their Literary Moulding in the Aggadah," in *Studies in Aggadah and Folk-Literature*, ed. Joseph Heinemann and Dov Noy (Jerusalem: Magnes Press, 1971), p. 151. As so often happens in literary approaches to *aggadah*, what Kagan has in mind is not NHD but the tales found therein. Her strong sense of this approach allows her also to say, "Every variant of an aggadah is an independent literary creation in its own right" (p. 151).

25. Birger Gerhardsson, *Memory and Manuscript: Oral Transmission in Rabbinic Judaism and Early Christianity* (Uppsala: C. W. K. Gleerup, Lund, 1961), since reprinted by Eerdman's Publishing, 1998.

26. Jaffee, *Torah in the Mouth* (see n. 13).

27. Ibid., pp. 211–28, which includes a number of his own many fine prior papers in this area. Though I have made reference before (see n. 11 above) to his outstanding paper "The Oral-Cultural Context of the Talmud Yerushalmi," which is not reproduced in *Torah in the Mouth*, it deserves further reference here because of its impressive conclusions about the importance of the disciple-sage relationship in shaping the Yerushalmi and other rabbinic works.

28. Jaffee, *Torah in the Mouth* (see n. 13), pp. 9–10.

29. Ibid., p. 140, and see the entire discussion there.

30. See the previous discussion of Kalmin's work nn. 17–18 above.

31. The citation is from his substantial statement in Yaakov Elmon, "Orality and the Redaction of the Babylonian Talmud," *Oral Tradition* 14, no. 1 (1999): 53, but there is also helpful material in the "introduction" to *Transmitting Jewish Traditions* (see n. 11), which he edited with Israel (Yisrael) Gershoni, and, to a lesser extent, since it treats of a time beyond our purview, his article in that book with Daphna Aphrat, "Geonic Yeshiva and Islamic Madrasa."

32. Elman, introduction (see n. 31), p. 12, and compare particularly Elman, "Orality and the Redaction" (see n. 31), p. 56 but also p. 81. However, he also indicates how late it was—the mid-eighth century—when much of "the redaction of many genres in Babylonian Jewish literary history" took place. Elman and Aphrat, "Geonic Yeshiva" (see n. 32), p. 109. It should be noted

that, as he regularly indicates in these papers, Elman is primarily concerned with the transmission of legal materials, whereas Kalmin's study focuses almost entirely on aggadic texts as does much of the attention in Gerhardsson and Jaffee.

33. Dan Ben-Amos, "Recent Books in Jewish Studies: The Hebrew Folktale, a Review Essay," *JS*, no. 35 (1995): 29.

34. Salo Baron, speaking of Max Kadushin's and other efforts to supply a structure of rabbinic thinking, dismissed them, saying, "[I]t will be difficult to construe a well-rounded system out of fragments of a consciously unsystematic folkloristic body of material." Baron, *A Social and Religious History of the Jews*, vol. 2 (New York: Columbia University Press, 1937), p. 434 n. 26.

35. Dov Noy, "The Jewish Version of the 'Animal Languages' Folktale (AT670)—A Typological-Structural Study," in *Studies in Aggadah and Folk Literature*, ed. Joseph Heinemann and Dov Noy (Jerusalem: Magnes Press, 1971), p. 188.

36. "Orality" here, as often in these studies, is being used as a synonym for folk-literature. Ben-Amos, "Recent Books in Jewish Studies" (see n. 33), p. 45. Dinah Stein has helpfully prefaced her survey of the evolution of Ben-Amos's distinctive approach to the issue of folklore and *aggadah* with an outline of the hermeneutic methods that preceded his. Stein, "Dan Ben-Amos's Studies of Folk Literature in the Midrash," in *Jerusalem Studies in Jewish Folklore*, ed. Tamar Alexander, Galit Hasan-Rokem, and Shalom Tzabar (Jerusalem: Magnes Press, 1998). The indistinct boundary line between the oral and the written is a major concern of Elman and Kalmin in the studies noted above. Various scholars have, however, minimized the folk element in the aggadic texts they have chosen to study, e.g., Shmuel Safrai, who argues that one detects in the tales about the sages "their genuine historical core." Safrai, "Tales of the Sages in the Palestinian Tradition and the Babylonian Talmud," in *Studies in Aggadah and Folk Literature*, ed. Joseph Heinemann and Dov Noy (Jerusalem: Magnes Press, 1971), p. 210. So, too, David Kraemer, stressing the level of literacy required to study the Talmuds and even the *midrash* books, says that these documents "most likely speak for rabbis alone and not for rabbinized Jews who were not rabbis." Kraemer, *Responses to Suffering in Classical Rabbinic Literature* (New York: Oxford University Press, 1995), pp. 215f., and see also his related discussion on p. 148. Eliezer Segal, who strongly argues for the synagogal as against the study-house origins of the classic midrashic collections, extends that line of reasoning to insist that they are not significantly folkloristic. Segal, *The Babylonian Esther Midrash* (Atlanta: Scholars Press, 1994), pp. 2–9, particularly his extensive n. 4 there. Yaakov Elman considers Segal's statement "a balanced view of the scholarly consensus." Elman, "How Should a Talmudic Intellectual History Be Written? A Response to David Kraemer's *Responses to Suffering*, *JQR* 89, nos. 3–4 (January–April 1999): p. 370.)

37. *Suk.* 28a, where he is termed the least of the eighty extraordinary disciples of Hillel the elder. He had, however, studied "Bible, Mishnah, Gemara,

Halakhah, Aggadah, Dikdukei Torah, Dikdukei Sofrim, [varieties of] Kal Veḥomer and Gezerah Shavah arguments, calendrical mathematics, uses of Gematria, the speech of Ministering Angels, the speech of spirits, the speech of the palm-trees, fuller's parables, fox fables, and great and small matters." Dan Ben-Amos, "Generic Distinctions in the Aggadah," in *Studies in Jewish Folklore,* ed. Frank Talmage (Cambridge, MA: Association for Jewish Studies, 1980), p. 50 and see the context.

38. Dan Ben-Amos, "The Idea of Folklore," in *Studies in Aggadah and Jewish Folklore,* ed. Issachar Ben-Ami and Joseph Dan (Jerusalem: Magnes Press, 1983), p. 15 and p. 17.

39. Galit Hasan-Rokem, *Web of Life: Folklore and Midrash in Rabbinic Literature,* trans. Batya Stein (Stanford, CA: Stanford University Press, 2000).

40. Ibid., p. 2. See also p. 10 and the context of n. 19 where she specifies that the "main sources of inspiration were structural, semiotic and hermeneutical," but not, I note, formalist, as in the work of Yonah Frenkel in n. 44, to be discussed below. Of interest as well is her distancing herself from Ben-Amos's reliance on the notion of genre, though she uses it as a partially helpful tool, and her suggestion that there are no complete bodies of folk literature, but folk literature is, "by definition, the study of an endless phenomenon..." (p. 40).

41. An indication of the popularity of this approach is provided by Joseph M. Davis's precisely titled article "Literary Studies of Aggadic Narrative: A Bibliography," which directs us to nearly five hundred modern studies treating of eleven different relevant themes (though his chronological range is much greater than our more limited one). In *New Perspectives on Ancient Judaism,* vol. 3, *Judaic and Christian Interpretation of Texts: Contents and Contexts,* ed. Jacob Neusner and Ernest S. Frerichs (Lanham, MD: University Press of America, 1987), pp. 185ff.

42. Heinemann, *Darkhe Ha-aggadah* (see n. 6), p. 1.

43. Ibid., pp. 275–76.

44. Yonah Frenkel, *Darkhe Ha-aggadah veha-midrash* (Masadah: Yad la-talmud, 1991). Two years later the Open University of Israel published Frenkel's *Midrash ve-aggadah,* a three-volume restatement of his prior academic work, for the use of radio students as well as general readers. Though a lengthy work, it often provides a simpler access to Frenkel's thinking.

45. Frenkel, *Darkhe Ha-aggadah veha-midrash* (see n. 44), pt. 2, with its emphasis on the primary situation of the scholar's study of text in the community of fellow scholars.

46. Ibid., pt. 3, though he must struggle somewhat to explain how the popular and folk aspects of this discourse become the concern of scholars and have so large a place in their traditions.

47. Ibid., chap. 12, pp. 395ff.

48. A good example of the former case is Richard Kalmin's persuasive critique, "The Modern Study of Ancient Rabbinic Literature: Yonah Frenkel's

Darkhei Ha'aggadah Vehamidrash," Prooftexts 14 (1994): 189–204.

49. David Stern, *Parables in Midrash: Narrative and Exegesis in Rabbinic Literature* (Cambridge: Harvard University Press, 1991). Note the limitation of aggadic focus in the subtitle.

50. Anthony Saldarini in his detailed review of Stern's work, some five years after its appearance, while appreciative of its accomplishment, is, in my eyes, too critical of Stern for not here employing the poststructuralist modes of literary study that became prevalent in the 1990s. Though Saldarini has provided a most helpful summary of the preceding scholarship in this area, in which the Gospel parables were often the focus of the scholarship, what Stern accomplished in advancing the study of this literary trope beyond what had been available to him is worthy of high commendation. For Stern's later contribution to poststructuralist literary theory and *midrash*, see notes 72–81 below. Anthony Saldarini, "Parables in Midrash: Narrative and Exegesis in Rabbinic Literature by David Stern," *RSR* 22, no. 2 (April 1996): 119–23.

51. Ibid., p. 9, and note the ensuing effort, pp. 10–16, to distinguish it from the Greek "parable" and the rabbinic *maaseh*, which he translates as "occurrence."

52. Some particularly impressive examples of the fruitfulness of these approaches deserve note here. Thus, Susan Shapiro's analysis of the deeper issues at stake in the Gadamer-Habermas debate, "Rhetoric as Ideology Critique," *JAAR* 62, no. 1 (Spring 1994), revisits two antagonistic positions founding the late twentieth-century turn to hermeneutic self-awareness in modern thought and literature. While her paper does not directly deal with religious texts, her well-established point is that "When we study contemporary interpretive theory, therefore, we are implicated with the history of its formation" (p. 147). Thus, we cannot by our new self-awareness leave out the recognition that this, too, is not value-free but inevitably comes to us, its users, encumbered with its own ideological freight. Gerald L. Bruns, acknowledging his debt to Gadamer, identifies in "The Hermeneutics of Midrash," in *The Book and the Text: The Bible and Literary Theory*, ed. Regina Schwartz (Oxford: Blackwell, 1990), the central thrust of this hermeneutic approach as not being concerned to "produce a theory that would lay bare its logic or deep structure or tacit rules," but to "clarify the conditions in which understanding occurs ... conditions [that are] social and historical rather than 'logical conditions of possibility'" (pp. 189f.). This leads to a rich sense of how to read *midrash*, which "is not a formal operation but a form of life lived with a text that makes claims on people.... This is why, as in legal hermeneutics, you find in the foreground of midrash the idea that interpretation is inseparable from application to a situation that calls for action" (p. 203). From this perspective, "Unfortunately, mainline research on midrash is just hermeneutically naive" (p. 210 n. 7). To a considerable extent, Ithamar Gruenwald's paper "Midrash and the 'Midrashic Condition': Preliminary Considerations," in *The Midrashic Imagination: Jewish Exegesis, Thought, and History*, ed. Michael Fishbane

(Albany: State University of New York Press, 1993), with its quite uncommon effort to set forth this social-intellectual "condition," albeit preliminarily, is instructive as to the practice of this hermeneutic approach. Though I approach NHD from a more philosophic concern with discourse than they do, my stance has much affinity with that of Bruns and Gruenwald, as will become clear later. Jack N. Lightstone, *The Rhetoric of the Babylonian Talmud: Its Social Meaning and Context* (Waterloo, Ont.: Wilfred Laurier University Press, 1994), examines the rhetoric with an eye to searching out its "stock rhetorical formularies" (p. x) but, aside from a peripheral comment on p. 168, seems to have no interest in how aggadic rhetoric might differ from the general flow of the Bavli's dialectic. Aryeh Cohen specifically indicates his approach in the subtitle to his book *Rereading Talmud: Gender, Law and the Poetics of Sugyot* (Atlanta: Scholars Press, 1998). Cohen carefully distinguishes his own hermeneutic from what may be called Frenkel's literary formalism, seen most clearly in Frenkel's isolated analysis of the structure of each aggadic story, whereas Cohen shows what greater insight is gained by setting the stories in their literary context, namely the *sugya*, the greater textual flow of dialectic, in which we find them (pp. 73–89). He then identifies his approach to the text with aspects of Daniel Boyarin's cultural poetics (Cohen, *Rereading Talmud*, p. 90; Boyarin's work will be discussed in the following section of this chapter). While Cohen has a refreshing interest in aggadic portions of the Bavli and his sugyetic approach adds a valuable approach to interpreting them, he is not directly concerned with the issue of what might distinguish aggadic from halakhic material in a *sugya*.

53. Jeffrey L. Rubenstein, *Talmudic Stories: Narrative Art, Composition, and Culture* (Baltimore: Johns Hopkins University Press, 1999); Alon Goshen-Gottstein, *The Sinner and the Amnesiac: The Rabbinic Invention of Elisha Ben Abuyah and Eleazar Ben Arach* (Stanford, CA: Stanford University Press, 2000). Note how the very titles indicate their break with the historical approach to these tales and their turn to them as literary creations.

54. Thus, Jacob Neusner indicates this even in works that might seem far removed from such a perspective. His *The Talmud of Babylonia: A Complete Outline* indicates in its preface the need for seeing the general plan of the work so as to be able to do a proper "literary analysis" of the work. I cite here the volume dealing with *Shevuot*, the tractate I studied as part of the sample of Talmudic aggadic material basic to this investigation: Jacob Neusner, *The Talmud of Babylonia: A Complete Outline*, part 3, *The Division of Damages, B: From Tractate Sanhedrin through Tractate Shebuot*, University of South Florida Academic Commentary Series (Atlanta: Scholars Press, 1995), ix.

55. Judith Hauptman, "Feminist Perspectives on Rabbinic Texts," in *Feminist Perspectives on Jewish Studies*, ed. Lynn Davidman and Shelley Tenenbaum (New Haven, CT: Yale University Press, 1994), p. 41.

56. Jacob Neusner, *The Unity of Rabbinic Discourse* (Lanham, MD: University Press of America, 2001), 3:xviii.

57. Particularly instructive in relation to what Neusner does and doesn't want to include in his study of rabbinic *aggadah* is his explanation of why his aggadic studies do not deal with parables that Stern, as we have seen, considers so illuminating an aspect of the discourse. Neusner writes, "I have not dealt with the rabbinic version of parables, because I do not know how they fit into the study at hand or contribute to the achievement of its goals. Parables ... do not figure in a documentary project such as this one, because they form *an infinitesimal proportion of the whole rabbinic literature* and do not impart their traits and presence to the definition of entire documents." Neusner, *Unity of Rabbinic Discourse* (see n. 56), 3: xii n. 2 (emphasis added). Thus, one cannot simply correlate Neusner's results with other works in this field without carefully keeping in mind his innovative definition of what he is seeking to do. By the same token, it should not be surprising that others will deem it valuable to study aggadic utterance, considering that some scholars have suggested that 20% of the Mishnah and $33^1/_3$% of the Bavli are NHD. These do not seem of only infinitesimal significance to many scholars but rather contribute importantly to the character of the work in which the NHD is employed. Besides, the rabbinic authors of this material understood all of it to be Oral Torah.

58. They may best be understood by attention to Neusner's introduction and "The Native Categories" and "Native Category-Formations" sections of his book *The Native Category-Formations of the Aggadah* (Lanham, MD: University Press of America, 2000). See particularly 1: xiii–xviii and, for his general theory of the proper approach to this literature, continue on 1: xviii–xxii. On 1: 134–36, he further specifies and clarifies his key conceptual interests.

59. Thus, Neusner occasionally makes references to further studies needed to fully carry forward his present investigations but for which he does not yet envision an appropriate plan. However, he also refers to works that grow out of ones he has completed. So he mentions his forthcoming *The Comparative Hermeneutics of Rabbinic Judaism,* vol. 1, in the preface to *The Native Category-Formations of the Aggadah* (see n. 58), 1: vii n. 3, which latter work he calls the prolegomenon to the former. And he concludes his *Dual Discourse, Single Judaism* by calling it the prolegomenon to his next project, telling the story of the divine narrative of Judaism whole and complete. Neusner, *Dual Discourse, Single Judaism* (Lanham, MD: University Press of America, 2001), p. 179.

60. While these works are primarily halakhic, they all contain a not insignificant amount of aggadic material, particularly when viewed as NHD, a matter discussed in prior chapters.

61. So his usage at Neusner, *Native Category-Formations of the Aggadah* (see n. 58), 1: vii. He feels some discomfort with this usage when dealing with the issue of where to classify the so-called Halakhic or Tannaitic Midrash books, *Mekhilta* (less so here), *Sifra*, and *Sifre*. See Neusner, *Unity of Rabbinic Discourse* (see n. 56), 2: xi.

62. Despite my familiarity with Neusner's writing, I found it took me quite a while to gain what seemed to me reasonable insight into his special use of the term.

63. Neusner, *Native Category-Formations of the Aggadah* (see n. 58), 1:xiii.

64. Ibid., 1:xiv, and see his n. 2.

65. Ibid., 1:133ff.

66. So the results of the first two volumes of Neusner's *The Unity of Rabbinic Discourse* (see n. 56). The third volume has a valuable summary of his findings in the entire three volumes (3: xii–xxi).

67. Neusner, *Dual Discourse, Single Judaism* (see n. 59), p. 179.

68. A striking testimony to his faithfulness to his task as he has defined it and to a recognition of its limits is found in his treatment of his findings concerning *Genesis Rabbah* in vol. 2 of Neusner, *Unity of Rabbinic Discourse* (see n. 56). While the key paragraph is not altogether clear to me, he notes that more than half of the halakhic passages inserted into this document "do not count as 'Halakhah in the Aggadah' at all" (p. 51 and see pp. 53f.). That is, they do not influence the Aggadah's own category-formation activity.

69. A biographical aside may perhaps be permitted here. My rabbinic training exposed me to several fine neo-Kantian thinkers. Mutatis mutandis, the theory and activity of the documentary approach reminded me of their concern with "regulative ideas," the ones they could create to show the rational structure inherent in every truly human achievement. In Kant, this approach of German idealist philosophy involved utilizing the notion of mental "categories" to explain the proper functioning of reason in relation to what we may simply here call "the world." I could not help but see in Neusner's effort a reminiscence of the grandeur and limitations of their rationalistic system-building.

70. Jonathan Culler, *Structuralist Poetics: Structuralism, Linguistics, and the Study of Literature* (Ithaca, NY: Cornell University Press, 1975), p. 137, as cited by Cohen, *Rereading Talmud* (see n. 52), p. 73 n. 6, introducing his discussion of the work of Yonah Frenkel. Cohen's self-consciousness about the issue of structure illustrates well that most of the authors of recent decades treated in the prior section of this chapter have been significantly influenced by the views discussed in this section. Thus, the divisions proposed here should be understood as heuristic impositions on the mongrel nature of culture.

71. F. David Peat, *From Certainty to Uncertainty* (Washington, DC: Joseph Henry Press, 2002).

72. Stern, *Midrash and Theory* (see n. 12), p. 1 of the introduction, entitled "The Midrash-Theory Connection," gives an astute understanding of what transpired in the previous fifteen years. Note that this citation indicates Stern's sense that the major impetus of this moment had passed.

73. Susan Handelman, *The Slayers of Moses: The Emergence of Rabbinic Interpretation in Modern Literary Theory* (Albany: State University of New York Press, 1982). The subtitle calls attention to her polemical argument that the

true rabbinic style of composition differed radically from that of the Greeks with their logocentricity and has emerged in the contemporary consciousness in the various anti-Hellenic hermeneutic of, particularly, Freud, Derrida, Lacan, and Bloom. This was one of the major areas of contention between Handelman and Stern referred to below.

74. David Stern, "Moses-cide: Midrash and Contemporary Literary Criticism," *Prooftexts* 4 (1984). Handelman responded in "Fragments of the Rock: Contemporary Literary Theory and the Study of Rabbinic Texts—A Response to David Stern," *Prooftexts* 5 (1985), and Stern rejoined in that issue, "Literary Criticism or Literary Homilies? Susan Handelman and the Contemporary Study of Midrash."

75. Both citations on p. 194 of Stern, "Moses-cide" (see n. 74).

76. Stern, *Midrash and Theory* (see n. 12), p. 6 and see the context.

77. Geoffrey H. Hartman and Sanford Budick, eds. *Midrash and Literature* (New Haven, CT: Yale University Press, 1986), front cover flyleaf.

78. Stern, *Midrash and Theory* (see n. 12), pp. 4–5. Here and in succeeding pages, Stern's rich discussion and interpretation of the falloff of the interest in a close relationship between midrashists and general literary critics is persuasive.

79. Ibid., pp. 8–9.

80. David Stern, "Midrash and Indeterminacy," *Critical Inquiry* 15, no. 1 (Autumn 1988) and republished, in somewhat different form, in 1996 as "Midrash and Hermeneutics: Polysemy vs. Indeterminacy," in Stern, *Midrash and Theory* (see n. 12), chap. 1.

81. Stern, "Midrash and Indeterminacy" (see n. 80), p. 23.

82. Steven D. Fraade, *From Tradition to Commentary: Torah and Its Interpretation in Midrash Sifre to Deuteronomy* (Albany: State University of New York Press, 1991).

83. Ibid., p. 68.

84. Gary G. Porton, "Rabbinic Midrash," *Judaism in Late Antiquity, Part One. Literary and Archeological Sources,* ed. Jacob Neusner. Leiden, Brill, 1995, p. 227.

85. Daniel Boyarin, *Intertextuality and the Reading of Midrash* (Bloomington: Indiana University Press, 1990).

86. Daniel Boyarin, *Carnal Israel: Reading Sex in Talmudic Culture* (Berkeley and Los Angeles: University of California Press, 1993).

87. Martin S. Jaffee, "The Hermeneutical Model of Midrashic Studies: What It Reveals and What It Conceals," *Prooftexts* 11 (1991): 67. Jaffee, noting his debt to William Scott Green, is forthright about his one significant reservation about Boyarin's and others' emphasis on intertextuality: "[T]he emergent hermeneutical emphasis in midrashic research tends to lose sight of the context of midrash in the historic development of rabbinic Judaism, even as it draws attention to the distinctive concerns of rabbinic readers" (p. 67). The remaining champions of the historicist approach no longer lay claim to hegemony in this field but,

conceding that to the hermeneutic researchers, they ask only for a significant place in the newly envisioned sense of the literature and its study.

88. Boyarin, *Intertextuality and the Reading of Midrash* (see n. 85), pp. 1–12.

89. Ibid., p. x, and see the context.

90. Boyarin bases himself on the current understanding "that all interpretation and historiography is representation of the past by the present, that is, there is no such thing as value-free, true and objective rendering of documents." Moreover, an interpreter necessarily "produces a representation in which the very image is generated by what the culture encourages and constrains her to see." Ibid., p. 12.

91. Ibid.

92. Boyarin, *Carnal Israel* (see n. 86), p. 14.

93. Ibid., p. 146. This is his summary of a detailed, sensitive discussion, beginning much earlier in the book, of a range of texts dealing with these issues.

94. One can detect something of this feminist attitude toward law as a particularly masculine activity in the hermeneutic of suspicion Judith Plaskow brought to bear on Jewish law (specifically as exemplified by its treatment of women) in her *Standing Again at Sinai* (San Francisco: Harper and Row, 1990), esp. pp. 171–210, but this needs to be counterbalanced by her more positive view of the democratic community as a proper authority in "Feminism and Religious Authority," *Tikkun* 5, no. 2 (1990).

95. Hauptman, "Feminist Perspectives on Rabbinic Texts" (see n. 55), p. 54.

96. Ibid., p. 56.

97. Charlotte Elisheva Fonrobert, *Menstrual Purity: Rabbinic and Christian Reconstructions of Biblical Gender* (Stanford, CA: Stanford University Press, 2000), a work that only concerns itself with *aggadah* in a passing comment while describing the *sugya* (p. 14), the basic Talmudic unit of argumentation. Judith Baskin's book is *Midrashic Women: Formations of the Feminine in Rabbinic Literature* (Hanover, NH: University Press of New England, 2002).

98. Baskin, *Midrashic Women* (see n. 97), pp. 4–5 and 7.

99. Elizabeth Shanks, "The Impact of Feminism on Rabbinic Studies: The Impossible Paradox of Reading Women into Rabbinic Literature," in *Jews and Gender: The Challenge to Hierarchy* (New York: Oxford University Press, 2000), pp. 114 n. 2 and 115 n. 11, provides a good list of some relevant publications (though her second group is only generally related to the specific issues of reading rabbinic text). Such major works as Miriam Peskowitz's *Spinning Fantasies: Rabbis, Gender and History* (Berkeley and Los Angeles: University of California Press, 1997) (who is particularly concerned with the special problems gender issues raise when one is dealing with rabbinic stories) and Judith Hauptman's *Rereading the Rabbis: A Woman's Voice* (Boulder, CO: Westview Press, 1998) (who here analyzes legal material) are not concerned with the different levels of authority rabbinic discourse imputed to aggadic and halakhic materials. Where Hauptman does deal with the halakhic-aggadic dichotomy in "Does the Tosefta Precede the Mishnah: Halacha, Aggada, and Narrative

Coherence," *Judaism* 50, no. 2 (Spring 2001): 236–37, it is only to attribute the paucity of *aggadah* in the Mishnah to Judah Hanasi's view that the two discourses should not be enmeshed but largely separated, a view that did not gain later approval. *Nashim: A Journal of Jewish Women's Studies and Gender Issues*, devoted its no. 4, Fall 5762/2001 issue to rabbinics. Its first section, "Feminist Interpretations of Talmudic Literature," had four studies, one of which was Charlotte Elisheva Fonrobert, "The Weeping Rabbi: On Reading Gender in Talmudic Aggadah." Her article and those of her colleagues concentrated on specific issues and their potential implications, but none of them moved on to the speculative systemic issue of gender as a possible basis for the bifurcation of rabbinic discourse as a whole or NHD as a genre particularly expressive of the feminine in all human beings.

100. For a good account of the early history of the distinction between the two genres of sacred literature, see Alf Hiltebeltel's article "Hinduism," in *The Encyclopedia of Religion*, ed. Mircea Eliade (New York: Macmillan, 1987), 6:342.b–343.a.

101. Prathavananda, as cited by Donald Bishop, writes that Bishop's own language is taken from his introduction to the book he edited *Indian Thought, an Introduction* (New York: John Wiley & Sons, 1975), pp. 13–14.

102. Ibid., p. 24. While Reddy in his article "The Vedas" does not specify the source, his citation is taken from Swami Shanananda, "The Vedas and Their Religious Teachings," in *The Cultural Heritage of India*, vol. 1, *The Early Phases* (Calcutta: Ramakrishna Mission Institute of Culture, 1937), p. 182. In the *Indian Thought* volume (see n. 101), T. Mahadevan in his article "Gandhi—A Modernist Heresy" polemicizes against universalist humanism in the course of arguing that Gandhi's teaching was "a modernist heresy." Sruti is "often the trump card in Indian philosophical disquisition. 'For the text says so' . . . is the final clinching argument. It can be refuted, if at all, by another text equally authentic. . . . Sruti in its purest sense denotes a completely independent means of cognition for the perception of philosophic truth" (pp. 360–62). In a somewhat similar effort to clarify matters for eager Western devotees of the Gita, Gerald James Larson writes, "[T]he Gita has never at any time had the status of sruti or sacred scripture. Only Veda is sruti, and the Gita, much like the Laws of Manu, is merely one more text of *smrti*—i.e., worthy to be remembered in tradition." Gerald James Larson, "The Bhagavad Gita as Cross-Cultural Process," *JAAR* 43, no. 4 (December 1975): 661.

103. William Cenlaver, "The Pandit: The Embodiment of Oral Tradition," *Journal of Dharma* 5, no. 3 (July–September 1980): 239, 245.

104. Muhammad Zubayr Siddiqi, *Hadith Literature* (Cambridge: Islamic Texts Society, 1993), p. 1, and see the description of the growth of reports about the Prophet on the next several pages. I largely follow Siddiqi in the discussion that follows, as amplified by various other writers. Thus, see the discussion by Munawar Ahmad Anees and Alia N. Athar, *Guide to Sira and Hadith Literature in Western Languages* (London: Mansell Publishing, 1986), p. xii. Their tribute to Siddiqi's work is found on p. xx, and their evaluation of the works

on hadith literature is primarily on pp. 205–8. J. Robson, in his excellent article, "Hadith," in *The Encyclopedia of Islam*, ed. Bernard Lewis, et al. (Leiden: E. J. Brill, 1971), 3:3ff., puts it this way: "an account of what the Prophet said or did, or of his tacit approval of something said or done in his presence."

105. Siddiqi, *Hadith Literature* (see n. 101), p. 5. For a discussion of the usual categories of hadith collections, see pp. 9–13.

106. Ibid., pp. 25–26.

107. Ibid., p. 110, and see the context. A fascinating description of the accepted techniques of analyzing and evaluating these traditions follows on his pp. 113–15. For a discussion of the uniqueness of this literature, see Anees and Athar, *Guide* (see n. 104), xiii–xiv.

108. Robson, "Hadith" (see n. 104), p. 24.

109. Reuven Firestone, *Jihad: The Origin of Holy War in Islam* (New York: Oxford University Press, 1999), p. 94. Writing about the main collections of this material, he adds, "In addition to religious ritual, law, rules of commerce, and aspects of public and private behavior, they ... contain Qur'an commentary and biographical information about the Prophet" (p. 95). He later makes incidental mention of nonlegal material in the later hadith collections, but neither he nor the other writers consider this significant enough to discuss.

110. Judith Romney Wegner, "Halakhah and Shari'a: Some Roots of Law and Norms of Conduct in Theocratic Systems," *CCAR Journal*, Fall 2000, has given a helpful indication of the insights yielded by a comparison of the similarities of the two legal systems. Some more direct encouragement for pursuing this on an aggadic level is provided by a (Hebrew) reference to the hadith as "the Moslem Aggadah" in Isaiah Tishby, *Mivhar Sifrut Hamusar*, with Joseph Dan (Jerusalem: M. Newman Publishing, 1970), p. 113. However, they do not there or later amplify this comment.

111. Even articles seriously treating the "logic" of the *aggadah* are rare. A notable exception to this rule is Heinrich Guggenheimer, "Ueber ein bemerkenswertes logisches System aus der Antike," methodos, *Rivista Trimestrale di Metodologia e di Logica Simbolica: A Quarterly Review of Methodology and of Symbolic Logic* 3, no. 10 (1951). The article does not limit itself to the *aggadah*, though it occupies a significant place in the paper, whose form of analysis may be judged from its being published in the journal's section on symbolic logic. Unfortunately the author's stated hope of returning to this topic was not, as far as I have been able to discover, fulfilled. Most scholarly books about how the rabbis reason concentrate solely on halakhic argument, ignoring the not inconsiderable attention the rabbis give to aggadic matters. See, for example, Menachem Fisch, *Rational Rabbis: Science and Talmudic Culture* (Bloomington: Indiana University Press, 1997), and, more recently, Leib Moscovitz, *Talmudic Reasoning: From Casuistics to Conceptualization* (Tübingen: Mohr-Siebeck, 2002). Neither work gives any attention to aggadic discourse.

112. Hirschfeld has been so thoroughly lost to later generations that Neusner can say, in speaking of Kadushin, he "is the only scholar, writing in any

language, who systematically attempted to bring order out of the chaos of the rabbinic writings by a sustained and articulated method that transcended mere collecting, arranging, paraphrasing and free-associating." Jacob Neusner, *From Literature to Theology in Formative Judaism* (Atlanta: Scholars Press, 1989), p. 5. *Pace* Neusner, Hirschfeld preceded Kadushin by almost a century. For data on Hirschfeld see the entry on him in the *Encyclopaedia Judaica* (in German) (Berlin: Verlag Eschcol, 1931), vol. 8, col. 103. I am grateful to Dr. Michael Meyer, who quickly responded to my request for help in finding information on Hirschfeld's thought. He directed me to Ismar Schorsch's paper "The Emergence of Historical Consciousness in Modern Judaism," *LBIY* 28 (1983): 427, whose paragraph on Hirschfeld and his writing provided valuable leads for further insight into his work.

113. H. S. Hirschfeld, *Der Geist der talmudischen Auslegung der Bibel,* pt. 1, *Halachische Exegese* (Berlin: M. Simion, 1840); its right-hand title page is *Middot Uderashot Hahalakhah, Halachische Exegese: Ein Beitrug zur Geschichte der Exegese und zur Methodologie des Talmuds*. The companion volume appeared seven years later as *Der Geist der ersten Schriftsauslegungen, oder Die haggadische Exegese: Ein Beitrag zur Geschichte und zur Methodologie des Midrasch* (Berlin: M. Simion, 1847). The page numbers hereafter cited in the text are to the latter work.

114. The first review of Hirschfeld's work was by Levi Herzfeld in *Literaturblatt des Orients*, nos. 41 (October 2, 1841) and 42 (October 9, 1841). It is a detailed critique of various aspects of Hirschfeld's volume, concentrating on individual matters of interpretation and decrying its poor organization and repetitiousness (this latter not without justice). The second review was by Abraham Geiger and occurred as part of a review of literature in a paper on the appropriate way to interpret the rabbinic interpretation of the Bible, "Das Verhältnis des natürlichen Schriftsinnes zur thalmudischen Schriftdeutung," *Wissenschaftliche Zeitschrift für Judische Theologie* 5 (1844).

115. The former citation is Geiger, "Das Verhältnis" (see n. 114), p. 54, and the latter is Geiger, "Das Verhältnis" (see n. 111), 55. This remark should be taken as the parallel to the prior comment in the text proper on that page that interpretation ought to be carried out in response to the *geschichtliche Moment*, "the present call for history." Surely there is something ironic in utilizing, even unconsciously, the post-Hegelian notion of the *Zeitgeist*, "the spirit of the times," to dismiss Hirschfeld for wanting to do an abstract Hegelian reading of the rabbis.

116. A brief aside about the vagaries of electronic library searches may be of some interest. My first Internet search of the catalogs of the Jewish Theological Seminary Library and the Hebrew Union College-Jewish Institute of Religion Klau Library, Cincinnati, turned up a copy of vol. 1 at the former and 2 copies of it at the latter, but no copies of the second volume at either institution. But, to my good fortune, the old Kiev classified holdings of the New York School of HUC-JIR, the original Library of the Jewish Institute of Religion,

a smaller library, had a complete set of the Hirschfeld work in its card catalog, but much of the Kiev collection had not yet been put on the electronic all-school catalog. When I reported my findings to Dr. Philip Miller, the librarian of the HUC-JIR Library, New York, he made an electronic search of all Judaica holdings in U.S. libraries and turned up five other copies of vol. 2. I am grateful to him for this, as for many other bibliographic favors, particularly as this one assured me that I did not have in my office the only known copy of this unusual work. Since then the Klau Library at HUC-JIR Cincinnati has found a copy in its Friedus collection and placed it on our electronic catalog. Perhaps other such old, electronically uncataloged collections will turn up other copies. But this relative paucity of copies as well as his "political" (read: intellectual) incorrectness may explain the lack of attention to Hirschfeld's thinking.

117. Dr. E., "Das Haus: Aus dem Aufzeichnungen des Kreisphysikus, Dr. E, [made available by his daughter] Ulla Wolf-Frank," *Jahrbuch für jüdische Geschichte und Literatur* 22, (1919): 132, and see the confirming comment at the bottom of that page.

118. See the final lines of the introduction to Hirschfeld's first volume, *Der Geist der talmudischen Auslegung* (see n. 113), p. x.

119. Hirschfeld, *Der Geist der ersten Schriftauslegungen* (see n. 113), see subsections 167 through 189, pp. 353–454.

120. Page numbers that follow in the text are to this work.

121. Max Kadushin, *The Theology of Seder Eliahu: A Study in Rabbinic Judaism* (New York: Bloch, 1932), a reworking of his doctoral dissertation. He was able to exercise more conceptual freedom in his next book, *Organic Thinking: A Study in Rabbinic Thought* (New York: Jewish Theological Seminary, 1938). His fullest exposition of his position came in *The Rabbinic Mind* (New York: Jewish Theological Seminary, 1952). He further applied his perspective to a number of issues in *Worship and Ethics: A Study in Rabbinic Judaism* (Evanston, IL: Northwestern University Press, 1964) and, less penetratingly, in his works on the *Mekhilta* in 1969 and the posthumously published one on *Leviticus Rabbah* in 1987.

122. Simon Greenberg's fine essay on Kadushin's work generally is particularly helpful for clarifying the thinkers Kadushin thought inadequate and whom his work sought to correct. Simon Greenberg, "Coherence and Change in the Rabbinic Universe of Discourse: Kadushin's Theory of the Value Concept," in *Understanding the Rabbinic Mind: Essays on the Hermeneutic of Max Kadushin*, ed. Peter Ochs (Atlanta: Scholars Press, 1990), pp. 19–44.

123. Kadushin may well have had a second apologetic agenda. His major research had been done in *aggadah*, and perhaps he sought to validate his scholarship in the eyes of the Jewish Theological Seminary faculty, which in those days set the academic standards not only for his movement but for much of American Jewry, and which denigrated *aggadah* and gave honor only to the *halakhah*. As a faithful alumnus of the seminary, he therefore sought to

show that his system embraced *halakhah* as well as *aggadah*. Note the second and third reasons Simon Greenberg gave, according to Theodore Steinberg, as to why Kadushin never received a faculty position at the seminary. Theodore Steinberg, "Max Kadushin: An Intellectual Biography," in Ochs, *Understanding the Rabbinic Mind* (see n. 122), p. 16.

124. Kadushin, *Rabbinic Mind* (see n. 121), p. 10. Echoes of this statement occur often in the book.

125. For Kadushin's change of terminology from "organic" to "organismic," see Steinberg, "Max Kadushin" (see n. 123), p. 4 n. 8.

126. *Cambridge Dictionary of Philosophy*, ed. Robert Audi (New York: Cambridge University Press, 1995), p. 551 s.v. "Organic."

127. Kadushin, *The Rabbinic Mind* (see n. 121), chap. 2, "The Organism of Rabbinic Value-Concepts," pp. 14–34, is about as comprehensive a statement as he ever made of this central notion, but it always remains elusive, particularly because he elucidates its many entailments all through his work.

128. Ibid., pp. 78–79 and very often in this work.

129. Kadushin apparently felt that *The Rabbinic Mind* best represented his point of view, for when his rabbinic organization, the (Conservative) Rabbical Assembly, sought to publish a volume on its most cherished notion, *Conservative Judaism and Jewish Law*, Kadushin helped in or approved the excerpting of statements from *The Rabbinic Mind* to serve as his article "Halakah and Haggadah," pp. 218–36 therein.

130. Max Kadushin, "Halakah and Haggadah" in *Conservative Judaism and Jewish Law*, ed. Seymour Siegel with Elliot Gertel (New York: Rabbinical Assembly, 1977), 221ff.

131. Ibid., p. 222. Kadushin, *Rabbinic Mind* (see n. 121), pp. 79–81 and see also pp. 258–59.

132. Kadushin, "Halakah and Haggadah" (see n. 130), p. 220.

133. Ibid., pp. 218–20, 225.

134. Ibid., 226–28. Aggadic statement seems indifferent to contradictions between authorities or even in a single master. Kadushin, *Rabbinic Mind* (see n. 121), p. 75f.

135. Kadushin, "Halakah and Haggadah" (see n. 130), pp. 223, 232. For the *pshat/derash* discussion, see p. 228f.

136. Ibid., pp. 227, 231f.

137. Ibid., pp. 221, 225, and passim.

138. Ibid. See the discussion of the characteristic aggadic term for a new interpretation of a previously treated matter, *davar aḥer*, in Kadushin, *Rabbinic Mind* (see n. 121), pp. 71f.

139. Theodore Steinberg, his devoted student, attributes Kadushin's lack of acceptance to his infelicitous literary style and mentions among those who have found his work useful E. P. Sanders, Moshe Greenberg, and Avraham Holtz, who has published a volume in Hebrew hoping to make Kadushin's work known to Israelis. He also points to the volume on Kadushin in which

his own paper appears: Ochs, *Understanding the Rabbinic Mind* (see n. 123), p. 17 and see its nn. 40–43. Steinberg's last bit of evidence, this volume, is unfortunate. Even the writers most positive to Kadushin (namely, Simon Greenberg and Peter Ochs), substantially take issue with him, and the rest who deal with rabbinic literature (Richard Sarason, Alan Avery-Peck, Martin Jaffee, and Jacob Neusner) subject him to withering criticism but not without appreciation for his intelligent and occasionally productive pathbreaking. Their deprecation continues a negative view of his work that goes back to Louis Finkelstein's review of Kadushin's first published book, *The Theology of the Seder Eliahu*. Finkelstein's review ends, "It is to be hoped that ... Dr. Kadushin may undertake other analyses of a similar nature, thus improving his method and at the same time giving us a better grasp of the thought of the sages." Finkelstein, "An Attempted Systematization of Rabbinic Theology," *Jewish Quarterly Review* 25 (1934): 13–16. In 1952, commenting on Kadushin's book and the *HUCA* article on the Mekhilta, Salo Baron wrote, "Some modification and even outright polarity of views may be explained by ... 'organic thinking' ... But this method too opens as many questions as it helps to answer.... Even then it will be difficult to construe a well-rounded system out of fragments of a consciously unsystematic folkloristic body of material." Baron, *A Social and Religious History of the Jews*, vol. 2 (Philadelphia: Jewish Publication Society, 1952), p. 434 n. 25. For two other, later, divergent lines of criticism, see David Stern, "Aggadah," in *Contemporary Jewish Religious Thought*, ed. Arthur A. Cohen and Paul Mendes-Flohr (New York: Scribner's, 1987), p. 11; and Leon J. Goldstein, "Conceptual Openness and the Rabbinic Mind," *JJTP* 3, no. 2 (1994): 303–30.

Chapter 8. Reconstruing the *Aggadah* Problem

1. As he noted in his late nineteenth-century *Introduction to the Talmud and Midrash*, Hermann Strack had this experience, even though he was looking for the more common notion of the limited applicability of the *aggadah*. Hermann L. Strack, *Introduction to the Talmud and Midrash*, 5th ed. (Philadelphia: Jewish Publication Society, 1931), p. 90 and n. 1. The recent Stemberger revision of this work says nothing different. And searches of the Talmuds and early *midrashim* substantiate their position.

2. A brief summary of this matter and positive assessment of Mordecai Margaliot's study is found in Menachem Elon, *Jewish Law: History, Sources, Principles* (Philadelphia: Jewish Publication Society, 1994), 3: 1543, para. 3 and notes thereto. See also the helpful discussion in Gerson D. Cohen, *A Critical Edition with a Translation and Notes of the Book of Tradition (Sefer ha-qabbalah) by Abraham Ibn Daud* (Philadelphia: Jewish Publication Society, 1967), pp. 182f. The primary source investigation is in Mordecai Margaliot, *Sefer Halakhot Hanagid* (in Hebrew) (Jerusalem: n.p., 1962), chap. 6, "The Introduction to the

Talmud Attributed to the Nagid Is Not by Him," pp. 68–73.

3. The paragraph "Vehaggadah" in the *Mevo Hatalmud*, which is on pp. 45b–46a of the appendices to the Romm edition printing of *Berakhot* that I consulted.

4. Thus, the term is defined as "command, esp. religious act, meritorious deed" in Marcus Jastrow, *Dictionary of Talmud Babli, Yerushalmi, Midrashic Literature and Targumim* (New York: Title Publishing, 1943), 2:823 and see the examples given there.

5. *Mevo Hatalmud* (see n. 3), p. 43b.

6. Adam Kamesar detects in Philo some support for this notion of the *aggadah* as a separate rabbinic body of tradition; and see his comments about Josephus and the early existence of an oral, distinct halakhic tradition. Kamesar, "The Narrative Aggada as Seen from the Graeco-Latin Perspective," *JJS*, 46, no. 1 (Spring 1004): 59–60.

7. Adin Steinsaltz, *The Talmud: A Reference Guide* (New York: Random House, 1989), p. 297, only discusses two of these, from which one may gauge the nature of such statements. A list of sixteen such statements is given by Moshe Sabar, *Mikhlol ha-maamarim Vehapitgamim* (Jerusalem: Mosad Harav Kook, 1971), 1:107.

8. My discussion in what follows is based primarily on Albert-Laszlo Barabasi, *Linked* (New York: Penguin, 2003); and Mark Buchanan, *Nexus: Small Worlds and the Groundbreaking Science of Networks* (New York: Norton, 2002). The former is a major researcher in the field yet explains his and others' findings with exemplary charm and clarity. The latter is an exceedingly well-informed and effective science writer. Just before the publication of the studies that opened up the new scientific understanding of networks, Mark C. Taylor, in his visionary evocation of the evolving condition of Western culture in *Hiding* (Chicago: University of Chicago Press, 1997), devoted some pages to his sense of the ten characteristics of network organization (pp. 325–33). In terms of the scientific data provided by Barabasi and Buchanan, I have found some of Taylor's insights helpful for my purposes here.

9. Barabasi, *Linked* (see n. 8), pp. 91–92.

10. Buchanan, *Nexus* (see n. 8), p. 15.

11. Edward N. Lorenz, *The Essence of Chaos* (Seattle: University of Washington Press, 1993), p. 5. Buchanan voices a similar sentiment in twice citing Herbert Simon's statement that the social and political scientists' mission "is to find meaningful simplicity in the midst of disorderly complexity." Buchanan, *Nexus* (see n. 8), pp. 12 and 198 (note the repetition of this notion).

12. Barabasi, *Linked* (see n. 8), p. 222. And he believes the new science of networks has involved us in a Kuhnian "paradigm shift" (p. 227).

13. See the second of Taylor's ten characteristics in Taylor, *Hiding* (see n. 8), p. 326.

14. Buchanan, *Nexus* (see n. 8), pp. 19 and 158.

15. Andrew Langowitz pointed out an interesting analogy to this network

logic of the whole making the individual parts largely dispensable. In a hologram, if part of the original figure is deleted and the remainder then exposed to the laser beam, the entire original figure will appear, though with some blurriness, and the neural network of the brain seems to operate in that fashion as well.

16. So Taylor's fourth through sixth of his list of network characteristics. Taylor, *Hiding* (see n. 8), p. 327.

17. Buchanan, *Nexus* (see n. 8), p. 103.

18. Barabasi, *Linked* (see n. 8), p. 83.

19. For a fuller statement of the simplest level of the rabbinic Covenantal dialectic, see my *Renewing the Covenant* (Philadelphia: Jewish Publication Society, 1991), pp. 217–20.

Afterwords

1. Franz Rosenzweig, "Apologic Thinking," cited here from its translation in *The Jew: Essays from Martin Buber's Journal, Der Jude, 1916–1928*, ed. Arthur A. Cohen (University: University of Alabama Press, 1980), p. 269. An English translation of Max Brod's book was published as *Paganism, Christianity, Judaism: A Confession of Faith* (University: University of Alabama Press, 1970). Leo Baeck's book went through many German editions, of which the sixth was published in English translation as *The Essence of Judaism* (New York: Macmillan, 1936).

2. Joseph Baer Soloveitchik, "Confrontation," *Tradition* 6, no. 2 (1964): 5–29. David Hartman sees halakhic overtones in this paper, but I think it damaging to his case that what finally put normative authority behind the Rav's position was not a ruling by the master but the statement adopted by the Rabbinical Council of America obligating the Orthodox community to follow his teaching. David Hertman, *Love and Terror in the God Encounter* (Woodstock, VT: Jewish Lights, 2001), vol. 1, esp. pp. 131–33.

3. An instructive example is found in Moshe Sokol's article "Is There a 'Halakhic' Response to the Problem of Evil?" *HTR* 92, no. 3 (1999): 311–23. This discussion of the Rav's position on this age-old problem centers on his assertion that, in keeping with Judaism's central concern with the Law, a believing Jew should be concerned not with theoretical issues of God and evil but what one needs to do about it. In that sense, the Rav's approach is "halakhic" but not in the sense that he draws upon what the *halakhah* mandates in specific instances or what the Rav defines as present duties in that regard. Sokol's interpretation of the Rav's approach in this essay is entirely drawn from contemporary philosophical positions, and it is these several aggadic considerations that lie behind his judicious use of quotation marks in the title to his paper.

4. At first my involvement with the *aggadah* merely provided me with a background for my primary engagement with contemporary Jewish thought. Much later, as *torah lishmah* had morphed into a book project, I realized that this work was the third aspect of my theological enterprise. Its centerpiece was the apologetic theology of Renewing the Covenant, but that was accompanied by a statement of its actional consequences, my writings in the field of Jewish ethics. What was yet missing was the textual study that lay behind it all, a foundation I had come to hope would someday reach publishable form. See my comment to this effect in *Renewing the Covenant: A Theology for the Postmodern Jew* (Philadelphia: Jewish Publication Society, 1991), p. xi. The relation between this work on aggadic discourse in general and my statement of a theology of Judaism without specific textual citation rests on my understanding of what textual citation can and cannot do in making a Jewish theology cogent. Classic Jewish texts always speak to a partial aspect of Jewish belief and do so, in the usual case, as a matter of personal opinion, albeit that of a rabbinic sage. Hence they can only illustrate that a given contemporary assertion has some relationship to classic Jewish teaching. They cannot claim, no matter how many such citations are adduced, that, as they usually seek to do, their view establishes what all rabbinic Judaism affirmed. The variety of aggadic opinions in rabbinic Judaism being so great, other teachings contrary or even contradictory to those cited could be adduced. Rather than adorn my apologetic theology with rabbinic texts that demonstrated some rabbinic opinion as my forebears, it seemed wiser to me to let that work stand on its intellectual own and one day give an illustration in depth of the textual acumen that stood behind it. This book fulfills that purpose.

Bibliography of Works Cited

Compiled by Tina Weiss

Albeck, Chanokh. "Hahalakhot Vehadrashot." In *Sefer ha-yovel li-khevod Profesor Aleksander Marks*, edited by David Frankel. New York: Jewish Theological Seminary of America, 1943.

Altmann, Alexander, ed. *Biblical and Other Studies*. Studies and Texts, vol. 1. Cambridge, MA: Harvard University Press, 1963.

Anees, Munawar Ahmad, and Alia N. Athar. *Guide to Sira and Hadith Literature in Western Languages*. London: Mansell Publishing, 1986.

Arazi, Abraham. "Shi-luv Aggadah Behalakhah." In *Sefer Hayovel Lerabi Chanokh Albek*. Jerusalem: Mosad Havav Kuk, 1963.

The Babylonian Talmud: Seder Nezikin—Sanhedrin. Translated by Jacob Shachter and H. Freedman. London: Soncino, 1935; *Seder Kodashim-Zebahim*. Translated by H. Freedman. London: Soncino, 1948.

Bacher, Wilhelm. *Erkhe Midrash: Ve-nilvah be-sofo kuntres leshon ha-RaMBaM be-sifro Mishneh Torah*. Translated by A. Z. Rabinovits. Jerusalem: Karmiel, 1969.

———. "The Origin of the Word Haggada (Agada)." *JQR O.S.*, 4 (1892): 406–429.

Baeck, Leo. *Aus drei Jahrtausenden: Wissenschaftliche Untersuchungen und Abhandlungen zur Geschichte des jüdischen Glaubens*. Berlin: Schocken Verlag, 1938.

———. *The Essence of Judaism*. Translated by Victor Grubwieser and Leonard Pearl. London: Macmillan, 1936.

Barabasi, Albert-Laszlo. *Linked: The New Science of Networks*. Cambridge, MA: Perseus Publishing, 2003.

Baron, Salo Wittmayer. *A Social and Religious History of the Jews*. Vol. 2. Philadelphia: JPS, 1952. First published 1937 by Columbia University Press.

Baron, S., et al., eds. *Sefer-yovel le-Yitshak Ber: Bi-mel'ot lo shiv'im shanah*. Jerusalem: Ha-Ḥevrah ha-historit ha-Yiśre'elit, 1960.

Baskin, Judith R. *Midrashic Women: Formations of the Feminine in Rabbinic Literature*. Hanover, NH: University Press of New England, 2002.

———. "Rabbinic-Patristic Exegetical Contacts in Late Antiquity." In *Studies in Judaism and Its Greco-Roman Context*, edited by William Green. Atlanta: Scholars Press, 1985.

Ben-Amos, Dan. "Generic Distinctions in the Aggadah." In *Studies in Jewish Folklore*, edited by Dov Noy. Cambridge, MA: Association of Jewish Studies, 1980.

———. "The Hebrew Folktale: A Review Essay." *JS* 35 (1995): 29–60.
———. "The Idea of Folklore." In *Studies in Aggadah and Jewish Folklore*, edited by Issachar Ben-Ami and Joseph Dan. Jerusalem: Magnes Press, 1983.
Berlin, Meir, and Shlomo Zevin, eds. *Entsiklopedyah Talmudit*. Jerusalem: Talmudic Encyclopedia Publishing, 1949.
Bialik, Hayyim Nahman. *Kol Kitve H. N. Byalik*. Tel Aviv: Dvir, 1947.
Bishop, Donald H., ed. *Indian Thought: An Introduction*. New York: John Wiley & Sons, 1975.
Borowitz, Eugene B. "The Rabbinic Conception of Torah: A Study in Jewish Theology." Rabbinic thesis, Hebrew Union College-Jewish Institute of Religion, 1948.
———. *Renewing the Convenant: A Theology for the Postmodern Jew*. Philadelphia: JPS, 1991.
———. "Universalism and Particularism in the Tannaitic Midrashim." DHL diss., Hebrew Union College-Jewish Institute of Religion, 1952.
———. "What Knowledge Does Judaism Think It Possesses?" In *Biblical Studies in Contemporary Thought: The Tenth Anniversary Commemorative Volume of the Trinity College Biblical Institute, 1966–1975*, edited by Miriam Ward. Burlington, VT: Trinity College Biblical Institute, 1975.
Boyarin, Daniel. *Carnal Israel: Reading Sex in Talmudic Culture*. Berkeley and Los Angeles: University of California Press, 1993.
———. *Intertextuality and the Reading of Midrash*. Bloomington: Indiana University Press, 1990.
Brod, Max. *Paganism, Christianity, Judaism: A Confession of Faith*. University: University of Alabama Press, 1970.
Bruns, Gerald L. "The Hermeneutics of Midrash." In *The Book and the Text: The Bible and Literary Theory*, edited by Regina M. Schwartz. Oxford: Blackwell, 1990.
Buchanan, Mark. *Nexus: Small Worlds and the Groundbreaking Science of Networks*. New York: W. W. Norton, 2002.
Cohen, Arthur A., ed. *The Jews: Essays from Martin Buber's Journal "Der Jude," 1916–1928*. Translated by Joachim Neugroschel. University: University of Alabama, 1980.
Cohen, Aryeh. *Rereading Talmud: Gender, Law, and the Poetics of Sugyot*. Atlanta: Scholars Press, 1998.
Cohen, Gerson D. *A Critical Edition with a Translation and Notes of the Book of "Tradition" (Sefer ha-qabbalah) by Abraham Ibn Daud*. Philadelphia: JPS, 1967.
Cohen, Shaye J. D. "The Significance of Yavneh: Pharisees, Rabbis and the End of Jewish Sectarianism." *HUCA* 55 (1984): 27–53.
Cohn, Haim Hermann. *Jewish Law in Ancient and Modern Israel: Selected Essays*. New York: KTAV Publishing House, 1971.
Culler, Jonathan. *Structuralist Poetics: Structuralism, Linguistics, and the Study of Literature*. Ithaca, NY: Cornell University Press, 1975.
Daube, David. *Alexandrian Methods of Interpretation and the Rabbis*. Basel: Helbing & Lichtenhahn, 1953.
———. "Rabbinic Methods of Interpretation and Hellenistic Rhetoric." *HUCA* 22 (1949): 239–64.
Davies, W. D. *Torah in the Messsianic Age and/or the Age to Come*. Philadelphia: Society of Biblical Literature, 1952.

Davis, Joseph M. "Literary Studies of Aggadic Narrative: A Bibliography." In *Judaic and Christian Interpretations of Texts: Contents and Contexts*, edited by Jacob Neusner and Ernest S. Frerichs. Lanham, MD: University Press of America, 1987.
Elman, Yaakov. "How Should a Talmudic Intellectual History Be Written? A Response to David Kraemer's Responses." *JQR* 89, no. 3–4 (1999): 361–86.
———. "Orality and the Redaction of the Babylonian Talmud." *Oral Tradition* 14, no. 1 (1999): 52–99.
———, and Daphna Aphrat, "Geonic Yeshiva and Islamic Midrasa" in *Transmitting Jewish Traditions: Orality, Textuality, and Cultural Diffusion*, ed. Yaakov Elman and Israel Gershoni. New Haven, CT: Yale University Press, 2000.
Elon, Menachem. *Jewish Law: History, Sources, Principles*. Translated by Bernard Auerbach and Melvin J. Sykes. Philadelphia: JPS, 1994.
Encyclopedia of Islam. New ed., S.v. "Hadith."
Encyclopaedia Judaica. Berlin: Verlag Eshcol, 1931.
———. S.v. "Hirschfeld, Hirsch S."
Encyclopedia of Religion. S.v. "Hinduism."
Ephrat, Daphna. "Orality and the Institutionalization of Tradition: The Growth of the Geonic Yeshiva and Islamic Madrasa." In *Transmitting Jewish Traditions: Orality, Textuality, and Cultural Diffusion*, edited by Yaakov Elman and Israel Gershoni. New Haven, CT: Yale University Press, 2000.
Falk, Ze'ev W. *Introduction to Jewish Law of the Second Commonwealth*. Leiden: E. J. Brill, 1972.
Faur, José. "Some General Observations on the Character of Classical Jewish Literature: A Functional Approach." *JJS* 28, no. 1 (1977): 30–45.
Feldman, Louis H. "Hengel's Judaism and Hellenism in Retrospect." *JBL* 96, no. 3 (1977): 371–82.
Finkelstein, Louis. "An Attempted Systematization of Rabbinic Theology." Review of *The Theology of Seder Eliyahu*, by Max Kadushin. *JQR* 25 (1934): 13–16.
Firestone, Reuven. *Jihad: The Origin of Holy War in Islam*. New York: Oxford University Press, 1999.
Fisch, Menachem. *Rational Rabbis, Science and Talmudic Culture*. Bloomington: Indiana University Press, 1997.
Fischel, Henry A. *Rabbinic Literature and Greco-Roman Philosophy: A Study of Epicurea and Rhetorica in Early Midrashic Writings*. Leiden: E. J. Brill, 1973.
———. "Studies in Cynicism and the Ancient Near East: The Transformation of a 'Chria.' " In *Religions in Antiquity: Essays in Memory of Erwin Ramsdall Goodenough*, edited by Jacob Neusner. Leiden: E. J. Brill, 1968.
Fonrobert, Charlotte Elisheva. *Menstrual Purity: Rabbinic and Christian Reconstructions of Biblical Gender*. Stanford, CA: Stanford University Press, 2000.
———. "The Weeping Rabbi: On Reading Gender in Talmudic Aggadah." *Nashim* 4 (2001): 56–83.
Fox, Marvin. "The Rav as Maspid." *Tradition* 30, no. 4 (1996): 164–81.
Fraade, Steven D. *From Tradition to Commentary: Torah and Its Interpretation in the Midrash Sifre to Deuteronomy*. Albany: State University of New York Press, 1991.
Frankel, Zecharias. *Mevo ha-Yerushalmi*. Breslau: Shletter, 1870. Reprint, Jerusalem: 1967.

Frenkel (or, Fraenkel), Yonah. *Darkhe Ha-agadah veha-midrash*. Masadah: Yad la-Talmud, 1991.

———. *Midrash ve-agadah*. 3 vols. Tel Aviv: Open University, 1996.

Gerhardson, Birger. *Memory and Manuscript: Oral Tradition and Written Transmission in Rabbinic Judaism and Early Christianity*. Translated by Eric J. Sharpe. Uppsala: C. W. K. Gleerup, Lund, 1968.

Ginzberg, Louis. *The Palestinian Talmud*. New York: Jewish Theological Seminary of America, 1941.

Goldin, Judah, *The Fathers According to Rabbi Nathan*. New Haven, CT: Yale University Press, 1955.

———. "The Freedom and Restraint of the Haggadah." In *Midrash and Literature*, edited by Geoffrey H. Hartman and Sanford Budick. New Haven, CT: Yale University Press, 1986.

Goldstein, Leon J. "Conceptual Openness and the Rabbinic Mind." *JJTP* 3, no. 2 (1994): 303–30.

Goodblatt, David M. *Rabbinic Instruction in Sasanian Babylonia*. Leiden: E. J. Brill, 1975.

———. Review of *The Sage in the Society of Late Antiquity*, by Richard Kalmin. *JQR* 90, nos. 3–4 (2000): 466–69.

Goshen-Gottstein, Alon. *The Sinner and the Amnesiac: The Rabbinic Invention of Elisha ben Abuya and Eleazar ben Arach*. Stanford, CA: Stanford University Press, 2000.

Greenberg, Simon. "Coherence and Change in the Rabbinic Universe of Discourse: Kadushin's Theory of Value Concept." In *Understanding the Rabbinic Mind: Essays on the Hermeneutic of Max Kadushin*, edited by Peter Ochs. Atlanta: Scholars Press, 1990.

Gruenwald, Ithamar. "Midrash & the 'Midrashic Condition.'" In *The Midrashic Imagination: Jewish Exegesis, Thought, and History*, edited by Michael Fishbane. Albany: State University of New York Press, 1993.

Guttmann, Alexander. "The Problem of the Anonymous Mishna: A Study in the History of Halakah." *HUCA* 16 (1941): 137–55.

Guttmann, Michael. *Zur Einleitung in die Halacha*. Budapest: Jewish Theological Seminary of Budapest, 1909.

Halbertal, Moshe. "Ilmale mikra katuv e efshar le-amro." *Tarbiz* 68, no. 1 (1999): 39–59.

Halevi, E. E. *Ha-Agadah ha-historit-biyografit: Le-or mekorot Yevaniyim Ve-Latiniyim*. Tel Aviv: Tel Aviv University, 1975.

———. *Olamah shel ha-agadah: Ha-agadah le-'or mekorot Yevaniyim*. Tel Aviv: Devir, 1972.

———. *Parashiyot ba-agadah le-or mekorot Yevaniyim*. Haifa: Haifa University, 1973.

———. *Sha'are ha-agadah*. Tel Aviv, 1963.

Halivni, David Weiss. *Peshat and Derash: Plain and Applied Meaning in Rabbinic Exegesis*. New York: Oxford University Press, 1991.

Hammer, Reuven. "Complex Forms of Aggadah and Their Influence on Content." *PAAJR* 48 (1981): 183–206.

Handelman, Susan D. "Fragments of the Rock: Contemporary Literary Theory and the Study of Rabbinic Texts—A Response to David Stern." *Prooftexts* 5, no. 1 (1984): 75–95.

———. *The Slayers of Moses: The Emergence of Rabbinic Interpretation in Modern Literary Theory*. Albany: State University of New York Press, 1982.
Harris, Jay M. *How Do We Know This? Midrash and the Fragmentation of Modern Judaism*. Albany: State University of New York Press, 1995.
Hartman, David. *Love and Terror in the God Encounter: The Theological Legacy of Rabbi Joseph B. Soloveitchik*. Woodstock, VT: Jewish Lights Publishing, 2001.
Hartman, Geoffrey H., and Sanford Budick, editors. *Midrash and Literature*. New Haven, CT: Yale University Press, 1986.
Hasan-Rokem, Galit. *Web of Life: Folklore and Midrash in Rabbinic Literature*. Translated by Batya Stein. Stanford, CA: Stanford University Press, 2000.
Hauptman, Judith. "Does the Tosefta Precede the Mishnah? Halacha, Aggada, and Narrative Coherence." *Judaism* 50, no. 2 (Spring 2001): 236–37.
———. "Feminist Perspectives on Rabbinic Texts." In *Feminist Perspectives on Jewish Studies*, edited by Lynn Davidman and Shelly Tenenbaum. New Haven, CT: Yale University Press, 1994.
———. *Rereading the Rabbis: A Woman's Voice*. Boulder, CO: Westview Press, 1997.
Hayes, Christine. "Response to Jacob Neusner." *JSJ* 27 (1996): 324–33.
Heinemann, Joseph. *Agadot Ve-toldotehen: Iyunim be-hishtalshelutan shel masorot*. Jerusalem: Keter, 1974.
———. "The Nature of the Aggadah." In *Midrash and Literature*, edited by Geoffrey H. Hartman and Sanford Budick. New Haven, CT: Yale University Press, 1986.
Heinemann, Yitshak. *Darkhe ha-agadah*. 2nd ed. Jerusalem: Magnes Press, 1954.
Hengel, Martin. *Judaism and Hellenism: Studies in Their Encounter in Palestine during the Early Hellenistic Period*. Translated by John Bowden. Philadelphia: Fortress Press, 1974.
Herford, Travers R. *Pirkē Aboth: The Tractate "Fathers" from the Mishnah, Commonly Called "Sayings of the Fathers."* 3rd ed. New York: Jewish Institute of Religion, 1945.
Herzog, Isaac. *Main Institutions of Jewish Law*. London: Soncino Press, 1936.
Hezser, Catherine. "Social Fragmentation, Plurality of Opinion, and Nonobservance of Halakhah: Rabbis and Community in Late Roman Palestine." *JSQ* 1, no. 3 (1993–94): 234–51.
———. *The Social Structure of the Rabbinic Movement in Roman Palestine*. Tübingen: Mohr Siebeck, 1997.
Hirschberg, H. Z., and B. Murmelstein. *Yaḥas ha-agadah la-halakhah*. Vienna: Kohut Memorial Foundation, 1929.
Hirschfeld, Hirsch S. *Der Geist der ersten Schriftsauslegungen, oder Die haggadische Exegese, Ein Beitrag zur Geschichte und zur Methodologie des Midrasch*. Berlin: M. Simion, 1847.
———. *Der Geist der talmudischen Auslegung der Bibel*. Berlin: M. Simion, 1840.
Hirshman, Marc. *A Rivalry of Genius: Jewish and Christian Biblical Interpretation in Late Antiquity*. Translated by Batya Stein. Albany: State University of New York Press, 1996.
Horgan, Maurya P. *Pesharim: Qumran Interpretations of Biblical Books*. The Catholic Biblical Quarterly, vol. 8. Washington, DC: Catholic Biblical Association of America, 1979.
Jacobs, Louis. *Studies in Talmudic Logic and Methodology*. London: Valentine, Mitchell, 1961.

———. "The Sugya on Sufferings in B. Berakhot 5a, b." In *Studies in Aggadah, Targum and Jewish Liturgy in Memory of Joseph Heinemann*, edited by Ezra Fleischer and Jakob J. Petuchowski. Jerusalem: Magnes Press, 1981.

———. *Teyku: The Unsolved Problem in the Babylonian Talmud; A Study in the Literary Analysis and Form of the Talmudic Argument*. London: Cornwall Books, 1981.

Jaffee, Martin S. "The Babylonian Appropriation of the Talmud Yerushalmi: Redactional Studies in the Horayot Tractates." In *The Literature of Early Rabbinic Judaism: Issues in Talmudic Redaction and Interpretation*, edited by Alan J. Avery-Peck. Lanham, MD: University Press of America, 1989.

———. "The Hermeneutical Model of Midrashic Studies: What It Reveals and What It Conceals." *Prooftexts* 11, no. 1 (1991): 67–76.

———. "The Oral-Cultural Context of the Talmud Yerushalmi: Greco-Roman Rhetorical Paideia, Discipleship, and the Concept of Oral Torah." In *Transmitting Jewish Traditions: Orality, Textuality, and Cultural Diffusion*, edited by Yaakov Elman and Israel Gershoni. New Haven, CT: Yale University Press, 2000.

———. *Torah in the Mouth: Writing and Oral Tradition in Palestinian Judaism, 200 BCE–400 CE*. New York: Oxford University Press, 2001.

Jastrow, Marcus. *A Dictionary of the Targumim, the Talmud Babli and Yerushalmi, and the Midrashic Literature*. New York: Title Publishing, 1943.

Kadushin, Max. *A Conceptual Approach to the Mekilta*. New York: Jewish Theological Seminary of America, 1969.

———. *A Conceptual Commentary on Midrash Leviticus Rabbah: Value Concepts in Jewish Thought*. Atlanta: Scholars Press, 1987.

———. *Organic Thinking: A Study in Rabbinic Thought*. New York: Jewish Theological Seminary of America, 1938.

———. *The Rabbinic Mind*. New York: Jewish Theological Seminary of America, 1952.

———. *The Theology of Seder Eliahu: A Study in Organic Thinking*. New York: Bloch, 1932.

———. *Worship and Ethics: A Study in Rabbinic Judaism*. Evanston, IL: Northwestern University Press, 1964.

Kagan, Zipporah. "Divergent Tendencies and Their Literary Moulding in the Aggadah." In *Studies in Aggadah and Folk-Literature*, edited by Joseph Heinemann and Dov Noy. Jerusalem: Magnes Press, 1971.

Kalmin, Richard. "Changing Amoraic Attitudes Toward the Authority and Statements of Rav and Shmuel: A Study of the Talmud as a Historical Source." *HUCA* 63 (1992): 83–106.

———. "Kings, Priests, and Sages in Rabbinic Literature in Late Antiquity." Paper delivered at the conference, "Intentionality in the Reworking of Rabbinic Texts," Association of Jewish Studies Conference. Boston. 17 December 2000.

———. "The Modern Study of Ancient Rabbinic Literature: Yonah Frenkel's 'Darkhei ha'aggadah vehamidrash [1991].'" *Prooftexts* 14, no. 2 (1994): 189–204.

———. *The Sage in Jewish Society of Late Antiquity*. New York: Routledge, 1999.

Kamesar, Adam. "The Narrative Aggada as Seen from the Graeco-Latin Perspective." *JJS* 45, no. 1 (1994): 52–70.

———. "Philo, Grammatike and the Narrative Aggada." In *Pursuing the Text: Studies in Honor of Ben Zion Wacholder*, edited by John C. Reeves and John Kampen. Sheffield: Sheffield Academic Press, 1994.

Kariv, Abraham. "Beyn Pshat Lidrash Be-aggadat Ḥazal." *Leshonenu Laam* 20, nos. 9–10. (1969): 233–40.
Kraemer, David. *Mind of the Talmud: An Intellectual History of the Bavli*. New York: Oxford University Press, 1990.
———. *Responses to Suffering in Classical Rabbinic Literature*. New York: Oxford University Press, 1995.
Lapidus, Rina. "Halakhah and Haggadah: Two Opposing Approaches to Fulfilling Religious Law." *JJS* 44, no. 1 (1993): 100–113.
Lapin, Hayim. "Catherine Hezser. *The Social Structure of the Rabbinic Movement in Roman Palestine.*" Review. *AJS Review* 24 (1999): 378–80.
Lieberman, Saul. *Greek in Jewish Palestine: Studies in the Life and Manners of Jewish Palestine in the II–IV Centuries C.E.* New York: Jewish Theological Seminary of America, 1942.
———. *Hellenism in Jewish Palestine: Studies in the Literary Transmission, Beliefs and Manners in the I Century B.C.E.–IV Century C.E.* New York: Jewish Theological Seminary of America, 1950.
———. "Me-agadah L'Halakhah." *Sinai* 4 (1939): 55–58.
Lieberman, Stephen J. "A Mesopotamian Background for the So-Called Aggadic 'Measures' of Biblical Hermeneutics?" *HUCA* 58 (1987): 157–225.
Liebes, Yehuda. *The Sin of Elisha*. Jerusalem: Hebrew University, 1986.
Lightstone, Jack N. The *Rhetoric of the Babylonian Talmud: Its Social Meaning and Context*. Waterloo, Ont.: Wilfred Laurier University Press, 1994.
Lorenz, Edward N. *The Essence of Chaos*. Seattle: University of Washington Press, 1993.
Margaliot, Mordecai. *Sefer Halakhot Hanagid*. Jerusalem: n.p., 1962.
Marmorstein, Arthur. *The Doctrine of Merits in Old Rabbinical Literature and the Old Rabbinic Doctrine of God*. New York: KTAV Publishing House, 1968.
Melamed, E. Z. "Ha'maaseh' Bemishnah Kimekor Lehalakhah." In *Torah shebe-'al-peh: Kinus ha-artsi le-Torah shbe-'al peh*. Jerusalem: Mosad Harav Kook, 1963.
Mielziner, M. *Introduction to the Talmud: Historical and Literary Introduction, Legal Hermeneutics of the Talmud, Talmudical Terminology and Methodology, Outlines of Talmudic Ethics*. 3rd ed. New York: Bloch, 1925.
Milikowsky, Chaim. "Further on Editing Rabbinic Texts." *JQR* 90, no. 1–2 (1997): 137–49.
The Mishnah. Translated by Herbert Danby. London: Oxford University Press, 1933.
Moore, George Foot. *Judaism in the First Centuries of the Christian Era: The Age of the Tannaim*. Cambridge, MA: Harvard University Press, 1927.
Moscovitz, Leib. *Talmudic Reasoning: From Casuistics to Conceptualization*. Tübingen: Mohr Siebeck, 2002.
Neusner, Jacob. *Are the Talmuds Interchangeable? Christine Hayes's Blunder*. Atlanta: Scholars Press, 1995.
———. *The Bavli's Unique Voice: A Systematic Comparison of the Talmud of Babylonia and the Talmud of the Land of Israel*. Vol. 1. Atlanta: Scholars Press, 1993.
———. *The Comparative Hermeneutics of Rabbinic Judaism*. New York: Academic Studies in the History of Judaism, 2000.
———. *Dual Discourse, Single Judaism: The Category-Formulations of the Halakhah and the Aggadah Defined, Compared, and Contrasted*. Lanham, MD: University Press of America, 2001.

———. *The Early Sasanian Period.* Vol. 2 of *A History of the Jews of Babylonia.* Leiden: E. J. Brill, 1966.

———. *The Fathers According to Rabbi Nathan: An Analytical Translation and Explanation.* Atlanta: Scholars Press, 1986.

———. *From Literature to Theology in Formative Judaism: Three Preliminary Studies.* Atlanta: Scholars Press, 1989.

———. *Introduction: Taxonomy.* Vol. 35 of *The Talmud of the Land of Israel.* Chicago: University of Chicago Press, 1982.

———. *Introduction to Rabbinic Literature.* New York: Doubleday, 1994.

———. *Judaism as Story: The Evidence of the Fathers According to Rabbi Nathan.* Chicago: University of Chicago Press, 1992.

———. *Mekhilta According to Rabbi Ishmael, An Introduction to Judaism's First Scriptural Encyclopedia.* Atlanta: Scholars Press, 1988.

———. *Native Category-Formulations of the Aggadah.* Lanham, MD: University Press of America, 2000.

———. *Sifra in Perspective: The Documentary Comparision of the Midrashim of Ancient Judaism.* Atlanta: Scholars Press, 1988.

———. *Sifre to Deuteronomy: An Introduction to the Rhetorical, Logical, and Topical Program.* Atlanta: Scholars Press, 1987.

———. *Sifre to Numbers: An American Translation and Explanation.* Atlanta: Scholars Press, 1986.

———. *Talmud of Babylonia: A Complete Outline.* Atlanta: Scholars Press, 1995.

———. *The Unity of Rabbinic Discourse.* Lanham, MD: University Press of America, 2001.

Noy, Dov. "The Jewish Versions of the 'Animal Languages' Folktale (AT 670)—A Typological-Structural Study." In *Studies in Aggadah and Folk-Literature,* edited by Joseph Heinemann and Dov Noy. Jerusalem: Magnes Press, 1971.

———. *Motif-Index of Talmudic-Midrashic Literature.* Bloomington: Indiana University Press, 1954.

Patai, Raphael. "Ethnohistory and Inner History: The Jewish Case." *JQR* 67, no. 1 (1976): 1–15.

Peat, F. David. *From Certainty to Uncertainty: The Story of Science and Ideas in the Twentieth Century.* Washington, DC: Joseph Henry Press, 2002.

Peskowitz, Miriam. *Spinning Fantasies: Rabbis, Gender and History.* Berkeley and Los Angeles: University of California Press, 1997.

Plaskow, Judith. "Feminism and Religious Authority." *Tikkun* 5, no. 2 (1990): 39–40.

———. *Standing Again at Sinai: Judaism from a Feminist Perspective.* San Francisco: Harper & Row, 1990.

Porton, Gary. "Rabbinic Midrash." In *Judaism in Late Antiquity,* edited by Jacob Neusner. Leiden: E. J. Brill, 1995.

Rubenstein, Jeffrey L. "Elisha ben Abuya: Torah and the Sinful Sage." *JJTP* 7, no. 2 (1997): 139–225.

———. *Talmudic Stories: Narrative Art, Composition and Culture.* Baltimore: Johns Hopkins University Press, 1999.

Saldarini, Anthony J. "The Adoption of a Dissident: Akabya ben Mehalaleel in Rabbinic Tradition." *JJS* 33, nos. 1–2 (1982): 547–56.

———. "[On] David Stern, 'Parables in Midrash: Narrative and Exegesis in Rabbinic Literature (1991).' Id., 'Hamashal be-Midrash; Sipporet u-Parshanut be-Sifrut ḤaZaL'" (Hebrew edition) (1995). *RSR* 22, no. 2 (1996): 119–23.

———. *Scholastic Rabbinism: A Literary Study of the Fathers According to Rabbi Nathan.* Chico, CA: Scholars Press, 1982.

Sanders, E. P. *Jewish Law from Jesus to the Mishnah: Five Studies.* London: SCM Press, 1990.

———. *Paul and Palestinian Judaism: A Comparison of Patterns of Religion.* Philadelphia: Fortress Press, 1977.

Sanhedrin. Trans. J. Shachter and H. Freedman. London: Soncino Press, 1935.

Sarason, Richard S. "Interpreting Rabbinic Biblical Interpretation: The Problem of Midrash Again." In *Ve-Emet: Studies in Honor of Ernest S. Frerichs*, edited by Jodi Magness and Seymour Gitin. Atlanta: Scholars Press, 1998.

———. "Toward a New Agendum for the Study of Rabbinic Midrashic Literature." In *Studies in Aggadah, Targum and Jewish Liturgy in Memory of Joseph Heinemann*, edited by Ezra Fleischer and Jakob Petuchowski. Jerusalem: Magnes Press, 1981.

Schorsh, Ismar. "The Emergence of Historical Consciousness in Modern Judaism." *LBIYB* 28 (1983): 413–37.

Schwartz, Baruch J. "On *Peshat* and *Derash*, Bible Criticism, and Theology." *Prooftexts* 14, no. 1 (1994): 71–88.

Sefer ha-yovel le-Rabi Ḥanokh Albek: Mugash al yede talmidav yedidav u-mokirav li-melot shiv'im shanah. Jerusalem: Mosad Harav Kook, 1963.

Segal, Eliezer. *The Babylonian Esther Midrash: A Critical Commentary.* Atlanta: Scholars Press, 1994.

———. "Law as Allegory? An Unnoticed Literary Device in Talmudic Narratives." *Prooftexts* 8, no. 2 (1988): 245–56.

Shanks, Elizabeth. "The Impact of Feminism on Rabbinic Studies: The Impossible Paradox of Reading Women into Rabbinic Literature." In *Jews and Gender: The Challenge to Hierarchy*, edited by Jonathan Frankel. New York: Oxford University Press, 2000.

Shepansky, Israel. "Hamidot Shehatorah Nidreshet Bahen." *Or Hamizrach* 42, no. 2 (1994).

Shimoff, Sandra R. "Hellenization among the Rabbis: Some Evidence from the Early Aggadot Concerning David and Solomon." *JSJ* 18, no. 2 (1987): 168–87.

Shochetman, Eliav. "Halakhah she-einah halakhah: Ha-im sovel ha-munaḥ 'halakhah' gam inyanei agadah." *Sinai* 120, no. 3 (1997): 183–92.

Siddiqi, Muhammed Zubayr. *Hadith Literature: Its Origin, Development and Special Features.* Edited by Abdal Hakim Murad. Cambridge: Islamic Texts Society, 1993.

Siegel, Seymour, and Elliot Gertel, ed. *Conservative Judaism and Jewish Law.* New York: Rabbinical Assembly, 1977.

Sifre: A Tannaitic Commentary on the Book of Deuteronomy. Translated by Reuven Hammer. New Haven, CT: Yale University Press, 1986.

Silberg, Moshe. *Talmudic Law and the Modern State.* Translated by Benzion Bokser. Edited by Marvin S. Wiener. New York: Burning Bush Press, 1973.

Simon, Solomon. "Stringent Aggadah—Lenient Halachah," *Judaism* 12, no. 3 (1963): 296–306.

Sokol, Moshe Z. "Is There a 'Halakhic' Response to the Problem of Evil?" *HTR* 92, no. 3 (1999): 311–23.

Solomon, Norman. "Extensive and Restrictive Interpretation." In *Jewish Law and Current Legal Problems*, edited by Nahum Rakover. Jerusalem: Library of Jewish Law, 1984.

Soloveitchik, Joseph B. "Confrontation." *Tradition* 6, no. 2 (1964): 5–29.

Steinberg, Theodore. "Max Kadushin: An Intellectual Biography." In *Understanding the Rabbinic Mind: Essays on the Hermeneutic of Max Kadushin*, edited by Peter Ochs. Atlanta: Scholars Press, 1990.

Steinsaltz, Adin. *The Talmud: A Reference Guide*. New York: Random House, 1989.

Steinschneider, Moritz. *Jewish Literature from the Eighth to the Eighteenth Century: with an Introduction on Talmud and Midrash: A Historical Essay from the German of M. Steinschneider*. London: Longman, Brown, Green, Longmans, and Roberts, 1857.

Stern, David. "Aggadah." In *Contemporary Jewish Religious Thought*, edited by Arthur A. Cohen and Paul Mendes-Flohr. New York: Scribner's, 1987.

———. "Literary Criticism or Literary Homilies? S. Handelman and the Contemporary Study of Midrash." *Prooftexts* 5, no. 1 (1984): 96–103.

———. "Midrash and Indeterminacy." *Critical Inquiry* 15, no. 1 (1988): 132–61.

———. *Midrash and Theory: Ancient Jewish Exegesis and Contemporary Literary Studies*. Evanston, IL: Northwestern University Press, 1996.

———. "Moses-cide: Midrash and Contemporary Literary Criticism." *Prooftexts* 4, no. 2 (1984): 193–204.

———. *Parables in Midrash: Narrative and Exegesis in Rabbinic Literature*. Cambridge, MA: Harvard University Press, 1991.

———. "The Rabbinic Parable and the Narrative of Interpretation." In *The Midrashic Imagination: Jewish Exegesis, Thought, and History*, edited by Michael Fishbane. Albany: State University of New York Press, 1993.

Strack, Hermann L. *Introduction to the Talmud and Midrash*. 5th ed. Philadelphia: JPS, 1931.

Strack, H. L., and G. Stemberger. *Introduction to the Talmud and Mishnah*. Translated by Markus Bockmuehl. Minneapolis: Fortress Press, 1992.

Taylor, Mark C. *Hiding*. Chicago: University of Chicago Press, 1997.

Teugels, Lieve. "Midrash in the Bible or Midrash on the Bible? Critical Remarks about the Use of a Term." In *Bibel und Midrasch zur Bedeutung der rabbinischen Exegese für die Bibelwissenschaft*, edited by Gerhard Bodendorfer and Matthias Millard. Tübingen: Mohr Siebeck, 1998.

Tishby, Isaiah, and Joseph Dan. *Mivḥar sifrut ha-musar: Perakim niḥarim be-tseruf, be'urim u-mevo'ot*. Jerusalem: M. Newman, 1970.

Towner, W. Sibley. *The Rabbinic "Enumeration of Scriptural Examples": A Study of a Rabbinic Pattern of Discourse with Special Reference to Mekhilta d'R. Ishmael*. Leiden: E. J. Brill, 1973.

Vermes, Geza. *Scripture and Tradition in Judaism*. Studia Post-Biblica, vol. 4. Leiden: E. J. Brill, 1961.

Visotzky, Burton L. *Fathers of the World: Essays in Rabbinic and Patristic Literatures*. Tübingen: Mohr Siebeck, 1995.

Wacholder, Ben Zion. *Messianism and the Mishnah: Time and Place in the Early Halakhah*. Cincinnati: Hebrew Union College Press, 1979.

Wegner, Judith Romney. "Halakhah and Shari'a: Some Roots of Law and Norms of Conduct in Theocratic Systems." *CCAR Journal*, Fall 2000, 81–95.

Zunz, Leopold. *Ha-Derashot be-Yisrael ve-hishtalshelutan ha-historit*. Translated by M. A. Zak. Jerusalem: Mosad Bialik, 1947.

———. *Die Gottesdienstlichen Vorträge der Juden: Historisch Entwickelt*. Berlin: A. Asher, 1832.

———. *Die Gottesdienstlichen Vorträge der Juden: Historisch Entwickelt ein Beitrag zur Alterthumskunde und biblischen Kritik, zur Literatur- und Religionsgeschichte*. 2nd ed. Frankfurt a. M. J. Kauffmann, 1892.

Index of Text Citations

BIBLE

Gen.
  1:3, 20
  1.20, 252n83
  2:7, 219n21
  2.19, 252n83
  2:22, 207n32, 219n19, 222n75
  3:9, 107
  3:19, 104
  4:9, 241n232
  5:3, 220n36
  10:8, 241n225
  14:14, 44, 220n34
  14:18, 73
  17:4, 242n259
  17:5, 55
  18:7, 86
  24:61, 46, 213, 213n96
  30:14, 12
  30:25, 202n80
  35:8, 26
  35:10, 55
  36:12, 12, 241n228
  38:2, 25
  38:12, 23, 202n93
  38:13, 202n82
  40:10, 227n2
  46:1, 18
  46:12, 23, 202n93
Ex.
  1:13, 22
  2:3, 23, 202n92
  2:8, 23
  3:14, 73
  4:24, 37, 73
  12:38, 107
  15:16, 72, 219n24
  15:26, 72
  19:8, 196n5
  19:9, 196n5
  20:1, 142
  20.2, 104
  20:2, 104
  20:8, 34
  24:12, 53, 222n83
  32:10, 227n7
  33:15, 230n47
  33:23, 73
Lev.
  2:13, 219n28
  5:1, 196n2
  13:45, 206n28
  16:3, 244n296
  16:30, 136
  19:15, 219n28
Num.
  13:20, 85
  15:30, 11–12
  21:30, 229n36
  27:11, 117
  33:3, 77
  35:5, 227n7
Dt.
  1:28, 94
  2:25, 23, 202n84, 202n84, 95
  4:7, 225n151
  4:8, 225n151
  4:24, 244n300
  4:34, 108
  5:12, 34
  7:10, 73, 220n34
  8:3, 9
  9:14, 75
  9:19, 218n12, 219n29
  13:17, 104
  14:1, 257n151
  16:1, 77
  17:8, 116, 197n26
  17:9, 196n2, 228n14

294 Index of Biblical Citations

Dt. *(continued)*
  22:6, 132
  23:23, 218n11
  29:13, 206n29
  32:13, 16
  32:14, 228n15
  32:47, 9
  33:29, 225n151
Josh.
  7:18, 234n130
  10:12, 202n84
  13:3, 227n3
  15:22, 86
  15:31, 86
Jud.
  14:1, 202n82
  19:2, 112
  20:18–28, 205n12
1 Sam.
  1:1, 202n81
2 Sam.
  22:12, 86
1 K.
  1:40, 94
  5:12, 45
  5:13, 104–105
  18:37, 219n24
  21:15, 92
  21:25, 127
  22:10, 86
  22:20, 92
2 K.
  2:23, 86
  4:10, 56
  4:27, 220n31
  19:35, 244n303
Is.
  5:18, 128
  6:6, 218n3
  10:16, 202n80
  19:5, 23, 202n92
  27:4, 218n12, 219n29
  49:3, 105
  54:6, 23, 202n94
  54:12, 202n80
  55:13, 202n80
  56:7, 218n13
  64:3, 202n80
  66:24, 218n4
Jer.
  5:16, 88
  9:18, 244n296

  9:26, 217n1
  13:7, 202n80
  18:22, 202n80, 232n92
  21:9, 202n80
  23:29, 84
Ezek.
  38:2, 53
Hos.
  6:3, 218n8
  14:8, 10
  14:10, 89
Amos
  5:2, 73, 220n35
  9:6, 257n151
Hab.
  1:13, 73
Zech.
  2:3, 127
Mal.
  3:16, 210n13
Ps.
  1:3, 87–88
  2:1, 218n14
  3, 56
  3:1–2, 218n14
  11:3, 232n101
  12:9, 222n82
  18:12, 86
  32:6, 220n42
  37:8, 218n12
  45:15, 242n257
  50:16, 132
  50:20, 128
  55:19, 206n24
  56:7, 206n26
  62:11, 84
  68:5, 20
  68:21, 220n41
  71:19, 20
  76:10, 12
  84:7, 39, 219nn26, 28
  91, 78
  93, 202n80
  102:18, 107
  104:35, 218n3, 219n25
  106:2, 24, 203n101
  106:3, 202n79
  107:10, 221n63
  109:14, 244n300
  119:26, 19
  119:47, 206n25
  119:96, 207n35

Index of Biblical Citations

119:147, 226n181
145, 72
145:16, 23, 202n91
Prov.
  2:20, 125
  3:12, 73
  5:19, 202n78
  14:34, 240n211
  16:5, 86
  23:2, 86
  23:5, 219n22
  23:15, 45
  25:12, 105
  28:11, 198n28
  30:32, 23
Job
  3:17, 218n11
  3:19, 86
  5:7, 72, 219n22
  16:13, 86
  22:25, 22
  37:6, 202n80
  40:30, 227n7
S. S.
  3:11, 105
  4:8, 105
  5:11, 104
  7:12, 219n30
  7:14, 73, 208n50
Ruth
  2:14, 202n77
Lam.
  1:1, 107, 242n259
  2:6, 244n300
  3:28, 25–26
  3:43, 20
Eccl.
  5:5, 132
  6:2, 12
  7:18, 240n210
  12:11, 142
  12:12, 72, 218n7
  12:13, 45, 220n39
Es.
  1:1, 84
  2.22, 249n48
  5:4, 84, 93
  5:11, 227n7
Dan.
  1:6, 202n83
  6:18, 244n296
  7:23, 218n9

  9:17, 222n86
  10:13, 218n3
Ez.
  1:3, 136
  7:8, 227n7
  9:4, 202n80
  11:13, 92
  47:12, 23
1 Chr.
  8:38–9:44, 86
  15:26, 232n98
  17:21, 73, 225n151
  21:15, 202n80
  23:15–17, 75
  29:23, 244n300

MISHNAH

Hag.
  1.8, 247n24, 247n26
  2.1, 133
Sot.
  5.5, 252n84
B. B.
  9.10, 248n41
San.
  10.1, 129, 130, 131, 132, 133, 256n138
  11.2, 121, 248n41
  11.9, 246n9
Ed.
  1.12–14, 249n43
  2.9, 204n110
Avot
  3.12, 256n138
  4.15, 256n142

TOSEFTA

tHag.
  2.3–4, 254n101
tSot.
  7.20–21, 200n52
tSan.
  7.7, 198n31
  12.9, 256n138
tEdu.
  1.14–15, 204n110

BABYLONIAN TALMUD (BAVLI)

Ber.
  1, 33

Ber. (continued)
  3a, 210n1, 219n20, 221n60, 222n75, 226n200
  3b, 205n17, 206n25, 210n3, 212n78, 216n228, 218n6, 223n105, 224n133, 225nn146, 152, 226nn180, 181, 193
  4a, 206n24, 209n65, 211n43, 212n77, 213nn105, 113, 214n123, 217n249, 219nn23, 24, 26, 220n45, 221n57, 223nn91, 105, 224nn116, 135, 226nn181, 189, 204
  4b, 204n5, 205n14, 210nn11, 84, 88, 89, 211n33, 213n102, 216n242, 218nn3, 6, 219n20, 220n35, 221nn59, 60, 65, 222nn82, 83, 223nn100, 114, 224n114
  4b–8b, 39–40, 205n19
  5a, 205n14, 20, 207nn33, 35, 209n61, 210n7, 211nn30, 34, 212nn62, 67, 69, 72, 213nn116, 121, 214nn135, 140, 216nn215, 216, 217, 219nn22, 28, 222n78, 80, 84, 223n99, 225nn152, 155, 157, 226n179
  5a–b, 73–74, 211n27
  5b, 204n5, 206nn25, 26, 207nn36, 37, 38, 39, 208nn49, 51, 209n51, 210n71, 211nn22, 24, 38, 51, 212n63, 214nn124, 142, 143, 145, 148, 149, 215n164, 216nn211, 234, 220nn43, 49, 221nn54, 57, 60, 222nn84, 89, 223n89, 224nn116, 122, 225nn158, 169, 170, 307nn37, 38, 39
  6a, 209nn56, 70, 210n13, 213n110, 215n164, 216n240, 218n15, 221n60, 222nn85, 88, 223nn88, 96, 225nn151, 153, 226n199
  6a–b, 206n25, 224n119
  6b, 206n25, 207n38, 209nn54, 59, 60, 62, 69, 210nn72, 74, 211nn26, 32, 44, 45, 49, 50, 214nn141, 146, 155, 158, 159, 163, 215n175, 216n205, 210, 213, 243, 218n8, 220n39, 221n52, 222n73, 225nn145, 164, 307n38
  7a, 206n26, 207nn33, 37, 209n58, 210nn2, 4, 17, 212nn57, 75, 213nn94, 109, 214n150, 215nn169, 171, 185, 216n218, 218n8, 221n69, 223nn88, 106, 224nn116, 123, 131, 132, 138, 225n159, 226nn197, 198, 307n37
  7b, 204n5, 208n46, 209n57, 210n15, 211nn31, 48, 212n61, 64, 213nn88, 93, 99, 214n152, 215nn170, 204, 216n207, 218nn14, 16, 219nn20, 26, 222n86, 223n101, 224nn128, 130, 136, 225nn147, 160, 165
  7b–8a, 208n47
  8a, 204n5, 206n24, 209nn51, 63, 68, 211nn23, 44, 49, 52, 212nn70, 73, 213nn106, 107, 108, 214nn144, 151, 156, 157, 160, 218n8, 220nn41, 42, 221n58, 223n110, 224nn113, 125, 140, 225n161, 226nn185, 194, 202
  8a–b, 211n28
  8b, 204n4, 209nn54, 56, 211nn49, 50, 212n65, 215n190, 217n254, 221n69, 222n76, 223n107, 224n139
  9a, 214n131, 225n166, 249n50
  9a–b, 222n81
  9b, 208n46, 210nn8, 16, 211n29, 212n76, 213n101, 214n147, 219nn24, 25, 221n57, 223nn104, 108, 224nn120, 121, 134, 225n150
  10a, 201n57, 207nn33, 37, 212n54, 213n98, 215n200, 216n206, 218n3, 222n78, 225n156, 226n205, 307n37
  10a–b, 208n43, 215nn176, 177, 183, 216n227
  10b, 209n56, 210n73, 213nn103, 104, 214nn153, 161, 215nn172, 198, 216n229, 219n30, 220nn31, 32, 221nn51, 58, 222n76, 223n95
  12a, 218n16
  12b, 204n3, 210n75, 213nn97, 117, 215n184, 217n245, 221n53, 225n154, 226n184, 249n44
  12b–13a, 223n92
  12b–13b, 223n93
  13a, 208n46, 213nn90, 92, 217n244
  17a, 234n130
  18a, 255n123
  18b, 211n47, 228n17
  20b, 231n75
  22a, 200n44
  23a–b, 201n70
  25b, 246n16
  31a, 248n36
  31b, 246n12
  31b–32a, 231n73
  32b, 232n80
  33a, 228n16
  33b, 125, 250n57
  34b, 202n80, 228n15
  35b, 227n9
  38b, 232n82
  44a, 246n16

Index of Biblical Citations

45b, 246n17
47b, 200n52
56b–57a, 229n38
58a, 256n145, 257n148
58b, 257n148
59a, 232n87
61b, 232n89
62a, 232n83
62b, 202n80
63a, 202n85
63b, 202n88

Tem.
14b, 199n37

Shab.
20a, 246n17
30b, 228n15, 256nn146, 147
31b, 229n39
33b–34a, 256n147
41b, 246n16
55a, 202n80
55b, 201n64, 229n42, 230n50
59a, 246n16
77b, 228n15
87a, 196n5
88a, 234n122
89a, 201n62
92a, 246n16
96b–97a, 256n134
104a, 229n36
105a, 229n42
113b, 202nn77, 80
118b, 234n130
120a, 200n52

Er.
2, 33, 35
2b, 248n35
13b, 247n22, 252n75
18a, 207nn32, 34, 208n47, 209nn52, 53, 54, 210n5, 212n85, 218nn5, 15, 219nn19, 21, 225nn149, 163
18a–19a, 38
18a–19b, 204n8
18a–b, 223n95
18b, 205n12, 206n28, 207n35, 208nn46, 48, 209n54, 210nn79, 85, 86, 87, 90, 211nn47, 49, 212nn54, 81, 213n96, 213nn96, 120, 214n125, 215nn174, 182, 191, 194, 196, 216nn209, 230, 238, 239, 217n252, 220nn36, 38, 221n66, 222n75, 223nn92, 109, 224nn130, 142, 225n167, 226nn190, 191, 192

19a, 206nn21, 28, 207n35, 208nn41, 45, 209nn59, 68, 210n76, 212nn58, 66, 215n188, 217nn246, 248, 253, 218n4, 219nn26, 28, 220nn38, 48, 221nn63, 69, 224nn124, 126, 129, 141, 225nn148, 162, 168, 226n186
21a, 207nn34, 35, 208n47, 210n77, 220n41, 222n79
21a–b, 210n78, 217n247
21b, 201n57, 206n29, 207n37, 208nn44, 50, 209nn66, 67, 210nn12, 80, 82, 83, 211nn41, 53, 212nn55, 68, 212nn55, 74, 79, 80, 82, 213n100, 214nn126, 129, 216n212, 217nn2, 255, 219nn17, 30, 222nn78, 80, 87, 223n98, 226nn187, 195, 307n37
21b–22a, 213nn112, 122
22a, 210n81, 211n20, 212n56, 213n119, 215n192, 218n3, 220nn34, 37, 222n75, 223n97, 226nn175, 188, 203
24b, 216n231
25b, 214n138
26a, 205n17, 213n118, 216n241, 226n196
32b, 250n54
37b, 246n16
47b, 200n42
51a, 227n7
53a, 235n133
53b, 250n58
54b, 200n52, 202n78
63a, 231n63
64a, 250n54
66a, 254n106
81b, 213n96, 254n106
85b, 254n106
88b, 246n16

Pes.
3a, 227n8
8a–b, 232n96
49a, 231n64
57a, 235n134
62b, 197n11, 229n35, 254n104
82b, 246n16
87a–b, 232n88
87b, 234n127
114a, 201n62
115b, 196n2
116b, 196n2
117a, 229n36

Yoma
4b, 233n113

Yoma *(continued)*
  10a, 251n74
  20a, 229n42
  38b, 201n57
  53b, 234n131
  54a, 232n84, 251n74
  67b, 247n19
  74a, 196n2
  75a, 197n6
  75b, 256n131
  75b–76a, 228n21
  76a, 252n78, 255n125
Suk.
  28a, 200n50, 263n37
  29a, 90
  35a, 229n40
  45b, 233n114
  52b, 251n73, 252n82
  53a, 201n57
Betz.
  4a, 248n35
  24a, 246n15
  25b, 231n77, 234n121
R. H.
  3b, 227n7
  17b, 231n65, 232n80
  25b, 228n14
  26a, 229n41
Taan.
  3b, 228n11, 234n131
  7a, 197n24
  8b, 202nn80, 91
  9b, 232n85
  10a, 229n37
  16a, 199n39
  20a, 202n84
  24b, 228n16
  27b, 24, 203n98
  30a, 197n15, 200n46
Meg.
  7b, 228n18
  10b, 134, 202n80, 230n49, 251n71
  11a–b, 232n94
  14a, 202n81
  14b, 233n118
  15a, 227n8, 228n14, 249n48, 251n74
  15b, 201n64, 227n4
  16b, 255nn119, 122
  21a, 232n80
  21b, 249n47
M. K.
  15a, 200nn42, 44
  16b, 231n72
  17a, 204n6

  21a, 197n14
  23a, 197n14
  25a, 255n11 8
  25b, 234n131
  28b, 201n59
Hag.
  3a, 197n19
  3b, 257n154
  5b, 202n80, 233n115
  11b–16a, 133
  12a, 232n86
  13a, 254n103
  14a, 200n42, 256n132
  15a, 131
Yev.
  11b, 255n114
  21a, 231n68
  24a, 255n114
  63a, 234n131
  77a, 234n128
  85b, 247n19
  109b, 234n128
  122a, 248n34
Ket.
  21b, 196n2
  39b, 231n67
  50b, 202n79, 249n47
  51a, 249n50
  79b, 246n16
  104a, 229n25, 248n30
  111a, 232n79
  111b, 229n30, 257n149
  111b–12a, 228n15
Ned.
  3, 33, 35
  3.11, 208n44, 218n6, 221n60, 247n19
  3:11, 34, 45, 204n9, 217n1
  3b, 213n115
  4.3, 199n39
  20b, 231n69
  21b, 209n55, 215n167, 218n7, 221n67
  22a, 205nn14, 17, 207n34, 210n19, 211n48, 215n179, 218n11, 221n60, 224n127, 226n183
  22a–b, 205n13, 215n180
  22b, 208n47, 212n71, 215n166, 224n117
  23a, 214n154
  24a, 209n54, 215n178, 216n208, 222n76
  25a, 207n38, 216n221, 216n233, 224n123
  26b, 215n201, 216n224
  31b, 211nn25, 39
  31b–32a, 37, 38, 207n34, 225n173
  31b–32b, 34

Index of Biblical Citations 299

32a, 209n64, 210nn6, 9, 10, 211nn37,
    42, 212n60, 213nn89, 91, 114,
    215nn181, 187, 195, 199, 216nn214,
    235, 236, 237, 218nn3, 10, 12,
    219nn19, 29, 220n34, 222n74,
    223nn90, 103, 225nn144, 149, 157,
    172, 226n176
32a–b, 205n19, 213n86, 220n41
32b, 206n28, 207n33, 210n14, 213n87,
    218n7, 219nn27, 29, 223n102
39b, 232n100
50a, 230n57, 234n131
51a, 229n36
Naz.
    23a, 231n65
Sot.
    4b, 247n20
    4b–5a, 229n27
    10a, 202n82
    10b, 230n48
    11b, 202n86, 234n125
    12a, 233n105
    12a–b, 202n92
    12b, 202n89
    13b, 202n93, 234n130
    16a, 247n26
    21a, 232n91
    21b, 233n108
    22a, 24, 203n99, 233n107
    30b–31a, 233n109
    34a, 235n133
    34b, 230n49
    35b, 232n98
    35b–36a, 232n97
    37a–b, 249n46
    40a, 198n28, 249n47
    41b, 234n130
    44a, 200n52, 248n31
    46b, 229n36, 233n111
    49a, 197n13, 228n12
Git.
    7a, 229n33
    23b, 246n17
    43a, 249n43
    46b, 246n16
    55b–58a, 230n55
    57a, 234n132
    57b, 234n131
    60a, 232n92
    60b, 201n69
    68a–b, 230n54
    68b–70b, 228n13
Kid.
    21a–b, 247n28, 248n28

30a, 200n42, 234n130
30b, 231n73, 233n112
36a, 232n90, 234n126
44a, 250n55
49a, 230n44
53a, 253n95
70b, 234n128
72b, 233n110
80b, 229n30
B. K.
    13a, 249n49
    16a, 228n17
    16b, 202n87, 232n92
    30b, 245n6
    37a, 230n59
    54b–55a, 201n60, 232n95
    60b, 197n12, 228nn12, 15
    81b, 229n34
    92a–93a, 231n70
B. M.
    19a, 229n40
    33b, 200n52
    35a, 250n52
    35b, 248n31
    58b, 246n17
    59a, 227n8, 231n71
    59b, 228n16, 230n60
    84a, 235n135
    85b, 229n31, 234n131
    86b, 229n26, 232n99
    116a, 201n71
B. B.
    4a, 233n104
    8a, 200n42
    9b, 234n130
    9b–10a, 197n21
    10a, 232n80, 234n130
    10b, 201n64
    15a, 229n22, 231n62
    15a–b, 232n93
    15b, 229n23
    16a, 232n80, 233n112
    16b, 202n80, 230n45, 255n121
    21a–b, 229n22
    23b, 248n32
    25a, 234n120
    52a, 201n71
    73a–74b, 230n58
    75a, 202n80
    78b, 229n36
    86a, 234n131
    91a, 230n53
    111a, 250n59
    111b, 246n13

B.B. (continued)
  123a, 24, 203n96
  123b, 202n80
  130b, 250n57
  134a, 200n50
  145b, 197n21, 23
  164b–165a, 227n9
San.
  4a, 247n26
  11.2, 248n41
  17a, 247n21
  22a, 202n94, 233n116
  24b, 248n28
  26b, 232n101
  27a, 234n130
  30b, 196n2
  33b, 15
  34a, 227n1
  37a, 230n50
  38a, 249n42
  38b, 230n47, 256n132
  42b, 230n52
  44a, 230n50, 234n130
  48b, 251n62
  49a, 256n138
  51b, 248n31
  56b, 227n8
  57b, 201n67
  58b, 234n131
  67b, 228n16, 256n133
  69b, 125
  71a, 248nn31, 34
  71b, 248n34
  75a, 204n7
  82a, 228n15
  86a, 227n8
  87a, 246n9
  90b, 229n43
  92a, 233n117
  92b, 230nn50, 61
  93b, 202n83
  95b, 230n50, 232n80, 251n71
  96b, 202n80
  97b–98a, 251n72
  99a, 255n122, 256n138
  99b, 138, 198n30, 199n40, 241n228, 252n86
  99b–100a, 256n144
  100a, 197n8, 202n90, 256n147
  100b, 200n52
  101a, 200n47
  102b, 233n106
  103b, 234n130
  106b, 254n105
  107a, 125
  109a, 255n121
  110b, 256n130
Mak.
  23b, 230n50, 250n59, 251n71
  23b–24a, 229n42
Shev.
  3a, 237nn152, 165
  4b, 237n160
  6a, 231n66, 237n159
  6b, 207n34, 214n136, 215n189, 217n256, 218n9, 221nn64, 69, 236n145, 237n180
  7a, 214n134, 237n164
  7b, 237nn152, 153, 155, 172, 179, 184
  8a, 211nn36, 40, 224n115
  9a, 219n23, 226n201
  10b, 214n137, 236n146, 237n178
  11a, 237n157
  11b, 209n51, 214n130, 221n71
  14a, 208n44, 237n161
  15a, 215n165
  15b, 96, 207n34, 226n174, 237n173
  16a, 96
  16b, 237n158
  17a–b, 237n171, 237n184
  17b, 237nn152, 170, 175, 177
  18a, 237nn151, 156, 182
  18b, 96, 205n19, 207n33, 211n21, 214n139, 215n193, 202, 218n10, 221n61
  20b, 204n9, 209n54
  23a, 216n226
  24b, 236n147
  26a, 214n128
  27b, 237n162
  29a, 206n29, 237n168
  29b, 207n38, 216n222, 224n123
  30a, 219n28, 226n178, 247n19
  31a, 96, 221n50, 237nn154, 174, 181
  31a–b, 236n145, 237n152
  31b, 237nn169, 183
  32b, 237nn163, 166
  34a, 204n10
  35a, 196n2
  35b, 96, 205n12, 208n47, 210n18, 215n173, 222n78, 224nn111, 137, 225n171
  36a, 34, 205n11, 213n95, 237nn150, 163, 167
  36b, 214n127
  37a, 208n44

Index of Biblical Citations

38b, 236n148, 237nn176, 183
39a, 96, 212n59, 221nn60, 70, 223n94,
   224n143, 236n149
39a–b, 204n10, 215n186, 224n112
39b, 207n31, 211n35
40a, 221n56
41b, 213n111
46b, 201n71
47b, 205n19, 209n55, 215n168, 220n33
111b, 255n122

A. Z.
3b, 233n103
4b, 234n131
5a, 227n10, 231n78, 232n95, 234n123
9a, 230n50
19b, 230n51
24b, 202n80
25a, 202n95
25b, 24, 203n97

Hor.
11b, 246n15

Zev.
62a, 24, 203n100
82a, 231n66
102a, 232n102, 233n119

Men.
29b, 250n61
37a, 248n33
45b, 251n63
53a, 227n7, 231n76
53a–b, 228n20
53b, 229n28
66b, 229n36
69b, 248n34

Hul.
4, 35
5a, 229nn24, 29
6a, 229n30
7a, 228n16
27b, 252n83
43a, 229n29
60b, 201n66, 227n3, 231n74, 232n80,
   252n87
68b, 205n15, 214n132
71a, 205n15, 214n128
76b, 206n27, 216n219, 220n47
77a, 205n16, 212n83, 214n133
77b, 204n9, 216n220
77b–78a, 224n118
78a, 206n28, 214n162, 216n225,
   218nn10, 12, 222n77
89a, 197n10, 234n124
90b, 235n136

91a, 24, 203n97, 232n80
91b, 228n16, 234n131
92a, 199n40, 201n64, 227n2
98a, 248n35
104b, 249n48
105b, 228n19
133b, 229n30

Bekh.
8b–9a, 230n56
57b, 228n15
58a, 232n81

Ar.
10b–11a, 235n136
11a, 234n129
15a–16b, 227n6
30b, 229n32

Ker.
7a, 256n137

Tam.
2:2, 94
3:4, 94
29a–b, 234n129

Nid.
19, 249n48
34a, 217n250
40a, 221n68
41a, 212n83
43a, 204n9, 220n44
44a, 222n74
44b, 215n203
45a, 205n11, 206n29, 208nn43, 46, 50,
   217n251, 221nn55, 72, 226n182
45b, 205n14, 206n30, 207n30, 215n197,
   218n10, 220n40, 223n95, 226n177
46b, 205n15, 220n46
47b, 216n232
53b, 249n43
69b, 200n45
70a, 200n45

Yerushalmi Talmud

yBer.
9.1, 24, 203n101
9.2, 24, 203n101
yPeah
1.1, 256n138
2.6, 198n31
yShevi.
9.1, 256n147
yMaas.
1.2, 81, 201n61
3.10, 12, 252n81

yShab.
  1.4, 199n38
  16.1, 201n68
yPes.
  5.3, 197n11, 254n104
  6.2, 256n138
yShek.
  5.1, 199n39
yYoma
  8.7, 256n137
yTaan.
  4.5, 246n14
yMeg.
  3.1, 200n51
  4.1, 199n39
yHag.
  1.8, 196n5, 198n31, 200n42
yYeb.
  4.2, 246n10
yYev.
  4.2, 201n61
  12.6, 197n25
yKet
  12.3, 197n26
yNed.
  10.8, 199n38
yGit.
  4.2, 196n2
yB. K.
  4.3, 200n42
yB. B.
  6.3, 201n53
ySan.
  3.9, 196n2
  4.2, 247n22
  10.2, 252n79
  11.3, 196n2, 197n26, 246n9
yShev.
  1:1, 237nn152, 165
  1:3, 237n160
  1:4, 237n159
  1:5, 236n145, 237n180
  1.6, 256n137, 237nn152, 153, 164, 172, 179, 184
  2:2, 236n146, 237n178
  2:3, 237n157
  3:4, 237n161
  3:5, 237n173
  3:7, 237n158
  3:8, 96, 237nn152, 155, 156, 170, 171, 175, 177, 182, 184
  3:9, 237n151
  4.1, 196n2
  5:2, 236n147
  5:6, 237n162
  6:2, 237n168
  6:5, 96, 237nn152, 154, 169, 174, 181, 183
  6:8, 237nn163, 166
  7:2, 96, 237nn163, 167
  7:3, 237n150
  7:7, 236n148, 237nn176, 183
  7:8, 236n149
  9.1, 256n147
yHor.
  3.4, 197n20
  3.5, 198nn28, 31, 199n38

MEKHILTA

Mekh. Beshallah
  6, 256n129
Mekh. Vayasa
  1, 15, 197n18
  3, 239n200
Mekh. Vayetze
  6, 239n200
Sifra Tazria
  13.2, 255n124
Sifre Num.
  69, 125
  75, 256n135
  112, 199n40
  112.3, 138
Sifre Dt.
  1, 255n125
  48, 197n7, 199n39
  49, 197n6, 199n40
  58, 200n52
  96, 257n151
  161, 200n52
  237, 246n12
  306, 197n9
  313, 200n52
  317, 197n17, 200n49

AVOT DE-RABI NATAN

AdRN
  8, 200n42
  14, 15
  18, 200n42
  27, 250n54
  28, 200n45

Index of Biblical Citations

29, 200n52
40, 200n42
AdRN B
  12, 200n48
  28, 200n50
Gen. R., 242n252
  1.4, 241n240
  1.9, 240n212
  1.15, 240n210
  3.4, 201n72, 202n76
  6.2, 240n210
  8.2, 254n103
  8.4, 243n264
  9.5, 203n108
  9.7, 105
  10.3, 240n212
  12.10, 201n72, 202n75, 202nn74, 75
  12.12, 243n266
  16.4, 200n43
  19.9, 242n256
  20.2, 233n234, 241n234
  20.10, 240n223
  21.4, 233n236, 241n236
  21.5, 256n129
  22.9, 241nn232, 238
  24.5, 242n257
  26.2, 247n22
  30.4, 243n285, 244n295
  30.5, 244n295
  30.8, 240n221, 244n295, 245n311
  33.3, 254n106
  33.7, 242n247
  34.5, 240n210
  36.1, 255n128
  37.1, 242n255
  37.3, 241n225, 243n282
  38.8, 244n290
  38.12, 244n289
  39.4, 240n210
  39.7, 240n210
  40.4, 243n266
  40.7, 199n39
  41.2, 203n105
  41.3, 241n243, 242n243
  42.3, 243n276, 243n283
  42.7, 244n293, 251n70
  44.8, 204n110
  44.9, 242n259
  44.17, 243n263
  44.19, 243n265
  46.7, 242n259
  47.9, 240n211, 255n126
  48.6, 243n271
  48.14, 243n269
  48.15, 109
  49.5, 243n270
  50.3, 242n252
  50.11, 244n290
  51.2, 243n278
  51.3, 243n281
  51.8, 109
  52.4, 243n282
  52.13, 243n270
  53.14, 233n235, 241n235
  53.15, 241n228, 243n272
  55.6, 243n286
  55.7, 240n210
  55.8, 255n127
  56.6, 252n77
  57.4, 240n210, 245n313
  58.3, 240n216
  58.5, 243n299
  60:3, 242n246
  60.15, 241n229
  61.4, 244n291
  62.4, 243n277
  62.5, 243n287
  64.4, 248n29
  65.15, 244n288, 255n120
  66.3, 199n39
  70.8, 240n210
  70.18, 241n231
  73.7, 243n287
  75.8, 243n262
  80.7, 240n210
  81.2, 197n25
  81.5, 203n109
  82.2, 243n269
  82.14, 241n228
  84.6, 203n106
  85.4, 240n220
  92.1, 106
  92.7, 243n268
  93.7, 240n219
  94.5, 201n65
  99.3, 240n210
Lev. R.
  1.2, 197n22
  2.2, 241n240
  2.5, 233n2.5, 241n233
  3.7, 200n42
  9.3, 199n39
  11.7, 203n105
  11.9, 242n257

Lev. R. (continued)
  13.3, 244n307
  13.5, 199n39
  15.1, 199n39
  18.2, 201n54
  19.2, 241n226
  19.6, 244n309
  20.2, 244n304
  20.10, 244n302
  21.5, 199n39
  21.9, 244n296
  22.1, 200n43
  22.10, 240n218
  23:10, 243n298
  25:8, 242n241
  27.1, 240n210
  27.5, 241n240
  27.6, 203n105
  27.7, 243n266
  27.8, 242n253
  30.2, 200n43
  30.3, 242n244
  31, 202n75
  31.1, 201n72
  31.7, 201n72, 202n76
  31.9, 242n245
  32.1, 255n125
  32.7, 241n239
  34.1, 243n285
  34.10, 240n215
  35.7, 244n301
  36.1, 199n39
  36.4, 240n213
  36.5, 106
  36.6, 106, 134, 243n280
Num. R.
  13.15–16, 247n22
S. S. R.
  1.1.5, 240n217, 244n296
  1.1.6, 243n274
  1.1.10, 244n300, 245N313
  1.2.1, 244n292
  1.2.2, 245n312
  1.12.1, 255n128
  1.15.3, 240n216
  1.16.2, 245n310
  2.4.1, 255n128
  2.14, 252n75
  2.14.6, 244n294
  3.4.2, 244n305
  4.7.1, 244n308
  4.8.1, 241n227
  5, 252n75
  5.14.1, 240n210
  7.8.1, 243n284
  7.9.1, 109
  9.1–4, 256n129
Eccl. R.
  12.1, 254n103
Lam. R.
  Pet. 21.8, 242n260
  Pet. 24, 241n237
  Pet. 31.16, 243n266
  Proem 5, 244n291
  Proem 8, 244n296
  Proem 15, 242n250
  Proem 20, 242n249
  Proem 24, 203n24
  Proem 25, 242n249
  Proem 30, 240n210, 244n303
  Proem 34, 241n243
  1.1.1, 242n259, 243n299, 244n299
  1.1.2, 240n214
  1.16.51, 244n306
  1.22.57, 242n242
  1.41, 201n72
  2.1.3, 243n279
  2.6.10, 244n300
  3.1.1, 241n240
  3.5.3, 242n248
  3.10, 203n107
  3.21.8, 240n211
  3.43, 201n72, 202nn75, 76
  3.90, 240n210
  4.1, 242n251
  4.18.29, 243n266
  5.18, 256n136
PRK
  1.3, 241n230, 243n297
  1.5, 109, 243n275
  1.7, 243n273
  1.8, 243n268
  2.5, 240n211
  2.7, 241n224
  3.1, 243n266, 244n300
  3.7, 244n292
  3.13, 201n55, 243n287
  4.3, 241n225
  4.10, 242n260
  6.4, 242n260
  7.4, 242n254
  7.5, 242n248
  7.8, 201n56, 243n287
  7.10, 243n272
  9.1, 242n258
  9.6, 243n266

12.1, 243n261
12.3, 198n29
12.14, 242n249
12.24, 243n267
12:24, 242n259
12.25, 199n39, 240n222
13.4, 242n251
15.10, 243n271
16.1, 243n268
16.8, 243n268
16.10, 242n248

17.1, 243n266
19.5, 243n269
20.6, 240n210
20.7, 108–109, 244n289
21.5, 201n72, 202n76
22.1, 242n251
27.2, 200n43
28.25, 198n27
42.6, 244n291
42.8, 244n291
appendix 2, 201n58

Index of Subjects and Proper Names

Abaye, R., 9, 56–57, 248n30, 250n59
Abba, R., 77, 109, 124, 205n14, 240n211
Abba b. Kahana, R., 12, 45, 136, 214n163
Abba b. Mattenah, R., 222n75
Abba Benjamin, 39, 45, 70, 206n25, 208n49, 223n89
Abbahu, R., 11, 93, 204n3
Abraham, 37–38, 44, 55, 136, 240n11
Adda b. Mattenah, R., 58, 124, 222n75
aggadah: aggregates of, 35–36, 36–40, 206nn24, 25, 26, 206nn24, 25, 28, 29; anonymous voices in, 9, 35, 78, 206n23, 227nn7, 8; anthropomorphism and, 75, 79–80, 105–106, 225n203, 241nn231–40; belief challenged in, 71–77, 89–90, 231n73; in biblical interpretation, 9, 20–21, 55–56, 73, 119, 201n72, 202nn76, 80, 204n110; boundaries of discourse in, 109, 128–29, 133–34, 255n128; critical studies of, 147, 154–57, 258n4, 264n41, 265n52; distribution of, 33–34, 35–36, 95–96; Greco-Roman influence on, 147–49, 155, 259nn8, 12; halakhah compared with, 115–18, 122, 125–28, 142, 168–69, 245nn5, 8, 246n10, 247n19, 251n68, 252n76; identification of, 4, 7–8, 14, 31–32, 126, 146, 180, 204nn4, 5, 257n2; in lists of components of Oral Law, 13–19, 199n39, 200nn42–52; *masoret aggadah*, 87, 109, 126; negative teachings in, 127–28; in nonhalakhic discussions, 23–25, 33–34, 180–83, 203n103, 204n110; philosophic analysis of, 169–70, 175–78, 272nn111, 112, 274nn121, 122, 123, 275nn127, 129, 139; readers' engagement with, 176–77; status of, 9–15, 91, 127–28, 197nn16, 26, 198nn31, 34, 232n99; thirty-two middot, 129, 134–35, 172, 174,

254n107; as written tradition, 18–19, 201n66. *See also* Babylonian Talmud (Bavli); literary analysis; midrash; Mishnah; Neusner, Jacob; rabbis; Talmud headings; Yerushalmi Talmud
Aha b. R. Hanina, 206n24
Aha b. Rava, R., 206n25
Aher (Elisha ben Abuya), excommunication of, 130–32, 156, 253n98, 254n101
Akabya ben Mehalaleel, 253n95
Akiba, R./Aqiba, R.: on challenges on interpretation, 105; dialogues of, 208n43; exaggerations of, 103; on the Exodus, 77; on Gen. R. 53.15, 241n228; *haggadah* used by, 204n110; in halakhic tales, 205n11; moral lessons of, 130, 207n37, 239n200; rebuke stories of, 90, 105, 136–37; rhetorical devices of, 42, 78–79, 204n110; sanctions on reading External Books, 129, 130; in Talmud Yerushalmi, 95
al ahat kamah vekamah, 108, 243n269
alav hakatuv omer, 229n34
Albeck, Chanokh, 248n27
aliba deman, 122
am haaret, 46, 55–56, 211n49
Ami, R., 9, 20, 21, 201n72
Ammi, R./Ammi b. Abba, R., 38, 73, 116, 204n5, 205n19, 206n28, 219n27
Anan, R., 202n76
"and it came to pass in the days of . . . ," 109
anonymous voices, 9, 35, 78, 206n23, 227nn7, 8
anthropomorphism, 75, 79–80, 105–106, 225n203, 241nn231–40
Arai, Abraham, 115, 245n5
Ashi, R., 46, 206n25

Ashkenazi, Samuel Jaffe, 236n145
asmakhta/asmakhtot, 118–19, 247n24, 248n27
Assi, R., 9, 56–57, 116
atonement, 39, 45, 208n44
Avery-Peck, Alan, 275n139
Avot, 100–101

Babylonian Talmud (Bavli): aggadah-halakhah interaction in, 84–85, 115–16, 233n110, 245n8, 265n52; aggadic material in, 21–22, 95–96, 103–104, 235n138, 236n144, 238n185, 245n8; culture reflected in, 149; oral tradition in, 152; radical treatment of a tradition, 117, 246n16; Yerushalmi Talmud compared to, 95–96, 116, 151–52, 235n138, 238n185
Bacher, Wilhelm, 7, 134, 230nn48, 50, 61, 251n62
Baeck, Leo, 127, 191, 198n32, 278n1
Barabasi, Albert-Laslo, 184, 277n8
Bar Kappara, R., 242n259
Baron, Salo, 134, 246n11, 263n34, 275n139
Barthes, Roland, 160
Baskin, Judith, 166–67
beduta, 117, 246n18
behavior, 41, 45–46, 58–60, 62, 71, 85, 200n45, 208nn41, 44, 221n67, 228n19
behedia ketiv beh, 119
Ben Aai, 45, 90, 107, 214n163, 242n259, 248n41
Ben-Amos, Dan, 152, 153, 263n36
Benjamin, Abba, 204n5
Benjamin b. Yefet, R., 90
Ben Sira, 254n103
Ben Zoma, 72, 223n92
Berakhiah, R., 240n211
Beruriah, 70, 197n11, 207n37, 218n3
Bialik, Hayyim Nahman, 115, 154–55
biblical texts: aggadah and, 9, 20–21, 55–56, 73, 84–86, 91–92, 119, 201n72, 202nn76, 80, 204n110, 228nn20–28; contradictions, reconciliation of, 92–93, 233n12, 233nn113, 114, 115, 116, 117; disparagement of, 90; exegetical freedom and, 86–87, 117–19, 126–35, 177, 247nn22, 24, 253n95; halakhah and, 34–35, 118–19, 205n14, 247n26; hyperbole in, 217n1; midrashim and, 104–106; verses as warrants for teaching, 68, 218nn8, 9, 10, 11; in yShevuot, 96, 237n152. *See also* grammar; midrash; word play

binyan av, 108, 243n271
bishlama leman deamar . . . ela leman deamar, 232n85
Bishop, Donald H., 167
Bloch, Renée, 258n4
Boyarin, Daniel, 164–65, 265n52, 269n87, 270n90
Brod, Max, 191
Bruns, Gerald L., 118, 139, 140–41, 247n22, 265n52
Buchanan, Mark, 277nn8, 11

Cenlauer, William, 167
circumcision, 37, 45, 73, 78, 136, 208n44, 217n1, 218n12, 219n19, 221n60, 222n74, 240n11
Cohen, Aryeh, 162, 265n52, 268n70
Cohen, Haim, 248n30
Cohen, Shaye J. D., 118, 129
common sense, 71, 74, 85, 91, 221n64, 228nn14, 15, 235n133
contradictions, reconciliation of/reconciliation tactics, 92–93, 233nn113, 114, 115, 116, 117, 118, 119
Culler, Jonathan, 160, 161

daateh, 244n294
Danby, Herbert, 196n4, 217n1
Daube, David, 134, 147, 259n8
davar aher, 69, 84, 102–103, 104, 117, 219n19, 247n19, 275n138
Davies, W. D., 198n34
Davis, Joseph M., 264n41
dayyecha, 136
deconstructionist literary theory, 160–61
derash, 135, 177; adding data, 69, 220n38; amplification of text, 219n19; comparisons (d-m-h) in, 71; *davar aher*, 69, 84, 102–3, 104, 117, 219n19, 247n19, 275n138; gemara, 71, 221n63; *ika de'amri*, 219n19; literal reading of names, 69, 219n26; missing letters or words, 69, 219nn21, 22; multiplication of confirming opinions, 71, 221n60; peshat impacted by, 69, 219nn28–37; reduplication of terms, 69, 219n24; shift of terms in passage, 69, 219n25; spelling or calligraphy, variations in, 69, 219n23, 229n36; splitting words, 69, 220n31; of straightforward meaning, 68, 218n7; wordplay, 70, 220nn39, 40; word splitting for, 69, 220nn31, 32. *See also* midrash

Index of Subjects and Proper Names

Derrida, Jacques, 160
devarim bego, 90, 232n79
dialogue form, 41, 208nn42, 43
Dimi, R., 9
disciples, 9–10, 18, 58, 126, 139, 201n57, 222n75
documentary approach, 157–60, 267n57, 268n69
Dorshe Haggadah, 8, 197n6
dream interpretations, 86, 229n38

eikhah, 107, 242n259
Elazar, R., 45, 77, 78, 105, 206n29, 224n143, 227n7
Elazar b. Azariah, R., 77, 136, 217n1
Elazar b. R. Shimon, R./Elazar b. R. Simeon, R., 93, 94
Elazar Hagadol, R./Eliezer the Great, 223n88, 234n130
Elazar Hamodai, R., 18, 126, 138, 239n200
Eliezer, R.: challenges to colleague, 75; excommunications of, 88; on the final redemption, 126; on fulfillment God's promises, 73; on names of God, 205n12; on night watches, 221n69; rebuke stories of, 136; on teaching women Torah, 92, 233n108; thirty-two middot (rules for discourse), 134–35, 172, 174, 254n107
Eliezer b. Eliakim, R., 249n47
Eliezer b. Jacob, R., 45, 59
Eliezer b. R. Yose Hagalili, R., 9, 87, 134
Eliezer Hamodai, 239n200
Elisha ben Abuya (Aher), excommunication of, 130–32, 156, 253n98, 254n101
Elman, Yaakov, 151, 235n137, 262n32, 263n36
Elon, Menachem, 121, 129, 246n10
en ... ela ..., 109, 134, 255n128
Ena Saba, R., 93, 233n118
en lemedin rules, 182
en mikra yote miyede peshuto, 135
en mukdam omeuhar batirah, 111
epukh, 117
etivun, 110
euphemisms, 42, 64, 73–74, 208n50, 223n114
Evil Yeter, 38, 89, 92, 105, 109, 233n112

Falk, Ze'ev, 125
Fathers According to Rabbi Nathan, The, 100–1, 239n201
Feldman, Louis, 259n10
feminism, 166–67, 270n99, 270nn94, 99

Finkelstein, Louis, 15, 199n41, 275n139
Firestone, Reuven, 168, 272n109
Fischel, Henry, 147, 254n102, 259nn11, 12
folklore, 42, 89, 153–56, 231n71, 263n36
Fonrobert, Charlotte, 166, 270n99
Fox, Marvin, 198n34
Fraade, Steven, 99, 162–63, 247n19
Frankel, Zechariah, 96
Freedman, H., 198n34
Frenkel (Fraenkel), Jonah/Yonah, 12–13, 155–56, 264nn40, 44, 265n52, 268n70

Gadamer, Hans-Georg, 160, 265n52
geerah shavah, 108, 109, 227n7, 243n270
Geiger, Abraham, 169–70, 273n114
Geist, 170, 172, 173
gemara, 71, 126, 221n63
gematria, 37–38, 70, 87, 108, 173, 220n41, 229n42, 242n259, 243n273
gender, 108, 166–67, 242n261, 270n94, 270nn94, 99
Genesis Rabbah, style of, 101–102
gentiles, in talmudic exegesis, 39, 97, 98
Gerhardsson, Birger, 151
Ginzberg, Louis, 95–96, 236n144
God: anthropomorphisms, 75, 105–106, 241nn231–40; Covenant faith, 188–89; in exile, 107; forgiveness from, 72, 223n94; fulfillment of promises by, 73; humankind's emulation of, 61–62; justice of, 52, 224n143; Max Kadushin on, 189–90; Moses' relationship with, 73; names of, 254n106; people of Israel's relationship with, 89–90, 231n73; providence of, 205n12; punishment, 52–53, 73, 211nn42, 48; rabbis' understanding of, 51–52; in rhetorical devices, 109; Shekhinah, 51, 93; as Shekhinah, 51, 93; tadik's relation ship with, 89
Goldin, Judah, 199n41, 239n201, 253n88, 257n153
Goodblatt, David, 139, 149, 150, 256n141
Goshen-Gottstein, Alon, 130, 157, 162, 253n98, 254nn101, 102
grammar, 107, 108, 173, 242nn249–55, 243n260
Greco-Roman influences, 108, 147–49, 155, 243n266, 259nn8, 12, 260n13
Green, William Scott, 269n87
Greenberg, Moshe, 275n139
Greenberg, Simon, 274nn122, 123, 275n139
Gruenwald, Ithamar, 128, 129, 139, 265n52
Guggenheimer, Heinrich, 272n111

guma, 120
Guttmann, Alexander, 249n49
Guttmann, Michael, 249n47

hadith genre, 167–68, 271n104, 272n109
haggadah, 7–8, 26, 180, 196n2, 197n6, 204n110
Haggai, R., 78, 218n3
halakhah: aggadah compared with, 115–18, 122, 125–28, 142, 168–69, 245nn5, 8, 246n10, 247n19, 251n68, 252n76; appeal of, 119–20; authority challenged in, 123–24, 249nn49, 50, 250nn54, 57, 59; biblical exegesis and, 118–19, 247n26; decision-making in, 121–24, 248n41, 249nn42, 47, 50; definition of, 14, 31–32, 121, 125, 126, 198n31, 204nn2, 3, 251n67; refutation of opinions in, 124, 126, 250n59, 251n73, 251nn62, 74, 252n75; sanctions in, 121–23, 129–32, 253n95, 254n101; Sinaitic revelation and, 8, 10, 53–55, 180, 189; terminology of, 117, 118–19, 122, 123, 246n18, 247n24, 249n44, 249n46, 250n56; value of, 10–11, 124–25. *See also* Babylonian Talmud (Bavli); Mishnah; rabbis; Talmud headings; Yerushalmi Talmud
halakhah lemaaseh, 123
halakha k . . . , 122, 249n44
Halbertal, Moshe, 106, 241n238
Halevi, E. E., 147
Halivni, David Weiss, 135
Hama berabi Haninah, R., 240n210
Hammer, Reuven, 99, 115n8, 245n8
Hamnuna, R., 45, 208n43
Hana b. Bina, R., 126
Hananiah, R., 10
Handelman, Susan, 160–61, 268n73
Hanina, R., 77, 94
Hanina b. Agil, R., 232n95
Hanina b. Dosa, R., 228n16, 234n131
Hanina b. Papa, R., 104
Haniniah b. Gamliel, 124
Harris, Jay, 95
Hartman, David, 278n2
Hartman, Geoffrey, 161
Hasan-Rokem, Galit, 153–54, 264nn38, 39, 40
hasorei mihasera, 117
hatakh, 122
Hauptman, Judith, 157–58, 166, 270n99
Hayes, Christine, 235n138
Heinemann, Joseph, 145, 163–64, 230n61, 235n137, 237n184, 238n186

Heinemann, Yitshak, 55, 105, 147, 154–55, 163–64, 241n229, 260n13
Helbo, R., 20, 39–40, 59, 201n72, 202n73, 206n25, 214n163, 218n8, 240n211
hemanuta beyadan, 87
Hengel, Martin, 147, 259n10
Herfeld, Levi, 169, 273n114
Herford, R. Travers, 239n202
Herog, Isaac, 251n65
hetivun, 110
Hezser, Catherine, 139, 149, 235n138, 253n95, 256n141, 261n21
Hillel, 117, 118, 252n75
Hinduism, 167, 271n102
Hinenah b. Papa, R., 11
Hirschberg, H. Z., 115, 245n4
Hirschfeld, H. S., 169–74, 272n112, 273nn114, 115
Hirshman, Marc, 148
Hisda, R.: as *baal aggadah*, 18, 19, 201n57; common sense of, 91; contradictions of accepted Jewish beliefs, 73; on entering the synagogue, 75–76; exegetical techniques of, 84, 217n2, 227nn5, 7; on halakhic exegesis, 121, 205n14; opposition to an aggadah, 91; prooftexts of, 206n24, 207n30; on Torah study, 45–46
Hiyya, R., 136, 234n131
Hiyya b. Abba, R., 11, 90, 205n19, 234n130
Hiyya b. Abin, 73
Hiyya b. Ammi, 40, 56–57, 79
Hiyya b. Ba, R., 10
Hiyya the Elder, R., 11, 126
Holt, Avraham, 275n139
Horgan, Maurya, 258n5
Huna, R., 18, 39–40, 59, 73, 124–25, 206n25, 207n37, 214n163, 240n211
Huna b. Judah, R., 40, 204n5
hyperbole: in aggadah, 43–46, 87, 103–104, 240nn213–22; Biblical example of, 217n1; exaggeration in, 94, 234nn129–36; *guma*, 120; logical agility, 117–18; in yShevuot, 96–97

i ba'et ema, 117
ika de'amri, 219n19
Illa, R., 78, 220n34
ilmale mikra katuv, i efshar le-omro, 106
im ba'et, ema, 91
ini, 233n116
intertextuality in reading of midrash, 163–65, 269n87
ipekha mistabra, 117

Isaac, R., 39, 44, 74, 136, 204n5, 205nn14, 20, 218n15, 223n88, 224n116, 228n16
Ishmael, R., 73, 84, 95, 117, 136, 217n1, 227n9
Islam, 167–68, 271n104, 272n109
Israel, people of: euphemisms, 73–74; in exile, 107; God's relationship with, 188–90, 222n78, 241n240; merits of, 61, 90, 93, 234n131; pagan practices adopted by, 74, 224n118; Sinaitic revelation and, 8, 53–55, 180, 189; Torah accepted by, 60–61, 73–74, 93–94, 241n240
Issi b. Yehudah, R., 240n210
itemar hakhi itemar, 117

Jacob b. Iddi, 223n91
Jacobs, Louis, 116, 245n8, 248n32
Jaffee, Martin, 147, 151, 238n185, 259n11, 260n13, 261n21, 262n27, 269n87, 275n139
Jastrow, Marcus, 249n46, 250n56
Jeremiah, R., 10, 74
Jeremiah b. Abba, R., 20
Jeremiah b. Elazar, R.: on Adam, 38–39, 220n36; aggadic compilation of, 206n28; hyperbole, 45, 79; mashal used by, 208n41; personification in aggadah, 208n48; *peshat* reading of, 218n5; on repentance, 224n124; surprise in aggadic anecdotes, 207n35; on Torah study, 46
Jonah, R., 201n61
Jonathan, R., 26, 133, 205n18, 222n88
Jose b. Zimra, R., 229n42
Joseph, R., 42, 43, 78, 86, 124, 248n30
Joshua, R., 9–10, 73–75, 126, 205n12, 207n37
Joshua b. Hananiah, R., 88, 197n25, 200n45
Joshua b. Korha, R., 73, 78, 217n1, 234n130
Joshua b. Levi, R.: on aggadah as Oral Torah, 18–19; contradictions of accepted Jewish beliefs, 73; on cursing the government, 7; as disciple, 9–10, 18; on the divine image, 226n203; exaggerations of, 45, 234n130; exhortations of, 204nn4, 5; on heavenly sanctions for rabbinic rulings, 250n59; on the importance of aggadah, 9–10, 18; *kiveyakhol* used by, 225n203; as *mesader aggadeta*, 201n57; on repentance, 74, 224n124; on the revelation at Sinai, 8, 234n130
Judah, R., 204n4, 218n10, 228n15, 230n61, 253n95
Judah b. Masporta, R., 234n130

Judah b. Menasiah, R., 220n31
Judah Berabi, 239n200
Judah b. Simeon, R., 74
Judah the Nasi, R., 8, 11, 14, 196nn2, 5, 205n14
Judah the Nasi II, R., 20, 21, 201n72
Justinia, story of, 206n29, 208n40, 221n55

Kadushin, Max: on aggadic v. halakhah, 177, 275nn134, 138; his American perspective on rabbinic discourse, 175, 274nn121, 123; biological paradigm of rabbinic thinking, 183–84; on God's covenant, 189–90; H. S. Hirschfeld and, 169–74, 272n112, 273nn114, 115; scholars' views on, 274n122, 275n139; on structuring rabbinic thinking, 175, 263n34, 272n112, 274n121; on value-concepts v. cognitive-concepts, 176–78, 275nn127, 129
Kagan, Zipporah, 150, 262n24
Kahana, R., 39, 90, 206n28, 221n71
Kalmin, Richard, 124, 148, 151, 235n137, 262n32, 263n36, 264n48
kal vehomer, 108, 243n268
Kamesar, Adam, 147, 260n13, 277n6
Kant, Immanuel, 268n69
Kariv, Abraham, 247n24
kashya, 244n293
kava, 122
ke'ilu, 79
keman, 122
keman ... keman, 232n97
keman ala hadetanya, 232n97
keman ala ha dikhetiv, 232n85
keneged, 108, 243n273
Kermode, Frank, 128
kidetani, 221n61
kiveyakhol, 79
kol makom she ..., 134
Kraemer, David, 235n138, 263n36
kushya hi le ..., 229n27

la kashya, 233nn116, 117
lamah li?, 227n5
Langowitz, Andrew, 277n15
Lapidus, Rina, 252n76
Lapin, Hayim, 261n21
Larson, Gerald James, 271n102
lashon havai, 94
lemai nafka minah, 122
leshamesh, 58
leshon havai, 94

Levi, R., 12, 105, 136, 197n25, 240n211
Levi b. Hama, R., 39, 53
Levi b. Sisi, 10–11
Lieberman, Saul, 115, 134, 147, 245n5, 259nn7, 12
Lieberman, Stephen, 134, 147
Liebes, Yehudah, 131, 254n101
Lightstone, Jack, 265n52
literary analysis: comparative religion, 167–68, 271n104, 272n109; deconstructionist theory, 160–61; feminism, 166–67, 270n99, 270nn94, 99; feminism in, 166–67, 270nn94, 99; folklore, 42, 89, 153–56, 231n71, 263n36; grammar, 107, 108, 173, 242nn249–55, 243n260; Hegelian approach to, 169–72, 272n112, 273nn114, 115; Neusner's form-criticism on, 157, 158; orality, 151–52, 153, 263n36; philosophic analysis, 169–70, 175–78, 272n112, 272nn111, 112, 274nn121, 122, 123, 275nn127, 129, 139; scientific paradigms for, 35–36, 143, 183, 184–86. *See also* word play
l'kayem mah sheneemar, 108–109
lo tavra, 110

maaseh, 245n7
maasim tovim, 200n52
Mahadevan, T., 271n102
mai havei alah, 122
mai kamashma lan, 88
mai taama d . . . , 232n97
man hu, 122
Manoah, 55–56, 213n96
mara deshemaata, 243n287
Mari b. Mar, 45–46, 220n41, 222n79
Marmorstein, Arthur, 256n129
Mar Ukba, 46
Mar Zutra, 205n14, 220n42, 225n152
mashal: defined, 88–89, 230n61; examples of, 231nn62, 65, 66, 71, 243n274; ideal human behavior taught, 41, 208n41; as interpretation, 108, 117; personification in, 42, 208n48; simile and metaphor used in, 42, 208n46; David Stern on, 156–57
matin, 123
matkif, 251n73
matkif ke, 233n106
Mattena, R., 220n47
may darasht beh?, 227n5
may dikhetiv, 72

may/may mashma, 72
megaleh panim batorah, 137–38
Meir, R.: challenges to colleagues' views, 74; Elisha b. Abuya and, 130; exaggerations of, 234n130; Judah, R. banning of his tudents, 253n95; logical agility of, 118; on mamerim, 106; moral lessons of, 207n37; nontextual statement/transmission of data, 70; his reading of Ps. 104:35, 218n3; Torah accepted by Israel, people of, 93
melitah, 108, 243n274
Menasseh b. Hikiyah, 11, 197n26–12
Meryon, R., 224n124
Miasha, R., 136
miba'eh leh (requiring a different Hebrew word), 72
midah keneged midah, 227n7
midrash: aggadah and, 4, 9, 16, 21, 35, 84, 103–104; boundaries of discourse in, 128–29; chronology in, 110, 244n299; critical studies of, 147–48, 258nn4, 5; *davar aher*, 102–103, 240nn210, 211; definitions of, 258n4; Greco-roman influences on, 147–49, 155, 259nn8, 12; halakhic midrashim, 15; homiletic midrashim, 109; intertextuality in reading of, 163–65, 269n87; juxtapositions in, 102–103, 109–10, 240n210; literary aspects of, 101–102, 154–55; midrash/halakhot pairings, 200n52; narrative of interpretation, 230n60; *petihta*, 103, 240n212; polysemy in, 161, 162, 165, 248n30; postmodernism and, 160–63, 265nn50, 52; readers' engagement with, 162–63; Samuel b. Nahman, R., 25, 203n103; status of, 12–13, 198nn31, 34; use of term, 146, 257n2. *See also* Stern, David
Midrash Agur, 134, 172, 254n108
Mielziner, Moshe, 235n137, 236n144
Milikowsky, Chaim, 258n4
minayin/minalan, 34, 74, 224n116
Mirmelstein, B., 115, 245n4
Mishnah: aggadah, comparative importance of, 16; *davar aher*, 117; on forbidden teachings, 133; halakhic texts of, 117–18, 180; in Oral Torah, 16–17, 199n39, 200nn42, 45
mistabra, 71, 221n64
miut, 108, 243n272
Moore, George Foote, 198n34

moral lessons, 41, 207n37
Moses, 73, 75, 78, 108, 218n12, 222n74, 243n261

Nahman, R.: on aggadah, 19, 20–21; comparisons used by, 222n75; dismissal of R. Zechariah's ruling, 250n59; on exaggeration in aggadah, 235n136; interpretations of, 204n5, 205n12, 206n28, 223n92; Shekhinah's position, 93
Nahman b. Isaac, R., 44, 59, 221n66, 223n92
Nahman b. R. Hisda, R., 136
Nahmanides, 124
Nahum of Gimo, 108, 243n272
Nathan, R., 75, 79
natural phenomena in talmudic exegesis, 63, 89, 94–95, 97, 228n15, 234n131, 235nn169–71
neha, 244n293
Nehemiah, R., 118, 217n1, 230n61
Neusner, Jacob: on aggadah, 158–59, 267n57; documentary approach of, 157–58, 266n54; on The Fathers According to Rabbi Nathan, 101, 239n201; his form criticism on rabbinic literature, 157, 158; on halakhah, 159–60, 249n47, 251n67, 268n68; on H. S. Hirschfeld, 272n112; on Max Kadushin, 275n139; Kantian philosophy and, 268n69; on origins of Midrash, 101–102, 239n208; on parable, 267n57; on rabbis' stature, 140; on Tannaitic midrashim, 99; on Yerushalmi v. Bavli Talmuds, 95–96, 98, 235n138
nimnu vegamru (ultimate determination of law by sages), 126
nirin, 124
Non-Halakhic Discourse (NHD), 27; feminism, 166–67, 270nn94, 99; folklore in, 153–56; Greco-roman influences on, 147–49, 155, 259nn8, 12; literary studies of/literary criticism applied to, 154–56, 265n52; networking/network as paradigm, 184–86; small-world structures and, 184. *See also* aggadah; halakhah; midrash
notarikon, 87, 108, 173, 229n42, 242n259
Noy, Dov, 152–53

Ochs, Peter, 3, 275n139
Oral Torah. *See* aggadah; Babylonian Talmud (Bavli); halakhah; Yerushalmi Talmud

Papa, R., 18, 46, 211n41
Pappus b. Judah, R., 136
parable. *See* mashal
pasak, 122
Patai, Raphael, 13
pelugta, 249n46
personification, 42, 208n48
peshat, 68–69, 135, 177, 217n2, 218nn3, 5, 13, 14, 16, 219nn28–37, 255n114
peshita, 229n33
Peskowitz, Miriam, 270n99
petihta, 103, 240n212
Pinhas b. Yair, 228n16
Plaskow, Judith, 270n94
Porton, Gary, 163
postmodern approach to Midrash, 160–63, 265nn50, 52
prayer, 46, 59, 221n66, 222n89, 234n131
proof-texts, 36, 205n24, 217n2

Qumran, 99, 147, 258n5
Qur'an, 167–68, 271n104, 272n109

Rabba b. Abbuha, 84
Rabbah, 46, 58, 85, 227n7, 228n18
Rabbah b. Bar Hana, 88
Rabbah b. Nahmani, 234n131
Rabbah bar Rav Huna, 249n43
Rabbi: *davar aher* (multiplication of textual meanings), 219n19; exaggerations of, 103, 235n133; *peshat* used by, 218n3; on unresolved differences of opinion, 78; wordplay of, 220n40, 225n157
rabbis: aggadic traditions of (gemara), 87–88, 230nn47–50; agreement of halakhists, 121–22, 248n41, 249n42; authority of, 43–44, 56–57, 70, 71, 123–24, 139–40, 221n60, 228n12, 249nn49, 50, 250nn54, 57, 59, 251n73, 256n144; as *baalei aggadah*, 9, 11–19, 197n26, 201nn53–70; code of behavior, 45–46, 58, 61–62, 85, 121, 208n44, 228n19; dialectical challenges of, 72–78, 117–18, 223n95, 224n124; disciples and, 9–10, 18, 58, 126, 139, 201n57, 222n75; divergent opinions of, 34–35, 74–75, 78, 90–91, 109–10, 111, 124, 126, 205nn14, 19, 232n47, 244nn292–94, 300, 250n59, 251nn62, 73, 252n75; excommunication

rabbis (continued)
  by, 88, 129, 130–32, 253n98, 254n101; exegetical freedom of, 86–87, 117–19, 126–35, 177, 247nn22, 24, 253n95; family sacrifice for, 222n75, 234n131; Greco-Roman influences on, 147–49, 155, 259nn8, 12, 260n13; hyperbole used by, 43–46, 87, 94, 103–104, 234nn129–36, 240nn213–22; on nature and natural events, 63, 94–95, 97, 234n131, 235nn169–71; realism of, 57–58; rebuke stories, 90, 105, 135–38, 255n125; sanctions of, 129–32, 253n95, 254n101; spiritual status of, 56–57; stories about, in Yerushalmi, 97, 131–32, 237nn157–63; study-activity of, 149–50; as transmittors of tradition, 71, 221n61; as wonder workers, 85, 228n16. *See also* aggadah; halakhah; midrash; Mishnah; Talmud headings
Rabin b. R. Adda, 39, 218n15
Rabinowitz, A. Z., 230n48
Randall, John Herman, 195n2
Rav: on the creation of Eve, 38, 207n32, 212n85; exegetical techniques of, 77, 218n10, 227n8; identification of halakhah by, 126; R. Kahana on, 90; on membership in Sanhedrin, 118; on rabbinic tradition, 87–88; Samuel and, 118; as wonder worker, 228n16
Rava: Abaye and, 118; on aggadah, 19; on the Aramean woman, 73, 75; dialectical challenge to aggadic teaching, 73; exaggerations of, 234n130; on family sacrifice for the scholar, 222n75; on government hierarchy, 218n9; on Israel's relationship with God, 222n78; legal acuity of, 220n47; nontextual statement/ transmission of data, 70; on rabbinical authority, 222n87; on Torah study, 46; unembellished counsel of, 227n8
Rava b. Hinena, 45, 79
Ravina, 201n57, 221n69
rebellious son, the, 248n34
rebuke stories, 90, 105, 135–38, 255n125
Reddy, V. Madhusudan, 167, 271n102
Resh Lakish, 252n87; on aggadah as Oral Torah, 19; on biblical texts, 90, 252n87; challenges of, 72, 74, 123, 136, 207n30, 222n83, 225n155; on human reproduction, 227n10; hyperbole used by, 43; on Israel's merits, 61, 90, 93; on Job's existence, 245n313; on location of Gehenna, 39; nontextual statements of, 70; *peshat* interpretations of, 218n4; on Pharoah, 93; reconciliation tactic of, 92; on repentance, 45, 74, 224n124, 226n186; rhetorical device of, 208n45; on Sinaitic revelation, 53
rhetorical strategies: anthropomorphism, 75, 79–80, 105–106, 225n203, 241nn231–40; question and answer, 78–79; questions, 42, 208n47. *See also* hyperbole
Robson, J., 168, 271n104
Rubenstein, Jeffrey, 130, 131, 157, 162

safek, 123, 250n56
Safrai, Shmuel, 263n36
Saldarini, Anthony, 239n206, 265n50
salka daatakh, 91
Samuel, 38, 78, 118, 207n32
Samuel b. Hofni, Gaon, 249n50
Samuel b. Inia, R., 233n115
Samuel b. Nahman, R. (Nahmani), 19–20, 20–24, 201n72, 202n80, 205n18; discourse techniques of, 26–27; exaggerations of, 234n130; on haggadah, 26; interpretations of, 104–105, 201n72, 202n80, 205n18, 245n313; legal writings of, 32–33; midrash, 25, 203n103; nonexegetic verse comments, 23–24, 203n101; nonhalakhic teachings without relations to biblical texts, 23–26, 203n103; rhetorical devices of, 109; Yerushalmi, 24–25, 203nn101, 102
Samuel b. Yudan, 98
Samuel the Nagid, 180–81, 182
Sanders, E. P., 121, 275n139
Sandmel, Samuel, 260n13
Sanhedrin, 121, 123
Sarason, Richard, 149, 258n4, 262n23, 275n139
Schorsch, Ismar, 169, 272n112
Schwartz, Baruch J., 135
Segal, Alan, 131
Segal, Eliezer, 115, 236n144, 245n5, 263n36
semukhin, 76, 226n205
Shammai, 117, 118, 252n75
Shanks, Elizabeth, 270n99
Shapiro, Susan, 265n52
shemaata (tradition), 125
shema mineh, lidrashah, 227n5
Sheshet, R., 71, 126, 140, 251n73, 257n148
Shimi b. Ukba, R./Shimi b. Ukva (Mar Ukva), 61–62, 201n57
Shimoff, Sandra, 147, 260n13

Index of Subjects and Proper Names   315

Shimon b. Yehotedek, R., 20, 201n72
Shochetman, Eliav, 251n67
Siddiqi, Muhammad Zubayr, 271n104
Simeon, R., 109
Simeon b. Avishalom, R., 42
Simeon b. Elaar, R., 78, 205n14
Simeon b. Eliakim, R., 249n47
Simeon b. Lakish. *See* Resh Lakish
Simeon b. Pazzi, R., 208n41, 219n21, 220n31, 231n74
Simeon b. Shetah, 204n10
Simeon b. Tarfon, 60, 205n19
Simeon b. Yohai, R., 39, 40, 104–105, 125, 206n24, 218n14, 227n9, 241n228, 241nn228, 232
Simlai, R., 9, 133, 197n11, 254n104
Simon, Herbert, 277n11
Simon, R., 109
Simon, Solomon, 252n76
Sinaitic revelation, 8, 10, 53–55, 180, 189
sirus (disarrangement), 107–108, 242n258
Sit und Leben, 149
Smriti literature, 167
Sokol, Moshe, 278n3
Solomon, Norman, 255n113
Soloveitchik, Joseph Baer, Rabbi, 191, 198n34, 278nn2, 3
Sruti literature, 167, 271n102
Stein, Dinah, 263n36
Steinberg, Theodore, 274n123, 275n139
Steinsaltz, Adin, 119, 125, 249nn50, 57, 277n7
Steinschneider, Moritz, 116
Stemberger, Günter, 96, 118, 246n11, 249n50, 254n107, 276n1
Stern, David: on biblical interpretation, 128; Greco-Roman elements in Rabbinic Judaism, 259n12; on the *mashal* form, 156–57; on midrash, 13, 161–62, 198n34, 230n61, 268n72; on parables, 267n57; polysemy in midrash texts, 161, 162; on postmodern approach to midrash, 160–62, 265n50
Strack, Hermann, 134, 276n1
"stubborn and rebellious son, the" 248n34
Symmachus, 118, 253n95

taameh, 244n294
Tahlia b. Abina, R., 19
talui, 123, 250n56
Tanhuma, R., 18, 240n210
Tannaitic midrashim, 99–100
tanu rabbanan, 228n12

Tarfon, R., 126, 136, 201n59
Taylor, Mark C., 277n8
teku, 124
Temple in Jerusalem, 56, 65
temurah, 173
terikha, 119
Teugels, Lieve, 257n2
textual reasoning movement (Ochs), 3
thirty-two middot, 129, 134–35, 172, 174, 254n107
tiyuvta, 124, 126, 251nn62, 74
Torah: disparagement of, 138; Israel's acceptance of, 60–61, 73–74, 93–94, 241n240; rabbis on, 45–46, 54, 212n73; Sinaitic revelation, 8, 10, 53–55, 180, 189; study of, 9, 45–46, 57, 92, 197n11; as understood by the rabbis, 50
Towner, Wayne Sibley, 238n187

Ulla, R./Aha b. Ulla, R., 34, 40, 56–57, 79, 205n11, 213nn95, 107, 218n7
ulpan, 126
uma ani mekayem . . . ela, 232n85
utena, 87

vehaamar, 233nn114, 117
vehaggadah k . . ., 122
veha imre inshe (introduction to adage), 231n71
vehakhamim omrim, 49
vehatanya, 221n60
vehilkheta k . . ., 122, 249n44
Vermes, Gea, 258n4
Visotzky, Burton, 148
vows, 79, 221n67, 222n76

Wacholder, Ben Zion, 258n4, 258nn4, 5
Wegner, Judith Romney, 272n110
Wittgenstein, Ludwig, 3, 4, 141
women: Akiba's wife, 234n131; feminism, 166–67, 270n99, 270nn94, 99; giving of Torah, 93–94; men walking in front of their wives, 76, 79, 221n66, 223n109; in Oral Torah, 61; otherness of, 61; sexism, 2, 89, 92, 233n108; social status of, 38, 46; Torah study for, 92
word play: in biblical text, 85–87, 228n20, 229nn34, 36, 37, 40, 42; foreign words in, 87, 229n42; juxtaposition, 76, 90–91, 102–103, 109–10, 223n92, 226n205, 232n85, 240n210; lessons derived from, 107–108, 242nn258, 260; missing letters or words, 69, 219nn21, 22; notarikon, 87,

word play *(continued)*
  108, 173, 229n42, 242n259; text anomalies in, 71–72, 222nn86, 87. *See also* hyperbole
world-to-come, 46, 52, 53, 64, 211n33
Written Torah. *See* biblical texts

Yaakov b. Aha, R., 19
Yannai, 228n16
Yavneh, 118
Yehudah, R., 87, 94, 118
Yerushalmi Talmud: aggadot in, 9, 95–97, 100, 236n144, 237nn164–68, 174–79; Babylonian Talmud compared to, 95–96, 98, 116, 151–52, 235n138; culture reflected in, 148–49; excommunication of Elisha ben Abuya (Aher) in, 131–32; oral tradition in, 152; rabbi stories in, 97, 237nn157–63
yetera, 227n5
Yishmael, R., 18
Yishmael b. Yose, R., 11
Yohanan, R.: on aggadah, 10, 19, 25; aggadic utterances used by, 205nn14, 19, 20, 25, 29; Akiba rebuked by, 136; on biblical basis of law, 118–19; challenges to colleagues' views, 74; in death, 71; differing views standing side by side, 77; exaggerations of, 235n133; on God's chastisements, 74; his rebuke of Resh Lakish, 136; identification of David's son, 70; knowledge of scripture, 220n43; *minayin* inquiry of, 224n116; *peshat* interpretations of, 218nn13, 14; on prayer, 59; prooftexts used by, 206nn24, 26; on Ps. 145 acrostic, 72; rhythm in discourse of, 209n54; Simeon b. Yohai and, 40; surprise in aggadic anecdotes, 207n35; on teaching halakhah, 9, 197n11; Torah accepted by Israel, people of, 93; unembellished counsel of, 227n8; unresolved differences of opinion, 78; on the wicked, 74; word play of, 86
Yohanan b. Dahabai, R., 250n54
Yohanan b. Narbai, R., 94
Yohanan b. Zakkai, 153, 263n37
Yose, R., 40, 206n26, 217n1, 218n13; as author of Seder Olam, 70; challenges to colleague, 75; on mamerim, 106; on Moses' sons circumcision, 73; on prayer, 74; unresolved differences of opinion, 78
Yose b. Betera, 239n200
Yose b. R. Hanina, 69, 220n31
Yose the Galilean, R., 136
Yosi b, Hanina, 59
yShevuot, 96–97
Yudan, R., 108

Zechariah, R., 250n59
Zeira, R.: on aggadah, 10, 12, 98, 127, 198n31, 202n88; on Benjamin b. Yefet, 90; on God's generosity, 208n41; midrashim of, 104; on natural phenomena, 228n15, 18; on prayer, 74; problem creation of, 120; on R. Huna's interpretation, 240n211; truth statement of, 70
Zeiri, R., 228n16
Zeorah, R., 240n211
Zunz, Leopold, 146, 169, 172